CANADA'S PRIME MINISTERS MACDONALD TO TRUDEAU

Portraits from the
Dictionary of Canadian Biography

CANADA'S PRIME MINISTERS
MACDONALD TO TRUDEAU

Portraits from the
Dictionary of Canadian Biography

Under the direction of
RAMSAY COOK
and
RÉAL BÉLANGER

UNIVERSITY OF TORONTO PRESS

© University of Toronto/Université Laval 2007
Printed in Canada

ISBN 978-0-8020-9173-4 (cloth)
ISBN 978-0-8020-9174-1 (paper)

Printed on acid-free paper

Library and Archives Canada Cataloguing in Publication

Canada's prime ministers, Macdonald to Trudeau: portraits from
the Dictionary of Canadian Biography/under the direction
of Ramsay Cook and Réal Bélanger.

Published in French under the title:
Les premiers ministres du Canada de Macdonald à Trudeau :
biographies écrites pour le Dictionnaire biographique du Canada

Includes bibliographical references and index.
ISBN 978-0-8020-9173-4 (bound)
ISBN 978-0-8020-9174-1 (pbk.)

1. Prime ministers – Canada – Biography. 2. Canada – Politics and government.
3. Canada – History. I. Bélanger, Réal II. Cook, Ramsay, 1931–

FC26.P7C365 2007   971.009'9   C2007-900930-1

Translation from French to English by Edward Baxter.

University of Toronto Press acknowledges the financial assistance
to its publishing program of the Canada Council for the Arts and
the Ontario Arts Council.

University of Toronto Press acknowledges the financial support for its
publishing activities of the Government of Canada through the Book
Publishing Industry Development Program (BPIDP).

Contents

Preface

The *Dictionary of Canadian biography/Dictionnaire biographique du Canada* is a major research and publishing project that has been in progress for more than 45 years as a collaborative undertaking of the University of Toronto and the Université Laval. More than 8,000 biographies of persons who died or flourished in the years from 1000 to 1930 are included in the 15 volumes of the *DCB/DBC* currently in print. The present work, entitled *Canada's prime ministers, Macdonald to Trudeau*, is published simultaneously in English and French by the University of Toronto Press and Les Presses de l'Université Laval respectively; it contains the biographies of the 15 men now deceased who have held the highest office in Canadian public life. The articles on the first four, Macdonald, Mackenzie, Abbott, and Thompson, who died in the last decade of the 19th century, first appeared in volume XII (1891–1900) of the *DCB/DBC*, which came out in 1990. Those dealing with the next three, Bowell, Tupper, and Laurier, were published in 1998 in volume XIV (1911–20). The biographies of Borden, Meighen, King, Bennett, St-Laurent, Diefenbaker, and Pearson have been available since 2005 in the *DCB/DBC*'s online version (*www.biographi.ca*). These 14 articles are now brought together in a compilation that also includes the previously unpublished biography of Trudeau, which has been written especially for the new volume and added to the online version.

The biographies already in the *DCB/DBC* have undergone a few changes. In the course of time the editorial teams in Toronto and Quebec, authors, and, on occasion, readers have discovered typographical and spelling mistakes and errors of fact; these have been corrected. Several features of the dictionary's editorial style that are inappropriate for a thematic volume have been adjusted. For instance, asterisks, small capitals, and editorial cross references, designed to direct the reader to related biographies in the series, have been deleted. Over the years, and especially since the publication of volume XII, the *DCB/DBC* has changed its editorial approach in certain respects, but minor differences in style and presentation have been allowed to stand. On the whole, corrections have been kept to a minimum to avoid creating versions very different from the originals. Readers interested in knowing more about the editorial style of the *DCB/DBC* with regard to personal names, place names, institutions, terminology, and so on should consult the Editorial Notes at the beginning of the printed volumes.

To do justice to the 12 scholars who prepared these biographies, we should mention that their texts are based on many diverse sources, including manuscripts in private and public archives, newspapers and journals, debates of the House of Commons and various legislative bodies, and printed and electronic works. In the volumes, and in the CD-ROM version of volumes I to XIV (2000) and the web-based publication (ongoing since 2003), each biography is followed by an exhaustive bibliography indicating the wealth of material examined by the authors. In the present work these authors provide instead a few, select sources in which interested readers may broaden their knowledge about these 15 fascinating individuals. Some of them have chosen the most pertinent of the titles listed in their original bibliographies; others have been able to cite new works published since their biographies first appeared in the *DCB/DBC*.

The production of these biographies has required the assistance, skill, and competence of many people whom we would like to acknowledge here collectively. Our gratitude goes first and foremost to the scholars who wrote, and during the initial editorial stages, more than once revised their articles. At that time each biography was carefully reviewed by several members of the two editorial teams, the anglophone one at the University of Toronto and the francophone one at the Université Laval. We wish to express our thanks to all those who played a part in editing, translating, and documenting the biographies, as well as to those were involved, over the years, in producing the original publications from which they have been taken.

DICTIONNAIRE BIOGRAPHIQUE   DICTIONARY OF CANADIAN
DU CANADA   BIOGRAPHY

Introduction

P rime ministers, the central figures in parliamentary government
and the leaders of political parties, fill dominant roles in Canada's
political history. Their importance is recognized in the *Dictionary
of Canadian biography/Dictionnaire biographique du Canada* by the space
devoted to them. Prime ministers usually fall into the top category of
8,000 words or more. Fifteen prime ministers, beginning with Sir John A.
Macdonald and concluding with Pierre Elliott Trudeau (written especially
for this volume) just over a century later, appear in *Canada's prime ministers,
Macdonald to Trudeau: portraits from the 'Dictionary of Canadian biography.'*
(Former prime ministers who are still living are not included.) Each political leader is presented by a recognized Canadian scholar who, following
the rigorous standards of research, writing, and critical judgement set by
the *DCB/DBC*, has brought life and understanding to the careers of the
individuals who have served in Canada's pre-eminent political office.
Bringing these well-written biographies together for the first time provides readers with an opportunity to reflect on the striking variety of
personalities who have succeeded in climbing the summit of Canada's
public life and the different challenges they faced in their determination
to stay there.

One wonders why these 15 men chose to spend their lives in politics,
and why they succeeded where others failed. Macdonald easily outplayed
the intellectually brilliant Edward Blake, though the seemingly ordinary
Alexander Mackenzie had already shown that Macdonald was not invin-
cible, given the right circumstances. After Macdonald died in office in
1891 four successive leaders, Sir John Joseph Caldwell Abbott, Sir John
Sparrow David Thompson, Sir Mackenzie Bowell, and Sir Charles Tupper,
each with some talent and experience, failed to keep their party in office.
Conservative leader Sir Robert Laird Borden seemed fated to remain
permanently in the shade of the charismatic Sir Wilfrid Laurier. But after
more than a decade and a half of Liberal dominance Borden's quiet

persistence finally won out. In the bitter 20-year battle between the ambiguous William Lyon Mackenzie King and the logical Arthur Meighen the Liberal tortoise repeatedly outran the Conservative hare. But Richard Bedford Bennett, a little like Alexander Mackenzie before him, took advantage of a socio-economic crisis to dislodge the seemingly indestruct-ible King, at least temporarily. And can the success of Louis-Stephen St-Laurent, a modest political neophyte of serene, fatherly self-confidence, be explained only by the years of prosperity over which he presided? Then John George Diefenbaker's resounding rhetoric unexpectedly con-vinced Canadian voters that their confidence was misplaced. Having vanquished the powerful 'governing party' of King and St-Laurent, Diefenbaker subsequently succeeded in preventing Lester Bowles Pearson from winning his ardently hoped-for majority. When these two warriors left the field to Pierre Trudeau and Robert Lorne Stanfield, the first a virtual newcomer to politics, the other an experienced provincial premier, the electorate gave the palm to the man who hoped to follow in the steps of Laurier. Obviously there is no standard mould that shapes Canadian prime ministers. Yet, despite their differences, each in turn found his powerful office a lonely one where increasing isolation from the people who had elected him almost inevitably became his fate.

What insights into the workings of our public life do the biographies of these 15 leaders provide? Did these contrasting men have anything in common that determined their success? Norman Ward, who taught political science at the University of Saskatchewan for many years, pub-lished in 1960 the book *Mice in the beer*, which included a witty essay entitled 'The fewer the higher: a field note on fecundity among politicians.' He summed up his argument this way: 'Close observers of the Canadian political scene can hardly have failed to remark (even though so far none of them have said anything about it) that in this country we have gone in heavily for politicians whose comprehension of their fellow-men has been unimpeded by the raising of large families of their own.' With tongue firmly in cheek Ward offered statistical support for his hypothesis: Macdonald with a son at the time of confederation – and later a daughter – was notably successful but, among prime ministers, stood near the high end of family size. The childless Laurier (discounting rumours about Armand La Vergne) and Borden and bachelors Bennett and above all King seemed to demonstrate 'Ward's Law' conclusively. Louis St-Laurent, the father of five children, may have raised doubts about it but his successor John Diefenbaker, who fathered no children, in 1958 won the largest electoral majority in Canadian history, thus restoring the law's validity. Lester Pearson, his two children grown up when he led successive minority governments, may be counted on either side. Pierre Trudeau, a bachelor when he became prime minister in 1968, immediately won a sweeping electoral victory. He then married and sired three sons during his long prime ministership; that may explain the gradual decline of his electoral magic. The truth, of course, is that 'Ward's Law' is best taken as its discoverer doubtless intended it: a learned, humorous refutation of the very idea that success in Canadian politics can be explained by social scientific laws. Prime ministerial success, as the *DCB/DBC* biographies presented here make plain, depends on, in the words of historian Donald Grant Creighton, both 'character and circumstance.'

Reading the *DCB/DBC* biographies of Canada's prime ministers suggests very few common motives other than an unstable mixture of personal ambition and a sense of obligation toward their country and their political party. For all of his rhetoric about service to his country – and it was more than mere rhetoric – no prime minister's ambition is more obvious than in the case of Mackenzie King, the longest-serving prime minister. Whether during the 1926 constitutional controversy – the King–Byng affair – or during the conscription crisis, 1942–44, King fought tenaciously and successfully for his political life. That his party's hold on office and, at least during the conscription crisis, the unity of the country were also at stake should not obscure the Liberal leader's powerful, intense ambition. But that was no less true, if sometimes less obvious, of his opponents. Arthur Meighen, for example, may have taken the correct constitutional stance in 1926 or a principled position on conscription during World War II but he, too, was fighting for his political life and his party's electoral success in both instances. Yet both King and Meighen could fairly claim that their actions on these and other occasions were motivated by what they believed was best for Canada. In 1926 King contended that Lord Byng's refusal of his request for a dissolution of parliament represented unacceptable imperial interference in Canadian affairs; Meighen held with equal fervour that, in supporting Byng's action, he was defending the constitution. In the debate over conscription King hoped to preserve the unity of his party and the country; Meighen believed that winning the war was the first priority. Yet pragmatism in making policy and in devising strategies of survival, rather than principle or ideology, often seems the guiding determinant in the success of Canada's federal political leaders.

For a Canadian prime minister there is usually no higher ground than the claim to be the defender of national unity against threats of disruption and disintegration. Sir John A. Macdonald was the first master of this strategy and confederation its first great test. Later he backed a costly plan for a transcontinental railway and a protective tariff as *national* policies required to build and bind together a vast, underpopulated territory. But the challenge of Louis Riel and the controversy over French and Roman Catholic language and education rights in the prairie west proved too much even for the adept Macdonald. His four Conservative successors struggled unavailingly to resolve the question of education rights until their party went down to defeat in 1896. Sir Wilfrid Laurier made 'national unity' the mantra that kept him in office for a record of more than 15 consecutive years despite cultural conflict over education and imperial relations. His example was emulated by successive Liberal prime ministers – especially King, St-Laurent, and Trudeau (Pearson never quite succeeded in adapting the ploy to his troubled times) – who articulated the formula in electorally appealing ways.

The claim to possession of the keys to national unity carried the damning implication that opposition parties lacked national virtue. Macdonald defined this strategy as 'I am a British subject and British born, and a British subject I hope to die,' while Mackenzie King emphasized Canada's autonomy; Laurier and Trudeau underlined the Canadian content of their policies, but all intended to brand their critics and opponents as antipatriotic or worse. Central to the national unity theme for successful prime ministers is the need to gain support in more than one region of the country and especially in Quebec. National unity is often personified in the idea of the special status of the 'Quebec lieutenant': Macdonald–Cartier, King–Lapointe. In a government led by a French Canadian prime minister, Laurier or St-Laurent, an anglophone often played a similar role: William Fielding for the first, and, sometimes, C. D. Howe or J. W. Pickersgill for the second. Only Sir Robert Borden in 1917 and John Diefenbaker in 1957, of the *DCB/DBC* prime ministers, gained office without strong Quebec support; neither was able to find a 'Quebec lieutenant.' No one English-speaking minister filled that notion-ally equal role under Pierre Trudeau. Leaders of regional parties have consistently failed to win office but, in their efforts to do so, have usually diluted their regional appeal hoping to attract national support.

While the national unity strategy most often was evoked to shore up domestic policies, it could also be rephrased as an appeal to the defence of the national interest in imperial and international affairs. Most obviously that was the case with Sir Robert Borden, who argued in 1911 that reciprocity with the United States threatened Canada's very existence. Then in 1917, despite the realization that national unity would be shat-tered, he enacted compulsory military enlistment for overseas service, convinced that Canada's interests depended on reinforcing the troops at the front. Of course, the decision also helped him and his coalition gov-ernment to win the 1917 election. Once again the Borden years provide examples of the entanglement of national interest/unity and personal/party interest. That perhaps is the key to prime ministerial success: a careful balance that skilfully links personal ambition with party goals and wraps both in the flag.

These are some of the themes that run through the *DCB/DBC*'s 15 biographies of Canada's prime ministers. But there is much more: details about personal lives, sketches of close associates, a narrative of major events, and an assessment of accomplishments and failures set against the backdrop of economic and demographic growth, the social crisis of depressions, and the impact of world events. Taken together, they recreate the political and social panorama stretching from the cam-paign for confederation in 1867 to the struggle to entrench the Canadian Charter of Rights and Freedoms in the new Constitution of 1982. Told through the lives of Canada's leading politicians this is a remarkable, engrossing, documented account of modern Canadian history.

RÉAL BÉLANGER   RAMSAY COOK

Biographies

Sir JOHN ALEXANDER MACDONALD,

lawyer, businessman, and politician; b. 10 Jan. 1815
(the registered date) or 11 Jan. (the date he and his family
celebrated) in Glasgow, Scotland, son of Hugh Macdonald
and Helen Shaw; m. first 1 Sept. 1843 Isabella Clark (d. 1857)
in Kingston, Upper Canada, and they had two sons; m. secondly
16 Feb. 1867 Susan Agnes Bernard in London, England,
and they had a daughter; d. 6 June 1891 in Ottawa.

John Alexander Macdonald was brought to Kingston at the age of five by his parents, in-laws of Donald Macpherson, a retired army officer living near Kingston. His father, who had been an unsuccessful merchant in Glasgow, operated a series of businesses in Upper Canada: merchant shops in Kingston and in Adolphustown Township, and for ten years the large stone mills at Glenora in Prince Edward County. Though never a man of wealth, Hugh Macdonald achieved sufficient local prominence to be appointed a magistrate for the Midland District in 1829. He and his wife saw to it that John received as good an education as was available to him at the time. He attended the Midland District Grammar School in 1827–28 and also a private co-educational school in Kingston where he was given a 'classical and general' education which included the study of Latin and Greek, arithmetic, geography, English reading and grammar, and rhetoric. His schooling provided appropriate training for his choice of profession, the law. In 1830, at age 15, he began to article in the office of a Kingston lawyer, George Mackenzie. He quickly distinguished himself. Two years later he was entrusted with the management of a branch of Mackenzie's office, in Napanee, and in 1833–35 he replaced his cousin Lowther Pennington Macpherson in the operation of the latter's legal firm in Hallowell (Picton). In August 1835 he opened his own firm in Kingston, six months before being formally called to the bar on 6 Feb. 1836. From 1843 he usually practised with one or more partners, first with Alexander Campbell and then, from the 1850s, with Archibald John Macdonell and Robert Mortimer Wilkinson.

As a lawyer Macdonald quickly attracted public attention, mainly by taking on a number of difficult and even sensational cases, including the defence of William Brass, a member of a prominent local family who was convicted of rape in 1837, and a series of cases in 1838 involving Nils von Schoultz and others charged with involvement in the rebellion of 1837–38 and in subsequent border raids. (In December 1837 Macdonald himself had served as a militia private.) Though he lost as many of these cases as he won, he acquired a reputation for ingenuity and quick-wittedness as a defence attorney. In fact he did not long find it necessary to depend on a practice dedicated to the defence of hopeless cases. In 1839 he was appointed solicitor to the Commercial Bank of the Midland District and was made a director. From that point on his practice essentially concerned corporate law, especially after he gained as a client Kingston's other major financial institution, the Trust and Loan Company of Upper Canada, founded in 1843. Though he acted at times for a wide range of businessmen and businesses, among them the company of Casimir Stanislaus Gzowski, the Trust and Loan Company for many years provided Macdonald with the bulk of his professional income.

Macdonald was himself an active businessman, primarily involved in land development and speculation. Throughout the 1840s, 1850s, and 1860s he bought and developed urban property, first in Kingston and subsequently in Guelph and Toronto, and he bought and sold, often through agents, farm and wild land in many parts of the province, in parcels as large as 9,700 acres at a time. He also acted as an agent for British investors in Canadian real estate. Connections formed with British businessmen who were directors of the Trust and Loan Company led to his being appointed, in 1864, president of a British-backed firm in Quebec, the St Lawrence Warehouse, Dock and Wharfage Company. He acquired directorships in at least ten Canadian companies, in addition to the Commercial Bank and the Trust and Loan Company, and he sat on two British boards. As well, he invested in bank stock, road companies, and Great Lakes shipping. Macdonald's business career was not, however, uniformly successful. He was caught at the time of the depression of 1857 with much unsaleable land on which he had to continue to make payments. In the 1860s he would suffer serious reverses because of the recklessness and sudden death of his legal partner, A. J. Macdonell, and the collapse of the Commercial Bank, which had advanced Macdonald loans. None the less, he managed to avoid failure, continuing to draw income from his law partnership and from the sale and rental of real estate.

Macdonald had a good many personal as well as business problems to deal with. In 1843 he had married his cousin Isabella Clark, who, within two years of their marriage, became chronically ill, suffering from mysterious bouts of weakness and pain. A modern medical examination of her symptoms concludes that 'she suffered from a somatization disorder, perhaps with a migrainous component, secondary opiate-dependence and pulmonary tuberculosis.' Isabella bore two children; in both cases the pregnancies and deliveries were extremely difficult. The first child, John Alexander, died at the age of 13 months. The second, Hugh John, would survive. Isabella herself died in 1857.

From an early age Macdonald had shown a keen interest in public affairs. He was ambitious and looked for opportunities wherever he could find them. At age 19, in 1834, he became secretary of both the Prince Edward District Board of Education and the Hallowell Young Men's Society. In Kingston he was recording secretary of the Celtic Society in 1836, president of the Young Men's Society of Kingston in 1837, vice-president of the St Andrew's Society in 1839, and a prominent member of the Presbyterian community. In March 1843, now well known as a lawyer, businessman, and public-spirited citizen, he was easily elected to the Kingston Town Council as an alderman.

Macdonald's three-year service at the local level was quickly over-shadowed by his entry into provincial politics in the general election of October 1844. He ran in Kingston as a conservative, stressing his belief in the British connection, his commitment to the development of the Province of Canada, and his devotion to the interests of Kingston and its hinterland. Again he was elected by a wide margin; provincially, con-servative winners outnumbered reformers by more than two to one.

It has been said that Macdonald's political views were influenced by his legal mentor, George Mackenzie. While Macdonald was in his office, Mackenzie had advocated a moderate conservatism which stressed com-mercial expansion but also adhered to such traditional tory notions as state support for religious institutions and leadership by an élite. At any rate, in his early years in the Legislative Assembly Macdonald proved to be a genuine conservative, opposing responsible government, the secularization of the clergy reserves, the abolition of primogeniture, and extensions to the franchise, because such measures were un-British and could weaken the British connection or the authority of the governor and also the necessary propertied element within government and society. Yet he was never an entirely reactionary conservative. His approach to politics from the first was always essentially pragmatic. The fact was that circumstances made it impossible for Macdonald, or any other conservative politician, to cling to political positions that had become outmoded. The transfer of power from the governor and his appointed advisers to elected colonial politicians and the gradual acceptance of party politics created a system in which exclusivist views could not be maintained, at least in public. Macdonald preferred conservative options but did not wish, he stated in 1844, 'to waste the time of the Legislature, and the money of the people, in fruitless discussions of abstract and theoretical questions of government.'

For six of the first ten years of his political career – between 1848 and 1854 – his party was not in power and his practicality was expressed mainly in efforts to promote the interests of his constituency. He regularly presented petitions and introduced legislation dealing with such matters as the incorporation of Kingston as a city; its debt; support for its charitable, religious, and educational bodies; and particularly the promotion of such Kingston-area businesses as road and railway companies, insurance companies, financial institutions, and gas, light, and water companies. (Macdonald had a personal financial interest in all of these businesses.) He was a conscientious and successful constituency man and would be re-elected from Kingston in seven consecutive elections for the assembly between 1844 and 1867 and in three for the federal house between 1867 and 1874.

Macdonald's first experience as a cabinet member was in 1847–48, when he served for seven months as receiver general and for three as commissioner of crown lands in the administrations headed by William Henry Draper and Henry Sherwood. In these posts Macdonald proved himself an able and even a reformist administrator, but his chief political initiative was devising and advocating the University Endowment Bill for Upper Canada in 1847. It did not pass but it reflected both his conservatism and his pragmatism. In an attempt to steer a middle course between the reform policy of a single state-supported, nonsectarian university and tory plans for a revived and strengthened Anglican King's College in Toronto, he proposed to divide the university endowment among the existing denominational colleges but to give King's College the largest share. In 1848 he resigned with the government to make way for the reform administration of Robert Baldwin and Louis-Hippolyte La Fontaine.

Macdonald did not hold office again until September 1854, when he became attorney general for Upper Canada in the newly formed coalition government of Sir Allan Napier MacNab and Augustin-Norbert Morin. His role in the formation of that coalition, from which some historians have dated the emergence of the modern Conservative party, is not entirely clear. The traditional version of the formation, which appears to have begun with John Charles Dent's account in *The last forty years* (1881), was that 'his was the hand that shaped the course' of the negotiations. Donald Robert Beer's well-founded modern view is that there is 'no direct evidence' of Macdonald's 'special contribution to these events.' The exact extent of his involvement will probably never be known, but it is certain that the expanded party created in 1854 exactly fitted his own plan, mentioned in a letter to James McGill Strachan in February of that year, to 'enlarge the bounds of our party' and was in line with his already established 'friendly relations with the French.' In 1861 Macdonald himself dated the existence of a solidly based Liberal–Conservative coalition from that occasion, 'when I took them [the Conservative party] up in 1854.'

As attorney general (a position he would hold until 1867 except for periods in 1858 and 1862–64) Macdonald assumed a heavy administrative load because the office not only oversaw the judicial and penal systems of Upper Canada but handled a constant stream of references from the other government departments on points of law. He again proved a competent, if somewhat spasmodic, administrator and was shrewd in his choice of expert and efficient deputies: Robert Alexander Harrison (1854–59) and Hewitt Bernard (1858–67). In the assembly he assumed an increasing share of the legislative load. His first major task was to steer through the act for the abolition of the clergy reserves, a measure that demonstrated his conservatism and his pragmatism by preserving a share of the revenues for clerical (mostly Anglican) incumbents but at the same time disposing of a long-standing, contentious issue. As he said in November 1854, 'You must yield to the times.' In the same session, in early 1855, he assumed responsibility in the lower house for a controversial bill on Upper Canada's separate schools, for which the Roman Catholic Church, led by Bishop Armand-François-Marie de Charbonnel, had lobbied the government. The bill was introduced first in the Legislative Council by Étienne-Paschal Taché and in the assembly only in May, near the end of the session, when many Upper Canadian members had already left Quebec (the capital). Though provision for separate schools in Upper Canada had existed since 1841, the act of 1855 really created the basis of the system that was to persist in Upper Canada and then in Ontario. It was defended by Macdonald on religious grounds – the right of Roman Catholics, according to the Toronto *Globe*'s report in June, 'to educate their children according to their own principles.' The bill itself and the manner of its introduction had been severely criticized by Joseph Hartman and others and ultimately opposed by a majority of Upper Canadian members, but it had passed on the strength of French Canadian Catholic votes. Macdonald was accused, probably rightly, of parliamentary manipulation and he laid the government open to a charge of 'French domination' of the administration. The issue also provided arguments for those in Upper Canada, led by George Brown of the *Globe*, who since 1853 had advocated the introduction of a system of representation by population in the provincial parliament, which would have given Upper Canada a greater number of seats than Lower Canada.

In 1856 Macdonald became, for the first time, leader of the Upper Canadian section of the government, replacing MacNab. The manner in which he assumed control has been the subject of some controversy. MacNab had come under increasing criticism within the coalition because of his lingering reputation as a compact tory and his growing ineffectiveness due to ill health. No doubt he should have resigned but he refused, making it necessary to force him out of office so that a reconstruction of the cabinet could occur. Macdonald does not appear to have acted purely out of personal ambition; he too had become convinced that MacNab had to go. He took part in the ouster, first by sending MacNab an ultimatum, which he rejected, and then by joining the Reform members of the cabinet, Joseph Curran Morrison and Robert Spence, in resigning from it on 21 May (the other Upper Canadian Conservative, William Cayley, soon followed) on the grounds that the government had been in a minority among the Upper Canadian members on a vote of confidence. MacNab had no choice but to place his portfolio at the disposal of Governor General Sir Edmund Walker Head. The cabinet was reorganized on the 24th, with Taché as premier and Macdonald as co-premier. Macdonald now assumed the leadership role he was to hold for the rest of his life.

John A. Macdonald, around 1856.

His approach to political power and responsibility was in practice highly personal. Before confederation he always shared the direction of the government and his party with a French Canadian leader, especially after November 1857 when the energetic George-Étienne Cartier took over from Taché. Macdonald himself kept a firm hand on the affairs of the party in his own section of the Province of Canada. He was its chief strategist, fund-raiser, and, during elections, campaign organizer. He intervened directly at the riding level to ensure that suitable candidates were nominated, often having to sort out the rival claims of as many as six potential Liberal–Conservative MLAs and if necessary 'buying off' (usually with the promise of a government appointment) those who might create a party 'split.' He advised candidates on policy and tactics and arranged election funding where necessary. He attempted to acquire the bloc support of a number of large groups, such as the Orange order and the adherents of the Methodist and Catholic churches, by appealing to the leaders of these organizations, including Ogle Robert Gowan, Egerton Ryerson, and bishops Rémi Gaulin and Edward John Horan, for their influence with their followers. Despite his best efforts, however, Macdonald was not notably successful in winning elections in Upper Canada before confederation. In 1861, after his first extensive speaking tour and a campaign in which he advocated a British North American federation and raised the old 'no looking to Washington' cry of loyalty, his candidates achieved only a small majority of Upper Canadian seats. In the other elections under his management, in 1857–58 and 1863, the Upper Canadian Conservatives were defeated.

Macdonald was nevertheless an adroit politician and a popular campaigner. He successfully combined political shrewdness with a talent for conviviality and for good-humouredly persuading his colleagues to follow his lead. On the platform he projected a no-nonsense political image, coupled with a flair for ridiculing the foibles of his opponents. Clearly, by 1855 colleagues recognized Macdonald's capacity for drink and soft sawder as important elements of his strength; others underestimated his skills because of them. But on occasion he was a hard drinker. The first time his drinking seems to have been a serious public problem was in the spring of 1862, at a time of government instability and during debate on a bill to expand the militia that Macdonald had introduced and defended. The *Globe* reported him as having 'one of his old attacks.' Because Macdonald took so much personal responsibility for leadership, when he went on a binge his party drifted. On 21 May 1862, after the defeat of the bill, the government resigned.

The truth was that the Upper Canadian Conservatives had usually been sustained in power by their alliance with Cartier and the Bleu bloc, which held a majority in Lower Canada. This relationship had obvious political advantages and reflected both Macdonald's belief in French–English cooperation and his long-standing commitment to the union of Upper and Lower Canada as an economic necessity. The relationship also meant that his brand of Conservatism had become more and more unpopular in his own section of the province and increasingly open to charges of 'French domination' of the ministry. Whether from conviction or necessity Macdonald had been forced to defend, against a hostile Protestant majority in the population of Upper Canada, the system of Catholic separate schools. He personally opposed representation by population as a basis for the distribution of seats in the assembly, even though most Upper Canadians and eventually many of his Upper Canadian Conservative followers, among them John Hillyard Cameron, came out in support of the principle. After 1851 the population of the western section of the province exceeded the east's so that adopting the principle would have reduced the effectiveness of the French Canadians as a political group. Macdonald also, like Cartier, showed limited enthusiasm for another popular Upper Canadian movement, the annexation of the vast territory west of Canada. Though the Taché–Macdonald government in 1857 made a vague claim to the lands then under the jurisdiction of the Hudson's Bay Company, Macdonald was not much concerned. In 1865 he was to state in a letter to Edward William Watkin, the former Grand Trunk president who had examined the question of confederation for the Colonial Office, that he was 'quite willing personally to leave that whole country a wilderness for the next fifty years.' Thus in the period 1854–64 he was in a kind of political trap of his own making. To stay in power he needed French Canadian support but that necessity in turn involved support for policies that were a political liability in his own section of the province.

Macdonald tried to compensate for the political weakness of Conservatism in Upper Canada in a number of ways. He insisted that the party officially remain a coalition of moderate Reformers and Conservatives and he always kept a succession of Hincksite Reform members, such as Morrison, Spence, and John Ross, or Reform defectors such as Michael Hamilton Foley or Thomas D'Arcy McGee in the cabinet to try to broaden his party's image and appeal. He also tried to compensate for political shortcomings by developing a centralized system of government patronage. Macdonald was, of course, far from the first politician to dispense patronage but, unlike his Conservative predecessors, he maintained a strong personal hold over office-giving while in power and he used offices, or the promise of office, in a deliberate attempt to strengthen the party at the local level, on the principle that reward should only result from actual service. By making sure that recommendations on patronage were 'attached to the legal department,' as Macdonald stressed in January

1855, and by working hard on behalf of people to whom he had made commitments, he was able to raise the level of loyalty to the party, and to himself, throughout the province.

Though never associated with legislation that produced dramatic or sweeping reforms, during the period when he was most influential as attorney general, party leader, or co-premier (1854–62), he oversaw, particularly in the late 1850s, the introduction of measures and administrative changes which contributed a good deal to the efficient running of a rapidly expanding and changing province. In the 1850s in Canada the state had just begun to assume responsibility for social welfare; the only existing provincial institutions in Upper Canada were the penitentiary at Kingston and the lunatic asylum in Toronto. Between 1856 and 1861 branches of the asylum were opened in Toronto, Amherstburg, and Orillia. An institution for the criminally insane was established in Kingston in 1858. The first reformatory for juvenile offenders began in temporary quarters in Penetanguishene the following year. By the act of 1857 that provided for the asylum for the criminally insane and the reformatory, a permanent board of inspectors was created to oversee and set standards for all state welfare and correctional institutions, including 52 local jails. Under Macdonald's leadership the basis of a public social-welfare system was laid down and gradually extended. In 1866 the Municipal Institutions Act (rescinded after confederation) required the establishment of a house of industry or a refuge for the poor in each well-populated county within two years.

During the same years a great deal of expansion and reorganization of the government's bureaucracy was undertaken. The question of a permanent seat of government, which had exacerbated urban rivalries for years, was settled by the ingenious device, on the part of Macdonald and others, of referring the issue to the queen in 1857. Announcement of her choice of Ottawa occasioned the temporary defeat of the Macdonald–Cartier government in July 1858, but when the Reformers under George Brown were unable to attract a parliamentary majority, it returned to office within 48 hours by means of the controversial 'double shuffle' manœuvre. In 1859 a parliamentary decision in favour of Ottawa was finally reached by a majority of five votes.

The Civil Service Act of 1857 established the rule that each major government agency would have a permanent, non-political head called a deputy minister. A first attempt to bring fiscal responsibility into government had been undertaken in the Audit Act of 1855 and the appointment of Macdonald's friend and former Conservative colleague John Langton as auditor of public accounts. Further financial change occurred in 1859 when the office of inspector general was elevated to a full-fledged Department of Finance, completing a long process by which the office of receiver general, who was originally the province's most important financial officer, was downgraded to a minor post. Two new departments were created. The Bureau of Agriculture and Statistics, established in 1857, became a full department in 1862. The previous year Macdonald had imposed a political head, the minister of militia affairs, upon the bureaucratic post of adjutant general of militia. In December 1861 Macdonald himself assumed the responsibility of being the first minister, a post which he held until May 1862, during the sensitive opening year of the American Civil War, and again in 1865–67, at the time of the Fenian raids. The expansion included the creation in 1857, within the Crown Lands Department, of a fisheries branch, charged with preserving and protecting fresh-water fish-stocks, and, more significant, the assumption by the province in 1860 of complete responsibility for Indian affairs, previously under imperial control.

Attempts were also made to develop areas of a province that was rapidly running out of accessible agricultural land. In 1858 two temporary judicial districts (Algoma and Nipissing) were established, tightening the government's control in these thinly populated northern areas. A network of colonization roads was planned under the direction of Crown Lands to encourage settlement in the southern section of the Canadian Shield beyond the existing areas of cultivation. These roads when built were never successful in their agricultural purpose (though they were helpful to the lumber industry), but the construction of several during Macdonald's period in office reflected his often-expressed view that there was a 'fertile back country' which only needed an improved transportation system to permit it to develop.

In the late 1850s, and especially in 1857, when more bills were passed than in any other year in the entire union period, the Macdonald–Cartier government undertook many legislative initiatives including the Independence of Parliament Act (1857), amendments to the Municipal

Corporations Act (1857 and 1858), an act for the registration of voters (1858), and amendments (1858) affecting the operation of the surrogate courts, the usury law, the composition of juries, and imprisonment for debt (it was abolished in most cases). As attorney general Macdonald was responsible for a number of significant reforms of the judicial system itself, among them the Common Law Procedure Act (1856), the County Attorneys Act (1857), and an act which permitted appeal in criminal cases (1857). In addition, this business-oriented government adopted a wide range of measures to stimulate economic growth. These included not only continued support of the Grand Trunk Railway but also, in the budget brought in by Inspector General William Cayley in 1857 and seen through the legislature by Alexander Tilloch Galt the following year, the first tariff system of 'incidental protection' for Canadian industry. This system, foreshadowing the National Policy of the 1870s, was responsible for 'numerous manufactories of every description which have sprung up in both sections of the province,' according to Macdonald in 1861. In 1859 Postmaster General Sidney Smith, one of Macdonald's closest political friends, concluded arrangements with the United States, Great Britain, France, Belgium, and Prussia for mail service to Canada and the United States. Macdonald and his colleagues also encouraged and supported a large number of acts incorporating new businesses and expanding the scope of existing ones, including road and rail companies, insurance companies, banks, mining, oil, and lumber companies, and many others, in some of which Macdonald and his parliamentary associates had a personal interest.

Macdonald went into opposition in 1862 when the Militia Bill was defeated in the assembly. He returned to office two years later, in very different political circumstances. The election of 1863 had returned almost twice as many Reformers as Conservatives in Upper Canada, but the situation overall, owing to the continued strength of Cartier's Bleus and the English-speaking Conservatives of Lower Canada, was a virtual stalemate. An administration led by the Reformers John Sandfield Macdonald and Louis-Victor Sicotte and then another formed in March 1864 by E.-P. Taché and Macdonald each failed to sustain majority support. A constitutional committee of the legislature chaired by George Brown, of which Macdonald was a member, reported on 14 June in favour of a federal system of government for the two sections of Canada or for all of the British North American provinces. This proposal received wide support in the Province of Canada because it offered a way out of the highly polarized political deadlock and would provide Upper and Lower Canada with separate provincial governments, thus allowing for greater regional freedom of action and a lessening of sectional and racial tensions. Macdonald, however, with two others from Brown's 20-member committee, refused to endorse its report, which was supported by almost all of the leading Canadian politicians of the day. Though he had been part of an administration which, as early as 1858, favoured a federal union, he had always been cool to the idea because, he stated in a public address in 1861, he feared a federation would have 'the defects in the Constitution of the United States' – a weak central government. Macdonald had always preferred a highly centralized, preferably unitary, form of government that would not be torn by jurisdictional disputes, which, he believed, had been 'so painfully made manifest' during the Civil War.

Despite these strong misgivings about federation, when Brown suggested combined action to bring about constitutional change, Macdonald reversed his stand. His shift came within two days, on 16 June 1864. The result was the formation on the 30th of the 'Great Coalition,' by which the majority of the Upper Canadian Reformers joined with Macdonald's Conservatives and Cartier's Bleus for the purpose of creating a federal union of British North America. The reasons for Macdonald's abrupt change of mind were both visionary and entirely practical. Federation would 'prevent anarchy,' 'settle the great Constitutional question of Parliamentary Reform in Canada,' and 'restore the credit of the Province abroad.' In other words, the united provinces would form a larger, stronger, more harmonious community and even a potential rival to the United States. More immediately the coalition allowed him to escape from serious political difficulties in his own section of Canada, where the Reform party appeared to be gaining unbeatable strength. 'I then had the option,' he wrote privately in 1866, 'either of forming a Coalition Government or of handing over the administration of affairs to the Grit party for the next ten years.'

From 1864 to 1867 Macdonald was preoccupied with two overriding concerns: the Civil War – its aftermath and its implications for Canada – and the not unrelated matter of the confederation of British North America.

In October 1864 a raid on St Albans, Vt, by Confederate soldiers operating from Canada and their later release on a technicality by Montreal magistrate Charles-Joseph Coursol caused a strong anti-Canadian reaction in the United States. In December its government demanded that all persons entering the United States from British North America be required to hold a passport and Congress began proceedings for the abrogation of the Reciprocity Treaty, in force since 1854. The Canadian government responded by calling out 2,000 militia volunteers to attempt to prevent further incidents along the border. As attorney general Macdonald authorized the creation of a small 'detective and preventive force' to gather information, using Canadian agents and American informants in several American cities. In charge of this first Canadian secret-service unit (which became the Dominion Police after confederation) Macdonald, in December, placed a 'shrewd, cool, and determined man,' a Scottish immigrant and former MLA named Gilbert McMicken. He reported directly and secretly to Macdonald, who in August 1865 once again added the responsibilities of minister of militia affairs to those of attorney general.

In 1864 Macdonald and McMicken were also forced to become concerned about the Fenian Brotherhood, an Irish-American paramilitary organization dedicated to the liberation of Ireland. There were fears of Fenianism spreading into Canada and there were rumours and a few incidents of armed organization on the part of the Hibernian Benevolent Society of Canada, but the menace turned out to be external. In 1866 raids were launched on Campobello Island in New Brunswick and, with more success, across the Niagara River at Fort Erie. Fenianism thereafter faded as a threat to British North American security but events of 1864–66 undoubtedly contributed to an 'atmosphere of crisis' which had an important effect on the rapid achievement of a federal union and on the form it took. The coalition government established in 1864 was under the titular leadership of Taché but Macdonald quickly became the mainspring of the confederation negotiations that followed. Brown had wanted the coalition first to pursue a federal union of the two Canadas alone. Macdonald insisted, and got his way, that the priority should be a union of all the provinces. An opportunity to further this aim presented itself, since the Maritime provinces had already begun preparations for a regional conference to discuss the possibility of a legislative union of Nova Scotia, New Brunswick, and Prince Edward Island. Viscount Monck, governor general of British North America, arranged with the lieutenant governors of those provinces to allow a Canadian delegation to attend the conference, planned for Charlottetown, to present informally a proposal for federation. During the summer of 1864 the Canadian cabinet prepared its proposals. When the delegation arrived at the conference in September, it was invited to present its case at once, before any discussion of Maritime union. Macdonald spoke first, beginning a process that was to culminate with the passage of the British North America Act three years later. It led to the Quebec conference in October 1864 between representatives of Canada, Nova Scotia, New Brunswick, Prince Edward Island, and Newfoundland, and eventually to the final meetings of the delegates of Canada, Nova Scotia, and New Brunswick with the British government in London between December 1866 and February 1867.

The extent to which Macdonald was personally responsible for the form and substance of the confederation agreement has been the subject of debate, but there is no doubt that he was the dominant figure throughout the events of 1864–67. At the Quebec conference he was the principal spokesman for the Canadian scheme, which had been worked out in some detail. He chaired the meetings in London in 1866–67 (in February 1867 he married there). The British North America Bill, for the federal union of Canada, Nova Scotia, and New Brunswick, was signed into law on 29 March 1867, to be proclaimed on 1 July. Macdonald's role was amply recognized in Great Britain. He was the only colonial leader to be awarded an honorary degree (from Oxford in 1865) or to be given a knighthood (conferred 29 June 1867, announced 1 July), and he was, of course, selected as the first prime minister of the Dominion of Canada. (He had been asked by Monck in May to form the first administration.)

Certainly much of the constitutional structure of the dominion was his creation. He could not say so publicly, but in private he claimed almost complete responsibility for the confederation scheme on the grounds that he alone had possessed the necessary background in constitutional theory and law. In the 'preparation of our Constitution,' he had told his close friend county court judge James Robert Gowan in November 1864, 'I must do it alone as there is not one person connected with the Government who has the slightest idea of the nature of the work.' His colleague

Thomas D'Arcy McGee said in public in 1866 that Macdonald was the author of 50 of the 72 resolutions agreed upon at Quebec.

Even at the time some played down Macdonald's role. George Brown challenged McGee's statement in the *Globe* and attributed the confederation plan to the collective efforts of the Canadian cabinet. Certainly there were aspects which Macdonald did not initiate and some of which he did not particularly approve. The financial arrangements, as he admitted, were the work of A. T. Galt. Representation by population, the principle that governed membership in the lower house, had long been advocated by Brown and was made a fundamental part of confederation at his insistence. The provisions for the official use of the French language in parliament, in the federal courts, and in the courts and legislature of Quebec, as well as the continuance of the *code civil* in that province, were clearly Cartier's contribution. The arrangements for the preservation of existing separate schools and for their establishment in new provinces were largely inspired by Galt. Before confederation Macdonald had never shared Brown's great enthusiasm for extending Canadian jurisdiction into the northwest, or for an intercolonial railway, which was provided for in an unusual constitutional clause insisted upon in London by the Maritime delegates, who included Jonathan McCully, William Alexander Henry, and Samuel Leonard Tilley. To what extent then can the BNA Act be said to have been 'the Macdonaldian Constitution'?

The terms of the act were not precisely what Macdonald would have wanted had he been allowed a free hand, but he believed that his main objectives had been achieved. His overriding goal had always been a system that, though federal in order to secure the assent of Quebec and the Maritimes, would be as centralized as possible, with a central government directed by a powerful executive. In the act the division of powers between the central and provincial governments reflected his aims. The federal powers were more numerous and contained the blanket phrase 'peace, order and good government.' In that phrase was the most sweeping grant of power known to the drafters at the Colonial Office, who supported Macdonald's centralist position. Macdonald intended to have ample room for anything he wanted to do. The federal powers were also concerned with those areas of jurisdiction where Macdonald believed real power lay: national defence, finance, trade and commerce, taxation, currency, and banking. As well the federal government was given the power (exercised by the imperial government before 1848) to disallow provincial legislation. (In June 1868 a justice department memorandum approved by cabinet for transmission to the provinces was to emphasize a new and exacting use of disallowance, so that even the strongest of provincial rights was to be subject to central surveillance.) The federal cabinet appointed its own provincial watch-dogs, the lieutenant governors, as well as the members of the Senate, the body designed by Macdonald to represent the well-to-do, propertied element of Canadian society, though the House of Commons would continue to be elected on a property franchise. Macdonald believed he had avoided the chief weaknesses of the American federation: universal suffrage and a weak executive. Canada would be run from the centre by people who had a genuine stake in the community. Macdonald's omission from the BNA Act of a formula for amending the structures and powers of the central government was probably not, as is often suggested, an oversight. Having seen to it that the local legislatures could amend their own constitutional arrangements within the tight constraints of section 92, Macdonald would not have neglected something analogous in section 91, on the powers of parliament, had he thought he needed it.

Macdonald's private agenda for the future of the new federation went much farther than the BNA Act revealed. It was not just that a provincial government was to be 'a subordinate legislature.' The provincial governments, he maintained, had been made fatally weak and were ultimately to cease to exist. He envisaged a Canada with one government and, as nearly as possible, one homogeneous population sharing common institutions and characteristics. In December 1864 he told Matthew Crooks Cameron that 'if the Confederation goes on[,] you, if spared the ordinary age of man, will see both Local Parliaments & Governments absorbed in the General Power. This is as plain to me as if I saw it accomplished but of course it does not do to adopt that point of view in discussing the subject in Lower Canada.' He was undoubtedly wise not to make such sentiments public, for among French Canadians, by whom the provincial governments were already being seen as the centre of what would become known as 'provincial rights,' there were even in 1864 suspicions of his intentions. Ottawa's *Le Canada*, edited by Elzéar Gérin, argued in 1866, 'The more the local legislature is simplified, the more its importance will be diminished and the greater the risk of its being absorbed by the federal legislature.' Macdonald thought he had set in motion an evolutionary constitutional process which in time would further alter the relative importance of the two levels of government. His colleague Hewitt Bernard, secretary of all the confederation conferences, had acquired an inner core of experience about how Macdonald's constitutional ideas could be translated into practice. Asked by Governor General Lord Dufferin in 1874 to comment on the BNA Act in the light of seven years of operation, Bernard directed his criticisms mainly at making still more explicit and restrictive the provincial powers covered in section 92.

In many practical ways the administrative structure of the new dominion government was that of the Province of Canada shifted into a new gear. The capital remained at Ottawa, of course, and many of the old province's deputy ministers and chief officers occupied senior positions in the federal civil service, among them Bernard, Joseph-Charles Taché, William Henry Griffin, Toussaint Trudeau, Edmund Allen Meredith, and John Langton. Macdonald was more ambitious than his colleagues to make not only constitutional room for central power but physical space as well. He wanted more land in central Ottawa than his colleagues would let him take. Macdonald wished, for instance, to take over Nepean Point for the governor general's residence, but his colleagues would have none of it. He told Joseph Pope years later that Rideau Hall had cost them more to patch up than a new residence would have cost at Nepean Point. Macdonald wanted to take the whole block between Wellington and Sparks streets east of Metcalfe for future departmental offices. His colleagues baulked at that too.

The Department of Justice was the portfolio Macdonald himself chose in 1867 and the one he retained until the resignation of his government in November 1873. He supervised the splitting of functions in 1867, consigning those of his former office, the attorney generalship of Upper Canada, to the provincial government in Toronto. The senior staff in his old office remained with the new department; no break in Macdonald's old departmental letter-books occurred.

His duties also tended to be a continuation of those he had carried as attorney general. The pardoning power, which belonged to the governor general, compelled Macdonald to review capital cases, and the penitentiary system was a federal responsibility. Federal involvement in both had been insisted upon by the Colonial Office; it is by no means certain that Macdonald wanted them. The penitentiary system he left to Hewitt Bernard, but in his policies he continued his tendency to be firm rather than charitable. The primary object of penitentiaries, he told John Creighton, the warden in Kingston, in 1871, was 'punishment, the incidental one, reformation.' It was possible to make prisons too comfortable, prisoners too happy. (Read *David Copperfield*, he said, particularly where Uriah Heep, in a model prison, is so much better off than poor people living outside it.) The power of release ought to be used sparingly. Certainty of punishment was of more consequence than severity of sentence. Macdonald attributed the high rate of crime in the United States to the ease with which pardons could be obtained through political pressure on state governors.

When Thomas D'Arcy McGee was shot on 7 April 1868, the full power of the dominion government was placed at the disposal of the attorney general of Ontario, in whose hands lay the responsibility for prosecution. The dominion shared the expenses of prosecuting Patrick James Whelan, and Bernard, as deputy minister of justice, took a prominent part in finding evidence in Ottawa. Although John Sandfield Macdonald was premier of Ontario as well as attorney general, Sir John virtually took over the case. He was implacable. Pressures arose for a stay of execution; even the prosecuting counsel, James O'Reilly, seemed uncomfortable; John Hillyard Cameron, the defence counsel, thought there should have been a new trial or at the least an appeal to the Privy Council. Yet Macdonald was ordinarily of milder mien, especially in cases where the evidence was ambiguous. The death sentence of Baptiste Renard, convicted in 1864 of rape, had been commuted, as usual, to life imprisonment. Three years later, after Bishop Edward John Horan of Kingston brought new evidence to Macdonald's attention, Renard was discharged.

The early sessions of the Canadian parliament showed Macdonald's strong centralist views about the assimilation of Nova Scotia, New Brunswick, and the Hudson's Bay Company territory. The new North-West Territories, to be carved out of Rupert's Land, were to become, Macdonald admitted, Canadian crown colonies, administered as such. He had things to learn; but the first year or so of confederation showed how firmly a central Canadian he was, sanguine about issues and difficulties that he was unfamiliar with. In the face of continuing anti-confederate sentiment in Nova Scotia, customs minister S. L. Tilley had to warn him in July 1868 from Windsor, N.S., 'There is no use in crying *peace* when there is *no peace*. We require wise and prudent action at this moment.' Macdonald was a realist, but realism with him took the form of perceptions forced upon a sanguine temperament. This odd combination gave him the incentive, dodger that he was, to adapt, shift, make expedients. He would not bow down to difficulties: he would try to work his way out of them. In the case of Nova Scotia, the recklessness of its premier, Charles Tupper, in pressing the province to enter confederation and his own central Canadian perspective had got him into trouble; when he moved it was late, but he acted with skill, courage, and resourcefulness. He travelled to Halifax in August 1868 in order to meet Joseph Howe to work out measures to ease the conflict between Nova Scotia and the dominion.

The application of an 'imperial screw' to Nova Scotia was not something he would willingly repeat. By 1869 he knew that as a mode for political unions it was counter-productive. At the end of that year Governor Stephen John Hill of Newfoundland suggested the colony might be added to Canada by imperial fiat. Macdonald would have none of it. Although terms of union had been negotiated with Canada by a delegation led by the island's premier, Frederic Bowker Terrington Carter, in the fall general election Newfoundlanders had definitely pronounced themselves against confederation. That, as far as Macdonald was concerned, was that. He would not impose Canadian rule on another colony without local opinion being tested and found willing. This attitude explains his readiness to negotiate at the first sign of trouble at Red River (Man.) in 1869. He would insist, for the same reason, on an election in British Columbia before confederation was cemented in place there in 1871. He would be endlessly patient with the demands, and elections, of Prince Edward Islanders. 'I see that you have quite a political ferment about your Railway,' he wrote in October 1871 to his doctor in Charlottetown, William Hamilton Hobkirk. 'I hope that the result of the increase of your pecuniary burdens will be your making a junction with the Dominion; but such a consummation … can be hastened by no action on our part, it must arise altogether from your own people.'

The acquisition of Rupert's Land was a major item on his 1869 agenda. This had been negotiated in London on Canada's behalf largely by Cartier. He and William McDougall, the minister of public works, arrived in London in October 1868; the latter was taken seriously ill almost at once. Cartier's negotiations crossed two ministries, Disraeli's on the way out and Gladstone's on the way in. Although McDougall was convinced that Gladstone's government would be more favourable to the Canadian cause, Cartier believed the opposite and he was right. Cartier left for Canada only on 1 April 1869, after six months of continuous negotiations. Under the dominion's temporary government act, assented to in June, a lieutenant governor and council were to administer the territories, which were to be transferred formally to Canada on 1 December.

After McDougall accepted the office of lieutenant governor of the North-West Territories (what Macdonald privately called his 'dreary sovereignty') Macdonald followed up a long conference with him by letters full of good sense. 'The point which you must never forget,' he advised sternly on 20 November, 'is that you are now, approaching a Foreign country, under the Government of the Hudson Bay Company. ... You cannot force your way in.' Macdonald encouraged him to retain Louis Riel (a 'clever fellow') for his 'future police,' and thus to give 'a most convincing proof that you are not going to leave the half breeds out of the *Law*.'

For the troubles that had already arisen in the Red River settlement over a federal survey and the transfer of the northwest, Macdonald, so far as he knew of them, put some blame on local priests. He also put some, privately, on Cartier for having 'rather snubbed' Bishop Alexandre-Antonin Taché of St Boniface that summer when he came through Ottawa on his way to Rome. Secretary of State Hector-Louis Langevin was thought to have patched things up, but Macdonald believed by late November that Taché's irritation had got back to Red River. The main burden of blame Macdonald put upon officials of the HBC. The dissatisfaction of the Métis was well known to its local council. The transfer had been planned and known of for months. HBC officer John H. McTavish had been in Ottawa in April, had seen Macdonald and others, and had been told of the transfer of the northwest to Canada with the same rights for its inhabitants as had existed before. Yet company officials gave no explanation to the people of Red River about what was to happen. 'All that those poor people know,' Macdonald said to Cartier on 27 November, 'is that Canada has bought the country … & that they are handed over like a flock of sheep to us; and they are told that they lose their lands. … Under these circumstances it is not to be wondered at that they should be dissatisfied, and should show their discontent.'

Macdonald's advice to McDougall that same day, in the light of what was then known, was good law and common sense. He told McDougall in a letter not to cross the 49th parallel and not to be sworn in as lieutenant governor. The policy should be to throw full responsibility for the unrest on the HBC and the imperial government. A proclamation from McDougall calling for the loyalty of the people in Red River would be well if it were certain to be obeyed. But if it were disobeyed, Macdonald reasoned, McDougall's weakness would be 'painfully exhibited' to the people and to the Americans. If he were not admitted to the country, a proclamation would create anarchy; it would then be open to the inhabitants of Red River 'to form a government *ex necessitate* for the protection of life and property, and such a government has certain sovereign rights by *jus gentium*.' The Americans might even be tempted to recognize it. This advice reached McDougall too late to save him from his own folly of 1 December, when he precipitately proclaimed the northwest to be part of Canada. A week later Riel established a provisional government. At about the same time, Macdonald sent emissaries, Charles-René-Léonidas d'Irumberry de Salaberry and Abbé Jean-Baptiste Thibault, when he thought reassurances were needed, and Donald Alexander Smith as a commissioner to negotiate the moment he saw that real mediation was going to be necessary. What he did not want was the British government sending out an imperial commissioner. He believed, as did the whole Canadian cabinet, 'that to send out an overwashed Englishman, utterly ignorant of the Country and full of crotchets as all Englishmen are, would be a mistake.'

When Taché came back through Ottawa in February 1870, Cartier ate as much humble pie as seemed requisite. But so sensitive was the northwest issue as a result of Thomas Scott's execution in March that two of the delegates sent east by Riel in March, Alfred Henry Scott and Abbé Joseph-Noël Ritchot, were arrested for complicity in the murder.

Macdonald hired John Hillyard Cameron to help get them off and made the $500 payment privately so that it would not appear in public accounts.

On 6 May, as the bill to create the new province of Manitoba was going through the House of Commons, Macdonald was struck down by the passage of a gallstone. He was so weak he could not be moved home, and his corner office in the east block became his sick-room. In early July Macdonald, his wife, his little daughter, his mother-in-law, Hewitt Bernard, Dr James Alexander Grant, a nurse, and a secretary went off to Charlottetown by government steamer from Quebec. The party arrived on 8 July and took up residence in a large rambling house in the suburbs. Macdonald was still so weak in the legs that he could not walk. It has been alleged that there, besides following the Franco-German War, Macdonald hatched the scheme to buy Prince Edward Island into confederation by getting its government to build a railway. Suspicions do not make evidence. What is certain is that Macdonald was not going to take the Island into confederation without a convincing display of local support. He was back in Ottawa on 22 September, impressing everyone with how well he looked.

He soon took hold of bringing British Columbia into confederation. Negotiations had been conducted by Cartier in June 1870. On 29 September Macdonald told the colony's governor, Anthony Musgrave, that though the terms Cartier had negotiated, including the construction of a transcontinental railway, could be justified on their merits, 'considerable opposition' could be expected in parliament because they would likely be seen as too burdensome to Canada and too liberal to British Columbia. He therefore told Musgrave to try to follow the course taken when the Newfoundland resolutions were going through parliament in 1869: have members of the colonial government come to Ottawa to discuss awkward points with the MPs, especially the Conservative caucus. In April–May 1871 Joseph William Trutch came east for that purpose and helped Cartier secure parliament's approval of the British Columbia terms of union.

Macdonald was again absent from the House of Commons. He had had to assume the thankless role of being a Canadian and an Englishman at the same time: as one of the British commissioners in the negotiations at Washington to settle outstanding Anglo-American differences, many of which affected Canada. One suggestion for a representative from Canada had been Sir John Rose, formerly Canada's finance minister, who had already conducted discussions on the same topic with American secretary of state Hamilton Fish. But Rose's interests were now London and New York and however much Macdonald trusted him – and that trust went a long way – his appointment was unacceptable politically. There seemed to be no one else for this ungrateful task but himself. He left for Washington on 27 February for what he would later describe as the 'most difficult and disagreeable work that I have ever undertaken since I entered Public Life.'

Macdonald had seen little of the United States for 20 years, and the commission was his first extended contact with American statesmen. He was surprised to find them agreeable socially; that did not make them less dangerous diplomatically. Of the pressing issues the *Alabama* claims was the most serious, but the commission, for the moment, could only agree to disagree on it. The full weight of negotiations then fell upon the Canadian inshore fisheries. Free access to those fisheries had ended when the Reciprocity Treaty lapsed in 1866 and the licensing of American vessels was now being rigorously enforced. Solving this issue became a matter of vital importance to Great Britain, which hoped to face the military and political consequences of the Franco-German War without the distraction of Americans being angry and belligerent. The United States, Macdonald told Tupper, wanted everything and would give nothing; his British colleagues, especially Lord de Grey, the chief commissioner, were ready to make Macdonald and Canada responsible for failure. They wanted a treaty in their pockets 'no matter at what cost to Canada.' Macdonald seriously weighed resigning as commissioner. De Grey strongly urged him not to, for the resignation of a plenipotentiary, especially the Canadian one, would endanger the treaty in the American Senate. Macdonald had been caught, as he admitted, between the devil and the deep blue sea, between his role as a British commissioner and as Canadian prime minister. Britain was so anxious to secure a treaty that, to help persuade Canada to ratify it, the British accepted Macdonald's suggestion that compensation be given by the imperial government for the Fenian raids, since the Americans had refused to consider any redress as part of the treaty.

Americans had accepted Canadian ratification of the treaty only because they thought that Canada would be a rubber stamp. If the British parliament ratified the treaty, that was that. As Macdonald put it to Tupper in April, 'When Lord de Grey tells them that England is not a despotic power & cannot control the Canadian Parlt. when it acts within its legitimate jurisdiction, they pooh! pooh! it altogether.' On 8 May, with much misgiving, Macdonald signed the Treaty of Washington.

In Canada he would face strong opposition from both political parties. He wrote to Rose some days after the signing, 'I think that I would have been unworthy of the position, and untrue to myself if, from any selfish timidity, I had refused to face the storm. Our Parliament will not meet until February next, and between now & then I must endeavour to lead the Canadian mind in the right direction. You are well out of the scrape.' He put it more sharply to de Grey: Canadian indignation in June and July was intense and pervaded all classes – parliament was certain to reject the treaty. If that happened, Macdonald suggested to Governor General Baron Lisgar in July, he would leave the government. His colleagues might or might not carry on without him. If they resigned, and a Liberal government were formed, it would oppose the treaty lock, stock, and barrel.

The fall of the Sandfield Macdonald government in Ontario in December 1871 did not augur well for the treaty, or for Ontario in the next federal election. Edward Blake, the new premier, and Alexander Mackenzie, his lieutenant, both opposed the treaty. It offered Ontario and Quebec nothing: no compensation from the United States for the Fenian raids on the Ontario and Quebec borders; free navigation of the St Lawrence for the Americans in return for the dubious privilege given to Canada of navigating three rivers in Alaska. The fisheries settlement offended most areas: Canadian fish would be admitted free to the American market, but access to the inshore fisheries was to be sold to the Americans for 10 years at a price to be set down by arbitrators. Macdonald had had to fight to avoid it being set down for 25 years. Scholars could later write about the treaty as an achievement in settling outstanding issues between Great Britain and the United States; it was another matter for the prime minister of a country that had to swallow critical sections of it. In the end, by waiting until May 1872, when Canadian public opinion had cooled down and the British had offered a guarantee for Canadian railways as compensation for the Fenian raids, Macdonald was able to get the treaty through the commons by 121 votes to 55. The vote did not mean, however, that the hustings had forgotten it.

Nor was this all. Riel would not go away. He had been got out of the country, but he drifted back. In the so-called Fenian attack across the Manitoba border in October 1871, Macdonald suspected him of playing a double game, first encouraging the leader, William Bernard O'Donoghue, and then switching sides when he saw that the raid would be damped down by the Americans. For that and other reasons Macdonald found Lieutenant Governor Adams George Archibald's shaking hands with Riel in apparent reconciliation unpardonable, and he wished that Archibald had had his political antennae sensitized by Ontario's reaction to the death of Thomas Scott.

These elements combined to make the general election of the summer of 1872 difficult, even treacherous, for Macdonald. He did not like to run a government out to full term, but after Washington an election in 1871 would have been folly. Even now the timing was not much better. Ontario farmers, he told Colonial Secretary Lord Carnarvon privately in September 1872, could not understand why the Maritime provinces should get free admission of fish to the United States while Ontario got nothing. And Ontario was even more important politically than before; after the 1871 census, redistribution gave it 88 seats, six more than it had in 1867. Macdonald worked at Ontario tenaciously. He went nowhere else (it was still the custom for ministers to pre-occupy themselves with their home provinces), leaving Quebec to Cartier and Langevin, New Brunswick to Tilley, Nova Scotia

Sir John A. Macdonald, 1872.

to Tupper, and Manitoba to A. G. Archibald and Gilbert McMicken, now dominion lands agent in that province. Macdonald also lavished money on Ontario. He got $6,500 from Conservative friends and received from Sir Hugh Allan some $35,000, plus an emergency draft of $10,000 on 26 August. The day after, in Toronto, he borrowed $10,000 on his own hook from Charles James Campbell and John Shedden at six per cent on a six-month note, a loan that alarmed Conservative campaign manager Alexander Campbell.

By this time Macdonald was very discouraged. He fought on as best he could, with those reserves of optimism that he always summoned up when the going was bad. His *modus operandi* in Ontario is suggested in his dealings with James Simeon McCuaig, MP for Prince Edward: 'Let me tell you that if [Walter] Ross goes in with money he will stand a great chance of beating you. You must fight him with the same weapon. Our friends here have been liberal with contributions, and I can send you $1000⁰⁰ without inconvenience. You had better spend it between nomination and polling.' McCuaig lost, and Macdonald got only 42 out of 88 Ontario seats, if that. In September he estimated his overall majority as 56. That was high, though how big his majority was depended on the issue. In April 1873, when Lucius Seth Huntington broke the first intimations of the Pacific Scandal, it would be 31.

At least three, possibly four, groups in Canada were interested in the Pacific railway by 1872, to say nothing of Americans. The main groups were those of Sir Hugh Allan of Montreal and David Lewis Macpherson of Toronto. Cartier had conceded in 1871, under opposition pressure and while Macdonald was ill, that the railway would not be built as a government enterprise but by a private company. Macdonald tried to bring the main groups together before, during, and after the election, but jealousies between Toronto and Montreal and mutual suspicions between principals made that impossible. In the late autumn of 1872 Allan was given the task of putting a company together to build the railway. Macdonald had made only one promise to Allan: the presidency of an amalgamated Canadian Pacific Railway Company, whenever it was formed. But there were commitments of which, as yet, Macdonald knew nothing, notably Cartier's to Allan in the summer of 1872, that Allan's group would be guaranteed the charter and a majority of stock in return for additional election funding, totalling more than $350,000. When Allan finally told Macdonald the amount, it seemed so fantastic that he did not believe Allan, and that fall he wrote to Cartier to confirm it. Cartier did, more or less; he was then in London fighting Bright's disease, which eventually would kill him, in May 1873. There was also Allan's commitment to American backers, of which Macpherson had been suspicious all along.

The Pacific Scandal was partly scandalous, partly not. All parties used money at election time. Macdonald would explain to Governor General Lord Dufferin in September 1873 how Canadian elections went. There were legitimate election expenses; because of the many rural constituencies, with sparse populations, these were large. Other expenses, long considered necessary, were in a half-light, being sanctioned by custom though technically forbidden by law, for example hiring carriages to take voters to the polls. Such expenses, in Macdonald's parliamentary experience, had never been pressed before an elections committee. No doubt the $1,000 McCuaig was to spend between nomination and polling day was partly for carriages. It was also no doubt for other things Macdonald did not mention: treating the voters could comprehend more than just carriages and whisky.

The Pacific Scandal broke in the commons on 2 April 1873. Huntington made a motion calling for a committee of inquiry and charging that Allan's original company, the Canada Pacific Railway Company, had been financed with American money and that Allan had advanced large sums of money to senior members of the government in the election. To his charges Macdonald ostensibly paid no attention; he brought in the members and voted down Huntington's motion; he called for a committee of investigation on his own. However, Conservatives were already uneasy. From then on Macdonald fought a stubborn, sometimes despairing, but often skilful rearguard action, hoping to rally his followers and to placate an uncomfortable, occasionally censorious governor general. But the telegrams published in Liberal newspapers on 18 July were damning, showing that Macdonald, and especially Cartier and Langevin, had accepted large sums of money, actions that were singularly inappropriate since the funds came from a financier with whom the government was negotiating a major railway contract.

WHITHER ARE WE DRIFTING?

Sir John A. Macdonald's denials and prorogation of parliament delayed investigation of the Pacific Scandal and raised public ire, as depicted by cartoonist John W. Bengough in *Grip* (Toronto), 16 Aug. 1873.

When parliament met in late October, Macdonald's colleagues were confident they would weather the storm, but almost at once defections began, including that of Donald Alexander Smith. Macdonald was urged to meet the opposition, to stop further haemorrhage while there was time. Dufferin and others believed that had the prime minister forced a vote of confidence early enough, he might have won by double figures. But Macdonald sank into a lethargy of gin and despair, waiting, glassy eyed, for some card he feared the opposition had up their sleeve. Finally, he made a great rallying speech on the night of 3 November, but he had been outgeneralled by fear and had left it too late. He and his government resigned 36 hours later, on the 5th.

Macdonald was in some ways glad to be out of it. He went to caucus the day after his resignation and offered to retire as leader, half hoping the members would accept, half fearing an abrupt plunge into private life. Caucus would have none of it. Perhaps retirement was not in his nature. When he was ill in 1870 Joseph Howe had suggested that he should retire to the bench, as chief justice of the proposed supreme court of Canada. Macdonald was contemptuous, exclaiming as Under-Secretary of State E. A. Meredith recorded in his diary, '"I wd. as soon go to H–ll!"'

Shortly after New Year's Day 1874 the new government of Alexander Mackenzie called an election and proceeded to wipe the floor with the Tories. Of 206 seats in the house the Liberals took 138. Macdonald held Kingston, by only 38 votes, but he was unseated in November on charges of bribery and other electoral malpractice. Yet the Conservatives' popular vote overall, even in this disastrous election, was still 45.4 per cent. Now in opposition (he was returned in a Kingston by-election), Macdonald needed income to live on. The money acquired in 1872 had never stuck in his pockets; he had bled freely with his own money, as well as with the funds of Allan, C. J. Campbell, Sir Francis Hincks, and others. He was only five years distant from having been flat broke.

Macdonald's private life in the 1850s and 1860s had demanded all his reserves of patience and sanguineness, hope and resilience. The spring and summer of 1869 marked its nadir. After a long and dangerous delivery, Agnes gave birth on 8 Feb. 1869 to a hydrocephalic girl, Margaret Mary Theodora, whose enlarged head undoubtedly contributed to the difficulty of her birth. A photograph taken in June shows Agnes and Mary; sad it is. Even sadder is one of mother and daughter in 1893 when Mary was 24. The cost in moral anguish to both parents can never be known, but any judgement of Sir John and Agnes should always have Mary in mind. By midsummer 1869 it was slowly coming to Macdonald – and with what infinite reluctance did he allow it – that Mary might never be normal. There were always hopes of some new medical treatment that would allow her to live like anyone else. It never came. She never did.

In 1869, too, Macdonald hit the bottom of his personal finances. He had been fighting off that dénouement for five years. One reason for the elaborate marriage settlement of 1867 was to protect Agnes against his creditors. The problem had begun in March 1864 on the death of his law partner, A. J. Macdonell. In May 1867 an estimated $64,000 (roughly $800,000 at 1988 prices) was jointly owed by Macdonald and the Macdonell estate, mainly to the Commercial Bank of Canada. As long as it would carry him – at rates of interest as high as seven per cent – Macdonald could stay afloat. But in September the bank failed; its assets and liabilities were taken over by the Merchants' Bank of Canada. Among the assets was Macdonald's debt, which in April 1869 was almost $80,000. Hugh Allan, president of the Merchants' Bank, did not press but indicated, when Macdonald raised the matter, that it would be useful to have the debt dealt with. The arrangements Macdonald was compelled to make in 1869 are by no means clear. He borrowed $3,000 from D. L. Macpherson to tide him over and, with Agnes, took out a mortgage on property at Kingston, payable to the bank, for $12,000. The money owed him by the Macdonell estate was largely uncollectable. (When Macdonell's widow died in 1881, Macdonald's Kingston factotum, James Shannon, told him that the estate still owed him $42,000.) In 1869 a case was pending in Toronto against Macdonell and Macdonald. It could have been settled out of court in 1865 for $1,000, but Macdonald did not like the counsel for the plaintiffs, Richard Snelling, whom he thought a shark. Finally Hewitt Bernard, again acting as a personal aide, was forced to negotiate a settlement in 1872, for $6,100.

At the time of confederation Macdonald had little income. As prime minister and minister of justice he earned $5,000 per year. His income from his legal partnership with James Patton Sr of Toronto, formed in 1864, was $2,700 between 1 May 1867 and 30 April 1868; the next year it was $1,760. What got Macdonald through was pride, and his friends. Macpherson discovered how bad Sir John's position was after Macdonald's attack of gallstones in May 1870; he set to work to develop a private sub-scription. He thought it unjust that a prime minister could not support and educate his family on his official income. In the service of his country he had become poor. By the spring of 1872 some $67,000 had been collected by Macpherson and invested as the Testimonial Fund, the income of which Macdonald could use in meeting the ordinary costs of living. Out of it, presumably, Macdonald's debt to the Merchants' Bank would be slowly discharged. Ever sanguine, in 1876 he told Thomas Charles Patteson of the Toronto *Mail* not to be upset at owing money. Treat debts as Fakredeen, in Disraeli's *Tancred*, treated his, Macdonald advised: he 'caressed them, toyed with them. What would I be without these darling debts.'

After the parliamentary session of 1874 was over, Macdonald began to feel that perhaps his fighting days were coming to an end. He sold his Ottawa house in September 1874 for $10,000 and began plans to move to Toronto, where his law firm and principal client, the Trust and Loan Company, were now located. Before he moved, he wanted the dispute over the contested Kingston election settled; he did not want it known that he would not be returning to Kingston. He won the by-election at the end of December by 17 votes. He then moved into a house on Sher-bourne Street in Toronto, rented from T. C. Patteson, and a year later into a more fashionable brick house on St George Street.

Macdonald in 1875 was determined to lie back, avoid factiousness, and ride the party with a loose rein. He lay back too much. One Friday in February, when Agnes was visiting in Niagara, he had been drinking brandy in the Senate bar, and by 3:00 P.M. he was already drunk. George Airey Kirkpatrick got him into the house for the speech he had to make. He spoke with sufficient clarity, though everyone present knew he was 'sprung.' Alexander Mackenzie followed. Macdonald, by now fractious, interrupted him constantly. Conservatives tried to get him out, but he refused to go. When he was drunk his temper went awry. Agnes would have kept him under control; left to himself, as Charles Belford of the *Mail* remarked, 'he is helpless as a baby.' She was called home abruptly by her mother's death that same evening. Macdonald had reason to try to turn over a new leaf. He did: he joined the Church of England on 2 March.

It may be well to confront the legend that Macdonald was a chronic drunkard. He was not. He was a spasmodic one: now and then, as the dialectic of life and politics went too savagely against him, or as the sheer strain of running or some inner compulsion, now beyond analysis, drove him. The numerous stories may be exaggerated but cannot be safely denied. A few examples suggest the general point. During the exertions and the parties of the Quebec conference of 1864, a friend discovered Macdonald standing in his room in front of a mirror, dressed in his nightshirt, a train rug thrown over his shoulder, practising lines from *Hamlet.* He was not sober. Such incidents were not always so innocent of effect. In the late stages of negotiations with the Manitoba delegates in April 1870, Macdonald, after having been on the wagon for several months, became quite *hors de combat* on a Friday, and could not be got working again until the Monday. He was tired from overwork, distracted by worries, and demoralized by the sudden death of a friend. In some ways that combination was typical. Still, it was also true that Macdonald was ill from gallstones. Perhaps the worst period of drinking occurred in 1872–73, at the time of the election and Pacific Scandal. In reviewing the fall of the government, Alexander Campbell told Alexander Morris, lieutenant governor of Manitoba and the North-West Territories, that Macdonald, 'from the time he left Kingston, after his own election, … kept himself more or less under the influence of wine, and … really has no clear recollection of what he did on many occasions at Toronto and elsewhere after that period.'

Macdonald's drinking had been serious enough that when he had consulted Hewitt Bernard about marrying his sister Agnes, Bernard replied that he had only one objection. Macdonald promised reformation. Another source said that Bernard tried to dissuade his sister from the marriage for that reason. Altogether, there is no doubt that Agnes had some idea of what she was getting into when she married Macdonald in 1867. And it was easier for Macdonald to promise reformation than to effect it. His reformations were spasmodic too. His having joined the Church of England in March 1875 did not prevent an unpleasant incident at a dinner party in T. C. Patteson's house in Toronto some months later. Macdonald got drunk, insulted Tupper, and finally went ropily upstairs to bed. Agnes went out the front door, and was still outside, sitting on the gate, when Patteson looked out at 6:00 A.M. Macdonald's political colleagues were philosophical; they would try to get him where he could sleep it off. Agnes could usually handle him, but, as this incident shows, not always. Of course people made allowances. His drinking may not have harmed him all that much in a world that tolerated a good deal of heavy drinking; it may even have had advantages in an age when men voted and women did not. What it did to him morally and physically is difficult to know; and one can only imagine what it did to Agnes. Some of her feelings surface in her diary.

The internal life of Macdonald's second marriage is as much a mystery as most marriages are. The main difficulty in knowing it is the absence of correspondence between them. One suspects that Agnes herself was the source of this hiatus, for she lived on until 1920 and had ample time to destroy not only Macdonald's letters to her but hers to him. Agnes was not greatly popular in Ottawa; she was acutely conscious of her lack of genial social graces, of deftness and ductility, and she finally seemed to take refuge in being something of a Tartar in the capital's society. But one must never forget her crippled daughter.

By 1875 Macdonald's law practice had become rather snarled. His agreement with Patton in 1864 was to last eight years. In the summer of 1871 a new agreement was drafted with a 20-year term. Macdonald's son, Hugh John, now 21 and a law student, was to enter the firm on 1 Nov. 1873. Of the profits from the Trust and Loan business Macdonald was to have one-third, Patton two-thirds; of general business Macdonald and his son were to have one-third, Patton one-third, and a new partner (Robert M. Fleming) one-third. The agreement defined Macdonald's participation as 'protecting & advancing the interests of the Firm, using his influence on their behalf & advising on important questions.' At the end of 1875 Hugh left the firm to go into practice on his own at Kingston, partly owing to a row with his father over his engagement to a young Toronto widow. The correspondence with his son does not show Macdonald to advantage. A softer and less vigorous edition of the old man, Hugh was, at least on paper, sweet reasonableness; Macdonald sounded like a heavy-handed father, gruff and unforgiving. He slowly got over it. By the end of 1877 Patton wanted out of the partnership. Evidence of the degree of bitterness is conflicting. Macdonald told T. C. Patteson on 18 Jan. 1878 that he and Patton were parting, but not amicably; the next day he told Hugh that any breach had been healed. The break became effective on 15 April. A formal indenture, dated 15 Oct. 1880, registered what had been a fact for two years.

In January 1877 Macdonald had told Langevin that he would resign the Conservative leadership when caucus met in Ottawa for the new session. His health seemed precarious, and he did not like to be an inefficient leader. But caucus would not hear of his resigning; Macdonald gritted his teeth and went on. He had already begun to think the Mackenzie government might be defeated. In the session of February–April 1877 he definitely adopted a protectionist policy, something he had been drifting toward for some years. Macdonald had once been a free trader; several of his Conservative colleagues were still free traders, Macpherson for one. But Liberals had occupied that terrain. Macdonald had to agree with Patteson of the *Mail*, as early as 1872, that the Conservative party had no option but to 'coquet with the Protectionists.' Of course that wicked word 'protection' should never be used, Macdonald told Macpherson privately in February 1872, but 'we can ring the changes of a National Policy; in paying the United States in their own coin.' In the summers of 1876–78 he was into political picnics, his hands 'full of these infernal things,' which were nevertheless an efficient means of popularizing protection and revitalizing his party.

The extent of its victory in the general election of September 1878 astonished even Conservatives. Macdonald's personal defeat in Kingston could not alter their elation. Nova Scotia, Prince Edward Island, Ontario, and Quebec all reversed positions from 1874. The most dramatic change was in Ontario, where Mackenzie had won 66 of 88 seats in 1874, and where Macdonald now won 63. Besides the obvious effects of the depression of the mid 1870s, the temperance question had in Macdonald's view done the Liberals great damage in Ontario. At the dominion level Mackenzie had passed the Canada Temperance Act in April 1878; at the provincial level Oliver Mowat's Liberal government passed the Crooks Act in 1876, which transferred authority for liquor licences from the municipalities to a provincial board. These acts alienated 6,000 licensed hotels and taverns in Ontario.

Subsequently elected in both Marquette, Man., and Victoria, B.C., Macdonald judiciously chose to represent the latter. His cabinet was built that fall from the same template he used to shape all his cabinets. It reflected Canada's national and religious composition and contained representatives of six provinces. Making such agglomerations work was the product of Macdonald's own peculiar make-up. First, he believed in politeness. Asking Langevin in 1879 to comment upon an enclosed letter, Macdonald noted, 'What answer shall I send? Let it be *soft*.' It made no sense to alienate people, merely for the sake of satisfying a principle, usually irrelevant. There were times to be tough and exigent: but they were far less frequent than people thought. If Macdonald returned few hard answers, he rarely promised, definitely, anything. Agnes had a frank word with T. C. Patteson on that subject. Patteson was interested in some office, perhaps for a friend. Agnes made it clear Macdonald was as costive with her as with everyone else. It was unlikely the office was already promised. Macdonald did not work that way. But she had no direct influence. 'Of Sir John's plans & purposes I know nothing, tho' the world ... persists in thinking I do. ... My lord & master who in his private capacity simply lives to please & gratify me ... is *absolutely* tyranical in his public life so far as I am concerned. If I interfere in any sort of way he will be annoyed. ... Sir John knows my opinion & wishes on the subject perfectly well. ... The other day ... I expressed it again with added decision – but Sir John, as is usual with him ... looked very benign[,] very gracious, very pleasant – but – *answered not one word!*' In 1890 Joseph Pope said much the same: Macdonald hated to be boxed in by promises, real or implied.

Under Macdonald patronage settled into a certain pattern. Nominations came from anyone, but ministers listened to those from party members of standing, especially from Conservative MPs or a Conservative who had fought an election and lost. Macdonald would never concede, and tried to prevent colleagues from conceding, that an MP had any *right* to be consulted about appointments. Fundamentally, it was a minister's responsibility to decide, and Macdonald rarely interfered. In his own departmental administration – as minister of justice (1867–73), minister of the interior (1878–83), superintendent general of Indian affairs (1878–87), and minister of railways and canals (1889–91) – Macdonald was cautious about appointments, and he would not have his deputy minister pushed around by cabinet ministers or MPs out for favours for their constituents.

When he was minister of justice, he paid particular attention to the appointment of judges; to some extent he always would. The argument that Macdonald never appointed to a judgeship anyone without a substantial record of party service is not true. Joseph Pope was basically right: Macdonald was after quality – mind, law, integrity, good health, even address. In 1882 he pushed Alexander Campbell, then justice minister, to appoint Lewis Wallbridge of Belleville, well known to Manitoba lawyers and an old friend, as chief justice of Manitoba, despite his Grit family connections. 'He will be a good judge,' Macdonald reasoned. 'It is so seldom one can indulge one's personal feelings with due consideration for public interests.' Macdonald's main concern was Wallbridge's teeth. He could not contemplate the prospect of a grave chief justice delivering judgement through a mouthful of black, decaying stumps. Mackenzie Bowell, a cabinet minister from Belleville, was set to work to get Wallbridge to have new teeth. It was a doubtful business, although, as Bowell put it irreverently, of '*gnashing* importance.'

The more important the judgeship, the less was Macdonald willing to let ordinary canons of patronage prevail. 'My rule,' he told one Nova Scotian in 1870, 'is to consider fitness as the first requisite for judicial appointments, and … political considerations should have little or no influence.' Perhaps the best example of this concern was his appointment of Samuel Hume Blake as a vice-chancellor of Ontario. In 1869 he thought the judges of its Court of Chancery, John Godfrey Spragge and Oliver Mowat, lacked authority; as Macdonald put it to J. H. Cameron, equity in Ontario needed heavier metal. He had wanted Edward Blake; solicited privately, Blake did not accept the offer, mostly because his private law practice was too lucrative. Macdonald tried other Liberals and in the end, in 1872, got Blake's brother to accept. 'There was,' he explained to Patteson, 'literally no Conservative fit for the position who was available.' Macdonald applied the rule of judicial qualification generally. Bliss Botsford was appointed a county court judge in New Brunswick in 1870, even though he had been an anti-confederate in 1865–66. Timothy Warren Anglin, a New Brunswick Liberal, noted that appointment and wondered if there were any possibility for himself. Macdonald answered promptly, stating that Botsford had been selected on 'special recommendation' and declaring his patronage principles: 'I think that in the distribution of Government patronage we carry out the true Constitutional principle.

Whenever an office is vacant it belongs to the party supporting the Government if within that party there is to be found a person competent to perform the duties. Responsible Government cannot be carried on in any other principle. I am not careful however what a man's political antecedents have been, if I am satisfied that he is really and bona fide a friend of the Government at the time of his appointment. My principle is, reward your friends and do not buy your enemies.'

In 1878 Macdonald took on the Department of the Interior portfolio because the west was the growing edge of the country. By 1881, however, the CPR was taking up so much of his time and energy that David Mills, one of the members of the Liberal opposition with whom he was always friendly, chided him with having largely left the department 'to take care of itself.' Macdonald was, as he was to admit in 1883, unprepared in debate and had to 'rely on memory and the inspiration of the moment.' That did not answer with a vigilant opposition. Macdonald was 66 in 1881, and his age was starting to show. He had been ill in 1880 and during the winter of 1880–81, when the CPR contract was going through parliament. He managed an expert defence of it in the house on 17 January, but after the session prorogued, on 21 March, he went to ground, pulse at 49, with liver and abdominal pain. His sister, Louisa, saw him early in May: 'I never saw John looking what I would call old till this time.' But he made no plans to give up. The CPR and the National Policy both needed the buttress of another election victory. He nursed his strength as best he could at home. Charles John Brydges, land commissioner of the HBC, found him there on 3 May looking 'very ill indeed' but determined to straighten out an ugly tangle with the HBC over a contract with the government for Indian supplies. Macdonald put the blame on Chief Factor John H. McTavish. In 1881 he still cherished hard memories of the HBC as partly responsible for the Red River rebellion. But his old friendship with Brydges allowed a sensible compromise that Brydges had suggested to go forward.

Macdonald by now needed help with the interior portfolio. D. L. Macpherson had become a minister without portfolio and government leader in the Senate in 1880, and the following year an ailing Macdonald began to get him to do the interior work when he himself was abroad for recovery. Macpherson liked the task and believed he was good at it.

From London in 1881 Macdonald watched Macpherson taking hold while he tried to build up his energies. Work was now his only pleasure. He returned to Ottawa in mid September a good deal more spry. A cartoon by John Wilson Bengough in *Grip* showed him passing his 67th birthday milestone with 'M.DCCC.L.XXX.II. JNO.A. O.K.' carved on it. This well-being was reflected triumphantly in the general election of June 1882. There were no major issues, and Canadians gave Macdonald (who was returned in the eastern Ontario riding of Carleton) nearly as large a majority as he had had in 1878.

Yet the next nine years of Macdonald's life would be a struggle to maintain his own strength, and that of his cabinet, against old age, illness, incompetence, or colleagues simply wearing out. Macpherson took over the interior portfolio officially in 1883 because he and other colleagues saw that Macdonald was carrying too heavy a load. But Macpherson soon flagged and was abroad for his own health in 1883 and again in 1884. When a question about British Columbia lands arose that year, of course Macdonald had to deal with it. He looked better than most of the cabinet but claimed that he felt the worst, with the possible exception of John Henry Pope. Although his face and voice did not betray his weakness, he was already thinking of easing back in the harness, especially when parliamentary sessions were on. But Tupper's retirement to England in 1884 as high commissioner left a gaping hole in the cabinet; a solid and capable replacement was a matter of urgency. It took a long time. 'We want new blood sadly,' Macdonald told Tupper in February 1885. Campbell and Archibald Woodbury McLelan wanted out, Tilley in finance was unwell and was away much of the time, Macpherson and Joseph-Adolphe Chapleau were ill and away, J. H. Pope was sick, John Costigan was often drunk. The work fell on Macdonald, that too-willing horse, and, he admitted to Campbell, 'much of it of necessity was ill done. ... If we don't get Thompson I don't know what to do.' Well before John Sparrow David Thompson came into cabinet, the Saskatchewan crisis, at the end of March 1885, was fully upon the government.

The issues in the Saskatchewan River valley were produced by a series of disappointments and an overstrained administration. The CPR pulled its main line far to the south in 1882; there were bad harvests in the valley in 1883 and 1884. The territory needed attention from Ottawa and there was no one to give it. Langevin went west in 1884 but he declined to make a 200-mile ride across the prairie to hear grievances from disaffected Métis at Batoche (Sask.) or whites in Prince Albert. In Regina Edgar Dewdney, lieutenant governor of the North-West Territories, did the best he could on skimped budgets and attempted so far as he was able to buffer Macdonald from difficulties.

Riel's arrival in the Saskatchewan valley in July 1884 created a stir among both Métis and whites. A large petition to Ottawa about grievances was got up by Riel, William Henry Jackson, and Andrew Spence in December. It was reviewed by Macpherson, now back on the job. On 28 January the cabinet concluded that it would have to assess the position of the Saskatchewan Métis, with full enumeration and probably land scrip in mind. Macdonald, who had always frowned on land grants and scrip as a solution, did not much like the decision, but he went along with forming a three-man commission to investigate the claims of those Métis who were still eligible but had not participated in land allocation under the Manitoba Act. The news was telegraphed to Dewdney on 4 February; Riel got it via his cousin Charles Nolin four days later. The appointment of a commission was not merely a shuffle. The government was looking to a strong commission; Macdonald and Macpherson were weighing up the men for it in early March. Once it was appointed and working, an insurrection would be pointless and any settlement of Riel's personal land claims unlikely.

In late March 1885, by an extraordinary combination of circumstances, two major problems landed on Macdonald's desk at the same time. The outbreak of fighting on the 26th at Duck Lake, between the Métis led by Gabriel Dumont and a North-West Mounted Police force under Lief Newry Fitzroy Crozier, occurred on the very day when Macdonald finally told George Stephen, president of the CPR, that the cabinet could not approve any further loan to allow its completion. By the next day it was becoming clear to Macdonald that the one problem could be made to relieve the other: further funding could be considered for the CPR because of its value in moving forces to quell the insurrection. As tactics the solution was brilliant: as government it was desperate.

In these circumstances, the introduction in April, not of relief for the CPR, but of the electoral franchise bill, might have seemed quixotic, not to say foolhardy. But with a rebellion on in the west, it was patent that, as things stood, whether the CPR survived or not, Macdonald could not win another general election, which was due within two years. Provinces controlled their own franchise and dominion elections were based upon provincially prepared voters' lists. Because Nova Scotia, New Brunswick, and Ontario were now under Liberal control, it was sensible to consider having a federal franchise, with federal voters' lists administered by county court judges or, where necessary, by local barristers. Macdonald wanted at least impartiality; he certainly wanted to negate Liberal partiality. Vigorously defended by Macdonald against a barrage of opposition attacks, the franchise bill passed in July, near the end of the session.

In dealing with the CPR, a private company dependent on the goodwill of the government, Macdonald could be more cavalier. The CPR was, as he had remarked in 1884, the government's 'sleeping partner (with limited liability).' In February of that year he suggested to Stephen that, in the war coming between the Grand Trunk and the CPR, it would be well to strengthen the latter's hand in sections of the country. 'The CPR *must* become political & secure as much Parliamentary support as possible.' Appointments to the Ontario and Quebec, the railway leased by the CPR from January 1884, 'should all be made political. There are plenty of good men to be found in our ranks.' In March Macdonald put the question more jocularly to Henry Hall Smith, the Ontario Conservative organizer. No one should be working on the CPR who was not – Macdonald used William Cornelius Van Horne's pithy remark – a 'fully "circumsised"' Conservative.

Stephen was not an easy-going confrère. He complained of manifold difficulties, but he did not always appreciate Macdonald's. For example, in 1885 the CPR wanted to institute a land buy-back scheme; being land rich and cash poor, it would sell some of its land back to the government. The cabinet was opposed and Macdonald reminded Stephen on 26 May that it had been only 'with *very* great difficulty' that he himself had gained acceptance for the loan package devised during the rebellion. 'The majority of our friends in Parlt and *all* our & your foes were in favour of the Govt assuming possession of the road, and my personal influence with our supporters and a plain indication of my resignation only got them into line. This was done by personal communication with every one of them. … You speak of having to come back next Session. I hope you have not done so to anyone else. A hint of that kind getting abroad would be fatal to you.' The CPR aid package, notice of which had been given by the prime minister on 1 May, was introduced in the commons on 16 June and passed in July. It is possible to wonder what would have happened to the CPR had Macdonald not been in power, or if he and Stephen had not worked together in utmost frankness. The line to the west coast was completed later in 1885 and in the summer of 1886 Macdonald travelled overland to British Columbia, his first trip west. Ironically, during the parliamentary session that spring the CPR did sell 6.8 million acres, valued at $10.2 million, back to the government to help repay the loan.

A glimpse of Macdonald's personal opinion about one of the most dramatic episodes of the North-West rebellion, Riel's trial and execution, emerges from his correspondence with his trusted friend J. R. Gowan, now retired from the bench, whom Macdonald had appointed to the

Sir John A. and Lady Macdonald pause at the Canadian Pacific Railway station in Port Arthur (Thunder Bay), Ont., 2 Sept. 1886.

Senate in January 1885. Macdonald confessed to him on 4 June 1885, two weeks after Riel was captured, that if Riel were convicted 'he certainly will be executed but in the present natural excitement people grumble at his not being hanged off hand.' When the question of clemency for Riel arose after his conviction in August, Gowan's legal and political view was much the same as Macdonald's. It would be, he told Macdonald in September, 'a fatal blunder to interfere with the due course of law in his case. The only plea he could urge was urged for him at the trial and found against him.' Macdonald's correspondence on this touchy subject is thin, but Gowan's letter to him of 18 November, two days after Riel was hanged, reveals Macdonald's perception clearly enough: 'From what you wrote me I did not doubt the result but I felt most uneasy to the last knowing how public men are often obliged to take a course they do not individually approve. The fact may affect you prejudicially with Lower Canada but looking at the subject with all anxiety to see the wisest course for you to take I felt it would have been an act of political insanity to yield, simply because the man was of French blood.' Thus, although it is sometimes averred that Macdonald sacrificed Riel to Ontario opinion, that is the truth inside out. Riel was a victim of the law. One way out might have been to bend before Quebec opinion. The *furia francese* spent its force eventually, but not without political damage. Though he won a comfortable majority in the federal election of February 1887, Macdonald lost ground in Quebec; provincially, the Conservatives lost control of Quebec to Liberal leader Honoré Mercier.

The west, after the rebellion, went on to become prosperous, with ranches, railways, immigration, and wheat. Ontario, on the other hand, took up fear of Catholicism and the French; Quebec took up fear of Protestants and the English. Anti-Catholicism had spilled northward from the United States, where a strong nativist movement arose in the late 1880s; but there was plenty of Protestant tinder in Ontario always ready for a satisfying and warming blaze, and Toronto's Protestant papers took fire after Mercier's Jesuits' Estates Act was given royal assent in July 1888. Protestant Ontario demanded disallowance, claiming papal intrusion into a settlement between the Jesuits and the province of Quebec (the estates' owner since confederation), but Macdonald and the minister of justice, Sir John Thompson, thought the act should stand. The Protestant 'equal rights' uproar followed in March 1889. William Edward O'Brien, MP for Muskoka, told Macdonald that he would move in the commons that the Jesuits' Estates Act be disallowed. Macdonald said he regretted such a motion but, he added in a typical gesture, he would be sorry if any Conservative should feel bound to separate from the party merely because he had voted for O'Brien's motion. He told William Bain Scarth, his right-hand man in Manitoba and MP for Winnipeg, to leave 'equal rights' severely alone. Many Conservatives might take it up but Macdonald felt they 'will be all right at election time. There is no use of reminding them of their mistake. It might, such is the perversity of human nature, have the effect of making them stick to their cry.' Macdonald had little stomach for recriminations.

In the commons debate in 1889 on disallowance, Thompson walked into O'Brien's outspoken ally D'Alton McCarthy with a cool, polite, but infuriating logic. Thompson was appalled at the sheer impolicy of the motion in a country like Canada, which was 40 per cent Catholic. Macdonald admired his performance but for one thing: it was too good. Thompson had angered McCarthy. Macdonald was thinking of a day when O'Brien and McCarthy, both Conservatives, would cool off and return to the party. Thompson had perhaps reduced that possibility. The government's overwhelming majority against disallowance, 188 to 13, was due not only to parliament's revulsion at McCarthy's argument but also to the French Canadians on the Conservative side having been told to keep quiet and let the common sense of the anglophone members prevail. Nevertheless, Macdonald did not like the drift of things. Canada, he told Gowan in July 1890, as a just punishment for ingratitude for the blessings that had been heaped upon it, was heading into trouble. 'The demon of religious animosity which I had hoped had been buried in the grave of George Brown has been revived. ... McCarthy has sown the Dragons teeth. I fear they may grow up to be armed men.'

On the Manitoba school question, which grew out of 'equal rights,' Macdonald agreed in 1890 with both Thompson and Edward Blake – the decision about the constitutionality of Manitoba's abolition of public funding for Catholic schools was best left to the courts, not to the House of Commons. He who had been so free with disallowing provincial legislation to protect the CPR from Manitoba or with Ontario over the Rivers and Streams Act, now capitulated to basic good sense. If Manitoba's school legislation was *ultra vires*, the courts would so declare it. If it were *intra vires*, what was the point of disallowance?

By 1890 many of Macdonald's colleagues had died off or retired, some of them too young. Thomas White died in 1888 at age 58, having won golden opinions as minister of the interior; Macdonald loved him like a son. John Henry Pope died in 1889; Macdonald mourned him as a trusted and salty companion. Others went to pasture: Tilley to Government House in Fredericton in 1885, Sir Alexander Campbell to Government House in Toronto in 1887. The weaknesses of Sir Adolphe-Philippe Caron, the minister of militia and defence, seemed to grow more apparent, as did Secretary of State Chapleau's thirst for a portfolio with blood in it. Macdonald had acquired younger men, enthusiastic and hardworking, but not very experienced: John Graham Haggart, Charles Carroll Colby, George Eulas Foster, and Charles Hibbert Tupper. They were awkward colleagues to handle sometimes, especially young Tupper, MP for Pictou, N.S., and minister of marine and fisheries from 1888 to 1894. He had much of the talent and all of the bumptiousness of his father. One of Tupper's importunate requests Macdonald endorsed with 'Dear Charlie, Skin your own skunks. JAMD.' In a characteristic argument in 1889 Tupper took exception to Conservative friends in Pictou being ignored in a coal contract for the Intercolonial Railway. Macdonald, then in charge of railways and canals, reminded him that chief engineer Collingwood Schreiber was responsible for the contract. Schreiber had no other interest than doing his duty. You can, Macdonald told Tupper, 'throw all the blame on me, if you like.' Still, he prefaced his letter with a touch of jocularity. 'I see we must find you a seat where there are no coal mines, or we shall have annual trouble.'

Foster also had a difficulty, though it was not with his Department of Finance. Macdonald was distressed over Foster's marriage to Adeline Chisholm in 1889. Her husband had deserted her and she had eventually got a divorce in Illinois. In a letter to former governor general Lord Lansdowne, now in India, Macdonald was frank. Mrs Foster would be shunned by Ottawa society, he said, and Rideau Hall would be closed to her. Foster would be stung to death in the next session of parliament. 'But,' Macdonald added, 'as Sir Matthew Hale long ago said, "There is no wisdom below the belt."' Macdonald judged wrong. If Lady Macdonald refused to see Mrs Foster, Lady Thompson would and did see her, and in 1893 Sir John Thompson persuaded Governor General Lord Aberdeen and Lady Aberdeen that the nonsense had gone on long enough.

Macdonald's heir apparent, after Sir Charles Tupper went to London in 1884 and McCarthy refused to enter the cabinet, had been Sir Hector-Louis Langevin. He had been groomed to replace Sir George-Étienne Cartier, upon whom Macdonald had relied so much. Cartier had been his Quebec lieutenant, respected, listened to, and with real authority. He had also been Macdonald's right hand in the commons, taking over the running of it when Macdonald was away. To this double role Langevin might have succeeded, but he was never really capable of filling either part of it. The political control of Quebec he was forced to share, reluctantly, with others. Hardworking in his department (Public Works), he was the senior minister but, despite Macdonald's urging, he seemed never quite to rise to mastering the general business of the house. He remained senior minister but by 1890 Thompson had become Macdonald's real lieutenant. He and Macdonald got on well together; he wrote admirable state papers and shouldered a great deal of the work. Macdonald was nevertheless devoted to Langevin, who had stood by him through many a dark hour. And he had always let tried and experienced ministers run their own departments. The obverse was that he could be caught by that trust. Of Joseph-Israël Tarte, Caron, and others, who by 1890 were bringing Macdonald allegations of wrongdoing in Langevin's department, Macdonald could only ask, what could he do? It was perhaps his inkling of a scandal involving Langevin and MP Thomas McGreevy, if not its details, that made him look early in 1891 for reasons to dissolve parliament. He now lived, according to Gowan, in daily fear that the searchlight would be applied to Langevin's department. Macdonald was not at all sure his government would survive.

The election of March 1891 would be fought on patriotic grounds, by meeting head on the Liberal call for unrestricted reciprocity with the United States. It was apparent to Macdonald that the American secretary of state, James Gillespie Blaine of Maine, was an expansionist interested in taking over Canada. Macdonald could strike the patriotic note hard. Asked for a dissolution, Governor General Lord Stanley was more than a little dubious about using, as a weapon of political war, the proofs of a pamphlet by journalist Edward Farrer on how American policies could be devised for driving Canada into annexation, but, with the Liberals getting the Langevin scandal hot and ready to serve, Macdonald did not want another session of parliament without an election first. He did not hesitate, in an enthusiastic address in Toronto on 17 February, to colour Liberal schemes of unrestricted reciprocity as fundamentally annexationist. Macdonald's famous remark in his electoral address on the 7th of that month, 'I am a British subject and British born, and a British subject I hope to die,' has to be read more as an expression of Canadian nationalism than as any lofty imperial sentiment. Indeed as early as 1884 he was looking to the day when Britain (now a rather 'shaky old Mother,' as he saw her) would be taken care of by her growing children. That year he was sorry to see New South Wales throwing over the chance to have an Australian federation; Canada and Australia together would have work to do ere long helping the mother country, he said in a letter to Gowan. But in 1889 cabinet expressed only mild interest in his proposals for a conference with the 'Australasian Colonies' and, perhaps following the lead of business, the possibility of trade relations.

Parliament opened at the end of April 1891 and on 11 May Tarte moved for the Langevin–McGreevy investigation. The next day, in an interview with the governor general, Macdonald suffered a slight stroke. Neither Thompson nor Lord Stanley liked the look of it; the election, which had produced a reduced Conservative majority, had taken a great deal out of Macdonald. Nevertheless, he rallied and in ten days was back in that all too familiar and sweaty harness at the Department of Railways and Canals, dealing, once more, on 22 May, with C. H. Tupper's importunities. It was almost the last business Macdonald did. Tupper wanted a policeman to control the crowds at the Pictou railway station when the trains came in. Macdonald patiently sent the letter to Schreiber, who replied that he could not believe the good people of Pictou had suddenly become all that uncontrollable! Few could know how toilsome were Macdonald's working days. Behind a life that seemed full of achievement and great projects were a mountain of detail, piles of paper, and long days of aching routines. In these last weeks, working in his department and in cabinet, he tried to keep his strength, avoiding late-night sittings of the house. He was chagrined at a ministerial defeat on 21 May on a motion to adjourn, by a vote of 65 to 74, because Conservative members were at dinner parties given by Chapleau and Dewdney. Such a defeat had not happened to Macdonald before, in 13 years of office. He himself had to come into the house. This defeat and the Langevin scandal gave the opposition new life and vigour.

Macdonald went the other way. While he was in bed recovering from a cold, a severe stroke overtook him on the afternoon of 29 May. He never spoke again. He died a week later, in the evening of 6 June 1891. There was a great state funeral in Ottawa and he was buried in Cataraqui Cemetery, near Kingston, beside his parents, his first wife, his sisters, and his long-dead child.

Under Macdonald's will, dated 4 Sept. 1890, rights of administration were given to Edgar Dewdney, Frederick White (a former secretary), and Joseph Pope, his secretary since 1882. The three men were, with Agnes, the official guardians of Mary, who would live until 1933. All of Macdonald's real estate and property in Ottawa (mainly Earnscliffe, the family's home since 1883) went to Agnes free of rent. Her current income was provided by her marriage settlement and by the testimonial gift of $67,000 presented to the Macdonalds in 1872. Macdonald's two insurance policies, each worth £2,000, were to be invested for the benefit of Hugh John, who also received some estate and stock left to Sir John by his sister, Louisa. Not counting the Earnscliffe property, Macdonald left about $80,000 plus the Testimonial Fund income.

Sir John A. Macdonald's widow and their daughter, Mary, May 1893.

Macdonald had an elasticity of mind and range of information rare in Canada and unusual anywhere. He joined to that a huge and irreverent sense of humour. He wore the dignity of his office, well and good; he had style, manners, and vocabulary, but they were often a mask and the real Macdonald would show through it, especially if he caught the eye of an old friend. With his friends, he rarely worried about being what later Victorians might have called respectable. He was never a later Victorian anyway. When his affairs were in a tangle, when he was depressed, when he was unable to put things off, he might get drunk: more often he would open up the truth in conversation. He often discovered that talk suggested, to his fertile mind, some way of escape. He had enormous patience. Sir Alexander Campbell, his old law partner and long a colleague, marvelled at it. To A. W. McLelan of Nova Scotia he gave the impression, even in 1889, that there were reserves of power yet unused.

J. R. Gowan reflected that of Macdonald's great aspirations, of his nobility of aim, there could be no doubt. But if Macdonald thought of the ends, he was insufficiently concerned with the means. The public service was affected. Lord Lansdowne, in India, was not surprised at the Langevin revelations, however much he was fond of Macdonald. In his own departments Macdonald would not tolerate a slack or disobedient deputy minister and he would back a fair and judicious official such as Schreiber in railways or a cabinet minister of the calibre of Thompson. But often he had to work with lesser men, of doubtful integrity or dubious intelligence. He may have trusted them too much, or his own capacity for using them. 'A good carpenter,' he told T. C. Patteson in 1874, 'can work with indifferent tools.' On 19 June 1891 the *Montreal Star* observed that as long as he was there, it did not much matter who was in the cabinet: 'His infinite capacity for getting well out of any scrape that his friends got him into ... [was] such as would have inspired confidence in a government composed of Montreal aldermen had he been at the head of it.' Macdonald's protean mind, his resourcefulness, his reserves of doggedness when the going was really rough – all gave him tremendous depth and resilience. He calls to mind an aphorism by Talleyrand, 'The stability of complicated natures comes from their infinite flexibility.' This quality could mean timidity, as with George Eulas Foster. Yet he was never a prig; his sense of humour could be wicked, and he loved old, even gamy friends and associations. It could also mean a tenderness that was both charming and touching. In April 1891 Tilley, his old finance minister, wrote from New Brunswick asking if he could continue for a while longer as lieutenant governor; if he stepped down, his and his wife's combined income would not be enough for them to live on. He would have to eat up his capital, and this, though Tilley did not say so, after 12 years of public service to New Brunswick and 24 to Canada. Macdonald sent the letter on to Foster, the New Brunswick minister in cabinet, endorsing it, 'My dear Foster, This is a sad letter. ... We must leave him in Govt House as long as possible.' Foster agreed. Tilley stayed until 1893.

The truth was, notwithstanding all the vicissitudes Macdonald had endured, he enjoyed his *métier*. He remembered faces and places, associations and names, and he kept them alive in mind and practice with an enormous and often personal correspondence. He listened to everyone, and led all to think that he set great store by their information. His own letters are a marvellous treasure: trenchant, whimsical, full of pith and substance, salt and savour – the way he was. 'He was the father and founder of his country,' said Sir John Thompson in 1891 in a rare interview, 'there is not one of us who ... had not lost his heart to him.' Even Liberals were not without grudging admiration; Conservatives, in parliament, in the country, loved the Old Man and at his death they mourned for him as if he had been taken from their very firesides.

J. K. JOHNSON AND P. B. WAITE

Further reading

D. [G.] Creighton, *John A. Macdonald* ... (2v., Toronto, 1952–55; repr. 2v. in 1, 1998).

P. B. Waite, *Macdonald: his life and world* (Toronto and New York, 1975).

Affectionately yours; the letters of Sir John A. Macdonald and his family, ed. J. K. Johnson (Toronto, 1969).

ALEXANDER MACKENZIE,

stonemason, businessman, militia officer, journalist, politician, and author; b. 28 Jan. 1822 in Logierait, Perthshire, Scotland, son of Alexander Mackenzie and Mary Stewart Fleming; m. first 28 March 1845 Helen Neil (d. 1852) in Kingston, Upper Canada, and they had two daughters, one of whom died in infancy, and a son, who also died as a child; m. secondly 17 June 1853 Jane Sym; they had no children; d. 17 April 1892 in Toronto and was buried in Sarnia.

Alexander Mackenzie was the third of ten sons, three of whom died as infants. The family was not well off, as frequent moves, from Logierait to Edinburgh and then in turn to Perth, Pitlochry, and Dunkeld, attested. Mackenzie's father was trying to improve his job prospects through these moves. He had done well as a carpenter during the high employment of the Napoleonic Wars; perhaps this success had expedited his marriage in 1817. However, employment and wage expectations had declined thereafter and by the 1830s his health was precarious. His death in 1836, at the age of 52, made the family's position difficult. Yet the steady industry of the three elder sons, Robert, Hope Fleming, and Alexander, positioned the family sufficiently well to obtain sensible apprenticeships for them. Alexander began working full-time at age 13, during his father's last year; he was apprenticed as a stonemason at 16 and began work as a journeyman less than four years later.

Mackenzie's deep sense of familial attachment was clear in both his early labours to garner income and, when he left home job hunting at 19, his quick adoption of a surrogate family in Irvine, the Neils. His attachment to them was strengthened by his affection for one of the daughters, Helen, who in 1845 would become his wife. He found it attractive to emigrate to the Canadas with this family in 1842, arriving in May 'with scarce 16 shillings in my pocket.'

To some degree Mackenzie and the Neils had fallen victim to roseate talk about the employability and high wages of stonemasons in the New

World. Though Mackenzie was offered a job at Montreal, he and the Neils chose to move on to Kingston, where, it was rumoured, better pay was available. This mistaken notion, and rock that was too hard for his tools, inadvertently set the footings for Mackenzie's business career as a general builder and building contractor. His ability to learn new skills quickly and his firm, direct way of handling workers rapidly enhanced his reputation. Over the next several years he served as a foreman or contractor on major canal and building sites in Kingston, St Catharines, and Montreal. A serious injury kept him out of work for nearly two months in 1844, but he was sustained in his positive outlook by his elder brother Hope, a carpenter-cabinetmaker who had come to Canada on Alexander's invitation in 1843. In 1846 Hope chose Port Sarnia (Sarnia), in Upper Canada, as the site where the whole family could settle; Mary Mackenzie and her remaining sons immigrated the following year. The family, so central to Mackenzie, was whole again.

Mackenzie now engaged in a successful career constructing public buildings and houses in the southwest part of the province and took on ancillary work as a developer and as a supplier of building materials. His construction included the Episcopal church and the Bank of Upper Canada in Port Sarnia and court-houses and jails in Sandwich (Windsor) and Chatham. Several of his brothers were involved with him in this activity and it assured him of prosperity. In 1859 Mackenzie, his brother Hope, contractor James Stewart, and Kingston plumber Neil McNeil submitted losing bids on the construction of the Parliament Buildings in Ottawa.

A firm Victorian piety complemented Mackenzie's attachment to family and the perspectives of his trade. Though born into a strongly Presbyterian family, at the age of 19 or 20, not long after he had left his family home, he found Baptists more attractive. Religious belief meant more to Mackenzie than institutional attachment, pious rhetoric, or a structure of acceptable moral norms. The afterlife was an ever-present reality, as his later letters to his second wife and to his daughter bear witness. He was widely considered to be honest and frank to a fault. His religious belief gave him a sense of strength and comfort which sustained him in periods of great stress.

Mackenzie's early introduction to the work world, his fierce commitment to the well-being of his family, and his religious background and

Alexander Mackenzie MP, May 1868.

convictions, indeed his Scottish culture, made him utilitarian. Even in maturity, he found little use for frivolous pursuits: he complained in a world-weary way to his wife in 1879 about the fuss people made over Edward Hanlan's latest rowing victory, which he termed an 'utterly useless trial of strength.' Had the test been 'cutting and splitting wood, hoeing corn, ploughing or any other useful occupation which would be of general benefit to mankind, I could have some sympathy with the excitement.' None of his contemporaries disputed the diligence with which Mackenzie pursued what he conceived to be his duty. Photographs of the man show an austere face, sharp eyes, and a tight mouth. He combined a physically compact frame with slightly reddish hair and a weather-beaten face. He did not dress well, most obviously at the beginning of his career in federal politics. This lack of sartorial concern reflected not only his utilitarian outlook but also his constant sense of personal budgetary constraint. In

1876, when he was prime minister, he lamented having to spend $128 for a politically necessary banquet and noted that he was avoiding entertaining on the score of cost. Here was the personal corollary of the political reformer's emphasis on financial retrenchment.

In public addresses and in frequent speeches in parliament, Mackenzie spoke extemporaneously, with only the briefest jottings to support him. He rooted his speeches in factual material culled through a voracious reading of newspapers, government documents, biography, and history, and they were delivered with a noticeable Scottish burr. Their occasional literary adornment did nothing to disguise a style both vigorous and acerbic. William Buckingham, Mackenzie's secretary during his prime ministership and his biographer, noted in retrospect that his humour wounded rather than healed.

Mackenzie had, in common with a wide range of other Reformers and Liberals, a consistent and relatively well-defined body of ideas: 19th-century liberalism. His egalitarianism was a deeply ingrained belief. He had absorbed some of his notions about equality from the meetings of moderate Chartists he attended when he was 19 and 20. Emigration to Canada enhanced and confirmed these views. Soon after he arrived in 1842, he engaged in lively political discussions in which he attacked the established position of the Church of England in Upper Canada. Established churches were symbols of the institutionalization of privilege, and meant, as was the case with the Roman Catholic Church in French Canada, a loss of individual freedom of choice. His ideal was the separation of church and state. Responding to celebrations in Scotland in 1875 of his prime ministership, he compulsively mentioned Britain's established church and its rigid class structure, though in his speeches on this visit he played down his dislike of each for obvious political reasons.

The potential for social and economic mobility offered by the Canadas appealed to his liberal economic notions and became part of his conceptual landscape. Like other Reformers, Mackenzie did not see enormous disparities of wealth and status in post-confederation Canada. The agrarian society of Ontario approached the ideal of Mackenzie and the Reformers because of the large number of hardworking, independent farmers, purportedly beholden to no one but themselves for their success and free of the strictures imposed on wage-earning classes. The Reformer in Canada should attempt to ensure the mobility of goods, labour, and capital nationally and internationally, and to prevent the development of institutionalized distinctions which limited the freedom of individuals, retarded their economic progress, and caused conflict between social groups. Indeed, these attitudes were reflected in the Reformers' horror at both the Pacific Scandal and the class privileges they felt were associated with the protective tariff imposed by the Conservatives in 1879. The legislation introduced by Mackenzie's own government was frequently marked by this ideological thrust.

Mackenzie was involved in politics in Canada from virtually the time he arrived. By late 1851, at Port Sarnia, he was a key Reformer, his position having evolved into secretary of the Reform Association of Lambton County. In September 1851 the Reformers of Lambton and Kent asked George Brown, the politically active owner-editor of the Toronto *Globe*, to oppose Arthur Rankin, a candidate supported by Malcolm Cameron, a Reformer of a ministerialist stripe, in the riding of Kent in the forthcoming general election. Mackenzie widened his political scope by campaigning strenuously, with Archibald McKellar and others, to obtain the nomination for Brown and then by helping bring about his election to the provincial assembly in December 1851. The basis of Mackenzie's own political career was laid.

When Brown ran in Toronto in the general election of 1857–58, Hope Mackenzie, not Alexander, took the Reform nomination in Lambton. Perhaps Alexander felt that his political reputation had been permanently besmirched by a libel suit that Cameron had brought against him in 1854. An editorial in the *Lambton Shield*, which Mackenzie had been carrying in editorial and financial terms from 1852, had suggested that Cameron had been involved in a clear-cut case of corruption. Mackenzie lost the suit, had to meet court costs and a £20 award, and, because of the financial pressure, was forced to close the newspaper. The case certainly brought him his first moments of political loneliness.

Hope was defeated by Cameron, but when Cameron moved on to the Legislative Council in 1860, Hope ran successfully in the Lambton by-election. He refused to run in the general election of 1861. There was a strong move to Alexander, whose activity as a census taker and as a member of Port Sarnia's fire brigade, temperance society, Dialectic

Society, and school board had broadened his knowledge of the community and enhanced his reputation. He was duly elected and represented Lambton in the provincial assembly until confederation.

Alexander Mackenzie established himself as a man of direct expression and forceful opinions. He developed a strong sense of parliamentary tactics, which later stood him in good stead. A companion-in-arms of George Brown, the Reform leader, he held views on representation by population, retrenchment and fiscal responsibility, the supremacy of parliament, and church–state relations that followed predictable paths, informed as they were by his egalitarianism, his economic liberalism, and his suspicion of unreasoned institutional authority. Yet his beliefs on such matters could be compromised when the special interests of his constituency or region were at stake. In the 1860s, for example, he lobbied for the oil-producers of southwestern Ontario, gaining lower excise taxes for them, which effectively increased the tariff protection they already had.

A crisis in the Reform movement qua party would come with confederation. It was widely believed that confederation solved the range of political issues over which party divisions had taken place: the old political parties thus no longer had any purpose. A fusion government was now required to pursue new and compelling national aims. The making of the 'Great Coalition' in 1864, into which Brown had taken most Reformers, with Conservatives, to bring about confederation, was seen as evidence of the propriety of the trend. This powerful argument, however, brought many Reformers to disagreement with their erstwhile party. Mackenzie had denounced the trend. Though he was one of Brown's most loyal followers and spoke in favour of confederation, he publicly expressed strong reservations about the formation of the 'Great Coalition.' Coalition involved compromising Reform principles. It weakened and divided the party, Mackenzie urged. He opposed anti-partyism because he believed parties to be intrinsically necessary to the political system, and because some issues, particularly those of parliamentary supremacy and fiscal responsibility, remained outstanding.

Brown had helped fashion a Reform or Liberal party that was explicitly regional and sectional, and therefore would not easily develop national alliances once confederation was in place. He had striven for more than a year after his resignation from the coalition cabinet in

December 1865 to create a Liberal opposition with national aspirations but he chose to give up elective politics in 1867. Liberals were left without a clear leader, only with a leadership group drawn from Ontario and Quebec: Edward Blake, Luther Hamilton Holton, Antoine-Aimé Dorion, and Mackenzie.

For a party that had roots in sectionalism and religious and ethnic hostility, anti-partyism and the loss of Brown were sharp blows. But the problems of constructing a national party were not these alone. The behavioural norms of the parliamentary Reform party were individualist and only loosely fraternal. Thus, while Mackenzie, who was elected for Lambton in 1867, openly performed the functions of a party manager in the House of Commons after confederation, he did not have any associated authority. His managerial role was likely a result of his reputation as a Reform purist and loyalist, a reputation compounded from his organizational activity, his diligence, his ideological commitment, and his identification with Brown. Only a safe man like Mackenzie could be entrusted with fostering a national party while keeping in check not only the leadership ambitions of unevenly talented men such as Holton but his own. At best Mackenzie could act in consultative concert with a small group of like-minded, leading Liberals, hoping that the disparate group of men calling themselves Reformers or Liberals would follow.

Given the above characteristics, the Liberals performed remarkably well in the general election in the summer of 1872, gaining good representation in Quebec and a majority of the seats in the Maritimes and in Ontario. Mackenzie campaigned in nearly 20 Ontario constituencies other than his own, a clear measure of his growing personal authority and of the increasing extent to which he was seen as party leader at that point. Issues such as the Treaty of Washington of 1871, the terms of union for British Columbia and the expenditures associated with it, and the troubles with Louis Riel in Manitoba told heavily against the Conservatives. Still, the Liberals did not form the government. Mackenzie had nevertheless demonstrated his ability, in the election and in his overlapping involvement at the provincial level. A member of the Ontario legislature since 1871 for Middlesex West, he served briefly as treasurer in the government of Edward Blake, from 20 Dec. 1871 to 15 Oct. 1872, in which year dual representation was ended in Ontario. His resignation from provincial politics was accepted in October, only a few days after he, Blake, and Brown, in a master stroke, had persuaded Oliver Mowat to become Liberal leader in Ontario.

When, finally, the federal party formally elected Mackenzie its leader in March 1873, he was intensely pleased. He had suggested that others – Dorion, Holton, and particularly Blake – were more worthy, and claimed that he sought only the best interests of the party. His self-effacing efforts went for naught. He was chosen leader by a group of peers who, in vesting new authority in him, more firmly defined the party. Whips were appointed and a national political committee was planned, forms of organization that Mackenzie had at one time resisted as vehicles for Holton's perceived ambitions.

Within a month of Mackenzie's becoming leader, the Pacific Scandal had broken. The Liberals uncovered the massive flow of money from Montreal capitalist Sir Hugh Allan to the Conservative party during the election of 1872 in presumed exchange for the Pacific railway charter. Mackenzie was scandalized by the rumours he heard as early as February 1873. Quebec Liberal Lucius Seth Huntington laid public charges against the Conservatives on 2 April. After a strenuous rearguard action, Prime Minister Sir John A. Macdonald abruptly resigned on 5 November. Mackenzie and the Liberals thus had power dumped into their laps.

The scandal precipitated and hardened Liberal suspicions about large concentrations of wealth and the influence of such wealth on government. A Liberal party with ideological leanings towards free trade and individual enterprise naturally pointed out that the scandal involved a rejection of the norms of competition and an assertion of monopoly power. The legislative expression of Liberal hostility towards monopoly and unfair competition was persistent after 1874. Mackenzie openly voiced that attitude, for example in relation to the Marine Electric Telegraphs Act of 1875, which regulated construction and maintenance. Liberals consistently associated their antagonism to protective tariffs with their fear of monopoly. Connected with their suspicions about monopoly was their fear of collusive, unparliamentary action on the part of the Conservative leaders.

Mackenzie was a fierce defender of the supremacy of parliament, as were his Liberal colleagues. The defeat of the government of John

An astounded Alexander Mackenzie (left) hears Sir John A. Macdonald glibly dismiss the Pacific Scandal, as cartooned by John W. Bengough in *Grip* (Toronto), 27 Sept. 1873.

Sandfield Macdonald in Ontario on 18 Dec. 1871 and the establishment of the Blake government, in which Mackenzie served, had revolved around the issue of parliamentary supremacy. Mackenzie's motion, on which the Sandfield government was defeated, accused it of being a corrupt coalition government intent on making patronage expenditures unregulated by parliamentary votes: a 'deliberately inaugurated ... system ... was destroying our Parliamentary system of Government.' The same issue was at the root of the Pacific Scandal. The powers that the Macdonald government had wanted in the charter of the Canada Pacific Railway Company in 1872 were attacked on the grounds that they pre-empted the right of parliament to decide on subsidies, routing, land grants, and conflict of interest. After the scandal broke, the intense struggle in parliament over the way in which it was to be investigated displayed the Liberals' faith in a parliamentary, as opposed to a judicial, inquiry.

On 5 November Mackenzie was requested by Governor General Lord Dufferin to form his first administration, amid some doubt as to his suitability as a prime minister. The most pressing decision he made, other than the difficult judgements involved in forming a cabinet, was to call an immediate election. The election of January 1874 had the scandal as its key issue, and the demoralized Conservatives were routed. Mackenzie had a huge majority.

Yet even at this point, and throughout its tenure of power in the mid 1870s, the Liberal party fell short of ideals of cohesion. Problems arose in part out of tensions underlying Mackenzie's leadership. Blake was widely regarded as a more natural leader for the party, though he had removed himself from consideration as its formal leader in early 1873. Yet Blake created a difficulty and for other reasons than his ability, personal problems, fluctuating ambitions, and occasionally overweening sense of self-importance. Although he and Mackenzie were united in their fundamental attitudes, Blake had a more radical reform agenda. This and his significant following, which encompassed the nationalist Canada First movement, including its protectionist elements, generated a rift within the party. The pressures for him to be in the cabinet, even to be prime minister, were intense. Blake sat, reluctantly, as a minister without portfolio from the time Mackenzie's first cabinet was formed, in November 1873, to February 1874, when he resigned. By the autumn of that year, however, because of disputes over the government's treatment of British Columbia, Blake had the temerity to suggest that Mackenzie step aside for him as prime minister. The exchange that followed between the two men soured their relationship: trust was lost over their differences on the terms proposed by Colonial Secretary Lord Carnarvon for the British Columbia difficulty and over their profoundly dissimilar recollections of events surrounding Mackenzie's appointment as prime minister in 1873. Blake believed that Mackenzie, *after* he had accepted Dufferin's request to form a government, had asked him whether he wanted the job. Refusal, Blake felt, was the only honourable response. Mackenzie, however, claimed the conversation, including Blake's refusal, had taken place *before* his acceptance. Moreover, when Mackenzie gave his explanation to Blake in September 1874, it led Blake, a master at the interpretation of nuance, to think that Mackenzie had been requested by Dufferin to ask him to consider becoming prime minister. Only on 15 October did Mackenzie explain that his talk with Blake had been undertaken on his own responsibility, over objections by Dufferin. It is not clear that Blake was satisfied by this account, as some significant misunderstanding had indeed taken place. In the interim, rebellion by a cave of Blake's supporters and allies culminated in the public excitement caused by Blake's enunciation of his radical program at Aurora, Ont., on 3 October. Though Blake may have been innocent of ill-will and though the speech may have held little that was new (Mackenzie believed both possibilities), from an outside perspective the statements set Blake up as an alternative leader to Mackenzie. It again became imperative to include him in the cabinet, something finally accomplished on 19 May 1875 by means of delicate negotiations through third parties. Blake served as minister of justice until 7 June 1877, when he resigned citing reasons of poor health, and then as president of the Privy Council, from 8 June to the beginning of 1878.

Blake was not the only highly competent Liberal whom it was difficult to lure into the cabinet. Luther Holton, the Montreal-based businessman-politician who Mackenzie thought would make a good finance minister, frequently refused to enter the cabinet. Mackenzie ascribed this reaction, at various times, to Holton's feelings of personal inadequacy, to his perceived desire to have the prime minister's job, to his purported plotting with Blake or Blake's friends, or to the long-drawn-out death of a daughter. Ironically, when Holton expressed a desire for a cabinet position, there was no available place.

Mackenzie's complaints about the inadequacies of his cabinet directly reflected the weaknesses of the Liberal party in his period of leadership. Few of the ministers, he thought, took on their fair share of parliamentary debate, but that partly reflected his own vigorous work habits. William Buckingham, his secretary, noted that he constantly took up the debating slack left by other ministers: he did not expect enough of them. Only five of his ministers held the same post throughout his administration: Mackenzie himself in public works, Albert James Smith in fisheries, Richard John Cartwright in finance, Isaac Burpee in customs, and Thomas Coffin as receiver general. Of this group only Cartwright was a powerful and regular speaker in the commons. Mackenzie felt the absence of good men in cabinet in another way. He made decisions on a consensual basis, explicitly so when he was *de facto* leader of the opposition between 1867 and 1873 and implicitly when he was prime minister. In letters to other leading Liberals he often sought advice about tactical and strategic political decisions: Holton, Alfred Gilpin Jones of Halifax, Cartwright, Dorion, and especially George Brown were among those he consulted. This process, which Mackenzie saw as a natural outgrowth of the character of his party, did not reveal any personal weakness, even though at times he was accused of still being Brown's second-in-command. Mackenzie rejected that notion and his correspondence with Brown gives it the lie. Brown was consulted on tactics because he had good, though consistently optimistic, judgement. Mackenzie used him and the *Globe* as political tools in turn, and Brown saw himself as no more than a stalwart and leading supporter.

To strengthen the party, adequate regional and ethnic representation in the cabinet was necessary, but that approach thinned the choices. Selection in Quebec was complicated by the need for a strong French Canadian lieutenant. Dorion, Mackenzie's first minister of justice, was ideal for the position, but his long service in law and politics and his wish for a more predictable life led Mackenzie to appoint him to the chief justiceship of Quebec in 1874. Thereafter, French Canadian leadership in the party floundered. Télesphore Fournier did not have an adequate following, and was named to the newly formed Supreme Court of Canada in 1875. Luc Letellier de Saint-Just was a senator and therefore inappropriate as a leader, and, in any case, Mackenzie named him lieutenant governor of Quebec in 1876. Félix Geoffrion, whom Mackenzie brought into the cabinet with the express desire to make him a Quebec lieutenant, became increasingly incapable of doing the work required by his Department of Inland Revenue. Joseph-Édouard Cauchon had some leadership credentials, but he had a sullied reputation on first entering cabinet. He lost his usefulness altogether once he had helped resolve the Liberals' difficulties with the Roman Catholic hierarchy in Quebec in

1876, following L. S. Huntington's attack in Argenteuil on clerical intervention in politics. He then was shifted to the lieutenant governorship of Manitoba. By 1876 Mackenzie was desperate for a stronger figure, particularly one from the Montreal region. The sign of his desperation was the choice of Toussaint-Antoine-Rodolphe Laflamme, first as minister of inland revenue. An able lawyer, Laflamme had none the less been closely associated with the Institut Canadien, which the Catholic hierarchy viewed as free-thinking and anti-clerical. Only a young Wilfrid Laurier, who had entered the commons in 1874, seemed to offer long-term relief, but he lacked experience for leadership and refused to enter cabinet until Cauchon left.

Good representation from the Maritimes was also difficult to obtain. Isaac Burpee, as Mackenzie saw it, was only willing to deal with matters directly pertaining to his Department of Customs. The minister of the interior, David Laird from Prince Edward Island, was appointed by Mackenzie in 1876 to the lieutenant governorship of the North-West Territories because of his abilities. A. J. Smith, William Berrian Vail, and Thomas Coffin were not the assets Mackenzie may have hoped they would be, and only by recruiting A. G. Jones in early 1878 as minister of militia and defence (he had previously taken a modest leadership role within the administration) was the representation from the region made more than acceptable.

Yet inherent in these troubles lay Mackenzie's achievement in forging a national Liberal party. His initial cabinet and later alterations welded not only personalities but regional coalitions to the Liberal party. In the Maritimes Smith, Vail, Coffin, and Jones had opposed confederation. Coffin and Burpee drifted on the fringes of the Conservative party, waiting for patronage, until the Pacific Scandal pushed them over to Mackenzie. Coffin's inclusion in cabinet was a price the prime minister was willing to pay for the support of a clique of Nova Scotian MPs. Burpee was representative of urban and commercial New Brunswick; Jones later performed that function for Nova Scotia. However, in New Brunswick, Burpee was overshadowed by Smith, who sat in the commons as an independent political chieftain until 1873, when Mackenzie garnered him. Smith, despite growing fat and lazy in office (Mackenzie's despairing opinion of him), delivered 12 of 16 New Brunswick seats to the Liberals in the election of 1874 and in the disastrous defeat of 1878 he still took 11. The process whereby Mackenzie established the Liberals as a national party in the Maritimes was symbolically completed by his speaking tour there with R. J. Cartwright during the 1878 campaign.

In Quebec a similar process of consolidation and growth took place. Through Cauchon and, more prominently, Laurier, Mackenzie began to defuse the hostility of the French Canadian Catholic hierarchy towards Liberals. He had already undertaken considerable efforts to draw Irish Catholics into the party. In Laurier he had recruited the key man of the next generation of Liberal leaders.

Mackenzie and his cabinets nevertheless faced significant limitations in the policies they could fashion and the problems they could solve. The general election of 1874 gave the Liberals a majority in Quebec and Ontario; indeed, they had an overwhelming preponderance in parliament. Cartwright pointed out to his fellow ministers in 1875 that 'no stable govt. is possible except in one of two ways, i.e. either by securing a decisive majority in Ontario and Quebec taken together, or by deliberately purchasing the smaller provinces from time to time.' Mackenzie agreed, at least in part. Rooted in Ontario, the Liberals faced possible tension in maintaining their position in Quebec and control over their Maritime representatives. The Maritimers could be bought off by patronage and log-rolling, but there was never enough of that. At times they could cause a decisive shift in party policy by acting in concert, as they did in 1876 when they forced the government to abandon its plan to adjust the tariff upwards.

Quebec was an even more difficult problem. The Liberal hold on the province was tested by several developments, the first of which concerned amnesty for Louis Riel. Sir John A. Macdonald, acting through Bishop Alexandre-Antonin Taché, had promised him amnesty for his activities at Red River in 1870. There was a general expectation in Quebec that the Liberal government would fulfil this promise, though it had been given before the death of Ontario Orangeman Thomas Scott at the hands of Riel's provisional government. Riel's election to the House of Commons for Provencher in January 1874 and the arrest, conviction, and sentencing of Ambroise-Dydime Lépine, Riel's lieutenant, on the Scott matter, made amnesty a lively issue. Mackenzie naturally prevaricated – although amnesty might soothe Quebec, it would provoke Ontario. But the Lépine complication actually brought a resolution to the difficulty, for his sentence of death was commuted by the governor general, Lord Dufferin. Here the Liberals hid behind imperial skirts. In February 1875 Mackenzie's government granted amnesty to all of those associated with the Manitoba problems, including a provisional pardon to Riel. Yet the issue made the Liberals extremely aware of their weaknesses in Quebec.

On the tail of the Riel question came another problem, even more crucial. As a result of the growth of ultramontanism in Quebec in the late 1860s and early 1870s, clerical hostility towards both Rouges/ Liberals there and Liberals in Ontario was commonplace. Ultramontanism, moreover, appeared to threaten the position of anglophone Protestants within Quebec. On 30 Dec. 1875 at a by-election in Argenteuil L. S. Huntington spoke his feelings on the relation of clerics and politics. Clerical intervention in elections was a wrong associated with the Tories, he declared. He called upon the Protestants of Quebec to align themselves with the Liberals in defensive reaction against ultramontanism. The repercussion among leading French Canadian Catholics was sharp. They feared that Huntington spoke for the Liberal government as a whole. Mackenzie chose the better part of valour and claimed that Huntington had expressed purely personal opinions, not those of the government or of the Liberal party. Yet, in private, he wrote to George Brown that what Huntington had said was absolutely true, though impolitic. In early 1876 the Liberals traced their defeat in three Quebec by-elections, including one in Charlevoix, to the Huntington affair. The party was being demoralized in the province. The Liberals counter-attacked on several fronts. First they undertook court challenges of clerical involvement in elections. These challenges did not profoundly alter clerical attitudes, so, through Cauchon, Mackenzie appealed to Rome for a papal legate (George Conroy) to investigate Canadian conditions. Laurier, intent on proving himself, worked hard to temper clerical involvement in electoral politics and clerical hostility to Liberals.

In economic terms, the dominant characteristics of the time the Liberals were in power were recession and depression. The downward trend of the economy had been signalled by the American crash of September 1873; by mid 1874 the effects of recession in Canada could not be mistaken. Conditions remained poor from then until late 1878, though the situation varied from sector to sector and from region to region. The agricultural sector in Ontario, which Mackenzie mistakenly believed would give his party hearty support in the general election of 1878, did relatively well, whereas towns and cities in which there had been substantial industrial expansion prior to 1874 suffered and showed electoral hostility to the Liberals. These negative economic conditions not only cost them seats in by-elections but enhanced key elements of their outlook on economic policy. The conditions made them tightfisted: this was certainly the case with railway policy.

A desire for fiscal restraint that derived from a concept of minimalist government had made Liberals, including Mackenzie, suspicious of the union and railway deal struck by the Macdonald government with British Columbia. When the deal was made public in 1871, the Liberals had recoiled in horror. To have promised to build, at enormous cost within ten years, a railway that would serve only a tiny population was an act bordering on fiscal insanity, Mackenzie would indicate in 1874. He did, of course, want westward expansion and railway construction. However, he and other Liberals objected to the poor planning of the railway and to the high cost associated with quick construction. Taxes should not be increased to pay for the railway: this assurance in the charter of the Canada Pacific Railway Company in 1872 was crucial from the viewpoint of the Liberals. Mackenzie returned repeatedly to this point in the tense discussions with British Columbia that followed.

Upon becoming prime minister he inherited a difficult situation. The railway had to go forward and consequently it had to be adequately financed. The Conservatives had not begun construction and the government of British Columbia had already issued complaints. Given fiscal restraints and a Liberal emphasis on avoiding tax increases, Mackenzie would have liked to see private financing. The Canadian Pacific Railway Act, passed in the spring of 1874, made such financing an available option. Preliminary discussions were actually held with George Stephen, who, however, told L. S. Huntington in December that he did not want to risk his own money. That response was not surprising in existing economic conditions. The depression, for example, involved some resounding American railway collapses. The Liberals had to go with direct government financing out of necessity. Mackenzie expressed goodwill towards

British Columbia, and indicated positive intentions, but he made it clear that the existing timetable for construction was impossibly short. Indeed, the pressure in Liberal ranks against quick construction was enormous. Blake was intensely opposed to extending a service at exorbitant cost to a tiny British Columbian population.

A circumspect policy of planning and surveying, and preliminary work on roads, waterways, and telegraph lines, with rail construction not too far in advance of the vanguard of settlement, was an obvious result. Mackenzie naturally wanted to utilize existing American lines south of the Great Lakes, rather than build through the uninhabited territory north of Lake Superior. The demands for lines in Manitoba and the need to provide patronage and log-rolling in the Port Arthur (Thunder Bay) region and in Manitoba could be met through contracts for preliminary railway work and for ancillary roads and telegraph lines. Mackenzie's strategy, notably the use of an American bypass, was similar to that of Macdonald prior to Riel's provisional government in Manitoba, and the plan appealed to interested capitalists.

In these circumstances Mackenzie called for a rescheduling of construction with British Columbia's consent. In February 1874 he commissioned party stalwart James David Edgar as the government's envoy to reach a readjustment with the government of British Columbia. Its premier, George Anthony Walkem, did not find the proposed readjustment acceptable; with specious reasoning he rejected Edgar as envoy in May and sent a sharp protest to Britain.

In this fashion the main provincial–federal struggle of Mackenzie's stay in power entered the realm of imperial relations. Colonial Secretary Lord Carnarvon suggested himself as arbitrator between the two levels of Canadian government. Despite Mackenzie's aversion to this apparent interference in internal Canadian affairs, Carnarvon proceeded, delivering in August terms for a basis of agreement that were less than those desired by British Columbia but much more than the Mackenzie government was willing to contemplate.

The Mackenzie government grudgingly accepted the Carnarvon Terms, but fiscal responsibility and constitutional problems prevented their full implementation. The Senate, dominated by Conservatives, refused to pass a commons-approved bill to finance one key element in the terms, building the Esquimalt–Nanaimo line in British Columbia. Carnarvon then refused to permit the enlargement of the Senate requested by Mackenzie. Disputes over what the government should do raged for months, as Governor General Lord Dufferin, the imperial government, and British Columbia tried to force further commitments from the Mackenzie administration. Only after recriminations so raw and furious that the diplomatic Dufferin felt a passing urge to hit his prime minister, was a compromise reached in 1876, by which Mackenzie agreed to start construction in British Columbia two years later.

This lengthy struggle over the Carnarvon Terms, and the caution generated by the Liberals' economic outlook and by depression conditions, has overshadowed what was actually an energetic program of railway undertakings. Total Canadian mileage increased from 4,331 in 1874 to 6,858 in 1879. This expansion was largely the result of the completion of the government-financed Intercolonial Railway, under engineer Sandford Fleming, and the construction of track under government contract in Manitoba and between that province and Lake Superior. The crucial process of surveying in the west was pushed ahead unremittingly. Some 46,000 miles of potential line were blazed between 1871 and 1877 and about 12,000 miles were actually surveyed. Construction of telegraph lines from Port Arthur to Edmonton was undertaken. In essence, the Carnarvon Terms, with the thorny exception of the Esquimalt–Nanaimo line, were met. These were impressive accomplishments under difficult circumstances.

Other economic policies pursued by the Mackenzie administration were also constrained by circumstances. In the case of reciprocity, the Mackenzie government felt that the previous administration had not sufficiently pursued improved trade relations with the United States. The Liberals intended to piggyback the trade issue on the outstanding issue of American payment for access to Canada's and Newfoundland's inshore fisheries, as specified in the Treaty of Washington. The Canadian hand would be strengthened further by having the chief negotiator appointed as the representative of Canada. George Brown got the job in January 1874. The eternal optimist, Brown negotiated hard with the American secretary of state, Hamilton Fish, but by the time a reciprocity treaty was agreed upon in June, the American Senate was close to adjournment and the agreement, much more extensive than that of 1854, slid into limbo. American political and economic conditions probably made it impossible to implement. However, the furore over the proposal in Canada served to highlight the key beliefs, strengths, and weaknesses of the Liberals. Mackenzie sought to ensure support for his party among farmers in Ontario, export-oriented merchants, fishermen, and shipping interests in the Maritimes. The agreement's inclusion of a large list of manufactures and the reduction of customs duties indicated that the Liberals were genuine free-traders. In terms of its contents and the methods by which it was reached, the agreement signalled the Liberals' wish to see Canada become more commercially independent from Britain. At the same time, the trade proposals generated a more unified protectionist outlook among Canadian manufacturers and to a lesser degree in the general business community, an outlook already partially precipitated by the depression.

The economic liberalism of the Mackenzie government was also made explicit in the tariffs of 1874, 1876, and 1877. Mackenzie, at pragmatic extremes, expressed a willingness in 1874 to keep protection in place and to increase it when the government needed revenue, but he made his distaste for these procedures obvious. None the less, tariff increases were made necessary by growing deficits rooted in the government's fiscal inheritance and in falling tariff revenues. Protectionists, recognizing the government's needs, mounted campaigns to gain their own ends. From their perspective, the 1874 tariff introduced by finance minister R. J. Cartwright was insufficient: designed to increase revenue, it virtually avoided all overt signs of protectionism.

Liberal free-trade proclivities were more severely tested in 1876, when inadequate revenue levels necessitated further tariff revisions. The government faced much protectionist agitation, which was expedited by a parliamentary committee on the causes of the current depression. The free-trade focus of the government wavered: Mackenzie heard Liberals argue for a tariff increase of as much as 5 per cent. Higher tariffs were indeed planned, but sectionalism within the party prevented them. Leading Maritime Liberals threatened open opposition to any tariff increases and this threat strengthened Mackenzie in his convictions. The 1876 tariff changes were minor. Protectionists then sought to influence the government on the basis of its apparent vulnerability to pressure from the Maritimes. Unified Nova Scotian coal interests demanded tariff protection, and protectionists used this demand as the Trojan Horse to attempt to gain generally higher tariffs. The 1877 tariff was, however, aimed only at garnering more revenue. The events of 1876 and 1877 formed a temporal dividing line, which separated protectionists from the Liberal party for almost the rest of the century.

Part of the Liberals' defence of free trade was that Canada's economic relationship with the mother country should not be broken by unnatural commercial restrictions. Mackenzie's sense of loyalty to the British empire was strong, both before and during his period in power. Thus he accepted the notion of a transcontinental Canadian railway as a link of empire; thus his loyalty to British constitutional practices. At the same time, however, he was eager to achieve greater powers of self-direction for Canada. Though he was cautious about an independent Canadian treaty-making power in the immediate aftermath of confederation, when advocates of such power (among them Sir Alexander Tilloch Galt, L. S. Huntington, and A. J. Smith) supported a parting of the ways with Britain, by 1882 he could support the idea.

The Treaty of Washington of 1871 had been decisive in Mackenzie's thinking on this issue. He felt that the Conservative leader, Macdonald, performed poorly for Canada as a British commissioner, and that the British negotiating team was so intent on smoothing relations with the United States that it ignored Canadian interests. Mackenzie saw the appointment of George Brown as *Canadian* plenipotentiary, for the negotiations on reciprocity with the United States in 1874, as a necessary step in achieving optimal results. His successful effort in having a Canadian, A. T. Galt, appointed as the British commissioner in arbitrage in 1875–77 over the fisheries dispute with the United States was similarly motivated.

Analogous approaches were apparent in non-commercial concerns. From a Liberal perspective, the Supreme Court of Canada was established in 1875 to create more effective Canadian decision making. Macdonald's government had initiated moves towards such a court, but it was the Liberal minister of justice, Télesphore Fournier, who actually introduced the Supreme Court Bill. Nationalist-minded Liberals amended it, with

Mackenzie's strong support, to limit sharply appeal to the Judicial Committee of the Privy Council in Britain. Disappointingly, the amendment became inoperative.

Mackenzie, and Blake to an even greater degree, had concerns about the activities of Lord Dufferin in relation to Canadian independence of action and parliamentary democracy. The suspicion was founded on the governor general's excessive support of Macdonald in the Pacific Scandal, which, Mackenzie felt, constituted a degree of British interference in Canadian domestic affairs. It was also apparent in the tension over the Carnarvon Terms and was manifest in Blake's hostility towards Dufferin for his undirected decision in 1875 to commute Lépine's sentence in the amnesty affair.

The blend of attachment to empire and stalwart Canadian nationalism that Mackenzie espoused was eminently clear in his approach to matters of defence. He himself had been a major of militia at Sarnia during the Fenian troubles prior to confederation, a decisive event in the formation of a sense of nationality among the thousands of Canadians who served. When Conservative cabinet minister and sometime Reformer William McDougall virtually accused Mackenzie of disloyalty to the crown during the 1867 election campaign, Mackenzie repudiated the charge by pointing to his militia service. He asserted in 1868 that the defence of Canada was not merely a matter of domestic concern but had to be fashioned in full cooperation with the British. However, the weakness he saw in the Canadian militia was leadership, which simply could not be provided by a thin array of British officers. Thus, as prime minister, he fully endorsed both the reorganization of the Department of Militia and Defence, of which W. B. Vail was minister, and the establishment of a military training college in Canada in 1874.

At the same time that Mackenzie's Liberals sought greater national powers *vis-à-vis* Great Britain, they reflexively stood as protectors of provincial rights in Canada. The strong sectional view that Reformers had displayed under Brown readily translated into a provincial-rights stance for the Liberals after confederation. In the case of the tensions over Catholic rights in education in New Brunswick Mackenzie's perspective was clear, if self-serving. It was, of course, politically convenient for him to claim that the issue lay entirely in the hands of New Brunswick.

Mackenzie espoused provincial rights in a way that might also be inter-preted as self-serving in the case of Luc Letellier de Saint-Just, lieutenant governor of Quebec in 1876. Saint-Just dismissed the provincial Con-servative government of Charles Boucher de Boucherville in 1878 on the grounds that it had not given the office of lieutenant governor its consti-tutional due, by issuing edicts and signing documents under his name without consultation. His actions were constitutional, but they transcended the commonly accepted notions of the lieutenant governor's powers, and so brought on the wrath of the federal Conservative party and demands for an inquiry and his dismissal. Mackenzie properly claimed that the electorate of the province was fully able to judge the case and that it was a matter of provincial concern. Even before they achieved power, the Liberals under Mackenzie had protested the giving of better terms of union to Nova Scotia on the assumption that this grant infringed on the financial arrangements other provinces had obtained at confederation. When Macdonald gave larger representation to British Columbia and Manitoba in the House of Commons than their populations warranted, the Liberals protested on the grounds that such action violated provin-cial rights and the sacred principle of representation by population. Mackenzie's respect for provincial rights did not mean that he gave way to the provinces on contentious issues. But he did avoid adversarial approaches. Rather than taking the issue of Ontario's boundary with Manitoba and the North-West Territories to the Judicial Committee of the Privy Council, as Macdonald had planned to do, he chose in 1875 to settle the matter by arbitration. Indeed, it was more by a process of negotiation between the federal and provincial governments that the matter was resolved in 1878, though Macdonald refused to honour the award.

Mackenzie's government established an enviable record of reform legislation, especially in its first two years of power. The most prominent of these laws was that on electoral reform, passed in 1874. Liberalism stimulated Mackenzie and his party to try to create a political context in which the popular will (as defined by those who had the right to vote) could find proper expression. This modestly democratic concept underlay not only the Liberals' ideas on Canada's relationship to Britain but also their position on electoral reform. Throughout the 1850s and 1860s Mackenzie had believed consistently that one reason the Liberals had difficulty gaining power was the electoral trickery of their opponents, who bribed, treated, and impersonated their way to victory. The electoral sins of the Conservatives in 1872 seemed to confirm this interpretation of their conduct. In 1873 the Liberals managed to force from the Macdonald government, in a weakened state after the election of 1872, feeble acts on electoral reform. In the aftermath of the Liberal victory of 1874 the Dominion Elections Act was passed. It included the secret ballot, the legal requirement to hold the election in all ridings on the same day to prevent engineered bandwagon effects, and the removal of property qualifications for candidates for the commons. To enforce this new law more effectively, justice minister Antoine-Aimé Dorion brought in a bill that placed the trial of controverted elections within the judicial system rather than within the scope of a parliamentary committee. In these laws, strong egalitarian notions were apparent.

The temper of the legislation passed during Mackenzie's régime was the temper of his Liberalism. Much of that legislation involved organizational and regulatory rationalization. The Post Office Act of 1875, which amended and consolidated the laws for regulating the postal system, introduced a number of important changes, including the compulsory prepayment of postage and a reduction of rates on certain classes of mail. This act was associated with the postal convention that year with the United States to expedite the passage of mail in North America. At the same time door-to-door delivery of mail, which had been established in Montreal in 1867, was extended to all major Canadian cities. The North-West Territories Act of 1875 not only brought together existing laws relating to the territories but provided the region with a practical constitution. (Mackenzie, who was responsible for the rough drafting of the bill, tacked on as an afterthought, in the section on taxation, provisions permitting separate Roman Catholic schools on the Ontario model. Only a sharp Senate debate on those provisions gave a foretaste of the controversy they would produce in later decades.) The Public Accounts Audit Act of 1878 affirmed and to a degree rationalized existing practice concerning lines of responsibility for governmental fiscal management. As well, the tariff changes of 1877 were accompanied by a wholesale revision of the regulatory structure of customs administration. The Collection of Criminal Statistics Act of 1876 and the Weights and Measures Act of 1877, both of which bore the mark of Edward Blake's precise mind, followed the same trend towards regulatory efficiency.

These and other laws were a signal contribution on the part of Mackenzie's government. Some of the legislation, for example the Weights and Measures Act, provided a regulatory context which tried to ensure fairer competition and protection for the consumer. The Inspection of Staple Articles Act of 1874, the Inspection of Petroleum Act of 1877, the Insolvent Act of 1875, the Customs Act of 1877, the Canada Joint Stock Companies' Act of 1877, and the insurance acts of 1875 and 1877 all reflected a drive to establish a more effective legal context for the free operation of market forces. The insurance acts, for instance, required federal licensing of insurance companies, deposits to cover a level of liability, and the publication of key financial data. The office of superintendent of insurance, established to deal with life insurance companies and first held by John Bradford Cherriman, had considerable powers of inspection. The Penitentiary Act of 1875 was intended to reform the running of penitentiaries through greater fiscal control and a more effective, better-controlled inspectorate.

Such legislation, which exhibits the ample scope of Liberal reformism under Mackenzie, was not as controversial as the Canada Temperance Act of 1878. Mackenzie personally disapproved of any use of alcohol as not only dysfunctional but immoral. Tipsiness or drunkenness in the commons appalled him. Yet he viewed temperance legislation with suspicion, largely because of the political divisiveness of enforced abstinence. He was, however, able to countenance the temperance act (also called the Scott Act after Secretary of State Richard William Scott) because it instituted a form of local option. Yet even that move was a political error: it alienated voters of all points of view and caused the liquor interest to campaign against the Liberals in the election of 1878.

Scandals also worked against Mackenzie that year. Although he was, within the boundaries of late-19th-century political life, a man of probity, he recognized the necessity and usefulness of patronage from the earliest stages of his political involvement. As prime minister he expected competence as well as service to the party from the beneficiaries of patronage. He had no intention of sweeping out Conservative appointments merely to benefit the Liberals. Besides, Lord Dufferin held very strongly to the principle of a permanent civil service. Still, the prime minister enjoyed rewarding his friends, and himself, within the scope of legitimate political practice. Sometimes the practice went beyond the pale of the acceptable: when he was treasurer of Ontario in 1871–72, he had a number of public buildings insured by the Isolated Risk Fire Insurance Company of Canada, which he had helped found in June 1871 and of which he was president. Mackenzie's brothers in particular were capable of administering soot to his reputation. In late 1874, falsely believing that the price of steel rails had fallen to an all-time low, he authorized the purchase of 50,000 tons of rails through a firm in which his brother Charles had a large interest. Alexander thought he had effected a saving for the dominion. He had not. When the matter came to light in 1875, he was accused not merely of nepotism but of nepotism at the expense of the country. He denied both: the bid accepted had been the lowest.

His efforts to create institutional probity in the Department of Public Works, the ministry he had compulsively undertaken when he became prime minister, had limited success. In that department his interests in construction, in fiscal retrenchment, and in rooting out what he conceived to be political corruption, fused. Though corruption continued in this large department, no real blame could be laid at Mackenzie's door except perhaps in terms of administrative practice. He swore to accept the lowest bids on public works contracts. Bids, however, were not required to be submitted on the same day and were opened as they came in, thus creating opportunities for contractors, through bribery, to cheat. He was more directly involved in the Neebing Hotel scandal of 1877, which developed from the government's selection of the Fort William town plot (Thunder Bay) as a terminus of the Pacific railway. A Liberal contractor had been selling land to the government at inflated prices. The contractor's partner was the evaluator who approved the prices. Mackenzie claimed ignorance, though he had appointed the evaluator.

The 1878 session of parliament, and the Liberals' mandate, ended on 10 May. Mackenzie called the federal election for 17 September. His own instinct had been to call it for the spring, when momentum could still be harnessed from the provincial victory in May of the Liberal party in Quebec under Henri-Gustave Joly. Some Liberals, however, recoiled from a spring election because their political machinery was not in place. The uneven preparation of the party was to some degree a product of Mackenzie's heavy work-load as prime minister and minister of public works. Taking on that department had been the egregious personal error of his political career. His ferreting instincts were too fully aroused by the finances of the department, so the burden of detailed work he faced as minister was enormous; furthermore, he did not effectively use the department to garner better financing and support for the party.

Mackenzie's strength as a party organizer, which had stood him in good stead in his early political career, was thus underutilized during his administration. By the mid 1870s a number of leading Ontario Liberals felt distinctly uneasy about the state of the party's machinery, even though Mackenzie had made efforts to give the parliamentary party some structure after he had gained full leadership. J. D. Edgar and others struggled to establish the Ontario Reform Association in 1876, with George Robson Pattullo as its full-time secretary and organizer, but without adequate support from Mackenzie. A national organization was not forthcoming. After the 1878 election Mackenzie would strongly support the formation of a central Liberal club fashioned after the United Empire Club of the Conservatives, thus indicating his concern about Liberal organization. Such a club, however, was not established until 1885 in Toronto.

Mackenzie not only moved sluggishly on organization, he had also misjudged the direction of public opinion. As he noted to William Buckingham with some puzzlement in September 1878, just before the election, 'My meetings have all been very successful, could hardly be more so, yet I find the Tories are everywhere confident, why I cannot under-stand.' He did not grasp the degree to which the voting populace had been swayed by protection or, to lesser extent, by issues such as the Letellier affair, the Scott Act, the sectionally divisive program for railway construc-tion, and the scandals that had marred his own reputation. Though he accepted the notion that the protectionist issue would mean a substantial loss in urban support, he did not apprehend the extent to which the issue appealed to rural feelings. Nor did Mackenzie sense how far the Liberals had fallen in public estimation, although the reception given to some of Richard Cartwright's unfortunate turns of phrase could have warned him. Fully committed to the tenets of economic liberalism, Cartwright declared in the commons in 1877 that governments could influence the business cycle no more than 'any other set of flies on a wheel.' The Conservatives thereafter derided Liberals as just such a set of incapable and uncaring flies. Mackenzie did little to improve this increasingly negative image of the party. Minor riots over work and food in Montreal in 1877 – symptoms of the intensity of the depression – led the municipal government to plead for the release of funds promised for public works in the city. Mackenzie refused, citing budgetary constraints. Even his humble beginnings were turned against him. Years after his death, Goldwin Smith could not resist repeating a barb often tossed, in various forms, at the prime minister for his obsession with detail, his unpolished manners, and his inflexibility: 'a malicious critic might have said that if his strong point was having been a stone-mason, his weak point was being a stone-mason still.' It was a cruel but telling caricature.

As a result of the election in 1878 the number of seats held by the two parties virtually reversed from that in 1874. Mackenzie himself was only narrowly returned in Lambton. After the election there was a muted debate within the party leadership as to whether the government should wait until it was defeated in the house to resign or whether resignation should take place earlier. The latter opinion won out. The prime minister indulged in a paltry list of last-minute appointments, and then gave Lord Dufferin his letter of resignation from office, effective 9 Oct. 1878.

Mackenzie had more than once complained of the enormous burden of office, and how pleasurable it would be to lay it down. Yet the loss of office pained him deeply. Some contemporaries thought he retreated into himself; certainly his leadership of the party was lacking: no caucuses were called until late in the 1880 session, and then, reputedly, by the chairman of caucus, Joseph Rymal, to consider the question of leadership. By early 1880 the leadership aspirations of Edward Blake, who had been defeated in 1878 but was returned the following year, were clear, and discontent among Liberal MPs began to crystallize. Mackenzie was aware of these trends, and either willingly or under direct pressure he announced his resignation as leader to the commons in the early hours of 29 April. Blake replaced him.

The scope of Mackenzie's political life narrowed significantly after 1880. The deaths that year of the men he had felt closest to in political life, Luther Holton and George Brown, distressed him deeply and enhanced his feelings of political isolation. His declining health during the 1880s reduced his activities. His voice began failing him in 1882 and in his last years of parliament he rarely spoke. He nevertheless remained a strong party man and retained a compelling interest in politics. Having moved to Toronto after his party's defeat in 1878, he was elected in 1882 in York East, which seat he would hold until his death.

Mackenzie's business activities had begun to shift focus as early as 1871, when he had given up contracting. His fire insurance company, which he formed that year and which he attempted to foster nationally, prospered and that success perhaps encouraged him to expand into life insurance. In 1881 he became the first president of the North American Life Assurance Company (it had been chartered in 1879); virtually all of its founding members were Liberal luminaries, among them Sir R. J. Cartwright, John Norquay, and Oliver Mowat. Almost from the first, the firm was national in scope, having agents in all provinces by 1882. And it was successful, with Mackenzie as its president until 1892, though for the last few years he was inactive.

Mackenzie also took to writing: in 1882 his *Life and speeches of Hon. George Brown* was published in Toronto. He wanted to erect a literary monument to Brown; at the same time he clearly wanted to reassert the Reform tradition. His previous writing had been adversative: his early journalism and the speeches honed for publication in the 1870s. So too was the sarcasm and invective in some of his private letters, where, for example, Samuel Leonard Tilley was dismissed as a 'man not above mediocrity' and Sir John A. Macdonald appeared as a 'drunken debaucher.' But this style of writing was ill suited to dealing with a close friend. It may have been also the sharp separation which Mackenzie made between his private and public life, and which he naturally extended to Brown in the biography, that rendered his depiction of the vibrant and intense editor of the *Globe* so wooden.

Throughout the gruelling public life that Mackenzie had fashioned, he drew sustenance from close family relations. The intensity and the hours of his work as prime minister and minister of public works had physically damaged him, he noted in letters to his brothers, to whom he remained close. His daughter, Mary, was also a correspondent and a confidante, though he avoided with her the sober political discussion to which he subjected his brothers. If not consistently, at least at various times during his administration, he lost a great deal of weight, a serious matter about which he could none the less joke light-heartedly with his second wife, Jane. She was his chief companion after their marriage in 1853. He had met her through his steady attendance at a Baptist church in the country near Port Sarnia, and Mackenzie took pleasure in sharing her piety. Reserved by nature, she had not functioned effectively as a political wife, unused, as a hard-working woman of rural origin might well be, to the requirements of fashionable entertaining at the apex of Canadian political society. The Liberal prime minister shielded her from those burdens as much as possible. His letters to Jane display an open affection and a gentle, broad humour, which was rarely discernible in the man at other times. They enjoyed several trips to Europe together after Mackenzie relinquished the Liberal leadership, one of which was financed by leading party members.

Alexander Mackenzie died on 17 April 1892, after being bedridden as a consequence of a fall near his home in early February. He did not have a state funeral. But attendances at services in Toronto and Sarnia were very large, and much public respect was paid the man.

BEN FORSTER

Further reading

D. C. Thomson, *Alexander Mackenzie, Clear Grit* (Toronto, 1960).

William Buckingham and G. W. Ross, *The Hon. Alexander Mackenzie, his life and times* (Toronto, 1892).

Sir JOHN JOSEPH CALDWELL ABBOTT,

lawyer, businessman, educator, politician, militia officer,
and gentleman farmer; b. 12 March 1821 in St Andrews
(Saint-André-Est, Que.), eldest son of the Reverend Joseph Abbott
and Harriet Bradford; m. 26 July 1849 Mary Martha Bethune,
daughter of the Reverend John Bethune, and they had four sons
and four daughters; d. 30 Oct. 1893 in Montreal.

J ohn Joseph Caldwell Abbott was the son of an ambitious, English-born Church of England missionary who believed in the ascendancy of the English in British North America. Abbott's early years were spent at various rural Anglican missions in Lower Canada, where his father was employed by the Society for the Propagation of the Gospel. A voracious reader, he was educated in his father's well-stocked library and under his exacting tutelage. He may also have spent some time at the school in Grenville which his father had helped establish.

His secondary education completed, he began work at age 17 with A. Laurie and Company, a Montreal wholesale and retail dry-goods firm. He did everything from selling cloth to packing apples. Within a few months, however, illness obliged him to return home. Upon his recovery he secured a position with a wholesale firm in Gananoque, Upper Canada, where he learned bookkeeping and accounting. In 1843 he went back to Montreal to study at McGill College. At the same time he read law with William Collis Meredith and Strachan Bethune (his future brother-in-law), and from 1846 with Christopher Dunkin as well. He took lessons to perfect his 'fine tenor' voice, sang in and directed the six-person choir at Christ Church, and assisted his father, who was bursar of McGill, with the college's accounts. Although a visitor's report for 1844 found their bookkeeping irregular and incorrect, Abbott was appointed deputy registrar and secretary to the bursar in 1845, protected from reprimand by his family's close friendship with the acting principal, Bethune, whose daughter Mary Martha he later married.

On his admission to the bar on 25 Oct. 1847 he entered into part-nership with William Badgley, professor of law at McGill, and he succeeded to Badgley's lucrative law practice when his partner was appointed to the bench in 1855. Through Badgley's good offices he began teaching at McGill in 1853 as a lecturer. The following year he received a BCL from McGill, and in 1867 a DCL, a degree available without examination to any graduate 12 years after his receipt of a BCL. In 1855 he succeeded Badgley as professor of commercial and criminal law and as dean of the faculty, a prestigious but not onerous position, given the small number of students, the limited formal teaching (most of the training took place in the professors' law offices), and the nominal admin-istrative duties; the deanship provided an annual stipend of £500 and a share of student fees. Although Abbott retained the title of dean until 1880, he had ceased teaching and relinquished his administrative respon-sibilities by 1876, when William Warren Hastings Kerr became acting dean. Upon Abbott's formal retirement, McGill named him emeritus professor in the faculty of law, and in 1881 appointed him to the board of governors of the Royal Institution for the Advancement of Learning. After a lengthy career he could count among his students many who became notable public men, including Adolphe-Philippe Caron, Toussaint-Antoine-Rodolphe Laflamme, Gonzalve Doutre, Wilfrid Laurier, and Eugene Lafleur.

Abbott's academic involvement grew naturally from his professional and business activities. A specialist in commercial law, he was mainly interested in contracts, bankruptcies, partnerships, and banking. Through intelligent and shrewd management he built his practice into one of the most substantial in Canada and he was believed to have 'enjoyed the lar-gest professional income of any advocate in the Province' for many years. In 1862 he was made a QC. Although he was said to have twice been offered the chief justiceship, a position for which he was considered particularly well qualified, acceptance of the post would have meant the loss of approximately four-fifths of his income. During his 46 years of practice he had numerous partners, including his sons John Bethune and Henry. In 1870 his legal business was sufficiently large to justify the creation, in conjunction with Joseph Doutre, of an Ontario agency, run by Toronto lawyer Herbert Chilion Jones, to facilitate 'business relations between the merchants of Montreal and the people of Ontario.'

John Joseph Caldwell
Abbott MP, April 1870.

Although Abbott's eulogists have made much of his strong sense of justice, claiming that the poorer his clients and the more just their cause, the harder he fought for their rights, most of his clients were wealthy and powerful men such as John Thomas Molson and Sir Hugh Allan and corporate interests such as the Bank of Montreal, the Merchants' Bank of Canada, the Hudson's Bay Company, the Séminaire de Saint-Sulpice, the Bell Telephone Company of Canada, the Standard Life Assurance Company, and the Canadian Pacific Railway. A private, dispassionate person, who avoided conflict, display, and emotion, Abbott preferred the quiet counselling of clients, the negotiation of agreements, and the drafting of contracts to the theatre of court-room pleading, especially before a jury. His most celebrated public court case was his defence, together with Laflamme and Kerr, of Confederate agents who had raided St Albans, Vt, from Canadian soil in October 1864 and were tried for extradition to the United States. Much to the annoyance of the Canadian and American governments, Abbott persuaded police magistrate Charles-Joseph Coursol that he lacked the jurisdiction to try the case, so Coursol set the prisoners free. After their rearrest Abbott again successfully defended the prisoners before judge James Smith, arguing that they were belligerents, not criminals. The highly publicized cases brought Canadian–American tensions close to armed conflict.

Railways were a passion which Abbott shared with his father and younger brother Harry Braithwaite, a well-known railway engineer. His father had been among the early promoters of a railway to circumvent the rapids at Carillon; the Carillon and Grenville Railway was incorporated in 1847 and both John and Harry purchased stock. In January 1859, when a more ambitious project, the Montreal and Bytown Railway, incorporated in 1853 and designed to absorb the Carillon and Grenville, ran into financial difficulties, Abbott and his associates purchased the line at a sheriff's sale for $21,000; it had cost its promoters some $400,000 to build. Five years later they sold it to the Ottawa River Navigation Company for a 'handsome profit.' Abbott also held shares in the Montreal Northern Colonization Railway, Nova Scotia's Eastern Extension Railway, and numerous others throughout his career. His most ambitious railway endeavour began with the Canada Central Railway, of which he was president for several years and his brother a constructor. Chartered in 1856 as the Lake Huron, Ottawa and Quebec Junction Railway, an amalgamation of several smaller lines, in 1861 it reorganized as the Canada Central and was seen by Abbott and Allan as a key link in a transcontinental line.

As Allan's legal adviser, Abbott became involved in the Montreal financier's efforts to secure a government contract to build a railway to the Pacific. Abbott drafted a charter for the Canada Pacific Railway, arranged for its incorporation, was named a provisional director, and left with Allan for London in late February 1873 to float bonds for its construction. News of the Pacific Scandal undermined their efforts, destroyed the company, and placed Abbott at the centre of one of the country's most sensational political scandals. Not only were the incriminating documents used by MP Lucius Seth Huntington to accuse the government of Sir John A. Macdonald of corruption stolen from Abbott's office by his confidential clerk, George Norris, but he had attended the meeting with Sir George-Étienne Cartier during which Allan had agreed to finance Cartier's election in 1872 in return for a contract to build the railway. Abbott had drafted letters to Cartier on the agreement and he had been the intermediary through whom requests from Cartier and Macdonald for additional funds had been made and met. A star witness at the royal commission established later in 1873 to investigate Huntington's charges, Abbott had advised Macdonald on the men best suited to serve on it, indicated what evidence ought to be destroyed, and attempted to purchase a witness to discredit his accusers. Political opponents never let Abbott, a Conservative MP, forget his sordid part in this political scandal. His enthusiasm for the construction of a transcontinental railway, however, was not dampened.

Indeed, Abbott was largely instrumental in the formation of another syndicate to build the Pacific railway. On Macdonald's return to power in 1878, Abbott began working on a plan which he submitted to the prime minister two years later, to extend the Canada Central so as to link it to the line from Port Arthur (Thunder Bay) to Winnipeg which had been begun by the government of Alexander Mackenzie. At Macdonald's urging Abbott revised his plan, enlarging the group of investors to include Duncan McIntyre, now the president of and a major shareholder in the Canada Central, George Stephen, Donald Alexander Smith, and others. Appointed the group's solicitor, a post he held from 1880 to 1887, Abbott once again drafted a charter and he secured the incorporation of the Canadian Pacific Railway on 16 Feb. 1881. In negotiating a contract with the government to build the line he had extracted far more generous concessions than Macdonald realized at the time and, according to Sir Richard John Cartwright, he clearly 'out-generalled Sir John Macdonald.' In February 1881 Abbott accompanied Stephen, McIntyre, and others to England in search of funds. Later that year the CPR purchased the Canada Central Railway. During the construction of the CPR Abbott proved to be a skilled advocate and frequent lobbyist for government assistance. Quite appropriately he was present at the completion of the line. Until this time he had refused to buy stock in the company, and much to Macdonald's annoyance would never speak or vote in the House of Commons on matters pertaining to the railway in order to avoid the appearance of conflict of interest. Privately, however, he pressed the CPR's claim whenever he could, and on its completion he purchased stock and accepted a position as director, which he retained until he became prime minister.

Abbott held shares in various other companies, including $20,000 in the Molsons Bank, $50,000 in the Merchants' Bank of Canada, $8,000 in the Bank of Montreal, and unspecified amounts in the Dominion Cartridge Company, the Dominion Transport Company, the Dominion Mineral Company, the Lake of the Woods Milling Company, and the Montreal Safe Deposit Company. He also had a $1,500 income certificate from the Minneapolis, St Paul and Sault Ste Marie Railway Company. He advanced over $68,000 and endorsed a bank loan of $86,000 to establish his younger sons, Arthur and William, in Abbott and Company, and later lent some $49,000 to the Metropolitan Rolling Mills, owned by Abbott and Company. During his early career he had served as secretary and treasurer of the City and District Building Society; in later life he was president of the Citizens' Insurance Company of Canada, and director of the Bank of Montreal, the Merchants' Bank of Canada, the Standard Life Assurance Company, and the Intercolonial Coal Mining Company.

Abbott's property provides further insight into his material success and social aspirations. In addition to owning a well-appointed home in Montreal, valued at $64,818 in 1898, and a more modest residence, valued at $3,000, for his sister Harriet, in 1865 Abbott purchased Senneville, a 300-acre country estate on the west end of Montreal Island, containing the remains of the stone mill built by Jacques Le Ber. This property, first known as Senneville Grange, and later more grandly as Boisbriant, was valued at $35,000 in 1898. On it he built a baronial house with a library and conservatories. He laid out farms, orchards, and gardens, and maintained a herd of Guernsey cattle, imported from 1878 to 1883 and thought to be 'the first direct importation' of this breed into Canada. Here he also indulged his passion for orchids, and is said to have possessed 'the richest variety at that time in Canada.' Boisbriant enabled Abbott to pursue his hobbies, secure solitude, and affirm his social standing among Montreal's merchant princes, in a way that his membership in the Rideau Club, Ottawa, and the St James Club of Montreal alone could not.

His social standing entailed obligations to the community. In 1860 he was one of the founders of the Art Association of Montreal (of which his eldest son, John Bethune, became a curator). A trustee for the estate of the Montreal merchant Hugh Fraser, Abbott spent over 15 years attempting to establish the free library, museum, and art gallery provided for in Fraser's will. After years of litigation between the trustees and Fraser's heirs, the Fraser institute, which contained the books of both the Mercantile Library Association and the Institut Canadien, was opened on 15 Oct. 1885, with Abbott, the institute's life president, delivering the inaugural address. In 1869 Abbott had helped establish the Protestant Institution for Deaf-Mutes and for the Blind.

Although Abbott had served in the local militia 'since boyhood,' in 1849 he was a signatory to the Annexation Manifesto, calling for union of the Canadas with the United States. His recruitment of 300 men, known as the Argenteuil Rangers, during the *Trent* affair of 1861 may have been designed to atone for what he later described as the 'sins of youth' and to enhance his political credentials, as much as to express his concern for his country's safety. Taunted by his political opponents in March 1889 for his 'disloyalty' in 1849, he explained that he considered his military service, and his commission as an officer and later commanding officer of the 11th Battalion of Rifles (Argenteuil Rangers), to be evidence that his youthful error had been forgiven.

Ironically Abbott is best remembered as a politician, a profession he claimed 'to loathe and detest.' 'I hate politics,' he explained in 1891, 'and what are considered their appropriate methods. I hate notoriety, public meetings, public speeches, caucuses, and everything that I know of that is apparently the necessary incident of politics – except doing public work to the best of my ability.' It is not surprising that Abbott entered politics in 1857, during a decade when 'railways were politics.' The constituency he chose, Argenteuil, was not an easy one. Its member, Sydney Robert Bellingham, a Liberal-Conservative, had held the seat since 1854. When Bellingham won again in the elections of 1857–58 by about 200 votes Abbott petitioned to have the election overturned on the grounds that men without property qualifications and from outside the constituency had been enticed to vote for his opponent. After a hearing before two judges that lasted two years, a select committee of the Legislative Assembly awarded Abbott the election, and he took his seat on 12 March 1860. That year he published the committee's proceedings in a work of 258 pages in which he argued that the enforcement of existing electoral laws rather than the enactment of additional ones was the best assurance of electoral probity. Although he had missed the first two years of his mandate, and was detained by professional business from regular attendance during the session of 1860, he was re-elected in 1861, and in May 1862 joined the moderate Reform government of John Sandfield Macdonald and Louis-Victor Sicotte as solicitor general for Lower Canada. During his year in office he initiated three important legislative measures: a bill to regulate the distribution of assets to creditors and relieve debtors from liability for debt – a measure which established his authority on the subject of insolvency and enhanced his professional reputation; a bill concerning juries and jurors in Lower Canada; and a bill to levy a stamp tax on judicial procedures. He also insisted upon acting personally as crown prosecutor, in spite of the fact that he had handled few criminal cases. He was re-elected in 1863, and although he refused to join the reconstructed ministry and subsequently voted against the government, Sandfield Macdonald invited him to pilot through the assembly his bill on insolvency, which had failed to pass before dissolution. The following year he published an annotated edition of the act entitled *The Insolvent Act of 1864, with notes together with the rules of practice and the tariff of fees for Lower Canada*, which demonstrated his thorough knowledge of French, English, and Scottish law.

In the following years Abbott was considered a loose fish. A reluctant supporter of confederation, he feared that it would reduce the English-speaking inhabitants of Lower Canada to political impotence. In consultation with William Collis Meredith, Christopher Dunkin, and others, he drafted a resolution calling on the government to protect the electoral borders of 12 English Quebec constituencies. Subsequently, Alexander Tilloch Galt endorsed the proposal, had the London conference accept it, and included it as article 80 of the British North America Act.

After confederation Abbott drifted into the Conservative party. Elected to the House of Commons for Argenteuil in 1867 and 1872, he remained interested in finance, especially in the revision of the Insolvent Act in 1869, and for some years he served as chairman of the house's banking committee. His implication in the Pacific Scandal led to his eventual defeat; although elected in 1874, he was unseated by petition, owing to irregularities in the voters' lists. Defeated in 1878 by 89 votes, he won a by-election in February 1880, only to have it declared void because of bribery by his officials. Re-elected in a by-election in August 1881, and returned in the general election of 1882 by acclamation, he held his seat until 15 Jan. 1887. On 12 May 1887 he was called to the Senate, an institution he argued had an important role to play in government. In recognition of his parliamentary skills and general usefulness, on 13 May Sir John A. Macdonald appointed him Senate house leader and named him to the cabinet without portfolio.

Abbott served as mayor of Montreal. Although his nomination as the English candidate was fiercely contested by George Washington Stephens, the city's energetic urban reformer, he was elected in 1887 by a comfortable majority of some 2,000 votes over Henri-Benjamin Rainville, and re-elected by acclamation the following year. Abbott's first act on being named to the Senate was to secure a charter for the Royal Victoria Hospital. Chosen the first chairman of the hospital's board, at the behest of its principal benefactors, Donald Alexander Smith and George Stephen, Abbott presided over the construction of a $650,000 building. He failed, however, to secure its amalgamation with the Montreal General Hospital, and incurred the wrath of conservationists by insisting that the hospital be built on the city's mountain parkland and using his position as mayor to achieve that end. The *Montreal Star* was especially critical of Abbott's civic administration, his insensitivity to the needs of his constituency, and the corruption in city hall during his tenure.

Inside or outside parliament Abbott's legal skills were in demand. In 1876 the Liberal government of Alexander Mackenzie had consulted him on revisions to its insolvency legislation. In April 1879 he accompanied Hector-Louis Langevin to London as legal adviser, to seek support from the Colonial Office for attempts of the Canadian government to remove Quebec's lieutenant governor, Luc Letellier de Saint-Just, whose dismissal of his Conservative cabinet had created an acrimonious political controversy in Quebec. While in London he transacted other government business, particularly the admission to Britain of American cattle in transit through Canada. In 1888 Macdonald asked him to go to Australia to negotiate closer links in trade and communication, a policy strongly backed by the CPR, but the mission was postponed and never accomplished.

Sir John A. Macdonald seems to have had a good opinion of Abbott, whom he considered a dignified, informed, dispassionate parliamentarian, 'distinguished for his lack of animosity and personal bitterness,' and one of the finest speakers in the house. Just before his death in 1891 Macdonald offered Abbott the presidency of the Privy Council. At the time he was apparently considering Abbott as the next prime minister; he had informed his minister of justice, Sir John Sparrow David Thompson, his most obvious successor, 'When I am gone, you will have to rally around Abbott; he is your only man.'

Abbott certainly did not want the prime ministership; in his opinion Thompson was the best person to lead the party. But in the end Thompson helped persuade Abbott to accept, Abbott consenting reluctantly on the condition that Thompson carry much of the responsibility, especially in the House of Commons. Abbott realized, and even exaggerated, his own limitations, and never ceased explaining to anyone who would listen that he had been chosen leader of his party simply because he was the man who divided it least.

'Venerable and well-mannered, fond of whist and cribbage,' as historian Peter Busby Waite has described him, the first Canadian-born prime minister 'was not without attractiveness' or social, administrative, and political skills. Even political opponents such as Cartwright conceded this. Moreover, as Waite has argued, Abbott's government was more than the caretaker, provisional administration so often depicted. A large backlog of work awaited him when he assumed power on 15 June 1891. Nor was it easy to lead a party grown tired and feeble in office, riddled by corruption and divided by religious, ethnic, and personal rivalries. The country, too, faced serious problems, not the least of which were a severe depression in trade, the Manitoba school question, the removal of Honoré Mercier from the premiership of Quebec, the Bering Sea dispute, and the Bond–Blaine convention. During the 17 months of his administration, Abbott, a tireless worker, cleared away much of the government business, shuffled his cabinet, forced Langevin to resign his portfolio until he was cleared of charges of corruption, endorsed a reform of the civil service, piloted important revisions to the criminal code through a recalcitrant Senate, pressed the Colonial Office to appoint a Canadian attaché to the British legation in Washington, and sent Thompson to Washington to discuss a broad spectrum of issues including a reciprocity treaty with the United States. Through his decisive and energetic leadership, notably his clever handling of the Mercier affair, his social diplomacy, and the assistance of friends, including William Cornelius Van Horne, who helped reconcile restless French Canadian colleagues such as Joseph-Adolphe Chapleau and Langevin, Abbott seems to have restored his party's confidence, inside and outside parliament. Of the 52 by-elections held during his brief term of office, the Conservatives won 42, increasing their majority in the House of Commons by 13 seats. In recognition of his public services he was created a KCMG on 25 May 1892.

Scarcely had he been a year in office, however, when his health began to fail. In August 1892 his doctors insisted that he take a prolonged rest to recover from what they described as 'cerebral conjestion and consequent exhaustion of the brain and nervous system.' Abbott, then aged 71, never returned to his office. In October he left for England to seek medical assistance. There, he wrote an undated letter of resignation to Thompson, whom he had left at the helm, to take effect at Thompson's convenience. On 23 Nov. 1892 Thompson met with the governor general and agreed to replace Abbott officially on 4 December; he was sworn in as prime minister three days later. Meanwhile, Abbott toured France and Italy vainly seeking health and relaxation. On his return to Canada his condition continued to deteriorate, and he died in Montreal. His funeral was held on 2 Nov. 1893 at Christ Church Cathedral, the bishop presiding over a congregation of the country's wealthiest and most powerful men. Although *La Minerve* generously pronounced Abbott a 'friend of our race,' he had not been popular among many of his French Canadian colleagues; he had simply been more acceptable than the extreme members of the Conservative party. A clever, persuasive, and discreet power broker, he had remained the seasoned advocate of English Quebec's powerful business community.

CARMAN MILLER

Further reading

There is no full-scale biography of Sir John Joseph Caldwell Abbott. The most accessible short account appears in the *Oxford dictionary of national biography*, ed. H. C. G. Matthew *et al.* (new ed., 60v. and index, Oxford and Toronto, 2004). B. J. Young, *Promoters and politicians: the north-shore railways in the history of Quebec, 1854–85* (Toronto, 1978), provides a very good summary of Abbott's career and places him in the context of his considerable business interests. His deanship at McGill is examined in R. A. Macdonald, 'The national law programme at McGill: origins, establishment, prospects,' *Dalhousie Law Review* (Halifax), 13 (1990): 211–363. Important for his political life are P. B. Waite, *The man from Halifax: Sir John Thompson, prime minister* (Toronto, 1985), which treats Abbott seriously and sympathetically, and, for context, D. [G.] Creighton, *John A. Macdonald* ... (2v., Toronto, 1952–55; repr. 2v. in 1, 1998), 2 (*The old chieftain*).

Sir JOHN SPARROW DAVID THOMPSON,

lawyer, politician, and judge; b. 10 Nov. 1845 in Halifax,
seventh and last child of John Sparrow Thompson and Charlotte
Pottinger; m. 5 July 1870 Annie Emma Affleck, and they had
nine children, five of whom survived infancy; d. 12 Dec. 1894
at Windsor Castle, England.

John David Thompson was educated at the Royal Acadian School and the Free Church Academy in Halifax. He was a demure, quiet lad whose shyness his father attempted, with some success, to overcome by having him give recitations of poetry at school ceremonies and later to meetings at the Halifax Mechanics' Institute, of which Thompson Sr was secretary for a number of years. He also taught his son a form of shorthand, one he had learned when he had first come to Halifax in 1827 and used when reporting speeches for Joseph Howe's *Novascotian, or Colonial Herald*. It was to serve both father and son for reporting trials and the debates of the Nova Scotia House of Assembly.

Of John David's six brothers and sisters only a little is known. His two oldest sisters died in the late 1840s; his brother William went to South Africa in 1859 after an unsuccessful career as deputy surveyor of Lunenburg County, and died there of drink – despite, or because of, the stern temperance principles of Thompson Sr. His other brother, Joseph, emigrated to Texas in 1866 and died the following year of yellow fever. Another sister married in 1867 and moved to Barrington. Thompson Sr died in October 1867. (At about this point, probably as a mark of filial reverence for his father and his father's Irish family, John David adopted the name Sparrow – he was to use the name John Sparrow David Thompson henceforth.) Thus, by 1867, when he was 22, Thompson's family had broken up. His one remaining sister and his mother were almost wholly dependent on him; the small family home on Gottingen Street was probably still carrying a mortgage. Thompson started his professional life young and with heavy burdens.

He had been admitted to the Nova Scotia bar in July 1865 after articling with Henry Pryor. In 1869 he went into partnership with Joseph Coombes, a lawyer with something of a court-room reputation, which young Thompson may have envied owing to his own diffidence. The partnership lasted until 1873. From 1868 to 1873 Thompson also reported trials and assembly debates.

Some months before his father's death Thompson had met Annie Affleck, who lived down the hill from his parents' home. She was his age, and may have been working in a Halifax shop or helping her mother with a still growing family. Thompson's courtship was long, intense, even arduous. Annie was a high-strung, vigorous, passionate young woman, intelligent and attractive. What she admired in Thompson was his intellectual capacity and his modesty joined to moral strength. He seemed to be a man she could lean on. As early as the autumn of 1867 Thompson was at Annie's home six nights a week, taking her for a walk or teaching her French and shorthand. The progress of their relationship is recorded in Annie's diary, important parts of which are in the shorthand Thompson had taught her.

The reason for Annie's shorthand was to keep the more intimate details of their courtship from her relatives. The Afflecks were Roman Catholics, and they were not sure they wanted Thompson, the son of a reputable but Methodist family, courting their eldest daughter. Thompson's intensity, and Annie's willingness to countenance it, seems to have been disconcerting to her family and some of their courting was carried on clandestinely. Thompson's frequent notes, with parts in shorthand, were 'smuggled' – Annie's word – into her house. His own family's objections may have been the more serious. Not only was Annie a Catholic, but Thompson was the sole support of his mother and sister. His mother was Presbyterian, and she may have found Roman Catholicism difficult to accept. Thompson's father had always been insistent upon toleration of Roman Catholics as a working principle for his Methodist faith, Irish Protestant though he was. He had specifically forbidden his children, for example, to have anything to do with the Orange order. Whatever the nature of his family's objections – the sources reveal only a void – Thompson did marry Annie Affleck, on 5 July 1870, in the bishop's parlour in Portland, Maine. An episcopal dispensation was necessary for

Annie's marriage to a Protestant, but the archbishop of Halifax was then in Rome and the closest bishop was in Portland. Annie's mother escorted her there for the wedding.

The newly-weds moved into Thompson's family home. Early in 1871 the dominion census-taker recorded them there, Thompson and his three women, his wife, his mother, and his sister: one Roman Catholic, one Presbyterian, and one Methodist. Thompson still called himself a Protestant, but he was not to remain so for long. In April 1871, when Annie was four months pregnant, he was christened a Roman Catholic (with his original name) in St Mary's Cathedral by Archbishop Thomas Louis Connolly.

The change had been coming for a long time. It seems to have been part of Thompson's search for certainties, a search that had taken him to the Anglican church as well as the Roman Catholic. He may have been seeking a better articulated eschatology, a faith whose philosophy comprehended more certainly the realities of earth and the mysteries of heaven. One major influence was Connolly, who in 1867 had preached a series of sermons on the Roman Catholic faith. Both man and argument attracted Thompson. Probably his mind was made up by the time he married Annie, but he deliberately waited nearly a year, to prove to his friends and clients that the decision was his, that he had not turned Catholic simply in order to marry a Catholic girl. Nevertheless it was risky professionally. Thompson seems to have believed that he had cut off his chances of professional success. Some of his friends thought so too. To his great satisfaction, not a single Protestant client left him. It speaks much about the respect he already enjoyed in Halifax.

In 1872 he was able to buy a house half a mile west of his old home, where his mother and sister continued to live. Willow Park was a large old frame-house on four or five acres of grounds that had once belonged to John Young. Thompson bought it for $12,000 – expensive, for in 1872 prices in Halifax were running high – of which he paid $2,000 down, perhaps using some small property he had picked up. All the children but the first (who had died at birth) were to be born there.

Thompson was elected in October 1871 as an alderman in Halifax's Ward 5, was re-elected three years later, and would remain an alderman until October 1877. Ward 5 was the largest and most populous in the city, and it gave Thompson his start in politics. He and Alderman Lawrence Geoffrey Power began by putting together an organized cumulation of all the laws of Nova Scotia that applied to the city of Halifax. It was typical of him. He liked to make order out of confusion, to clean up, clarify, codify, and throughout his later career he would do the same. The monuments he left behind him were characteristic: besides Halifax's charter, the Nova Scotia Judicature Act of 1884 and the Canadian Criminal Code of 1892.

He served as secretary for the commission that ran the new Point Pleasant Park, an area of some 200 acres taken over by the city in 1873 from the British army, which he was partly instrumental in getting under way. He was on several committees, but his most important work was on the Board of School Commissioners, 1873–78, jointly appointed by the province and the city. Thompson tried so far as possible to mitigate the contentious issues of the 1870s between Catholics and Protestants that racked New Brunswick and Prince Edward Island, and inevitably crossed into Nova Scotia. In part it was owing to him that the working of Catholics and Protestants within one single school system (begun in 1865) survived this troubled period. Nova Scotia did not then have a legal separate school system, nor has it, in all essentials, today; it has an informal one.

In the summer of 1877 the Halifax Fisheries Commission met, pursuant to the arrangements made by the Treaty of Washington in 1871. Canada had been given rights in the American shore fisheries, Americans were given access to the Canadian, and the patent difference in value in favour of the Americans was to be the subject of arbitration. The American delegation, conscious of their weakness in knowledge, hired Thompson to help them prepare their argument. They did not, however, do well in the 1877 arbitration; the basic reason was the weakness of their case, but contributing were the conduct of the American on the arbitration tribunal, Ensign H. Kellogg, fatuous and bibulous, and chairman Maurice Delfosse's sympathy for the Canadian member, Sir Alexander Tilloch Galt.

That autumn, on completion of his term as alderman, Thompson was persuaded by Conservative friends in Halifax to stand in a provincial by-election for Antigonish County. Thompson's political development had been slow. His father had been a close friend of Joseph Howe for many years and he had grown up in a reform household. Father and son followed Howe into anti-confederation, but in 1869, when Howe joined the cabinet of Sir John A. Macdonald, Thompson seems to have accepted confederation as inevitable. By the time of Howe's death in 1873, Thompson was already in the Conservative camp, influenced to some degree by Charles Tupper's invention, around 1869, of what Tupper called the National Policy.

Thompson did not really want to go into politics in 1877; if he did go, he preferred a constituency where he was known. Antigonish was almost *terra incognita*. But it was open, and the group around the Halifax *Morning Herald*, a Conservative paper started in 1875, succeeded in getting Thompson to offer himself. A strong push would be needed; Antigonish, like many counties in Nova Scotia, did not welcome outsiders, and for some years it had been held by the Liberals. Thompson, however, got a good deal of help from John Cameron, then bishop of Arichat, a strong-minded Scotsman, vigorous and well trained. Cameron was a redoubtable figure, convinced he was right, who herded his flock with intelligence, forthrightness, and assiduity. He had come to be very impressed by Thompson, whom he had met in Halifax some years before, at Archbishop Connolly's. Thompson's cause in 1877 looked bleak; a complete stranger in Antigonish, with a manner cool and lacking *bonhomie*, he was a man you had to know in order to respect. After some difficulties, and undoubtedly helped by the full backing of the bishop, Thompson won the by-election.

Thompson's relationship with Cameron was to continue a long time; it was almost like that of son to father, although the bishop was no more than 18 years Thompson's senior. Cameron advised him in the long quarrel between the Sisters of Charity of Halifax and Michael Hannan, who succeeded Connolly as archbishop of Halifax in 1877. It was a bitter religious feud over the right of the archbishop to control the sisters. Thompson was the order's lawyer. In 1879, presumably on Thompson's and Cameron's advice, the case was taken by the sisters to Rome. They won; Hannan came within an ace of losing his archbishopric altogether, and the sisters were grateful to Thompson ever afterward.

In September 1878 the provincial government of Philip Carteret Hill, Liberal but at times masquerading under a non-party label, had gone to the polls. It had hoped to ride to victory on the coat-tails of the anticipated victory of Alexander Mackenzie's government in Ottawa. Both elections, Nova Scotia and dominion, were disasters for the Liberals. Mackenzie was badly defeated, and Hill's government was swept out of office just as decisively. Thompson was elected in Antigonish by acclamation. The new Conservative premier of Nova Scotia was Simon Hugh Holmes of Pictou County. Thompson joined the cabinet as attorney general, a post he would retain for the duration of the government. Having taken a post of emolument under the crown, he had to stand for election again but, despite rumours of stern opposition, he again won by acclamation.

The role and function of attorney general, in spite of the long history of the office, has been largely ignored by historians. The administration of criminal law was a provincial responsibility and, as attorney general, Thompson was the chief law officer of the crown, the head, in fact, of the law enforcement system. The office had fallen rather into neglect, mostly because of the incompetence of post-confederation appointees. Thompson worked very hard, and the best source for the nature of the office is the correspondence he received. The work-horse of the Nova Scotia judicial system at the grass-roots level was the justice of the peace, paid only by fees, who could be anything from a cooper to a merchant to a fisherman. Lawyers could make more money defending criminals than acting as JPs. Thompson was frequently asked by the justices for advice, especially with difficult cases.

The most important duty of the attorney general was to prosecute for the crown in all serious criminal cases. This was a duty manifestly impossible to discharge, and different attorneys general took different views of it. Thompson did all the important criminal prosecutions for the county of Halifax, the largest and most populous in the province. One of the cases he did take outside Halifax was that against Joseph Nick Thibault of Annapolis County, accused of murder in 1880. There was much circumstantial evidence and great care was required in developing the case. Thompson feared a miscarriage of justice if he did not handle it himself. Patiently, quietly, he tied together the circumstantial and eye-witness evidence, with the result that Thibault was convicted.

Thompson worked so hard, both as attorney general and as a member of the government, that he frequently had to stay downtown until the wee hours and then walk the mile and a half to Willow Park after the last horse-drawn omnibus had gone. Annie complained that he was always doing other people's work for them. He helped pilot through the assembly the County Incorporation Act of 1879, a measure designed to give independent taxing powers to the Nova Scotia counties, making municipalities of them in fact. It was designed to relieve the strain on the provincial budget for roads and bridges. But it was long overdue in any case, though mightily resented by Nova Scotia taxpayers, who had never been enthusiastic about paying taxes, even on their own behalf. The government, however, had a big majority, and it was confident that when the next elections came the good points of the act would be more apparent than the bad.

The government's chronic shortage of funds made it difficult to effect what Premier Holmes dearly wanted – a consolidation of all private and publicly owned railways in the province (outside the Intercolonial Railway, which was run by the federal government) under one aegis, called the Nova Scotia Railway. It was the premier's pet project, but the whole cabinet was necessarily involved in trying to make it a reality. The legislation was put in place in 1881 and 1882, but by that time Holmes had lost so much credit both with his colleagues and with the party that on the eve of new elections in May 1882 he was forced to resign. Thompson had to step in and become premier.

It was the last thing he wanted. He was fed up with politics and only the full pressure of the party, provincial and federal, kept him in. Thompson took his government to the polls in June 1882, and was defeated. It was not a bad defeat; immediately after the election he believed he could patch a government together, with the help of some of the more versatile and high-minded members of the opposition. He had the respect of both sides of the house, and the attempt might have succeeded, had it not been for one fatal handicap: an opening on the Supreme Court of Nova Scotia that everyone believed was waiting for him. In fact, the appointment was promised to him as a reward for taking the party through the election. There was no way that Thompson could form a coalition government without a firm commitment that he would stay in office. Since he could not make it, the coalition collapsed and he resigned, in July 1882. He was appointed at once, by Sir John A. Macdonald, to the Supreme Court.

For the next three years he was what Macdonald used to call a legal monk. He liked the role; he was as good a judge as he had always imagined he would be. His first court must have seemed very odd, for Thompson, at 36 years of age, was the youngest man in the room. His decisions were liberal rather than narrow and technical. In criminal cases, he was apt to be charitable where the evidence was uncertain, but firm, even unforgiving, where it was clear. His particular *bête noire* was cruelty, especially against women or children. As a judge he found time to help found the Dalhousie law school. In the spring of 1883 Thompson, Wallace Nesbit Graham, and Robert Sedgewick went to see how things were done at the law schools of Harvard, Boston, and Columbia universities. Thompson came back convinced that the human resources existed in Halifax to fashion a good law school; what was really needed was a first class law library, and he and others set out to get it together. During the law school's first terms, 1883 and 1884, he gave lectures on evidence. They were so good that even eminent lawyers from downtown Halifax used to come to listen to him. Thompson's talents were in fact sufficiently noteworthy that the Nova Scotia Liberal government, which had defeated him two years before, asked him to draw up a plan for re-organizing the provincial Supreme Court. Thompson's Judicature Act of 1884 was a thorough reform of its working procedures, so well done that it stood unchanged until the 1950s. Thus Thompson happily continued the even tenor of his way. His children were born at Willow Park; his salary though not large was solid; he could look forward to another 40 years of genteel poverty, no doubt becoming in time chief justice of Nova Scotia. He had no ambitions other than to be a well-read judge, learned in the law.

In 1885, however, the government of Sir John A. Macdonald was looking for new men. The work of Macdonald's cabinet was not being handled well, either in administration or in parliament. Too many ministers were old, or sick, or worn out. Especially was this true of key members, Sir Samuel Leonard Tilley in the Department of Finance, Sir Alexander Campbell in Justice, Sir David Lewis Macpherson in the Interior. Few of the others were capable of performing the business of the government in the commons. Much of this fell upon Macdonald's shoulders; of necessity it could not all get done. A major reconstruction was clearly required. Before that could be effected the North-West rebellion broke out, and the government now hung on for its very life.

Macdonald needed, among other ministers, a new one from Nova Scotia. The normal post-confederation complement of cabinet members from Nova Scotia was two. Tupper had resigned in 1884 to become salaried high commissioner in London. The other minister was Archibald Woodbury McLelan, not too popular in his native province and getting old. There were not many good candidates among the Conservative MPs from Nova Scotia, and they were apt to be jealous of each other; but they all agreed that there was one man who, if he could be persuaded, they would willingly accept: John Sparrow David Thompson.

Thompson had no interest in leaving the bench to go back into the 'slime,' as he put it, of politics. Overtures in 1884 and early in 1885 he turned down politely and firmly. Halifax MPs begged Macdonald to be persistent; Thompson's presence in the government would more than make up for the trouble in getting him. The three most powerful persuaders were not politicians. One was John James Stewart, editor of the Halifax *Morning Herald*, the leading Conservative paper in the province; another, Bishop Cameron; and most important, Annie. Cameron told Tupper, another of the many persuaders, that there would have to be conditions: especially that Thompson should go straight into the most senior portfolio in the government, the Department of Justice. Such a proceeding had never occurred before, especially not with a young, new minister wholly inexperienced in dominion politics. It was a measure of Macdonald's determination that he was willing to go this length, and to push Campbell, his old friend and colleague, out of Justice into the Post Office. But even that move would not have been sufficient to bring Thompson to Ottawa had it not been for Annie.

Thompson liked his life as a judge, and he already had a provincial reputation for being fearless, independent, and able. But Annie looked at his colleagues on the Supreme Court – 'those old crows' she called them – and felt that her young and able husband needed more challenges than those supplied at the Supreme Court on Spring Garden Road. Annie was a woman high-mettled, ready to dare anything; and in the end, when the question was fairly on the line, it was she who decided that Thompson should take the plunge into federal politics. He was sworn in as minister of justice late in September 1885, in Ottawa. He would have to have a constituency. The current member for Antigonish was Angus MacIsaac, a Liberal, which was awkward, but MacIsaac dearly wanted a county court judgeship, something eminently in Macdonald's power to offer. A deal was made. MacIsaac resigned his seat and took the Antigonish County judgeship; Thompson, after a hard fight, was elected for Antigonish in October 1885.

He arrived back in Ottawa later that month, in time for the long cabinet meetings on the Riel crisis. What to do with Louis Riel, who the previous August had been sentenced to hang, was the primary responsibility of the minister of justice, but the decisions in the first instance had already been made by Thompson's predecessor, Campbell. Although it was Thompson's opinion that whoever had raised up the 1885 rebellion, French or English, white or Métis, deserved the full punishment of the law, his function, so far as Riel was concerned, was simply as another voice in cabinet. On 8 November he was suddenly taken ill with a severe attack of kidney-stones, and was out of action for the next fortnight. By the time he was back, Riel had been hanged and the storm was on in Quebec in full fury. Parliament opened on 3 March, and on the 11th Conservative member Philippe Landry proposed a motion expressing the regret of the house at Riel's execution. Thompson made his first major speech to parliament during the ensuing debate, saying that anyone who encouraged the Indians to go on the war-path could not escape justice. If Indians were to hang for murdering white men, so should Riel. He concluded, 'I am not disposed to be inhumane or unmerciful ... but in relation to men of this class ... I would give the answer to appeals for mercy which was given those who proposed to abolish capital punishment in France: "Very well, but let the assassins begin."'

Thompson's speech brought him into the forefront of the party. He was not known at all when Macdonald first brought him to Ottawa. Some MPs had beseeched Macdonald not to appoint him; Campbell thought he looked like a failed priest, a too innocent Christian who would never survive the lions in the House of Commons. But the commons is a curious place. It distrusts rhetoric and high-flown style; whatever flourishes it tolerates have to come from the strength of the argument. Thompson did not seek to convince the house by declamation or sounding phrases, but by the force of his facts, by the reasonableness of what he was saying, and by his transparent fairness. From the very beginning he had its ear.

He spoke courteously, quietly, with a low, clear, musical voice, as if he were trying only to get at the truth. And parliament was persuaded. The vote defeating the motion of regret for Riel's execution, 146 to 52, surprised everyone, including the Conservatives, for until Thompson's speech they had made a poor fist of defence.

Thompson worked hard at his parliamentary career. He became master of the order-paper and of the government business before the house. Macdonald badly needed a good generalist. Other ministers, Mackenzie Bowell, Joseph-Adolphe Chapleau, Sir Adolphe-Philippe Caron, McLelan, and Tilley, were all capable of answering questions about their own departments, Sir Hector-Louis Langevin perhaps capable of rather more; but there was no one really, not since Tupper had gone to London, who could be counted on to help cope with an opposition in full attack. By the end of that first session in 1886, Thompson had shown his mettle, and Macdonald began to lean more and more upon this minister who was always master of his own department, of himself, of government business, and who was willing to shoulder whatever he was asked to do. Within two years Thompson was indispensable.

Thompson's administration of the Department of Justice was also exceptional. Few ministers of justice worked as hard. The main bent of his administration can be summed up as care, courtesy, and concentration. He was a stickler for getting departmental work done and done well. He was not a martinet; he drove himself, and expected others to do their best. There was no side to him, nor did he throw his weight around. He believed in giving credit where due, to his junior officers as well as to others. He would promote a good man from within the public service, resisting patronage claims for someone on the outside. Especially was this true of the prison system, where the political pressures on, say, the appointment of a warden, were fierce. He was also conscientious in going over the files on capital cases. He recommended that at least two men be reprieved from the death sentence, despite the advice of his departmental officers, because he felt the evidence against them justified conviction but not execution. Thompson was sentimental, soft in some ways, but he was capable of steeling himself; in cases of cruelty to women or children he could be implacable.

In May 1888 Justice William Alexander Henry of the Supreme Court of Canada died and there was immediate speculation that Thompson would succeed him. Several vacancies occurred in the court over the next few years; Thompson's name was associated with all of them. He thought about them, for he still did not like political life, but nevertheless he appointed others, including one of his deputy ministers, Robert Sedgewick. Macdonald and the party needed him, and Thompson simply endured political things he disliked. Macdonald put him through his paces doing the political circuits in southwestern Ontario in the fall of 1886; familiarity with public speaking made Thompson like it no better. 'You have to give your best and your worst,' he used to say, and he found that difficult. Audiences seemed to him always at the boiling point. You could not reason: you could only fire off shots.

Thompson's performance in 1887–88 at Washington during the fisheries negotiations between Canada and the United States made him more indispensable. Tupper was the main Canadian delegate, and technically Thompson was only a legal adviser; but Tupper was not a lawyer, just a knowledgeable, noisy politician, and he needed someone like Thompson who knew the legal side. Thompson's experience advising the Americans at the Halifax arbitration of 1877 made him especially valuable. Joseph Chamberlain, the senior plenipotentiary for the British–Canadian side, was impressed, so much so that although Thompson was the youngest member of cabinet, he was awarded a KCMG in 1888 with the assent of two grateful governments. The treaty of 1888, so laboriously put together, was rejected by the American Senate. Both governments then fell back upon a usefully arranged *modus vivendi*.

In weighing questions of copyright, North American fisheries, the projected Alaskan boundary, Bering Sea sealing – all of which arose between 1885 and 1894 – Thompson could be counted on to make the subject his own and produce an elegant state paper. Macdonald never had a minister like him for handling tasks that required mastery of detail and a clean, clear, firm, and exhaustive argument of the government's case. Macdonald had been Canada's minister of external affairs long before that department was invented; but in 1890 he was 75 years old, and by that time Thompson had become Canada's unofficial but real second-in-command in external affairs. He and Macdonald did not always agree; Macdonald was more disposed than Thompson to the spirit of *quieta non movere*. Thompson was more positive and aggressive, his nationalism more sensitive.

Thompson's recommendations to cabinet as minister of justice were of the same quality. Every provincial statute was gone over by his department, and controversial or awkward sections were looked at by the deputy minister or Thompson himself. Many of his predecessors in the office simply put 'approved' on the departmental recommendations, but Thompson outlined many of them himself. After his appointment some long feuds with the provinces ended, or were put to the test of court arbitration. Most notably was this the case with Ontario. Macdonald had kept up a running battle with Oliver Mowat, premier of the province, through the early 1880s; when Thompson got fairly into the saddle, a correspondence began, courteous, tractable, but firm. Mowat was willing to take all the power he could get; Thompson was willing to argue such matters on their legal merits, and to put them to the arbitration of the courts. Mowat and Thompson had an agenda of discussion between them from time to time when Thompson was in Toronto. Their relation became cordial, polite, respectful of each other's position and capacity. In 1892, when Thompson's name was being suggested for the chief justiceship of the Supreme Court of Canada, Mowat wrote him that he would be delighted to see him in that office and would trust his decisions, tory though he unfortunately was.

The feud with Manitoba's railway legislation also eased off with an end to the Canadian Pacific Railway's monopoly in the late 1880s. A major area of disagreement was with Honoré Mercier, premier of Quebec, whose district magistrates acts of 1888 and 1889 were disallowed. It is noteworthy, however, that after Macdonald's death in 1891 not a single statute was disallowed by Thompson. The place for constitutional warfare, he believed, was not political cabinets but the courts. He was confident, perhaps too confident, that courts would produce proper answers. It was the same with the Manitoba school question, which pitted the hard-headedness of the Manitoba government against the intransigence of the Catholic Church. The policy behind the Canadian government's response to the Manitoba education acts of 1890 – referring the matter to the courts – was suggested by prominent Liberal Edward Blake in the house in April 1890, but it was cheerfully accepted by Thompson as the only way to dispose of an awkward, intractable piece of legislation, affecting many interests, and both difficult and delicate to deal with politically. If these acts were constitutional, then *ex parte* decisions by the federal cabinet disallowing them were wrong; if the acts were unconstitutional, the courts would so declare and they would fall to the ground, useless.

By this time Thompson's family was fully established in Ottawa. They had stayed in Halifax until 1888, and the years of Ottawa boarding-houses had been misery for him. Thompson was passionately devoted to his family; an uxorious husband, a solicitous, devoted father, he found Ottawa without his wife and children terrible. Sundays were the worst. He would walk the streets after mass looking in the houses where other men had their wives, their children, and there he was, getting on for 45 years of age, wandering Ottawa like a minstrel. Finally the family came to Ottawa, and Thompson took a house near Metcalfe and Lisgar. They would live in four different rented houses in that same area between 1888 and 1894.

He sent his two boys, John Thomas Connolly and Joseph, to the Jesuit-run Stonyhurst School in Lancashire, England, when they arrived at the age of 13 years or so. It was a hard decision, dictated by his own experience. All his life he felt the lack of a well-rounded education; he knew how hard it was to try to get it on one's own. His Halifax colleague, Thomas Edward Kenny, MP, had gone to Stonyhurst and commended it. Thompson's two eldest girls, Mary Aloysia, 'Babe' as she was known, and Mary Helena, he sent to the academy for young ladies run by the Religious of the Sacred Heart at Sault-au-Récollet (Montreal), so that they would learn French properly, something he had set himself to work on after he came to Ottawa. He thought it churlish not to be able to acquit oneself in French. His third daughter, Frances Alice, 'Frankie' as everyone called her, seems to have been his favourite. Born in 1881, the last of Thompson's children to survive into maturity, Frankie began to suffer a disease in her hip joints. She went through operations and treatments from about 1890 onward, with the best orthopaedic advice available, from Dr Thomas George Roddick, professor of surgery at McGill University. Frankie was at death's door in October and November 1891. She always required looking after, but, unlike Macdonald's daughter Margaret Mary Theodora, who was hydrocephalic and mentally retarded, Thompson's Frankie was bright, intelligent, vivacious, and charmed everyone. Her operations and illnesses were expensive, and kept Thompson perpetually worried about her. He was always hoping that one of those operations would restore her to the bustling little girl who used to hurtle down the path at Willow Park into his arms to welcome him home. A crisis in Frankie's life came at the time of Macdonald's final illness; she was undergoing operations in Montreal, and Thompson was stuck in Ottawa.

Thompson was the last minister to visit Macdonald before the devastating stroke of 29 May 1891. Following Macdonald's death a week later, there was a cabinet crisis, with Thompson close to the centre. It was partly owing to Governor General Lord Stanley, who was sure that Macdonald had indicated his successor in a will, but no such will could be found. There was a delay of two weeks with the party in a turmoil about who should lead. Stanley finally called on Thompson to form a government; he declined, perhaps having no real appetite for power, but also knowing that a considerable section of the Ontario Conservatives would be unhappy with a Catholic prime minister. Thompson recommended John Joseph Caldwell Abbott, who, after hesitation, accepted.

In the mean time the inquiry into corruption in Langevin's Department of Public Works was being laundered in the House of Commons committee on privileges and elections. However, Thompson in the commons and Abbott in the Senate were determined to get to the bottom of the issue; there would be a comprehensive investigation. The government hired lawyers to advise Langevin, who seemed unaware of being in any danger; it offered lawyers to Joseph-Israël Tarte – the principal prosecuting MP – to help get at the facts. The inquiry went on that whole summer of 1891, while on the floor of the commons Liberals tried to make as much capital as they could. Only 27 seats separated them from power; 14 defections from the government's side would bring it down. Thompson's policy of getting everything into the open made it possible to rally the Conservatives in the commons. Langevin was forced by the cabinet to resign his portfolio, though he kept his seat. With the Langevin scandal hot and ready to serve, the Liberals had protested a large number of elections; the first by-elections came early in 1892, and as they went on they became a Liberal disaster. Some 50 took place, and the net result was to strengthen the Conservative majority to something like 65 by the end of 1892. Conservatives had not had a majority like that since the palmy days of 1878.

This big majority ensured passage of Thompson's new Criminal Code in 1892. The legislation had been introduced to the commons in 1891, then circulated to the judges for comments, and, in revised form, put through the house. Compiled by Justice George Wheelock Burbidge, Thompson's former deputy minister, and Robert Sedgewick, his present one, the Canadian Criminal Code built upon English and Canadian precedents and represented a considerable simplifying of Canadian criminal law and procedure. The anachronistic distinction between felonious crimes and misdemeanours was abandoned; a suspect was allowed to testify on his own behalf; and an attempt was made to lighten the punishment of juveniles. Thompson brought the legislation through in the commons in relative ease, but Abbott had to fight hard in the Senate.

In August 1892 Abbott was taken ill and in October he went overseas for consultation. Many in the Ontario wing of the Conservative party wanted to keep him as prime minister, a feeling cleverly parodied in the Toronto satirical weekly *Grip*:

> Dear Sir Abbott, we implore you, do not leave us in the lurch,
> In the face of rising clamor o'er the influence of the Church. …
> We will give you leave of absence, and however long you're gone
> We will do the business for you and your stipend will run on;
> Let no public cares annoy you – heed not shouts of praise or blame,
> We don't want your able counsel – all we ask for is your name.

Thompson could cheerfully echo that sentiment. Especially was this true after the nearly inexplicable decision of the Privy Council in July 1892, in *Barrett* v. *the City of Winnipeg*, declaring the school acts of Manitoba *intra vires*. The Supreme Court of Canada, by a unanimous decision, had said the opposite. Unlike some Conservatives who saw the Privy Council decision as a happy release from the afflictions of the Manitoba school question, Thompson knew that the decision closed off the government's only door of escape. Now it would have to take action under the appeal clauses in section 93 of the British North America Act. And, Thompson argued to himself (and doubtless to close friends), how could a Conservative government with himself as a Catholic prime minister act in a way seen to be fair to everyone? The party at this stage seemed to worry too. As Louis Henry Davies observed from the Liberal sidelines,

'There must have been kicking ... or ... keeping a poor sick man in office would not have been resorted to.'

A cabinet sub-committee was struck to hear argument about a government appeal to the courts under section 93. Did perhaps the wording of the Manitoba Act of 1870 supervene the 1867 BNA Act? The hearing was set for 25 Nov. 1892. Five days before, letters were received in Ottawa by the governor general and Thompson that extinguished any hope of keeping Abbott on. The London doctors had told him his health demanded an instant resignation. He enclosed it, and he recommended Thompson as his successor, even though Thompson had suggested someone else, perhaps John Graham Haggart. The old cabinet was kept in being for another fortnight, while the sub-committee heard argument, and it was only on 7 December that Thompson was officially sworn in as prime minister. Little opposition to Thompson from within the party remained. There was no one else. 'They will find,' said Annie at one point in this long process, 'that they cannot do without you.' It was an oddly prophetic remark.

Cabinet changes were made. Thompson thought Chapleau might usefully retire to the comfort and security of the lieutenant governor's residence in Quebec. Chapleau was not unwilling, but the premier of Quebec, Charles Boucher de Boucherville, an old ultramontane, would not serve under Chapleau. Thompson tried hard, but old men can be stubborn. Chapleau became lieutenant governor, Boucherville resigned, and Thompson persuaded Louis-Olivier Taillon to take up the reins of the Quebec premiership. Auguste-Réal Angers, whom Chapleau had replaced, came to the Thompson cabinet, the one minister from Quebec of unquestioned probity. The Ontario contingent was not very satisfactory either, and Thompson did not have good cabinet timber available. He thought John Carling, who had been minister of agriculture for years, should retire. But Carling carried a deal of political clout in southwest Ontario, and had recaptured London for the Conservatives in a recent by-election. He was furious at being asked to retire, talked of resigning his seat, which would have fairly put the cat among the pigeons in the several closely fought constituencies around London. The governor general was brought in, and eventually, after hints of a KCMG, Carling consented to give up his department, staying on as minister without portfolio. The knighthood came the next year. Mackenzie Bowell was created minister of trade and commerce, with two controllers as assistants, one for inland revenue and the other for customs. To his great satisfaction, Bowell was sent to Australia to develop Canadian trade, one of the results being the 1894 Colonial Conference held in Ottawa.

Thompson gave his first major speech as prime minister in Toronto in January 1893. It was about tolerance, and about Canadian nationalism, both natural enough. He was a nationalist and a passionate one. He had difficulty, as did all sincere Canadian nationalists, in equating this conviction with independence. It was not that Thompson did not want to see a Canadian nation, but he believed the moment Canada was independent of British protection, she would be taken over by the United States. American actions in Hawaii were not reassuring, then or later; the tenor of some American newspapers was openly annexationist. It was also clear to Thompson – confirmed through a Canadian secret agent sent to New York at the end of 1893 – that a small section of the Liberal party was prepared to deliver Canada into American hands if it could. Among this group, called the Continental Union Association, were both Ontario and Quebec Liberals: Sir Richard John Cartwright, John Charlton, Mercier, and François Langelier. Thompson was sure in 1893 that most of the Liberal party was loyal, Wilfrid Laurier included; and in the end he realized that the conspiracy to make Canada part of the United States was confined to a small, not very quiet section of the opposition. His own view was that the real independence of Canada would have to wait until Canada was stronger, with numbers big enough to be able to sustain it. He thought that might be when the population reached 50 million.

In March 1893 Thompson went to Paris as one of the British judges on the international tribunal to settle the Canadian–American dispute over sealing in the Bering Sea. There were seven judges in all: two British, two American, and three European; the chairman was French. From late March until early July the tribunal heard argument from both sides. The result was a vindication of the position Thompson had taken ever since the first American seizures of Canadian sealing vessels in 1886: there was no justification for the United States claim that the Bering Sea was closed to all foreign sealers. Thompson feared, however, lest the regulations the tribunal was authorized to bring in be inimical to the seal hunt in the future, and opposed them so far as he could. But the regulations, though awkward, were no disaster: a year or two later Canadian sealers were doing better than ever.

Outside of the downward revision of the tariff, which was designed to spike Liberal guns, and the Manitoba school question, which was in train in the courts, Thompson's major concern in 1893 and 1894 was the North-West Territories school question. There the government's course was made easier by the fact that the territories assembly was under dominion tutelage. Nevertheless Thompson found the going difficult, between the Roman Catholic episcopacy in the west, led by the archbishop of St Boniface, Alexandre-Antonin Taché, who looked to Quebec as the model for a separate school system, and western Protestants, many of

Sir John S. D. Thompson, February 1894.

whom were from Ontario and believed that a system analogous to the Ontario separate schools was as far as they could go. The question was not helped by extreme statements from newspapers. Some Catholics in the northwest did not know they had any grievances until told about them from outside, or by their bishops; some Protestants were not aware of the 'awful' concessions to Roman Catholics until they read about them in the Protestant papers of Ontario. Thompson sometimes despaired of getting bishops, or Protestants, to be sensible. The former were almost worse, for they expected more of a Catholic prime minister than Thompson in good law and conscience could deliver. But in the end the North-West school question was largely solved to Thompson's satisfaction. Evidence of its effectiveness was the fact that the system was not essentially disturbed until 1905.

By 1894 the Manitoba school question had gone through its own evolution. The Thompson cabinet decided to determine judicially the important legal questions raised by section 93 of the BNA Act. At issue were the rights of redress, if any, of Manitoba Roman Catholics in the light of the Privy Council decision in *Barrett* v. *the City of Winnipeg*. This issue became the reference case later known as the Brophy case, which finally came before the Supreme Court of Canada in February 1894. The court had a difficult problem, construing *Barrett* against section 93. It decided the Roman Catholics had no right of appeal, that remedies were at an end. Some in the Conservative party greeted this decision with relief. The Supreme Court had taken away from the government any power of action. To get rid of the whole Manitoba school question, all the Thompson government had to do was, as Caron put it, 'sit back and wait.' Many in the party hoped that would happen. Thompson did not see it in this way. He believed there would have to be an appeal to the Privy Council in the Brophy case. There was. It was being argued, in fact, when Thompson was in London in December 1894.

Thompson had gone to London at the end of October 1894, ostensibly to be sworn in as a member of the imperial Privy Council, an honour given for his performance at Paris the previous year. But he also wanted to consult London doctors. The session of 1894 had been long and hard; the government had a powerful majority, but the Liberal opposition, believing this would be the last session before a general election, made as much noise as it could. The session began in February and ended only in July. George Eulas Foster, the minister of finance, and really Thompson's right-hand man, was away ill during part of the budget presentation, and after his illness he, with Bowell, helped run the Colonial Conference held in Ottawa in June. Thompson had a great deal on his shoulders and the strain was showing. He had never been thin. He was 5 feet 7 inches tall and in 1885 had been about 190 pounds. Over the years he had punished his excellent constitution with massive doses of work, and food; those vast, delicious French luncheons and dinners of 1893 had not made him thinner. By 1894 he was 225 pounds. At the end of the session there was swelling in his lower limbs; he took a holiday in the Muskokas for two weeks, then visited doctors. At first they were optimistic, but before his departure for London they seem to have become less so. At this point, in October 1894, Annie suggested he resign. Thompson, however, could

A moment of mirth: Sir John S. D. Thompson (sitting left) with family
and friends (Mackenzie Bowell standing left), vacationing on Lake Rosseau,
Ont., summer 1894.

not do that. He had never forgotten how the Nova Scotia party felt when
he left them in 1882 to go to the bench. He would have to stay until
after the 1895 election; if the government won, he could retire with
honour. In the mean time he would see what the London doctors said.

In London, medical opinion was optimistic, so much so that Thompson
gave himself three weeks holiday on the Continent, travelling with his
daughter Helena, and Senator William Eli Sanford and his daughter, to
Italy. Thompson was feeling well enough to climb all the way to the top
of St Peter's dome. That was unwise. He returned to London, unwell, on
1 December and started discussions with the Colonial Office on a long
agenda, especially Canadian copyright, about which he felt strongly.
There were social events. He was invited to go to Hawarden Castle to
meet William Ewart Gladstone. His health seemed uncertain, but on
11 December he said he was feeling better than he had for some months.

On Wednesday, 12 December, he went down to Windsor Castle to be sworn in as the Right Honourable Sir John Thompson. The ceremony was not long; afterward, sitting down to lunch, he fainted. Taken to a room near by, he recovered, saying, 'It seems too absurd to faint like this,' and returned to the table; before he could eat anything, suddenly, without a sound, he fell backward into the arms of Sir John Watt Reid, the queen's doctor, who had been placed beside him. Thompson did not move or breathe again. A massive heart attack had killed him.

Thompson's death shocked the country, stunned the cabinet, and devastated his family. Not least affected were Governor General Lord Aberdeen and Lady Aberdeen, who had become family friends. The British government sent his body home to Halifax in the warship *Blenheim* as a token of its esteem. The government of Canada buried its prime minister with an imposing state funeral at Halifax, on 3 Jan. 1895.

Few lawyers greater than Thompson have ever come out of Nova Scotia. He was not widely read, a weakness he recognized and deplored, but he had an incisive and rapid mind. He grasped facts quickly and remembered them with facility, and best of all sorted them out in his own mind. This ability, joined to a vast capacity for work, gave him an extraordinarily powerful intelligence. Yet he wore his power quietly and with modesty; it came from his mind, not his manner. There was another thing about Thompson: he really loved justice, as he hated iniquity. Justice for him was not merely a profession but a fire that burned inside him, a passionate hatred of injustice and cruelty, which made him remarkable among both lawyers and judges. He radiated the strong sense of a mind unclouded by prejudice, concerned for truth. Albert Martin Belding, in the *St. John Daily Sun*, gets Thompson right in this memorable eulogy:

No dreams of glory dwarfed his loftier aim,
To whom his country's good was more than fame;
No sheen of gold obscured his clearer view,
Who saw the right, and held the balance true.

What Canada lost, as the poet truly said, was the 'onward look of that untrammelled mind.'

P. B. WAITE

Further reading

P. B. Waite, *The man from Halifax: Sir John Thompson, prime minister* (Toronto, 1985).

Sir MACKENZIE BOWELL,

newspaperman, militia officer, Orangeman, and politician;
b. 27 Dec. 1823 in Rickinghall, England, son of John Bowell
and Elizabeth Marshall; m. 23 Dec. 1847 Harriet Louisa Moore
(d. 1884) in Belleville, Upper Canada, and they had four sons
and five daughters; d. there 10 Dec. 1917.

Mackenzie Bowell emigrated to the Canadas with his parents in 1833. It took them eight weeks to reach Quebec City and another week to go from Montreal to the Bay of Quinte, on the north shore of Lake Ontario. They settled there in the village of Belleville, where John Bowell had relatives. He was a cabinet-maker and Mackenzie learned that trade. Though he continued to help his father in the evenings, in 1834 or 1835 he went to work as a printer's devil for George Benjamin, editor and owner of the Belleville *Intelligencer*.

Young Mac served as Benjamin's right hand, especially when Benjamin was in politics. In 1848 he became a partner in the *Intelligencer*; the following year he and his brother-in-law took over its printing business. Bowell assumed sole proprietorship of the weekly in the early 1850s. In 1867 he launched a daily edition and in 1875 the Intelligencer Printing and Publishing Company was incorporated. A founding member of the Canadian Press Association in 1859, he was its president in 1865–66.

Bowell's rise came as much from steady public involvement as it did from journalism. The chair for several years of both the board of school trustees and the grammar school board, he was also a member and vice-president of the local board of agriculture and arts. In 1865, with Henry Corby, Billa Flint, and others, he established a board of trade; Bowell himself was a president or director of several companies besides the *Intelligencer*. A keen supporter of the militia in Hastings County, he helped organize the Belleville Volunteer Militia Rifle Company in 1857; he saw active duty at Amherstburg, Upper Canada, during the American Civil War, and at Prescott during the Fenian disturbances of 1866. He would retire from the militia in 1874 with the rank of lieutenant-colonel in the

49th (Hastings) Battalion of Rifles. During these decades Bowell gained recognition too as a leading member of the Orange order, which he had joined in 1842. In 1870–78 he was grand master of the lodge in British North America, and in 1876, in Londonderry (Northern Ireland), he was elected president of the order's Imperial Triennial Council.

When George Benjamin chose not to run for re-election in Hastings North in the provincial election of 1863, Bowell decided to try his hand there as the Conservative candidate. Helping him campaign was Benjamin's last major effort – he would die the following year. Bowell was defeated but he was elected for the same constituency to the new House of Commons in 1867. He would hold Hastings North for the next 25 years.

Bowell first came into political prominence in April 1874, when, as an Orange spokesman, he moved for the expulsion from the commons of Louis Riel, leader of the uprising at Red River (Man.). A casualty of that event had been Thomas Scott, an Irish Orangeman from Hastings whose execution stirred passions there. In 1878, after the Conservatives' electoral victory, Sir John A. Macdonald appointed Bowell minister of customs, a portfolio he would retain until after the prime minister's death. His principal task was the supervision of the main source of government revenue. As a consequence of the National Policy tariff of 1879 many new rules were established and a number of new rates based on the *ad valorem* principle were adopted. A board of dominion customs appraisers was created in June 1879, including appraisers from Halifax, Saint John, Quebec, Montreal, Kingston, Toronto, and London. Bowell believed it was essential to have common policies; it was already apparent that different ports gave different evaluations for the same goods. Moreover, an *ad valorem* determination of duties meant that invoices could be, and often were, deliberately understated. The Customs Act clearly laid down that the invoiced value had to be based on fair market price in the country of origin. The board of appraisers reported to Bowell that its actions provoked grumblings and some enmity from importers, but customs was like that. As the board's secretary, Charles Belford, noted, 'The "ignorant impatience of taxation" is not confined to the thoughtless or the uneducated.'

In the political side of his office, Bowell dealt mainly in the small change of politics: jobs, salary increases, promotions, and patronage. He seems to have been scrupulous in following government rules, but there were exceptions. Macdonald frequently enquired of him, in benign fashion, when, where, and if the rules might be bent. A minor customs appointment was suggested in a covering letter from Macdonald in 1884: 'If you can *possibly* do this for the Bishop do it. It is of very great importance just now to keep him not only friendly but *Earnest* in the cause.' Even more headstrong members of cabinet learned to write in the same vein. Sir William Young, former chief justice of Nova Scotia, asked railways minister Sir Charles Tupper if two iron summer-houses being made in Glasgow for Point Pleasant Park in Halifax could be brought in free of duty. Tupper sent the letter to Bowell, asking 'What can you do for Sir William?'

Bowell would not always bend before political requests. Paul-Étienne Grandbois, MP for Témiscouata, Que., came to Macdonald in July 1884 with a plea for a constituent, a Captain Charette, whose vessel had been seized for smuggling spirits from Saint-Pierre and Miquelon. It was a clear case. The cargo was condemned, but Grandbois pleaded for the restitution of the vessel to Charette on the ground that he was a simple-minded man of good character. Macdonald sent affidavits to Bowell 'so that you may if possible have mercy upon the owner of the schooner and let him off as easily as your conscience will allow.' Bowell in return sent Macdonald a full documentation of the seizure. After reading this dossier Macdonald backed Bowell completely, agreeing that 'the most rigorous steps should be taken to condemn the vessels [apparently more than one was involved] and to bring all the parties to justice.'

Bowell's talents were administrative: he was conscientious, hard-working, and scrupulous. Customs, with its large bureaucracy, steadily changing schedules of rates, stream of demands from manufacturers and importers, and detailed fiscal components, required such talents. Moreover, Bowell was patient at unravelling patronage problems. The postmastership of Belleville in 1880 is a case in point. Senator Robert Read of Belleville wanted it for his son-in-law, both men from large families of Conservatives. The brother of Sir Alexander Campbell, the postmaster general, was also a candidate. Belleville distiller Henry Corby wanted it for a nominee of his and wrote Macdonald accordingly. It was this letter, passed on to Bowell by Macdonald, that occasioned Bowell's revelation of the actual situation in Belleville. He calmly gave his chief a *tour d'horizon* of the postmastership and then added, almost as an afterthought, that 'the

Mackenzie Bowell
MP, May 1889.

position is *not vacant* nor do I know when it will be as the present Post Master Mr. [James Hubbard] Meacham is to all appearances as capable of performing the duties as he has been for years past and has *no intention of resigning*, and cannot under the law be superannuated not being a Civil Servant but paid by fees.'

After Macdonald's death in 1891 Bowell retained his customs portfolio under John Joseph Caldwell Abbott. In addition, he was acting minister of railways and canals from June 1891 to January 1892, at which time he was made minister of militia and defence. On the accession of Sir John Sparrow David Thompson as prime minister in December 1892, Bowell was elevated to the Senate and became government leader there, with a newly created portfolio, trade and commerce. He was assigned two controllers as assistants: John Fisher Wood for inland revenue and Nathaniel Clarke Wallace for customs.

When Thompson went to Paris in March 1893 as a British representative on the arbitration over sealing in the Bering Sea, Bowell, as senior minister, became acting prime minister. His selection had nothing to do with his talents; it was simply the custom that the senior minister assumed this duty. It may be a measure of Thompson's lack of full confidence in Bowell that much of the significant correspondence, while Thompson was in Paris, is with George Eulas Foster, acting leader in the commons.

In September 1893 Bowell, as minister of trade and commerce and duly instructed by cabinet, went to Australia with Sandford Fleming to talk about trade between the Australasian colonies and Canada and the proposed Pacific cable. He went by the new Vancouver–Sydney steamship line, itself a point of discussion, and returned in January 1894. The results of his work were so encouraging that Canada took the initiative in calling an intercolonial conference, to meet in Ottawa at the end of June, to discuss intercolonial trade and imperial preference. The conference was really Bowell's idea. Six of the seven Australian colonies sent delegates, as did Fiji, the Cape Colony, and a still independent Hawaii. The British government sent an observer, not a delegate; it was not at all sure it liked such colonial initiatives.

The conference of 1894 may well represent the best reach of Bowell's talents. He was 70, an age when many think of honours, reputation, and coasting. The Australian adventure had been a great fillip to his self-esteem. Younger cabinet colleagues called him Grandpa Bowell; he looked the part, with his full white beard, but the appellation may also have signified intellectual limitations. There is evidence that Thompson was looking for ways to ease him out of cabinet when Thompson died suddenly on 12 Dec. 1894 in England.

Governor General Lord Aberdeen now had a difficult choice. The cabinet had been held together, disciplined one might say, by Thompson's strength, suavity, and knowledge. It now fell back into constituent parts, each with members who displayed individual prejudices and jealousies. Thompson had left no intimations about a successor, and there was no clear choice. Foster was able but waspish. John Graham Haggart was able but lazy, and, as Lady Aberdeen said, 'a Bohemian.' Neither would serve under the other. Sir Charles Hibbert Tupper, probably the most capable and resolute member of cabinet, was self-willed and headstrong. None of the others offered much. The one person in the Conservative party left out of the consideration was old Sir Charles Tupper, then in London as Canada's high commissioner. Thompson had grown to dislike Tupper Sr, his pushy ways, his penchant for the improvement of Tupperdom.

Thompson's view was shared by his widow, Annie Emma, and, even more important, by Lady Aberdeen. Any prejudice that Lord Aberdeen had acquired against the elder Tupper via Sir John Thompson had ample domestic reinforcement.

When Thompson had gone to London in 1894, Bowell was again acting prime minister. On 13 December, the day after Thompson died, Lord Aberdeen invited Bowell to discuss the position of affairs with his cabinet colleagues, and with him. Bowell said he would not consult his colleagues. He doubtless knew what their opinions were on his becoming prime minister, but he would see the governor general, leaving Lord Aberdeen free afterward to consult whomsoever he chose.

After conferring with a prominent Roman Catholic senator, Sir Frank Smith, about Bowell's political suitability, the governor general asked him on the evening of the 13th to form a government. By the 21st Bowell had put a government together, with himself as president of the Privy Council as well as prime minister. The new administration included all the ministers from Thompson's cabinet save Sir John Carling; eight members kept their previous positions. Bowell was delighted with his accession to the highest political office in the country. Knighthood came to him on New Year's Day 1895. He had never been guilty of underestimating his own capacity. Now his vanity expanded beyond reason. He had seen a good deal of Sir John A. Macdonald's methods of governing the party and he believed he could emulate him. But to imitate Macdonald demanded a reach of intelligence and a finely tuned discrimination wholly unavailable to Sir Mackenzie Bowell. What to him was cleverness was, to others, evasion, weakness, unreliability, and fatuity. The governor general found that Bowell liked to have a trapdoor for escape in case of danger. Moreover, it was difficult to hold him to a point of policy because he had not sufficiently possessed himself of it in the first place or, if he had, he had forgotten. Aberdeen thus had reason to become uneasy about so slippery a prime minister, one who found it difficult to be frank and could not be trusted.

In Bowell's defence, it has to be said that his ministry was split into factions and that the Canadian ship of state had in these months a very hard helm. One difficulty was Manitoba. There the Roman Catholic minority clamoured for federal remedial legislation to restore the public support to their schools that had been abolished by the provincial government of

Thomas Greenway. The decision of the Judicial Committee of the Privy Council in the Brophy case, delivered on 29 Jan. 1895, forced the federal government to redress their grievances. Bowell's Orangeism did not block his willingness to do whatever the law said he must do for the aggrieved Catholics. But what action was to be taken? How was it to be implemented? Should there be, as some wanted, a general election first? To these questions the members of the Bowell cabinet returned different answers. If ever a government needed a firm, judicious hand, it was now.

One member, minister of justice C. H. Tupper, succeeded in persuading his colleagues to accept the principle of the remedial order. It was issued on 21 March as an order in council, which declared that Manitoba must pass new legislation restoring to Roman Catholics their separate school privileges. At first the government went along with Tupper, that, having issued the remedial order, it would go to a dissolution at once. But several English-speaking members of cabinet then urged upon Bowell the ingenious idea of a further session, in 1896, which would delay the whole nasty issue and perhaps even allow time for it to be solved without a plunge into an election. Tupper did not like this course; indignant over the repudiation of a clear-cut policy, he tendered his resignation on the 21st. Bowell replied that to appeal to the country when the heather was afire would be inexcusable. Tupper retorted angrily on the 25th that 'the beginning of the blaze is a more auspicious period than the middle. ... You cannot, I fear, keep Parliament together long enough to see the end of this fire.' The intervention of the governor general, Senator George Alexander Drummond, and Sir Donald Alexander Smith, brought Tupper back at the end of March with the proviso that if no settlement with Manitoba was reached, remedial legislation would be introduced in the 1896 session.

Bowell seems to have believed that a political settlement with Manitoba was possible and that there was going to be no need to put a difficult and complex constitutional issue to the arbitrament of the hustings. Manitoba's clever reply in June 1895 to the remedial order held out hopes that, with more information and negotiation, some compromise could be reached. By January 1896, however, things had turned for the worse. Senator Auguste-Réal Angers, the minister of agriculture, had resigned in July 1895 and Bowell could not find a French Canadian to replace him; the government had lost two critical by-elections in Quebec over the school issue; and Nathaniel Clarke Wallace, Orange grand master and the great anti-remedialist in the ministry, had resigned in December. Parliament opened on 2 Jan. 1896 with the government in furious disarray. Within 24 hours there was a revolt against Bowell by about half the cabinet; seven ministers resigned on the 4th and urged the governor general to replace Bowell with old Sir Charles Tupper. The seven were led by Foster, Haggart, and Walter Humphries Montague. Thomas Mayne Daly, a loyal cabinet colleague, encouraged Bowell to be reasonable for the sake of the party. The session would be a rough one and strong men would be needed on the government side. However much Bowell disliked the seven 'traitors,' he needed them. He would not be able to get others, not on the eve of a divisive session over which hung a sinister cloud: the general election that had to be called by 25 April 1896. Furthermore, Daly pointed out, if Bowell did not have a government the governor general would soon have to find another one.

Aberdeen's actions in helping to patch up this cabinet rupture were based on his dislike of calling in Tupper as prime minister. As important was his mistaken belief that the seven rebels had, as the basis of their insurrection, the aim of avoiding remedial legislation, to which the cabinet was pledged. Here the governor general was almost certainly misled by Bowell, whose vanity could not allow that the rebels disliked him personally. Bowell therefore alleged the policy difference. Hence, Aberdeen pressed him to try to reconstruct. But after four days, 4–7 January, Bowell had to give up. Early on the 8th he formally tendered his resignation.

Then an odd event occurred. That afternoon, in room 25 of the Senate, Angers, Joseph Bolduc, and Philippe Landry were talking with three MPs when the governor general's aide-de-camp knocked on the door, asking to speak to Angers. Aberdeen wanted private advice from him on what to do about Bowell's resignation. Angers's advice was given at once: refuse the resignation on the grounds that the house had not yet voted its reply to the speech from the throne. This position is precisely the ground Aberdeen took later that day in refusing Bowell's resignation.

Several rebels then learned that Aberdeen had not been given the true state of affairs by Bowell. They went to Government House with their version, that they and certainly old Sir Charles Tupper were not anti-remedialists. This account was news to Aberdeen. Next the newspapers reported that Aberdeen's aide had been seen visiting Wilfrid Laurier, leader of the opposition. The rebels jumped to the conclusion that Aberdeen was thinking of calling on him to form a government. That did it. As C. H. Tupper said, 'We all turned in like sheep into the fold, at the very rumour.' The 'traitors' returned to cabinet on 15 January with the exception of C. H. Tupper, who was left out in the reshuffle of ministers because of his father's likely return. Thus did the rebels come back, with the compromise that Tupper Sr would lead in the commons and that, when the session was over, Bowell would resign as prime minister and Tupper would take over the government and go to an election.

That was what happened. Still, there were hopes, never abandoned by the governor general or the government, that Manitoba might agree to a compromise before any election, that remedial legislation, though introduced in parliament on 11 February, might still not have to be passed. Even after the motion for second reading came up three weeks later, hopes and negotiations were not abandoned. But the determined opposition of the Liberal party to the remedial bill, which was withdrawn on 16 April, and the simple fact that the government had to dissolve before 26 April, made the running. Bowell's resignation on the 27th, as promised, was not much regretted. So well did Tupper fight the election of June 1896 that he actually got more popular votes than Laurier (46 per cent against 45), but Laurier won on the basis of seats in Quebec, which went 49 to 16 for the Liberals.

Bowell returned to the Senate, never forgetting or forgiving the 'traitors' of January 1896. He was anything but a *fainéant*. Instead of retiring in decent obscurity to Belleville, he stood loyally to his work in the Senate. For the next two decades its *Debates* are full of his interventions. In 1896 too he resumed active control of the *Intelligencer*, which he had relinquished in 1878. At his 90th birthday in 1913 he was still going to his office at the newspaper, still inordinately vain, proud, for example, at people not guessing his age. He looked only 65, almost the age of his eldest daughter. In 1916, at 93, he set out to visit his son in Vancouver and then go on to the Yukon. The following year he died quietly at his William Street home in Belleville of old age and pneumonia, and was buried in Belleville Cemetery, just west of the city.

Sir Mackenzie Bowell began his career with lusty Orange prejudices, but by the 1880s his fighting spirit was subsumed within Conservative politics and his Orange positions had softened. According to the Toronto *Globe*, it was Bowell who succeeded in making the Orange order more friendly to Catholics. That tolerance was born of political necessity. At Bowell's death, the Belleville *Daily Ontario* noted that he was not a great lawmaker or parliamentarian; he had no independent cast of mind. But mere mediocrity could not have taken him as far as he went. His aptness for public life was 'administrative rather than constructive ... he administered the affairs of that department [customs] honestly, fearlessly, efficiently. He left to others the long speeches and the framing of the statutes, while he kept the machinery of the government in motion.' That is about as good an epitaph as Bowell, vain as he was, could have asked for. Others, Lord Aberdeen not least, set him down more harshly. Unreliable as Bowell was, his honesty seemed to them to be not the triumph of a strong mind, but the refuge of a weak one.

P. B. WAITE

Further reading

There is little published material specifically on Sir Mackenzie Bowell, aside from the biographical articles that appear in the standard reference works of the late 19th and early 20th centuries, such as *The Canadian men and women of the time: a handbook of Canadian biography*, ed. H. J. Morgan (Toronto, 1898; 2nd ed., 1912). For his year and a half as prime minister, the best source is [I. M. Marjoribanks Hamilton-Gordon, Marchioness of] Aberdeen [and Temair], *The Canadian journal of Lady Aberdeen, 1893–1898*, intro. J. T. Saywell (Toronto, 1960). No archival record of Bowell's birth has been found. The date has generally been given as 27 Dec. 1823; however, the parish registers held by the Suffolk County Council record a marriage in Rickinghall between John Bowell and Elizabeth Marshall, possibly Bowell's parents, on 19 March 1824, which may indicate a birth date of 27 Dec. 1824.

Sir CHARLES TUPPER,

doctor and politician; b. 2 July 1821 near Amherst, N.S.,
son of Charles Tupper and Miriam Lowe, née Lockhart;
m. 8 Oct. 1846 Frances Amelia Morse in Amherst, and they
had three daughters, two of whom died in infancy, and three sons;
d. 30 Oct. 1915 in Bexleyheath (London), England.

O f Planter descent, Charles Tupper was born on his father's small farm outside Amherst. Since his father was a co-pastor of the local Baptist church and his mother 'a pious, devout woman,' Tupper was taught the merits of hard work and self-discipline, but his childhood appears to have been happy. When the young man fell victim to the 'demon rum,' with 'a look of horror' his father simply exclaimed, 'Is it possible?' Tupper's father was a formidable scholar and much of Tupper's education took place at home, although he attended local grammar schools. In August 1837 he entered Horton Academy in Wolfville, where he became 'fairly proficient' in Latin and Greek and acquired a reading knowledge of French and a smattering of science. In 1839–40, after teaching for a time in New Brunswick, he studied medicine with Dr Ebenezer Fitch Harding of Windsor, N.S., and then, using borrowed funds, he entered the University of Edinburgh to obtain the best medical training available. He received a diploma from the Royal College of Surgeons of Edinburgh on 20 April 1843 and became an MD on 1 Aug. 1843.

While living with Dr Harding, Tupper had undergone a conversion experience, but the years in Britain introduced him to a world of temptations, to many of which he yielded, drinking Scotch for the first time and going to the theatre. He never entirely abandoned his Baptist upbringing, but his commitment to the Baptist faith weakened. After returning to Nova Scotia he broke off an engagement he had entered into at age 17, briefly became engaged to the daughter of a prominent Halifax merchant, and on 8 Oct. 1846 married Frances Morse, a granddaughter of one of the founders of Amherst. By all accounts the Tuppers were a close couple.

Frances – described by Edward Whelan in 1864 as 'a very fine and hand-some woman' – was always at her husband's side, re-establishing the family home wherever political necessity dictated and accompanying Tupper whenever possible on his travels. In recent years, upon the flimsiest of gossip, Tupper has acquired the reputation of being a womanizer. He certainly enjoyed the companionship of women, but there is no evidence that he was anything more than mildly flirtatious and his affection for his wife was genuine. Their children were brought up in her Anglican faith and Tupper acquired a pew in St Paul's Church while living in Halifax, although on the campaign trail he would frequently attend Baptist meet-ings, dropping substantial sums in the collection plate.

After returning to Amherst, Tupper established a medical practice and opened a drugstore. The life of a country doctor involved long and frequently arduous journeys on horseback and he had to turn his hand to everything from surgery to pulling teeth. Like most doctors trained in the 'heroic' methods, he may not always have helped those he sought to heal – staying up all night to administer half-hourly doses of champagne to the ailing wife of a political enemy may have won him respect but whether it contributed to her recovery is less certain. Yet Tupper bragged that he never 'refused a sick call' and his patients believed that 'if Tupper gave you up, you might as well turn your face to the wall.' As even his sympathetic biographer, Edward Manning Saunders, admitted, however, 'It may be that his political success created an exaggerated belief respecting his professional skill.'

Upon becoming provincial secretary of Nova Scotia in 1857 Tupper handed the practice over to his brother and partner, Nathan, but after the Conservative defeat in 1859 he established a lucrative practice in Halifax. He became city medical officer, served on the surgical staff of the Prov-incial and City Hospital, and was chairman of the committee responsible for establishing a medical school. As one of the best-trained doctors in the province, he was concerned to increase the status of the profession by driving out the unqualified. In 1863 he was elected president of the Medical Society of Nova Scotia and in 1867–70 he served as first pres-ident of the Canadian Medical Association. He transferred his practice to Ottawa in 1868, and during the period in opposition after 1873 he practised there and in Toronto. But medicine occupied less and less of his time, although he carefully nurtured his professional image, storing a medical bag under his desk in the House of Commons.

Tupper had become involved in politics through the influence of James William Johnston, the leader of the Conservative party in Nova Scotia, a prominent Baptist, and a family friend. He first stood for election in Cumberland County in 1855, when he defeated the leading Liberal, Joseph Howe. Overall, however, the election was a disaster for his party and at its first caucus on 30 Jan. 1856 he called for a new strategy, which involved courting the Roman Catholic minority and embracing government construction of railways. According to Tupper's account, Johnston accepted this change of direction, surrendering the effective leadership to Tupper. In fact, the transfer of power took place more gradually. Johnston spoke frequently in the House of Assembly during the 1856 session. Yet it was Tupper who led the attack on the government, in speeches so acerbic and partisan that Howe dubbed him 'the wicked wasp of Cumberland.' As Howe's relations with the Roman Catholic members of his party became increasingly strained, Tupper encouraged defections to the Conservatives in 1857. Deprived of their majority, the Liberals under Premier William Young resigned; the Conservatives took office on 24 Feb. 1857 and Tupper became provincial secretary.

In his very first speech to the legislature Tupper had made clear his commitment to 'this new accompaniment of civilization – the railroad.' Now in charge of the Railway Board, he appointed James Laurie, a civil engineer, to prepare a detailed study of Nova Scotia's railways. Tupper's enthusiasm is partly explained by the fact that few counties were better situated to benefit from railways than Cumberland. But he would base his political career on the belief that Nova Scotians (and later Canadians) should play down ethnic and cultural differences and focus on developing their vast resources. Nova Scotia, he believed, with its 'inexhaustible mines' and its strategic 'geographical position' could become 'a vast manufacturing mart for this side of the Atlantic.' Tupper did not yet advocate protection. What he did see as necessary was access to the markets of Canada and the United States, a substantial influx of capital, and the steady growth of population through immigration. To open the way for development Tupper persuaded Johnston in 1857 to negotiate an end to the General Mining Association's monopoly over the mineral resources of the colony. In June of the same year he initiated discussions with New Brunswick and Canada to secure an intercolonial railway and in September 1858 he went to London seeking imperial support for the project. The negotiations failed, partly because the Canadians seemed more interested in federal union, which Tupper did not feel authorized to discuss, but primarily in his view because the British were 'too much engaged with their own immediate interests.' He returned to Nova Scotia convinced of the need to restructure the imperial relationship and to seek closer ties with the other British North American colonies.

The election of 12 May 1859 was marked by an unusual degree of sectarian conflict. The Conservatives carried the Catholic vote but there was a larger switch of Protestants to the Liberals. In Protestant Cumberland, Tupper barely retained his seat. After losing a vote of no-confidence, the Conservatives appealed to the lieutenant governor, Lord Mulgrave, for another dissolution and, when he refused, resigned on 7 Feb. 1860. Tupper did not take defeat graciously. He believed that five of the Liberals elected should have been disqualified and he petitioned for Mulgrave's recall. During the next three years Tupper ferociously attacked the Liberal government both in the assembly and in editorials in the *British Colonist* (Halifax). Clinging to power with a small majority, the Liberals moved to restrict the franchise, but Tupper persuaded the assembly to delay the change and in 1863 the Conservatives were returned to power with the largest majority in a decade, winning 40 of the 55 seats. Johnston became premier and Tupper provincial secretary on 11 June 1863, and on 11 May 1864 Johnston went to the bench and Tupper became his successor.

During the campaign Tupper had committed his party to an expanded railway network and an improved system of public education. Both policies were risky – railway building unleashed sectional tensions; education reform aroused sectarian rivalries – and both were expensive. The provincial economy was buoyant, however, and Tupper was able to push ahead with the Pictou extension of the Nova Scotia Railway. He placed great faith in Sandford Fleming, who was hired as chief engineer early in 1864, and when construction by local contractors proceeded slower than projected, in January 1866 he awarded Fleming the contract to complete the line, ignoring the provincial statute that called for public tendering. Judged by its results the contract, though controversial, was a good one, for on 31 May

Charles Tupper,
premier of Nova
Scotia, 1864.

1867 the entire line from Truro to Pictou Landing was completed ahead of schedule and on budget. Tupper had less immediate success with the line from Annapolis Royal to Windsor. The first company failed to fulfil its contract, but in 1866 Tupper reached an agreement with the Windsor and Annapolis Railway Company, which completed construction in December 1869. Initially Tupper also sought to finish the line from Truro to the New Brunswick border but he did not seriously pursue negotiations after confederation, and the intercolonial railway, became likely.

Tupper's achievements in the field of education were equally impressive. In 1864 he had passed his first Free School Act, establishing a system of state-subsidized common schools, subject to regulation by a superintendent of education under the direction of a Council of Public

Instruction, composed of the members of the Executive Council. The act did not introduce local taxation; it simply promised greater financial support to school districts which instituted compulsory assessment. When fewer than half did so, Tupper introduced another act in 1865 imposing compulsory taxation. He attempted to appease Protestant opinion by stressing that the new schools, while non-denominational, would still provide Christian instruction. Partly to rebuild his reputation among Baptists, alienated by his support for the resuscitation of Dalhousie College in 1863, he appointed Theodore Harding Rand as the first superintendent of education. These actions aroused Catholic concerns and one of his own supporters moved an amendment in 1865 to allow state-supported separate schools. Tupper had already placed control over educational policy in the hands of the cabinet, where Catholic representation was virtually guaranteed, and he opposed the creation of publicly funded separate schools. But he indicated to Catholic archbishop Thomas Louis Connolly that, so long as they followed the prescribed course of study, Catholic-run schools could offer religious instruction after hours and still receive public grants. This compromise ensured to Nova Scotia a degree of religious harmony unparalleled in the other colonies.

In 1858 Tupper had been unwilling to make a formal commitment to union with Canada but in 1860, when he spoke in Saint John on 'The political condition of British North America,' he openly advocated it. He was motivated in part by frustration and a desire for a larger political arena in which to exhibit his talents. Yet personal ambition will only go so far in explaining the determination with which he pursued his goal. Certainly he expected important 'commercial advantages' for Nova Scotia, but again his concern was with more than economic development. What Tupper wanted was greater influence for his colony within the empire. His speech in Saint John reflected his anger at imperial policies which did not recognize the potential value of the colonies. 'What is a British-American,' he declared, 'but a man regarded as a mere dependent upon an Empire which, however great and glorious, does not recognize him as entitled to any voice in her Senate, or possessing any interests worthy of Imperial regard.' Tupper had concluded, he later said, that the Maritimes 'could never hope to occupy a position of influence or importance except in connection with their larger sister Canada.' Confederation held out the promise that 'British America, stretching from the Atlantic to the

Pacific, would in a few years exhibit to the world a great and powerful organization, with British Institutions, British sympathies, and British feelings, bound indissolubly to the throne of England.' Within a few years his view would be reinforced by his conviction that the impending victory of the North in the American Civil War made union necessary for 'the existence of our country as a British Province.'

On 28 March 1864, arguing that British North American union could not be achieved for some years, Tupper pushed through the assembly of Nova Scotia a resolution calling for a conference to discuss Maritime union, which he saw as a preliminary to a larger union. In view of the anticipated hostility of Prince Edward Island, Charlottetown was selected as the site. Tupper and Premier Samuel Leonard Tilley of New Brunswick acted as the joint secretaries there in September, but because of the arrival of a Canadian delegation the conference abandoned discussion of Maritime union, endorsing instead a plan for confederation. This decision owed little to the inspired oratory of the Canadians for they were preaching to the converted. Agreement in principle was easily achieved and the delegates reconvened at Quebec in October to work out the details.

At Quebec, Tupper again headed the Nova Scotian delegation. Although his own preference was for a legislative union, he knew this was unacceptable to French Canadian representatives such as George-Étienne Cartier and Hector-Louis Langevin. Therefore, he strongly supported the Canadian proposals for a highly centralized federal union, while opposing efforts to alter the form of the local legislatures and insisting that the provinces should have the sole right to levy duties on their natural resources. He was also concerned to offset 'the great preponderance of Canada' in the proposed House of Commons by ensuring equal regional representation for the Maritimes (exclusive of Newfoundland) in the Senate. Tupper may be forgiven for misjudging the value of the Senate as a guardian of regional interests. Harder to justify is the compromise he accepted on the issue of compensating Nova Scotia for surrendering control over customs duties. Nova Scotia was more dependent on customs revenues and collected more per capita than the other colonies; yet in order to reach an agreement with the Canadians Tupper underestimated the potential shortfall in provincial revenues and accepted an annual subsidy of 80 cents per capita. This decision not only ensured that Nova

Scotia would enter confederation with a deficit, but also sowed the seeds of future disparities between the large and small provinces. The sincerity of his faith in confederation notwithstanding, Tupper proved a much less effective negotiator for the financial interests of Nova Scotia than Tilley was for those of New Brunswick.

Tupper was convinced that he could persuade the assembly of Nova Scotia to accept the Quebec resolutions, but opposition quickly mounted across the colony. Although supported by the imperial government and by Liberal leader Adams George Archibald, he was reluctant to move a motion in favour of confederation, and the defeat of Tilley in the New Brunswick election of 1865 justified his caution. Tupper therefore marked time for a year. In 1866, in order to fragment the anti-confederation forces, he promised that changes would be made in the Quebec resolutions and persuaded the assembly on 18 April to endorse by 31–19 a motion in favour of union. He then proceeded to London where, while awaiting delegates from the other colonies, he wrote pamphlets and letters to newspapers to counteract Howe's efforts to arouse British public opinion against confederation.

At the London conference in December 1866 few changes were made to the Quebec resolutions. The federal government was given the authority to pass remedial legislation to protect separate schools where they had been established by colonial legislation prior to confederation. Although Archbishop Connolly strongly lobbied for constitutional guarantees for separate schools in the Maritimes, Tupper refused his consent. Tupper did agree to strengthen the federal authority by turning the coastal fisheries from an area of joint responsibility into one controlled solely by Ottawa. Since Nova Scotia was likely to enter confederation with a much higher debt than had been predicted, due largely to his own policies, he pushed for a revision of the subsidy formula but only minor changes were made. Once again he appears to have been convinced that the advantages of union would offset the immediate financial difficulties of the province. Tupper returned to Halifax and began to prepare for confederation. The assembly and the Executive Council were reduced in size to reflect their more limited responsibilities, senators were selected, and an act was passed preventing dual representation in the provincial and federal parliaments. On 4 July 1867 Tupper handed over power to a revamped provincial administration under Hiram Blanchard. He undoubtedly expected to be included in the new federal cabinet but when Prime Minister Sir John A. Macdonald ran into difficulty in forming it Tupper persuaded Thomas D'Arcy McGee that they should both step aside in favour of an Irish Catholic from Nova Scotia, Edward Kenny. Tupper may have been motivated by his awareness of the electoral débâcle that was to follow, for in the first federal elections in September he was the only pro-confederate in Nova Scotia to win a seat (Cumberland), and then by a very narrow margin.

Although offered the chairmanship of the Intercolonial Railway Commission, Tupper declined the post because it 'would weaken my influence in rendering the Union of the Provinces acceptable to the people of Nova Scotia.' In the commons he spoke frequently on Nova Scotian issues and attempted to rebuild his political base. When Howe went to London in 1868 to push for repeal, Tupper was sent by Macdonald to present the opposite case and did so effectively. Tupper also met with Howe and offered to assist him in obtaining 'better terms' for Nova Scotia if Howe would agree 'to make the best of union.' When Howe did just that and entered the federal cabinet, Tupper appealed to the Conservatives in Hants County, N.S., to re-elect Howe and even offered to resign his own seat for him if necessary. Howe and Tupper thus became allies, although the relationship was not free of friction.

As Howe's health declined, the need to find Tupper a cabinet position grew stronger and on 21 June 1870 he became president of the Privy Council and on 2 July 1872 minister of inland revenue. His influence was soon felt. Tupper was convinced that the United States would never agree to a fair resolution of the Atlantic fisheries dispute unless the Canadian government adopted a firm policy. Prior to confederation he had unilaterally doubled the licence fees for Americans fishing off Nova Scotia, in 1868 he had persuaded the British government to allow Canada to raise its fees, and he strongly pushed for the decision in 1870 to end the licensing system. This action precipitated the appointment of a joint commission, which met in Washington in 1871 and on which Macdonald sat. Tupper acted as the prime minister's liaison with the cabinet during these negotiations and, although not entirely happy with the Treaty of Washington, he loyally stood by it and Macdonald in the commons. In the federal election of 1872 Tupper organized the campaign in Nova Scotia and he boasted of 'not a single Anti-confederate being elected.' Indeed, of the province's 21 members, only one was clearly an opponent of the government, although several more were former repealers whose loyalty to the Conservative party would be found wanting during the Pacific Scandal of 1873.

On 22 Feb. 1873 Tupper replaced Tilley as minister of customs and, although he held the office only until 5 November, when the government was brought down by the scandal, he was responsible for establishing the British system of weights and measures as a uniform standard across Canada. In the disastrous election of 1874 only he and one other Conservative were elected in Nova Scotia. None the less, the Pacific Scandal brought unexpected political benefits for him. Macdonald contemplated resignation and a number of prominent Conservatives abandoned ship. A vacuum existed at the very heart of the Conservative party and Tupper moved to fill it. He was not involved in the Pacific Scandal – as a Maritimer excluded from the inner circle of the cabinet he had been unaware of the substantial contributions made by Sir Hugh Allan to the Quebec and Ontario ministers – but he defended those implicated and he stood by Macdonald during and after the election. For four years Tupper campaigned in virtually every by-election in Canada, and in the commons he became the party's most effective critic of the Liberal government of Alexander Mackenzie. It is easy to make fun of Tupper's 'reputation for parliamentary blather,' but his command of detail and his memory were outstanding and there were few speakers who could match him. After one series of public debates, George William Ross declared that Tupper left him wondering if he 'was even remotely qualified to be a party politician.' Although Macdonald's self-confidence gradually returned, his health was not good and Tupper was the heir apparent.

Tupper's influence in the formulation of Conservative policy during this period was critical. It would be foolish to assign to any individual responsibility for the growth of protectionist sentiment among Conservatives, for this was an inevitable reaction to economic circumstances. But Tupper was an early convert. In 1868 he had presented to parliament a memorial from Nova Scotia coal-owners demanding a higher duty on imported coal, partly as a means of persuading the Americans to renew the Reciprocity Treaty, abrogated in 1866. Gradually he became convinced that such a duty should be part of a larger 'national policy,' a term he used (though certainly did not coin, as he later claimed) in debate, and his conviction was reinforced by the refusal of the Americans to renegotiate reciprocity in 1871. As the recession of the 1870s deepened and Liberal efforts at renewing reciprocity proved futile, Tupper focused increasingly on protection. There is an apocryphal story that he came to the debate on Richard John Cartwright's budget in 1876 prepared to advocate free trade in the event that the Liberals adopted protectionist policies. Certainly he came prepared to attack across-the-board tariff increases, but there is no doubt that he was deeply committed to selective increases to protect Canadian industries, more deeply indeed than Macdonald or Tilley.

Similarly, it was more than political opportunism that led Tupper to attack the Liberals' railway policies. He had strongly supported the efforts of Sandford Fleming to construct the Intercolonial to the highest possible standards and he viewed the Liberal policy of raising freight rates and using contractors from outside the Maritimes as a betrayal of the economic benefits promised by confederation. He was equally critical of the Liberals for not giving greater priority to the completion of a railway to British Columbia over an all-Canadian route. Although not solely responsible for these positions, Tupper placed them at the centre of the Conservative party's platform. His speeches were distributed to party organizers across the country, the Nova Scotia Liberal-Conservative Association which he had established in 1874 was used as a model elsewhere, and he actively campaigned in both the Maritimes and Ontario during the election of 1878, which saw the Conservatives returned with a healthy majority and 16 of the 21 seats in Nova Scotia.

The interests which contributed to the Conservative victory in Nova Scotia were rewarded in Tilley's 1879 budget, although the tariff on coal was not raised as high as the Nova Scotians wished because of opposition from Ontario. Tupper's personal reward was appointment as minister of public works on 17 Oct. 1878. The burdens of the office were so heavy that on 20 May 1879 railways and canals were hived off as a separate department with Tupper as minister. Tupper's greatest challenge was the completion of the Pacific railway, which he viewed not merely as a

Canadian railway but as 'an Imperial Highway across the Continent of America entirely on British soil.' He made several popular changes in its route and began to distribute contracts for further work. He hoped to raise funds through the sale of public land in the west and in the summer of 1879 he travelled to London to get a British guarantee for the sale of bonds. He returned without it but with 50,000 tons of steel rails purchased at a bargain price. Although in opposition he had rejected building the railway as a public work, he was now committed to government construction at the lowest cost possible. The revenues from land sales proved disappointing, however, and, as costs spiralled, so did criticism of the chief engineer, Sandford Fleming. Tupper reluctantly put pressure on Fleming to reduce the costs – and therefore the quality – of construction but he could not save his old friend and in May 1880 was forced to remove him. Mounting evidence that the long depression of the 1870s was lifting and signs of interest from a syndicate headed by George Stephen persuaded Tupper that the railway could be given over to private enterprise and in June he induced the cabinet to agree. Tupper and Macdonald handled the negotiations and on 21 Oct. 1880 Tupper signed a formal contract with Stephen's group on behalf of the government. The terms were controversial and with hindsight it is possible to conclude that they were unnecessarily generous to the syndicate. Yet if one accepts as valid Tupper's concern that the railway be constructed quickly to the highest possible standards but at the lowest possible cost to the government and that it follow an all-Canadian route, the initial terms do not seem unreasonable; indeed, the actual grant to the Canadian Pacific Railway Company was lower than the amount Tupper had originally forecast as necessary. Moreover, Tupper's experience had convinced him that a private company whose profit would come from operating the railway would be more committed than the government to high quality construction. Tupper believed it was in the national interest for the company to succeed and his commitment to the CPR was virtually limitless. His violent partisanship in its long and bitter competition with the Grand Trunk helped prevent the two railways from arriving at some form of cooperation. When the CPR required additional financial support in December 1883, he worked out a rescue plan and persuaded the caucus and the commons to agree to it. On 24 Feb. 1885, during another crisis, he wrote to Macdonald from London pleading with him not to 'let the

CPR go down' and offering to resign as high commissioner and return to Canada. Indeed, his commitment to the early completion of the railway led him to recommend more generous terms for a government loan than the cabinet was prepared to accept.

The Liberals were critical not only of the costs of the CPR but also of Tupper's policy of subsidizing 'local railways.' In fact, Tupper recognized that an expensive railway-building program in the west could be sustained only if counterbalanced by expenditures on railways in the existing provinces. Shortly after assuming office he had removed as general superintendent of government railways Charles John Brydges, whose operation of the Intercolonial had antagonized business interests in the Maritimes. Tupper lowered freight rates as a means of increasing traffic and revenues and made substantial reductions in operating costs; by the early 1880s the railway was operating at a profit. At Tupper's insistence the Grand Trunk was coerced into selling to the Intercolonial a branch line to Rivière-du-Loup, Que., to complete the link between Halifax and the St Lawrence. Moreover, he refused to give the CPR running rights over the Intercolonial to Halifax but 'cajoled' Stephen into building the 'Short Line' to Saint John. Tupper's generosity was not limited to his own region for Quebec and Ontario received even more in subsidies for railway building than did the Maritimes and huge sums were spent on widening the Welland Canal and deepening the St Lawrence channel. That there were many benefits to the Conservative party from these policies is undeniable and it is hardly surprising that the Liberals dubbed Tupper 'the High Priest of Corruption.' But, according to the Toronto *Daily Mail*, 'Develop our resources' was Tupper's motto, and he defended his policies on the ground that 'I have always supposed that the great object, in every country, and especially in a new country, was to draw as [many] capitalists into it as possible.'

During the latter part of 1879 the relations between Tupper and Macdonald had deteriorated, particularly over the issue of Fleming's dismissal. Although the breach was eventually healed, Tupper was no longer clearly the heir apparent and his health was not good. As early as March 1881 he asked Macdonald to allow him to replace Sir Alexander Tilloch Galt as Canadian high commissioner in London. In the election of 1882 Tupper campaigned only in Nova Scotia, where the Conservatives won 14 of the 21 seats; Tupper was acclaimed and his son Charles

Hibbert, already being groomed to take his father's place, was returned for Pictou. On 30 May 1883 Tupper, without surrendering his cabinet post, became unpaid high commissioner. He was based in London but returned to Canada repeatedly to deal with ministerial business and there was increasing criticism of his holding two incompatible offices. In May 1884 he resigned as minister and on 24 May became salaried high commissioner, abandoning his seat in parliament. His absence from the commons, Tilley noted in 1885, was 'very much felt' and in 1886 Macdonald appealed to him to return and assist the party in the forthcoming federal election. Partly to combat the secessionist cry raised by William Stevens Fielding in Nova Scotia, on 27 Jan. 1887 Tupper became minister of finance, while continuing to act as high commissioner, and in the election of 1887 he campaigned vigorously in Nova Scotia, carrying 14 of the 21 seats. Tupper not only defended protection but in a bold move extended it to the iron and steel industry in his 1887 budget. In part he hoped to undermine secessionist sentiment and consolidate Conservative support in eastern Nova Scotia, where the prospects 'of a great iron industry' were good. But he also believed that Canada was ready to move to the next stage of industrial development.

In 1885 the American government had abrogated the fisheries clauses of the Treaty of Washington and the following year the Canadian government retaliated by imposing a strict interpretation of the fisheries convention of 1818, precipitating a crisis in American–Canadian relations. As high commissioner, Tupper had pressed the British government for a 'firm and unflinching maintenance of our rights.' When a joint commission was established in 1887, he helped draft the British terms of reference and was chosen to represent the Canadian government as one of the three British commissioners, while Joseph Chamberlain represented the British government. Tupper worked closely with John Sparrow David Thompson, who acted as legal adviser, but he was clearly the dominant figure. Indeed, the American secretary of state, Thomas Francis Bayard, complained that 'Mr. Chamberlain has yielded the control of the negotiations over to Sir Charles Tupper, who subjects the questions to the demands of Canadian politics.' Although Tupper could not persuade the Americans to discuss reciprocity, in February 1888 he secured a treaty that included significant concessions to Canada, so significant that the treaty was rejected by the American Senate; however, the *modus vivendi* worked out by the commission temporarily resolved the crisis. Later that year, at Chamberlain's request, Tupper, who had been created a CB in 1867, a KCMG in 1879, and a GCMG in 1886, would be made a baronet of the United Kingdom, much to the annoyance of Thompson, who felt Tupper had grabbed all the credit. Tupper's star was clearly on the rise again. Macdonald appealed to him to remain in the government and even promised to reinstate him as the heir apparent. But Tupper knew that his chances of succeeding were uncertain and he felt that Macdonald should carry out his pledge, made during the crisis over Louis Riel, to recommend Sir Hector-Louis Langevin as his successor. On 23 May 1888, after resigning from the cabinet, Tupper resumed the office of high commissioner in London.

Tupper's influence with the Canadian ministry placed him in a position of unusual strength during his terms as high commissioner and he extended his duties to include an ever-wider range of activities. He was particularly concerned with promoting immigration and to this end toured the British Isles and made occasional trips to Europe. He was no less active in advancing Canadian commercial interests. Indeed, he made an important contribution to the cattle industry by demonstrating in 1883 that Canadian herds were free from disease and by persuading the British government to exempt Canadian cattle from restrictions applied to American cattle. Tupper encouraged Canadian exporters to communicate directly with him and he put them in touch with British importers. He also negotiated loans for the Canadian government and the CPR, eliminating the costly expenses of British middlemen. Prior to the Colonial and Indian Exhibition in London in 1886, which he helped to organize, he visited the boards of trade in all of the provinces to ensure that Canada was well represented. He also obtained a mail subsidy for a steamship from Vancouver to the Orient and pushed for an all-British Pacific cable and a fast Atlantic steamship service.

Tupper moved in high social circles, meeting British statesmen and members of the royal family on intimate terms. He was constantly in touch with the colonial secretary and even helped draft British commercial legislation affecting Canada. He also played an increasingly active role in international negotiations. In October 1883, although not a full plenipotentiary, he represented Canada at a conference in Paris and disagreed openly with the British delegation. The following year he persuaded the British government to allow him to carry on commercial negotiations with Spain, and in 1893 he concluded a trade arrangement with France. When tensions had mounted in 1889 over American efforts to prevent Canadians from fishing for seals in the Bering Sea, Tupper returned to Washington to assist in the negotiations, antagonizing the British government by his uncompromising defence of Canada's rights. In 1890 he successfully urged London to reject a fisheries treaty that Robert Bond of Newfoundland had negotiated with the United States. Tupper thus acquired considerable influence, but it was not always possible to distinguish between his work as high commissioner and his activities as a politician. In the election of 1891, for example, he returned to Canada to campaign for the National Policy. So flagrant was his partisanship that a resolution condemning his conduct was narrowly defeated in the commons. The non-political nature of the high commissioner's office was established only with his successor, Sir Donald Alexander Smith.

Equally controversial were Tupper's attitudes toward imperial unity. Although proud of being a citizen of 'the mightiest Empire in the world,' he believed that the attempt to turn it into a federal union was impracticable, and at the founding meeting of the Imperial Federation League in London on 29 July 1884 he denounced a resolution which held that the only options were federation or the disintegration of the empire. He agreed, however, to a modified resolution declaring some – presumably more limited – form of federation 'indispensable' and he served on the league's council and executive committee. After 1887 the league was racked by internal dissent over the question of regular colonial contributions to imperial defence, which Tupper opposed, and it was dissolved on 24 Nov. 1893. Tupper was blamed by some for its collapse, but he believed that the best way to strengthen the imperial connection would be through a mutual preferential trading agreement. In 1889 he had clashed with Macdonald by advocating such an agreement, causing, Macdonald reported, 'dissatisfaction in Quebec.' In 1891 and 1892 Tupper published articles in the *Nineteenth Century* (London), in which he again advocated the merits of preferential trade. He thought it 'mischievous' of England to expect Canada to reduce its tariff except as part of a larger agreement, and he strongly criticized Prime Minister Sir Wilfrid Laurier in 1897 for introducing imperial preference without getting anything for Canada in return. Yet Tupper viewed the empire as much more than a commercial enterprise. 'Preferential trade,' he once declared, 'may or may not be a good thing, but it is not and never has been the foundation-stone of Canadian loyalty.'

The death of Macdonald in 1891 offered Tupper an opportunity to become prime minister. He recognized, however, that his appointment would not be universally welcomed, he enjoyed his influence in London, and he urged his son Charles Hibbert, then minister of marine and fisheries, to give 'hearty support' to Sir John Thompson. After Thompson's sudden demise in December 1894, Tupper was the logical candidate to succeed, but his health was not good and Governor General Lord Aberdeen and his influential wife disliked him. Aberdeen asked Mackenzie Bowell to form a government. As it became clear that Bowell was incapable of resolving the conflict within the Conservative party over the Manitoba school question, the pressure for Tupper's return mounted, and by the end of 1895 he was back in Ottawa. On 4 Jan. 1896 seven members of the cabinet resigned and compelled Bowell and a reluctant Aberdeen to agree that Tupper would enter the cabinet as secretary of state on 15 January and become prime minister upon dissolution. On 4 February he was elected in a by-election in Cape Breton and effectively took charge of the government.

On the critical issue of restoring separate schools in Manitoba, Tupper never wavered. Although personally opposed to them, he believed a promise had been made to the Catholic minority and it should be honoured. When the Judicial Committee of the Privy Council had ruled in 1895 that the federal government had the power to use remedial legislation, Tupper advised his son to stand by this decision even if 'it would close your political career.' In February 1896 he introduced a remedial bill into the commons, where it was filibustered by a combination of extreme Protestants, led by D'Alton McCarthy, and Laurier's Liberals. Two months later, having pushed through only 15 of the 112 clauses, Tupper was forced to abandon the bill. On 24 April parliament was dissolved and on 1 May Tupper became prime minister. He successfully developed a party program which at least partially neutralized the Patrons of Industry and he insisted that the 'real issue' in the election was 'our great fight to protect the industries of Canada.' But try as he might he could not turn the election of 1896 into a rerun of 1891. So bitterly were the Conservatives divided over the schools issue that at every party rally Tupper was faced with a barrage of criticism. At Massey Music Hall in Toronto, for example, there was 'a constant din of meaningless interruptions,' but he still spoke for two hours and ended with a ringing declaration that 'we must do right' even if it meant 'the downfall of the Conservative party.' In the end Tupper won more votes than the Liberals, carrying about half the seats outside Quebec. It was the 'unexpected' Liberal landslide in Quebec that gave Laurier his majority. Tupper had tried in vain to persuade Sir Joseph-Adolphe Chapleau to return to active politics, but even with a strong Quebec lieutenant he would have had difficulty in inducing Quebeckers to vote for someone so clearly identified as an enthusiastic imperialist. None the less, after the election Tupper declared that he would support a remedial bill if Laurier introduced one.

Although the results of the election were known on 24 June, Tupper clung to office, insisting that Laurier would be unable to form a government. When he sought to make a number of appointments, however, Lord Aberdeen refused to confirm them and on 8 July Tupper resigned, complaining that Aberdeen had acted unconstitutionally. For the next four years Tupper worked to rebuild his party, as he had done after its defeat in 1874. Although he had not abandoned hope of winning seats in Quebec and he vigorously attacked Laurier for failing to fulfil his promises to the Manitoba Catholics, his primary concern was to woo back those traditional Tories who had deserted the party. This strategy involved questioning the loyalty of the Liberal leadership to the empire. Tupper strongly supported Canada's participation in the South African War, but Laurier managed to defuse the issue and by the time of the election in November 1900 the war was of limited significance. Tupper's strategy paid off in Ontario, where the Conservatives gained 17 seats, but Laurier carried the rest of Canada. Tupper himself went down to defeat and two days after the election he announced his resignation, selecting as his successor his fellow Nova Scotian and friend Robert Laird Borden.

For the next 15 years Tupper resided mainly at Bexleyheath in England, at the home of his daughter Emma (whom he had rushed to the northwest to rescue in 1869, when her husband was imprisoned by Louis Riel's provisional government); but he made frequent trips across the

Atlantic to visit his sons. On 9 Nov. 1907 he was appointed a member of the British Privy Council. His major preoccupation continued to be Canada's relationship with Britain and he served on the executive committee of the British Empire League and wrote articles and public letters promoting closer economic ties. He remained opposed to imperial federation and to the demand that Canada make a direct contribution to imperial defence costs, although in 1912 he supported Borden's proposal to make an emergency contribution of Dreadnoughts to the Royal Navy. Gradually his health declined, but even at the age of 84 on a visit to Rome he possessed sufficient energy to begin the study of Italian. The death of Lady Tupper on 11 May 1912 was, however, a severe blow, as was the death of his eldest son in April 1915. On 30 Oct. 1915 the last of the original Fathers of Confederation died at Bexleyheath. He was buried beside his wife in St John's Cemetery, Halifax, after a state funeral with a procession a mile long.

In 1867 the Halifax *Morning Chronicle* had described Tupper as 'the most despicable politician within the bounds of British North America.' Throughout his career Tupper was variously described as 'the Boodle Knight,' the 'Great Stretcher' (of the truth), 'the old tramp,' the 'Arch-Corruptionist,' and 'the old wretch.' All of these epithets contain a grain of truth and much of the abuse Tupper brought upon himself by his combativeness, his partisanship, and his pomposity. 'In big issues,' a private secretary noted, 'Sir Charles was chivalrous and courageous' but 'in trivialities … he sought an alibi.' None the less, his faults were blown out of proportion by his political foes. Given that patronage was the way in which local loyalties were harnessed to the national interest, there was nothing unusual about Tupper's concern to reward supporters, especially since when he arrived in Ottawa Nova Scotians occupied a tiny proportion of federal posts. Except perhaps during his early career in Nova Scotia he normally acted upon the principle that civil servants should not be dismissed unless they had been active politically, and both in the civil service and in the party he showed a real desire to appoint and advance men of talent. In the interests of holding power he could be ruthless. He believed in using the resources of the state to encourage private investment and he expected those who benefited from the party's policies to support the party. Whenever possible he awarded contracts to companies that made contributions, although there is no evidence that he distributed contracts in order to get contributions. He used his personal fortune to encourage loyalty but he operated within the framework of the law: only one of his elections was overturned upon petition and that because a supporter had given a 50-cent railway fare to a constituent. His standards of political morality were low but so were those of his contemporaries.

Tupper became a very wealthy man, how wealthy it is impossible to know since his private papers contain virtually no information on such matters. Initially his income was derived from professional fees but he was soon loaning out money for mortgages and making speculative investments in the coalmines at Springhill, N.S., whose interests he assiduously promoted. He apparently earned more from his medical practice after 1874 than he had as a cabinet minister; as his political influence increased, however, so did the opportunities for corporate directorships in such companies as the Crown Life Insurance Company, the Bank of British Columbia, and the General Mining Association. While opposition leader after 1896 he made numerous trips to London to act as chairman of New Gold Fields of British Columbia Limited and the Klondike Mining, Trading and Transportation Corporation Limited, two highly speculative gold-mining ventures. The salaries he received for such activities were not large, but insider knowledge provided the chance of windfall profits from stock investments and most of his fortune seems to have been derived from this source. Tupper had no reservations about using political influence to advance developments in which he had an interest and he acquired the reputation of 'feathering his own nest.' All three of his sons became successful lawyers, two of them after studying at Harvard, and all three benefited from their father's connections. James Stewart and William Johnston became partners in a Winnipeg firm, whose clients included the CPR, and Charles Hibbert operated out of Halifax and later Vancouver, often in alliance with his father. For his daughter's husband Tupper secured the position of commandant of the Royal Military College of Canada in Kingston, Ont. Tupper's brother and various nieces and cousins all received government patronage, becoming what the Toronto *Globe* described as 'public-kept Tuppers.' In an age with only the haziest notion of conflict of interest, Tupper operated upon the fringes of what was acceptable but it is not clear that he ever overstepped the bounds and he was hurt by allegations of misconduct. In retirement he went to great lengths to set the record straight (at least as he saw it). In 1912 he gave a series of interviews to a Vancouver journalist, William Arthur Harkin, who published them as the *Political reminiscences of the Right Honourable Sir Charles Tupper* in 1914, the same year in which Tupper published his own *Recollections of sixty years*.

Longevity brings many rewards and by the time of his death Nova Scotians had become reconciled to confederation and had come to see Tupper as one of their most distinguished sons. At the national level, too, respect for Tupper grew over time. In 1925 Hector Willoughby Charlesworth compared him with Laurier and declared Tupper 'the greater man, – one of the greatest and most far-seeing statesmen this continent has produced.' Modern Canadian historiography has been less generous. Tupper is praised for his essential role in confederation but thereafter is made a mere appendage of Macdonald. Yet Tupper was at least as responsible as Macdonald for rebuilding the Conservative party after 1874 and for designing and implementing the 'national' policies with which the party became identified and which most historians accept were, however imperfect, appropriate policies for the times. Tupper was also responsible for turning the office of high commissioner into one of real importance and for gaining considerable international recognition for Canada. In every position he held he added important measures to the statute book. If Tupper does not inspire much enthusiasm today, it is undoubtedly because his vision of Canada was always tied up with his commitment to the empire, a commitment which French Canadians could not share and which has come to be seen as inconsistent with the creation of a distinctive Canadian national identity. Even recent Maritime historiography has turned against him. The anti-confederates have become the heroes and Tupper is viewed at best as self-interested and at worst as a *vendu*. But just as Tupper did not see his loyalty to the empire as incompatible with his loyalty to Canada, so he did not see his loyalty to Canada as incompatible with his loyalty to his native province. He was an imperialist and there were limits to his tolerance, yet he was prepared to make compromises to incorporate into the political system Canadians of every religion and of different ethnic origins. He was no provincialist but he sought to ensure that national policies brought economic benefits and opportunities to all the provinces. 'No intelligent man ...,' he believed, 'can feel for a moment that, as a Canadian, he does not occupy a far higher status than he ever could have done as a New Brunswicker, a

Prince Edward Islander, or a Nova Scotian.' There is much not to admire about Tupper: his ethnic chauvinism, his relentless pursuit of power and fortune, his partisanship, his social conservatism, and what the *Globe* once described as his 'tendency to boastful self-assertion.' But as the Toronto *News*, a Liberal paper, declared in 1903: 'With all his faults he was essentially a policy-maker and a constructive statesman.'

PHILLIP BUCKNER

Further reading

P. A. Buckner, 'The 1860s: an end and a beginning,' in *The Atlantic region to confederation*, ed. P. A. Buckner and John Reid (Toronto and Fredericton, 1994), 360–86, and 'The 1870s: political integration,' in *The Atlantic provinces in confederation*, ed. E. R. Forbes and D. A. Muise (Toronto and Fredericton, 1993), 48–81.

Ben Forster, *A conjunction of interests: business, politics, and tariffs, 1825–1879* (Toronto, 1986).

The life and letters of the Rt. Hon. Sir Charles Tupper, bart., K.C.M.G., ed. E. M. Saunders (2v., Toronto, 1916).

K. G. Pryke, *Nova Scotia and confederation, 1864–74* (Toronto, 1979).

P. B. Waite, *Canada, 1874–1896: arduous destiny* (Toronto and Montreal, 1971).

Sir WILFRID LAURIER
(baptized Henry-Charles-Wilfrid),

lawyer, newspaperman, and politician; b. 20 Nov. 1841 in the parish
of Saint-Lin (Laurentides), Lower Canada, son of Carolus Laurier
and Marcelle Martineau; m. 13 May 1868 Zoé Lafontaine
in Montreal; they had no children; d. 17 Feb. 1919 in Ottawa.

According to some sources, Wilfrid Laurier's ancestor François Cottineau, *dit* Champlaurier, a native of Saint-Claud, France, came to New France with the Régiment de Carignan-Salières. He took up farming and on 7 Jan. 1677 in Montreal married Magdelaine Millots. Thus began the long line of Lauriers in North America. Sometime around the spring of 1834 Wilfrid's father, Carolus, a sixth-generation Laurier, moved to Saint-Lin, which was a predominantly agricultural parish with a population of about 2,000, largely French Canadian but including a handful of British immigrants. A farmer and surveyor, Carolus was bilingual, literate, and dynamic, and he quickly grasped the possibilities for socio-economic mobility in that part of the country. Inspired by his father, Charles, a surveyor whose hobbies were astronomy, philosophy, and mathematics, he set his sights high in his community despite his very modest income. Charles lived with the family from 1840 and, full of the scientist's fervour, went around the parish showing some of his inventions. Carolus was a natural leader who held several important offices and in 1855 became the first mayor of the municipality. Above all, he and his father were interested in politics, especially the policies of Louis-Joseph Papineau's Patriote party, which they had defended at home among friends and in their correspondence. At the time of Wilfrid's birth on 20 Nov. 1841, the two men were fulminating against the recent union of Lower and Upper Canada. To a family still grieving over the loss in 1839 of the first-born, Marie-Honorine, the arrival of this second child brought healing.

Laurier began elementary schooling on 5 Sept. 1847, not long before his beloved mother died of tuberculosis on 7 March 1848. In September 1852, when he was not yet 11, his father removed him from the school in Saint-Lin and sent him to one in New Glasgow, a few miles from his home, where the English language and British customs prevailed. Here Wilfrid became immersed in a culture that would always have a place in his heart, and he soon learned English, which he would speak with a slight Scottish accent. In 1854 Carolus took him to the Collège de L'Assomption to begin his classical education. There Wilfrid discovered a rigid universe run by priests who made the Roman Catholic religion both a program of studies and a rule of life. The teachers glorified ultramontanism and denounced liberalism. Although he occasionally skipped classes to go and hear Rouge speakers talk about politics, Wilfrid did well at L'Assomption. In 1859, for instance, he won prizes in seven of his eleven subjects. He had already developed a passion for politics and had pinned his hopes on liberalism. In 1861 his long years at the college came to an end. He would never forget its oppressive, conservative atmosphere – or the taste for literature he had cultivated there. He decided to study law, a natural choice, given his interest in the field, his personality, and the eloquence he had displayed at school.

In September 1861 Laurier enrolled at McGill College. The Montreal milieu and the English establishment had a permanent influence on his future. At the home of Dr Séraphin Gauthier, where he was boarding, he met Zoé Lafontaine, who was to be his wife. A piano teacher of modest means, she too was a boarder there. It was also during his student years that he discovered, to his horror, the gravity of an illness which was sapping his energy. His frequent coughing spells and blood-stained handkerchiefs convinced him he had tuberculosis, a malady of unhappy memory for the Laurier family. In 1862–63 his condition frequently confined him to bed and brought him to the brink of depression. Only later, while living in the Bois-Francs region, would he learn he was suffering from chronic bronchitis, a 'germ of death' which would be with him for the rest of his life. During his time at university as well, Laurier established lasting ties with Rouge activists in Montreal. Second in his class of 11 students in his first year, and tied for second at the end of his third year, he soon attracted the attention of one of his professors, Toussaint-Antoine-Rodolphe Laflamme, who was a radical Rouge. Laflamme took him into his law office as an articled clerk. On 2 Oct. 1862 he also introduced Laurier to the Institut Canadien, a literary society and centre of Rouge activity in Montreal, of which he was an influential member. Laurier fitted in so well that he served as first vice-president from May 1864 until the fall of 1866. In the society Laurier rubbed shoulders with Joseph and Gonzalve Doutre, Louis-Antoine Dessaulles, Médéric Lanctot, and Antoine-Aimé Dorion. He worked with them, in vain, to smooth out the problems that it was experiencing with Bishop Ignace Bourget of Montreal, who fiercely opposed liberalism and the Rouge party. Laurier would never forget his skirmishes with Bourget.

On 3 Oct. 1864, shortly before his 23rd birthday, Laurier passed the law examinations set by the Lower Canadian board of examiners. This son of an ordinary surveyor, who had finally achieved professional status, cut a striking, even astonishing figure. Slim and more than six feet tall, he took meticulous care of his wavy, chestnut hair, which threatened to spill over his broad forehead. He was genuinely handsome. He had the face of a thinker and artist, marked with a certain nobility, but his pale complexion and gentle, delicate features gave a disquieting impression of fragility. His good looks never matured and left him and others some-what anxious about his health. None of his friends had any doubts as to the man's calibre, however. Intelligent and ambitious, although easygoing and a bit of a daydreamer and romantic, he cultivated benevolence and affability. He was capable of disarming frankness and admirable loyalty to his friends, and he defended his convictions stubbornly, with implac-able logic, while showing great tolerance of different opinions. His calm, reserved, almost timid appearance concealed his capacity for leadership. A realist who liked to take men and things as they were and who may already have lost his religious faith, he feared two things: the swift flight of time, and death. They were recurring causes of anguish to the young lawyer. At heart he was an intellectual with little inclination to physical exercise but a passion for political action.

Laurier practised law initially in Montreal but experienced periods of difficulty there. His first office, which he opened in partnership with Pierre-Amable-Oscar Archambault on 27 Oct. 1864, closed within a month; his second, established with Archambault and Henri-Lesieur Désaulniers, had to shut down after only three months for lack of clients. On 11 March 1865 Laurier was alone and penniless. Médéric Lanctot, who was busily attacking the proposed confederation of British North America in his newspaper *L'Union nationale* (Montréal), rescued him from this abyss; on 14 March Lanctot and Laurier announced their partnership. In their law firm Laurier did the work of two men and was highly regarded by Lanctot, who saw him as 'a man of the future,' according to the poet Louis Fréchette. But Laurier's health, which was still frail, soon thwarted these high hopes. At the end of October 1866 the cruel illness required drastic treatment that was made possible by a combination of circumstances within which politics played a key role.

Laurier had, in fact, been involved in politics ever since he finished university. In August 1864 he had joined with the Liberals of Lower Canada, both radicals and moderates, in denouncing the proposed confederation. They argued that it would give too many powers to the central government and lead to the annihilation of the French Canadians, who should at least be consulted. He took part in a study group that published a devastating critique of the scheme, he spoke at several public meetings, and he wrote articles for *L'Union nationale*. It was all in vain. On 10 March 1865 the Legislative Assembly of the Province of Canada approved the plan by 91 votes to 33. In November 1866 Antoine-Aimé Dorion invited him to replace his recently deceased brother Jean-Baptiste-Éric Dorion as editor of *Le Défricheur* in L'Avenir. There Laurier would find the opportunity to pursue both his struggle against confederation and the drastic treatment – fresh country air – essential for his bronchitis. He left Montreal for L'Avenir on 18 November, but it was in Victoriaville, where he published *Le Défricheur* from 1 Jan. 1867, that he wrote his finest articles opposing both the union of 1841 and confederation. On 7 March 1867, when the plan was under discussion in London, Laurier wrote scathingly: 'Confederation is the second stage on the road to "anglification" mapped out by Lord Durham. ... We are being handed over to the English majority. ... [We must] use whatever influence we have left to demand and obtain a free and separate government.' Rouge and separatist, this was the position taken by the man who some 30 years later would lead the country whose creation he was now trying so hard to prevent. On 21 March, however, *Le Défricheur* had to shut down, a victim of the editor's illness, its heavy financial problems, and the opposition of the local ultramontane clergy, who labelled Laurier a liberal revolutionary. On 1 July confederation was officially proclaimed. At the age of 25 Wilfrid Laurier suddenly had to reorganize his life.

Once the shock of these set-backs had subsided and his health had improved, Laurier accepted the challenge without delay. He decided to settle permanently in the Bois-Francs region, at Arthabaskaville (Victoria-ville) where he took up residence in mid September 1867. The administrative and judicial seat of the county, Arthabaskaville, with its storybook landscape, had a population of about 730, of whom 96 per cent were French-speaking. Laurier would have a large house built there in 1876–77 at a cost of $3,000 and established firm connections with Liberals and artists. He became so well integrated into local society that he was elected alderman, mayor, and, in 1881, county warden. He looked after the affairs of the parish community and church on a regular basis. In 1897 his political responsibilities made it necessary for him to move to Ottawa, but, as his correspondence shows, he would never forget the charm and tranquillity of Arthabaskaville, to which he would return at Christmas and during seasonal holidays.

After he had established residence, Laurier's next move was to take a wife. On 13 May 1868 he married Zoé Lafontaine in the cathedral of Saint-Jacques in Montreal. He had always refused to ask for her hand on the grounds that he was too ill and poor, but when Dr Gauthier told him she was about to marry another suitor even though she still loved him, he hurried off to Montreal. That very evening, without Carolus or any of his family being present, he was married, and he then immediately returned alone to Arthabaskaville, where an urgent case awaited him. No children would ever be born to him and Zoé, a fact he deeply regretted. On the whole it was a happy marriage, though not always. There was Laurier's passionate attachment to Émilie Barthe, the wife of his law partner Joseph Lavergne. After 1876 he became infatuated with this bril-liant and highly cultured woman, who shared his literary tastes and his interest in things English. Their romantic liaison was the most famous in Canadian political history. Their letters bear witness to a genuine love, but was it platonic? No one knows for certain. It was rumoured at the time, though never confirmed, that Armand La Vergne was their son. Their involvement apparently lasted until about 1900, when political necessity took precedence. Wilfrid and Zoé resumed their close relation-ship and remained devoted to each other for the rest of their lives. Zoé outlived her husband and died in Ottawa on 1 Nov. 1921.

Sir Wilfrid and Lady Laurier with some friends.

In the summer of 1867 Laurier had also reorganized his professional life. He opened his law office in Arthabaskaville, where he would practise for 30 years with four different partners: Eugène Crépeau (1867–69), Édouard Richard (1869–74), Joseph Lavergne (1874–97), and Philippe-Hypolite Côté, who joined the firm in 1889. His practice concentrated mainly on general law and never had the advantage of any famous cases. Peers recognized his competence by electing him to the council of the Arthabaska bar in 1888 and making him *bâtonnier* of the district in 1889. Undoubtedly the star of his firm, Laurier to his great regret gradually had to reduce his share of the day-to-day work because of ever-increasing political obligations. The practice of law did not make him wealthy or enable him to accumulate the money he needed for his growing responsibilities within the Liberal party. He found this situation trying and complained about it regularly.

The financial security Laurier wanted so badly would become his after the election of 23 June 1896, which brought him to power in Ottawa. The next day William Mulock, the MP for York North in Ontario, asked his authorization to raise a fund of $50,000 to $100,000 to keep him free of financial worries for the rest of his life. Laurier accepted, just as in 1897 he would accept the Liberal party's offer of a luxurious home in Ottawa. He closed his law office in Arthabaskaville and appointed his partner Joseph Lavergne to the bench. This ideal situation did not mean, however, that he made no investments after 1896. Although he claimed not to have any skill in financial matters, he had in the past attempted to put his money to work. Along with others, he set up the Syndicat Agricole d'Arthabaskaville in 1880 to produce beet sugar. In 1889 he and four partners founded the Compagnie Minière Laurier to 'carry on mining business and operations in the counties of Arthabaska, Mégantic, and Wolfe.' After 1896 he accepted several company directorships without much hesitation, but for the most part he simply invested his money, as he did in the Canada Cement Company near the end of his life. At his death he was worth at least $25,000, in addition to his life insurance policies, movable property, and real estate.

From the summer of 1867 Laurier's personal and professional life had grown increasingly secure, but he had one more dream – to enter politics. On 1 Aug. 1867 he confided to Zoé, 'I am actively involved in election work. ... Now they want me to be a candidate and I will not refuse. I might as well work for myself as for others.' Most provincial Liberals belonged to the Reform Association of Lower Canada, an organization formed that year to encourage their divided forces and sketch out a program which would bring them together. In the end, probably to avoid deepening rifts among them, Laurier decided not to run in the general election of late August and early September 1867; the first contest held since confederation, it was to choose members for the Quebec Legislative Assembly and the Canadian House of Commons. Like the Rouge and Liberal he had always claimed to be, he fought to the end in the party struggles that brought his Liberal–Conservative opponents to power in Canada and in Quebec.

Before making his official entry into public life, Laurier had to settle two prerequisites for his future success. First he had to make up his mind whether he would accept once and for all the confederation he had but recently been denouncing. Having taken a step in that direction in the summer of 1867, he opted for the affirmative. Like his leader Antoine-Aimé Dorion and many other Liberals, he chose to recognize the *fait accompli* and work within the new Canada to make it less disastrous for French Canadians. Second, he had to decide whether he would continue adhering to the Rouge philosophy articulated by the now nearly defunct Institut Canadien, whose popular support was dwindling. This time he answered in the negative. Radical liberalism was for him a thing of the past to be replaced by moderate liberalism of the classic British Whig type, which respected the popular will and was, he hoped, less threatening to the Roman Catholic clergy. From then on Laurier could think of nothing but the day when he would be elected to the provincial legislature.

This day came in the summer of 1871, a crucial year that marked the turning-point in his life. From 28 May Laurier conducted an intense campaign for the riding of Drummond and Arthabaska. He had nothing in his favour but his own fiery spirit, his network of Liberal friends, and his budding prestige; there was scant support from the Liberal party of Henri-Gustave Joly, which was merely a coalition of small regional groups, with no organization or program. To the local Catholic clergy, who called him a Rouge and a revolutionary obsessed with liberty, Laurier responded with a balanced platform addressing the current major election issues. It touched on education, colonization, and agriculture, for which funding had to be increased, on the abolition of the Legislative Council, and on industrial development, the cure for the scourge of emigration. On the evening of 11 July his 750-vote majority took some of the sting out of the provincial Liberals' defeat.

During the two and a half years he laboured in the Quebec legislature, Laurier nevertheless usually behaved as if he were still a university freshman, watching, listening, learning, and conforming (not always cheerfully) to the demands of parliamentary life which, as his letters to Zoé show, he did not really like. One of the youngest assemblymen, Laurier was not the opposition's star performer. In fact, he took an active part only in the first session, in November and December 1871, but he did good work then. In his maiden speech, on 9 November on the address in reply to the speech from the throne, he stated with the conviction of a prophet that the province's 'true progress' and 'true prosperity,' along with the promotion of political reforms, were the cornerstones of his involvement in public life, and that they required industry and the immigration of workers and skilled artisans. On 22 November Laurier attacked the double mandate, which allowed members to represent federal and provincial ridings simultaneously and which in 1871 enabled no fewer than 17 MLAs to hold seats in Ottawa as well as at Quebec. His terse comments stood out in the debate. 'With the single mandate, Quebec is Quebec; with the double mandate, it is no more than an appendage of Ottawa.' The speech was well organized and quite meaty, setting out in clear terms the doctrine of provincial autonomy, which was central to the problem. Many people felt that a formidable orator had made his mark, yet except for rare occasions Laurier made no further appearances. Perhaps he was too disappointed with the milieu. Perhaps he succumbed to boredom or was too busy with his law practice. One thing is certain: he was distressed by the lamentable state of his party.

The Liberal party was indeed in a sorry condition. With no real program and no extra-parliamentary organization, it was still bearing the heavy burden of its radical past. Like other members, Laurier realized the time had come for serious thinking and dramatic action. The future lay in a renewal of Liberal thought and in a dynamic party that would bring together both Liberals and Conservatives who were eager to seize the reins of power and put principles ahead of selfish interests. From the time he entered politics, the member for Drummond and Arthabaska devoted himself to this endeavour.

Initially Laurier chose to wield the pen. In December 1871 he reaffirmed in an Arthabaskaville newspaper what he had maintained during the previous election campaign: 'The Liberals of 1871 cannot be the same, in terms of men or principles, as they were in 1848, a time of liberal renaissance.' That month he moved into action, joining with other young men such as Louis-Amable Jetté, Frédéric-Ligori Béïque, and Honoré Mercier to found the Parti National, which was born of the desire to make a fresh start. Though hesitant at first, veteran Liberals rallied to it. Focused on reform and autonomy, it sought to become a meeting ground for moderates in the province who were capable of 'putting the national interest' ahead of everything else. Older supporters soon realized that, as *Le Canadien* pointed out, the Parti National was 'the Liberal party reorganizing itself, rejuvenating its 1847 program.' In this Liberal resurgence, Laurier undeniably played a role. He was, in fact, one of the main forces behind it. The results of the federal election in the summer of 1872 did not, however, measure up to the hopes of the youthful members. Sir John A. Macdonald, though greatly weakened, was returned to power in Ottawa and the Liberal party gradually absorbed the Parti National. Nevertheless, Laurier and the other young men had given their original party an impetus it could not entirely overlook.

In the fall of 1873 fate intervened on Laurier's behalf. The Macdonald government, rudely shaken by the Pacific Scandal, resigned on 5 November and was replaced by the Liberals under Alexander Mackenzie. In the ensuing election at the end of January and the beginning of February 1874, Laurier seized his opportunity. He gave up his provincial seat and ran in Drummond and Arthabaska. His campaign was short – only 27 days – as was his platform, which was simply a denunciation of Conservative corruption. There was no room this time for learned definitions of political liberalism. Victory was the only aim. It came for Laurier and the Liberals on 29 January. That evening Liberal party workers of Drummond and Arthabaska took their new MP from parish to parish in a long parade. The 32-year-old Laurier thrilled with joy.

When he entered the House of Commons on 26 March 1874, he must have felt quite humble in the vast chamber occupied by 205 other MPs; some of them, both among his opponents led by Macdonald and among his political friends such as Mackenzie, Antoine-Aimé Dorion, Luther Hamilton Holton, Edward Blake, and Richard John Cartwright, were impressive figures. He had to begin, of course, by emerging from his semi-anonymity and earning his stripes one by one if he wanted to gain recognition in the Canada which was still to be built but whose foundations were as yet fragile, indeed contested. Laurier devoted the first phase of his parliamentary career, from 1874 to 1878, to the task of carving out a place for himself. To win the attention of his colleagues, he relied on his eloquence. He attracted notice as early as 30 March 1874 when he spoke in support of the address in reply to the speech from the throne. In French, he made a threefold profession of faith – in his country, in his party, whose liberalism he immediately identified with liberalism as practised in England, and in his government. His speech was an instant success. He took the floor again on 15 April on the question of an amnesty for Louis Riel, the new Métis MP for Provencher, Man. In flights of oratory in English, he opposed Riel's expulsion from the commons, even though he felt no sympathy for the man, as he later noted to his fellow MP James Young on 16 September. Like other Quebec Liberals, he simply

used the issue to weaken the Conservatives still further. In the
commons on 15 April, however,
his speech was all greatness of soul
and beauty of expression. On
12 Feb. 1875 he returned to the
Riel fray in support of a government proposal to amnesty everyone
involved in the Manitoba troubles
except the Métis leader and two
others. Here again, Laurier struck
a chord that was deeply moving.
But he also used the occasion to
explain the basis of his stand on
all political questions. Avoiding
both extremes, he shared the
opinion of 'moderate men' who,
he was sure, 'would seek a medium
course for justice and truth.'

Wilfrid Laurier MP, April 1874.

Increasingly, until 1877, his performance in the house revealed him in
public as a centrist and a lucid, unusually able politician who had the
parliamentary community in the palm of his hand.

There was more to be done, however. He had to make a name for
himself within the Liberal organization, to become the Quebec solution
to the problems faced both by the party as it evolved and by the government it had formed in Ottawa. Over time the Mackenzie administration
lost much of its vigour, getting mired in the economic depression and in
short-sighted policies. Moreover, Quebec was not adequately represented
in the cabinet after Antoine-Aimé Dorion's resignation in May 1874. To
make the situation even more intolerable, the ultramontane wing of the
Catholic clergy gradually resumed its activity, further obscuring the distinction between doctrinaire and moderate liberals and interfering
improperly in elections. And so Laurier began again, this time resolutely
and seriously, the lengthy process of winning Quebec for the Liberals.
In 1875, for example, he took an active part in the provincial election.
On 6 June at Sainte-Croix in the county of Lotbinière, he confronted a
supremely confident Joseph-Adolphe Chapleau, the rising star of the

Conservatives, and delivered a message indicative of what was to come. 'When the Conservative party wraps itself in the mantle of religion, that is nothing but a mask. ... We, on the other hand, are liberals in the English tradition.' Most important was the powerful address on political liberalism he delivered at Quebec on 26 June 1877. It was a historic moment. Laurier could have destroyed his career at this point. His leaders even tried to dissuade him from speaking, for Bishop George Conroy, the apostolic delegate, was conducting an inquiry in order to make a ruling on the politico-religious conflict between the Catholic Church and the Liberals in Quebec. But Laurier set aside this deceptive caution, which had led to the existing problems. He recognized, of course, that he should not provoke Conroy, but he also knew the time had come to explain his party's liberalism as clearly as possible. His approach was pragmatic, his ambition partisan in that he wanted to help create a modern party system and a modern form of government where the Liberal party would occupy its rightful place on the political chessboard of the province. He spoke brilliantly, sometimes with passion but more often with logic, occasionally resorting to easy eloquence. No, he assured some 2,000 listeners, 'Liberal Catholicism is not political liberalism.' No, the Liberal party is not 'a party composed of men holding perverse doctrines, with a dangerous tendency, and knowingly and deliberately progressing towards revolution.' No, there is no 'moral difference' between Liberals and Conservatives. To make his own position clear, he defined his liberalism: 'I am one of those who believe that in all human affairs there are abuses to reform, new horizons to discover and new forces to develop.' One country – England – had put these principles into practice. The Liberal party there had 'carried out a series of reforms which have made the English the freest of peoples, the most prosperous and the happiest in Europe.' Then, as a democrat aware that respect for individuals and their choices and for the separation of church and state was necessary, he laid down, though in moderate terms, the proper role of the clergy in politics. Their 'right of intervening ... ends when trespassing on the rights of the elector. ... It is ... perfectly permissible to change the opinion of an elector by reasoning and all other means of persuasion, but never by intimidation.' He concluded: 'The policy of the Liberal party is to protect [our] institutions, to defend them and spread them, and, under the sway of those institutions, to develop the country's latent resources. That is the policy of the

Liberal party and it has no other.' Laurier had expressed ideas that would satisfy Bishop Conroy in powerful words which he would repeat through the best years of his political career.

It was a triumph for Laurier. Overnight he became a national figure, but even more, he became the leader the Quebec Liberals had awaited. Prime Minister Mackenzie understood this impact and on 8 Oct. 1877 made him minister of inland revenue. Henceforth Laurier would have a seat in the inner circle of Canadian politics and be considered, moreover, the true successor to Dorion and 'the real leader of the Liberals in Lower Canada.' He remained a minister only a year and a day, however. It was to be a rather turbulent and stressful year. The first hurdle was his re-election in Drummond and Arthabaska, as custom dictated. The relentless battle waged against him by the Conservatives brought about his defeat on 27 October. He then ran in Quebec East where, regarding himself as 'the last card of the party in this province,' he encountered the same difficult struggle and the same abuse from the Conservatives. Nevertheless, the Liberals were better organized and gave him enough support that on 28 Nov. 1877 he won by 315 votes. From that day until his death in 1919, Laurier would forge such solid links with Quebec East that it would never desert him. But the joy of victory would soon fade. The parliamentary session of the winter and spring of 1878 brought him back to harsh reality. The Mackenzie government could not muster the energy to give adequate leadership to the country and Laurier suffered a recurrence of his illness, which several times kept him confined to bed. He still made some fine speeches in the house and appropriately defended his work and the administration of his department, but that was all. He was more spirited during the campaign leading up to the federal election of 17 Sept. 1878. In full control of his party's Quebec wing, Laurier made every effort, but to no avail. The Liberals lost by 78 seats to the Conservatives and their National Policy. Although he himself was re-elected, Laurier had not been able to prevent his opponents from winning a majority of 29 seats in Quebec. At the age of 36 he was once more an ordinary MP in a shrunken group of 64 Liberals, only 18 of whom were from his province.

Now began the difficult years from 1878 to 1884. Disillusioned and discouraged, Laurier often gave the impression of having lost interest in politics and in his own party, which suffered one set-back after another.

Certainly he had some successes and occasionally attracted attention, for example when he pointedly called on Mackenzie to resign in 1880, and when that year he and others founded the Quebec newspaper *L'Électeur* to bolster the Liberal rank and file. He published his famous article 'La caverne des 40 voleurs' in *L'Électeur* on 20 April 1881, which touched off a sensational lawsuit by referring to Louis-Adélard Senécal, a Conservative and a close friend of Chapleau, as a swindler and accusing him of trying to rob the province. There were also his contributions to the work of the house. He seldom expressed new ideas, however. He defended the moderate protective tariff, provincial autonomy, and Canada's ties to the British crown. Opposing the Conservative policy of aiding the Canadian Pacific Railway, he supported the theory of laissez-faire and of a reduced role for the state in economic matters. In a word, there was nothing overly impressive, certainly not to journalist John Wesley Dafoe, who saw Laurier at work during the 1884 session and drew this unflattering portrait: 'Laurier's political activities consisted chiefly of being an acting secretary of sorts to the Liberal leader [Blake]. He kept his references in order; handed him Hansards and blue-books in turn; summoned the pages to clear away the impedimenta and to keep the glass of water replenished. ... There were memories in the house of Laurier's eloquence; but memories only.' Such was the level to which Laurier's public image had sunk by 1884. His only real interests seemed to be the peace and quiet of Arthabaskaville, where he could read to his heart's content, his law practice, his friends, and, of course, Émilie Lavergne.

Suddenly, in 1885, Laurier's career entered another spectacular and dazzling phase. Once more unexpected events bore him into prominence. The key factor was the North-West rebellion led by Louis Riel, which threw the whole country into turmoil. Riel surrendered in May, went on trial in July, was sentenced to death in August, and was hanged on 16 November. These events aroused powerful emotions; Ontarians, haunted by the ghost of Thomas Scott, felt he had to be avenged, and French Canadians were indignant to the depths of their souls. The trial and hanging, the whole attack on the Métis leader, heaped scorn on their ancestry and their French Canadian culture. Motivated equally by sincerity and by the hope of weakening the Conservatives as much as possible, Laurier returned to the political struggle. He first demonstrated his newly regained aggressiveness in the House of Commons on 7 July 1885, when he delivered the longest address of his parliamentary career. He spoke as the active leader of the Quebec Liberals. Pointing a vengeful finger at Macdonald, he accused him of contempt for the Métis and of ultimate responsibility for the rebellion. Laurier next took action outside parliament along with Honoré Mercier's provincial team, which was better organized and more nationalist than ever. It was now ready to transform the French Canadian movement of sympathy for Riel into a true Parti National that would bring together Liberals and Conservatives furious at Macdonald and his French-speaking ministers, Chapleau, Sir Hector-Louis Langevin, and Sir Adolphe-Philippe Caron. In September and October 1885 Laurier spoke at no fewer than six public meetings, but the most telling at the time was his great address at the Champ-de-Mars in Montreal on 22 November, only six days after Riel had been hanged. Speaking to a crowd of nearly 50,000, he was so carried away that his words touched the collective imagination. 'If [I] had been on the banks of the Saskatchewan when the rebellion broke out,' he reportedly said, '[I] would have taken up arms [myself] against the government. ... Riel's execution was a judicial murder. How could M. Chapleau ... have been a party to this cold-blooded murder of a compatriot?' On that day Laurier had identified himself with the innermost sorrows of French Canadians and undoubtedly won them over. To be sure, he had not defined his nationalism, but it was unquestionably close to Mercier's. Never since entering politics had Laurier gone so far in his remarks as on 22 November, nor would he ever do so again.

The crowning moment of Laurier's political recovery, however, was still to come. On 16 March 1886, during debate on a motion by the Conservative Philippe Landry that the house express its regret at the death of Riel, he found his first opportunity to point out the only path to be followed in the difficult process of building Canada. 'We cannot make a nation of this new country by shedding blood,' he asserted, 'but by extending mercy and charity for all political offences.' To charges that French Canadians were disloyal to England, he replied, 'It would perhaps be best, from a utilitarian point of view, to have only one language; but ... French is the language of our mothers, the language which recalls to our minds the most sacred associations and so long as there are French mothers the language will not die. Yet these sentiments are quite consistent with our loyalty to England.' In Toronto on 10 December he elaborated this concept of the country again, obviously with the intention of making his position clear to Ontario. He justified his actions and words of the preceding months and then, on a somewhat provocative note, went so far as to scold the crowd. 'If you had been yourselves ... on the banks of the Saskatchewan ... what would you have done?' He unhesitatingly supported the attitude of French Canadians towards the Riel affair and openly defended their right to exist in Canada. Proclaiming his definition of the Canadian nation, he declared: 'We are Canadians. Below the island of Montreal the water that comes from the north from [the] Ottawa unites with the waters that come from the western lakes. But uniting they do not mix. There they run parallel, separate, distinguishable, and yet are one stream, flowing within the same banks, the mighty St. Lawrence, and rolling on toward the sea ... a perfect image of our nation.' Liberals in Ontario listened with surprise to this 'silver-tongued' orator who had been written about in the press after his speech of 16 March. More significantly, they made the acquaintance of a politician who wanted to offer Canadians a carefully considered path which was based on moderation but could become an inspiration. On that day, 10 Dec. 1886, Laurier reached the zenith of his political ascent.

When Macdonald called a general election for 22 Feb. 1887, Laurier, now out of the shadows, led the attack. He directed the campaign in Quebec with renewed confidence. Mercier, the new provincial premier, and some nationalist (and even ultramontane) Conservatives came with him as he travelled through a number of regions with the ghost of Riel blithely in tow. It was no use. On 22 February Macdonald edged back into power. Edward Blake, weakened, ill, sleepless, and with little enthusiasm for heading the party, resigned on 2 June 1887.

The federal Liberals' leadership problem was now plainly exposed. As was the custom of the time, Blake had the last word about a successor. Instead of Oliver Mowat, who was not available, or Sir Richard John Cartwright, who was unpopular with French Canadians and manufacturers, or David Mills, who lacked nerve, he unhesitatingly picked Laurier. His choice was a surprise to the many Liberals who saw Laurier as too frail, easygoing, and flexible, or too tainted in Ontario by the Riel affair, or too threatened in Quebec by the clergy, who still remembered him as a Rouge. It was certainly a surprise to Laurier, who categorically refused. On 11 June he wrote to his friend Ernest Pacaud: 'I do not want to be leader. That is not my aspiration ...; but there remain two objections. ... I am not a wealthy man, and my health is poor ... my friends are imposing too heavy a burden on me.' The clear-sighted Blake did not give up. In his opinion the party needed a leader with integrity, sound judgement, and courage, one able to look at problems not from a racial or religious point of view, but strictly from the standpoint of the national interest, and one who could stir crowds, but also persuade Quebeckers to join the Liberal ranks in overwhelming numbers, an essential condition for taking power in Ottawa. On 18 June 1887 Laurier yielded to the pressure and accepted, though he made it clear that he was assuming the leadership temporarily and would relinquish it as soon as Blake had recovered his health. In fact, he believed that it would be very difficult for a French Canadian to hold such a position in a federal party. He was definitely not enthusiastic at the time, but, as his correspondence also shows, he was, at the age of 45, amply endowed with nerve, determination, and the will to succeed.

Laurier would spend the next nine years of his life convincing Canadians that he was capable of guiding their destinies. Once again he found circumstances suggested a threefold strategy. First he had to provide the party with an economic policy that could reinvigorate its demoralized organization, divert Canadians from their intercultural quarrels, and defeat Macdonald's ageing Conservatives, who were incapable of creating a climate that could halt Canadian emigration to the United States. By 14 July he had hit on such a policy: commercial union with that country. His choice was inspired by the widespread free-trade sentiment in the party, which gathered around the tireless Cartwright and was central to the continentalist thinking beloved of many Canadians. In the winter of 1888, apparently thanks to James David Edgar, the measure, which assumed the establishment of a common tariff regime, was watered down to unrestricted reciprocity: the free movement of all products between Canada and the United States. It was then introduced in the House of Commons and defeated on 6 April, with some 20 Liberal MPs abstaining. Disappointed but not crushed, Laurier retained the option. He believed the vast market of 60 million Americans was an important outlet and he refused to allow the possibility that Canadian industries might be destroyed. He also dismissed the accusation of disloyalty towards England, a country whose civilization he admired greatly but from which, he declared, the colony would have to detach itself progressively in order to become a full and complete nation. Until 1891 he did his best to resist the attack on unrestricted reciprocity, regarded by many as equivalent to commercial union, which they believed could deprive Canada of its identity. He held out against Blake and other influential Liberals, and against the members of the Imperial Federation League, who were constantly crying treason to the empire and conjuring up annexation to the United States. He even had to defend himself against the Americans, who were shutting themselves off in a policy of narrow protectionism. Despite his efforts, reciprocity did not become as effective a tool for mobilizing the rank and file as he would have liked.

Nor did it do anything to calm intercultural conflicts. Canada in 1888–90 was a cauldron about to boil over. The problem was basically one of national identity. Some saw the nation as closely linked to the British empire, while others saw it as attached to the North American continent. But there was more to the conflict. A number of Protestant anglophones favoured an exclusively English-speaking and Protestant Canada. Fearing the strength and ambition of the Catholic French Canadians, which Mercier expressed so vigorously, they set out on a crusade against Canadian dualism. On the other hand, French Canadians, with the support of some anglophones, dreamed mainly of a bilingual and bicultural Canada. They too set out on a passionate crusade.

The agitation was soon felt in parliament. Laurier had to intervene in order to clarify both the position of his party and his definition of the nation that was to be built. This was the second objective he had in mind, and not the least important. Laurier used the prudence called for, but above all he pinned his hopes on frankness and made a sweeping defence of respect for provincial autonomy, for the country's two basic cultures, and for freedom. On 28 March 1889, in the name of these principles, he took a stand against the proposal that the house condemn the Jesuits' Estates Act passed by the Mercier government. He spoke out even more strongly on 22 Jan. 1890 when D'Alton McCarthy, a Conservative MP from Ontario, introduced a bill to abolish guarantees for the French language in the North-West Territories Act. Laurier fine-tuned a strategy based on the defence of provincial autonomy, even at the risk of sacrificing the spread of Canadian duality across the country. How could he prevent a province with an English-speaking majority from creating exclusively English and Protestant institutions? He recognized the realities, but he put his faith in the magnanimity of the majority partners. Thus on 21 February he supported an amendment moved by Sir John Sparrow David Thompson giving the assembly of the North-West Territories the power to decide the matter for itself. It was tantamount to saying that the territories could abolish the use of French in their assembly when it suited them. The subordination of the fate of the two cultures to the principle of provincial autonomy left a number of people puzzled at the time. For their part, French Canadian nationalists would never forgive Laurier for it but, as leader of a federal party, he had concluded that he was obliged to bow to political reality.

The same political realism had kept Laurier from acting when early in 1890 the Liberal government of Manitoba under Thomas Greenway had introduced two bills, one abolishing French as an official language and the other setting up a non-denominational school system controlled and financed by the state. Among French Canadians, who by then made up only about one-tenth of the population of Manitoba, and among the province's Roman Catholics generally, there was consternation. But in Ottawa, Laurier, who like Macdonald and many others was anxious to calm premature agitation, quickly agreed with the government decision to allow the courts to deal with this delicate matter, and he washed his hands of it.

There remained his third objective. Laurier had quickly identified its importance after June 1887, since it was a matter of revitalizing and reorganizing the party. Despite his ongoing intention to give up the leadership, he worked harder than ever. He put great weight on the creation of strong provincial organizations and the establishment of close ties to the provincial parties. With Edgar in particular, he prodded the parliamentary organization committee, which raised funds, produced and distributed election pamphlets, and monitored the party newspapers such as Toronto's *Globe* and Quebec's *L'Électeur*. In his home province he maintained the tradition he had established in 1875–77, adroitly taking advantage of the ground Blake had gained over the years. Quebec's conversion to the Liberal party gradually acquired an irresistible momentum. To some extent Laurier was the architect of this success, but he was also its beneficiary, reaping the fruits of his predecessor's labours. In Ontario he managed to render himself the indispensable arbiter for a caucus split into various factions. He also made some courageous political speaking tours in that province which, although not in themselves successful, nevertheless enabled him in the long run to become the only real rallying point for the rank and file.

The Liberal defeat in the general election of 5 March 1891 dampened the enthusiasm of many, even though the party had made substantial gains in Ontario, and Quebec had sent more Liberals than Conservatives to Ottawa for the first time since 1874. Macdonald had skilfully campaigned on loyalty to Canada and the empire, which he declared were being betrayed by unrestricted reciprocity, the main election issue. This defeat, Laurier's first as head of the party, hurt him, and he was hurt even more the following day when Blake, in a direct attack on his leadership, published an open letter against his trade policy. Laurier was disillusioned, and became increasingly so in 1892, a year in which nothing seemed to go right for the Liberals. He fought off his weariness by extensive reading and writing. Sometimes he would relax by going for a walk in Ottawa. Too often, he raised the question of his resignation, an obsession constantly on the tip of his tongue, but his colleagues protested each time, especially after Blake left Canada in June 1892.

Not until 1893 did a new lease on life really begin for Laurier, bringing revived hope. At this crucial stage he experienced a restored desire for action and benefited from a political situation that presented him with the opportunity of a lifetime. Borrowing an idea from John Stephen Willison, the editor-in-chief of the *Globe*, and with the solid support of James Sutherland, the party's chief whip, Laurier convened a great national convention in Ottawa on 20 and 21 June, attended by no fewer than 1,800 Liberals from all parts of the country except British Columbia and the North-West Territories. On the keynote of duality and under the distinguished chairmanship of Mowat, the convention brought forth a new program in which unrestricted reciprocity, watered down to satisfy Mowat and a number of other Liberals, was set in the context of developing the country's natural resources and maintaining a customs tariff to generate revenue for Canada. The party, now officially 'the Liberal party of the Dominion of Canada,' gave thought to its organization and held out to Canadian voters, and especially to protectionists and industrialists, the prospect of an increasingly credible alternative. Laurier was recognized as the undisputed, indeed indisputable, leader of all the country's Liberals. He undertook a series of speaking tours to give more momentum to the results of the convention and show he was equal to the dream of making Canada a nation. Aware of the growing importance of the agricultural west, he visited it in September and October 1894 and offered it a threefold program: loosening the grip of the National Policy, opening the American market, and increasing immigration. He did not win the west at this time, but he did gain respect and sympathy.

Laurier rose to the summit of political life as a result of one of the greatest tragedies of Canadian political history: the Manitoba school question, which resurfaced once and for all on 29 Jan. 1895. On that day the Judicial Committee of the Privy Council decided the federal government could intervene: Ottawa did have the right to remedy the injustice caused in 1890 by the Greenway government's creation of a non-denominational school system, which was so abhorrent to the largely French-speaking Roman Catholic minority. Suddenly the ball had bounced back into the court of the federal politicians. Through all the twists and turns of this affair, Laurier never played the hero. He never issued a firm public statement, although he regularly expressed sympathy for the right of the minority to have their own schools and declared his desire to protect that right as well as he could. Instead, setting his sights on party unity and power, he stepped up manoeuvres to embarrass the Conservatives, who were so divided they had to make the ageing Sir Charles Tupper leader of their party in order to restore a modicum of harmony. On 11 Feb. 1896 the government introduced a remedial bill aimed at restoring separate schools in Manitoba in both principle and practice. It was a courageous and generous gesture. Laurier vacillated, but held himself up as the defender of provincial rights and the symbol of hope for the minority. He moved that consideration of the measure be postponed for six months, and then went to great lengths to prolong debate unduly by systematic obstruction, thereby killing the bill. On 16 April, in an indescribable scene, Tupper withdrew it. For many, Laurier had come to represent moderation and conciliation in a troubled Canada, and although he had been more opportunistic than statesmanlike, leaving the minority leaders flabbergasted and believing they had been betrayed, he had won the last round but one before his final coronation. There remained the general election, called for 23 June.

Even though he considered resigning as leader in order to strengthen the unity of the grass roots, Laurier made the most of his opportunity. Prime Minister Tupper waged an excellent campaign, but Laurier appeared the only one capable of solving the country's social and economic problems and giving it a fresh start. He had solid backing from three provincial premiers – Mowat of Ontario, Andrew George Blair of New Brunswick, and William Stevens Fielding of Nova Scotia – and support from Quebec, where, in spite of a number of troublesome bishops, both Liberals and some Conservatives who had been won over by his personality presented him as an idol. By attacking on all fronts and not committing himself to a clear-cut position on the Manitoba school question, the main but not the only issue in this historic election, he won a majority of 30 seats, even though the Conservatives received 46.1 per cent of the popular vote to the Liberals' 45.1. He had gained a broad national mandate with a solid base in Quebec, which gave him 49 of his 118 MPs. At the age of 54, Wilfrid Laurier became prime minister of Canada, the first French Canadian to hold this office since confederation.

Laurier now had to shoulder his destiny. He would serve four successive terms as head of the government of Canada over a period of 15 years to fulfil it. His quarter-century of experience in active political life, in close contact with the country and with people such as Macdonald, whom he greatly admired as a master of politics and a leader of men, provided him with a grounding, as did his moderate liberalism. He exploited to the utmost the many, often contradictory aspects of his personality. With his exceptional charm and charisma, he could convince, captivate, and listen to each individual as at that moment the most important person in the world, or keep firm control of the members of his party. He also fell back on his habitual easygoing manner, both to gain respite from the fiery furnace he faced every day and to let time do its work. Skilful, opposed to taking rigid positions, and occasionally manipulative, he cultivated the art of ambiguity, of mental reservations, of blending into the surrounding air. In dealing with issues, he refused to worry about details, preferring to concentrate on the essential, guided by a pragmatism that accepted men and things as they were. Above all, he elevated compromise and quiet diplomacy almost to a dogma. Some regarded this penchant as a lack of conviction, an exaggerated nonchalance. In fact it was a strategy for achieving his purposes more readily in a dog-eat-dog environment. All in all, the man was a politician, but most of the time he was open, tolerant of opposing views, and conciliatory, except when there was a question of disloyalty. He never allowed a minister to thwart his plans. He could then become firm, abrupt, and willing to sacrifice his best men for the sake of his goals – cabinet solidarity and the integrity of his government, to which he clung tenaciously. For 15 years only one person held the reins of power in Ottawa. All the same, Laurier succeeded in winning the sincere friendship of his colleagues, of the party rank and file in general, and even of his opponents. Some saw him as a benevolent father, some as a disarmingly frank, close, and loyal friend, and still others as a noble soul. Almost all were impressed by the dignity of this great seigneur, this rallier of men.

To keep the upper hand in his government and his party, Laurier never forgot one key factor: patronage. He put it to every conceivable use: to show gratitude to a friend, draw an opponent into his camp, or get rid of an unwanted member of his inner circle. He attended to every detail, even to assigning a post office to a village. He played this role in Quebec especially, noting in 1899 that there he was 'the first and the last judge.' With the English-speaking provinces, he usually signed documents after the decisions had been made by the regional ministers. In this way, little by little, Laurier shrewdly wove an effective network of reliable friends and loyal organizers.

On another level, he took on the task of building alliances. He sought close links with leading capitalists and with Ontario, a problem province. He attempted to cajole influential members of the ultramontane clergy in Quebec, counting of course on the moderate bent of his liberalism but aware that his efforts in this direction risked antagonizing radical Liberals, who were perhaps more numerous than historians have indicated. He was careful in his choice of cabinet ministers, and in 1897 even tried to dictate the appointments to be made by the Liberal premier of Quebec, Félix-Gabriel Marchand. At the same time, he did his best to inspire Marchand to be conciliatory in his proposed school reforms. Despite the occasional serious clash, his actions gradually bore fruit, though people on both sides remained on their guard. The best proof of his success would be the good relations he enjoyed in the long run with Archbishop Paul Bruchési of Montreal. In the province of Quebec also, Laurier shrewdly managed to gather under his protective wing the moderate Conservatives of the school of Sir George-Étienne Cartier. The likes of Arthur Dansereau, Chapleau, and Joseph-Israël Tarte were notable in this regard. The conquest of Conservative Quebec, at this stage, was due to Laurier more than anyone else.

From the day of the election Laurier had resolutely set about the task of getting his vast country moving again, after the economic depression and cultural and religious conflicts which had badly shaken it. His first concern was to choose his cabinet. He took into account regions, ethnic groups, and religions; he showed sensitivity to the feelings of industrialists by keeping Sir Richard Cartwright, the leading spokesman of reciprocity, out of the finance ministry and calmed the fears of the clergy by leaving radical Rouges out of important positions; he flattered the moderate Quebec Conservatives by appointing one of them and drew on the administrative experience of three former provincial premiers in preference to colleagues of opposition days. As a result there were loud screams in the wings from the old guard, but between 13 and 20 July 1896 Laurier had put together a talented team of 11, including Mowat in the justice portfolio, Fielding in finance, Blair in railways and canals, Cartwright in trade and commerce, Tarte in public works, and Mulock as postmaster general.

The first item on Laurier's agenda was to settle the Manitoba school question. He at once shelved the inquiry that had been so often promised before 1896 and opted for negotiations with the Greenway government, to be conducted mainly by the highly credible Mowat. The ultimate objective was compromise or, in plain terms, to yield to the will of the stronger party and then hope to satisfy the weaker through minor adjustments. On 19 Nov. 1896 the Laurier–Greenway agreement, a veritable pact between victors, was made public. It confirmed that separate schools would not be re-established but provided for religious instruction in the schools between 3:30 and 4:00 P.M., if requested by the parents of 10 children in rural areas or 25 in urban ones. At least one Roman Catholic teacher was to be hired if the parents of 40 children in urban areas or 25 in rural ones so demanded. In schools where there were 10 children who spoke a language other than English, instruction could be given in English and in the mother tongue, according to the bilingual system.

That was all. Gone were the minority rights written into two constitutions. Almost nothing had mattered except an 'English' peace, to be preserved at all costs, and a narrow view of Canada, a country the majority wanted to have reflect its own image. After a violent reaction from the Catholic hierarchy, there was a period of calm imposed by the encyclical *Affari vos*; it was issued following an inquiry conducted in Canada by Monsignor Rafael Merry del Val, the papal legate who had been sent at Laurier's request to study the situation in Manitoba. He concluded that the Laurier–Greenway compromise was imperfect and inadequate, but that it must be accepted and improved over time by moderate means. Laurier had won. Never again would he allow the Manitoba question to come before parliament, although he occasionally tried to collect a few crumbs in concessions from Greenway. Laurier could boast of having restored national harmony, but at an enormous price. Whatever may have been said about it, this agreement stood as a dangerous precedent since it marked the emergence of an increasingly unicultural and English-speaking Canada, a truncated vision of the country foreseen by the Fathers of Confederation. The accord revealed as well the willingness of the federal government to abdicate its role as protector of minorities, to recognize the primacy of provincial rights over minority rights, and to bow to the weight of numbers.

The Laurier administration also searched for harmony on tariff reform. After appropriate consultations Fielding unveiled its decision to the house on 22 April 1897. The main feature was the immediate institution of a two-level rate. The one already in effect was maintained for any country that imposed a protective duty against Canada; a preferential reduction of 12.5 per cent (which could be increased to 25 per cent the following year) was applied to any country admitting Canadian goods at a rate equivalent to the minimum Canadian charge. There was almost universal satisfaction. Though annoyed by the preferential principle, industrialists and protectionists could see that the National Policy was being maintained. Many advocates of free trade saw preference as a step in the right direction. And imperialists quickly realized that, for practical purposes, Great Britain with its free trade policy would gain the most from preference. All in all, it was a master-stroke that helped restore the confidence of Canadians, even though farmers, who benefited little from the change, were somewhat soured by the process.

But Laurier and his team still needed a grand plan for material progress, one that could become the symbol of their optimism and be part of the economic recovery dawning in the western world. For Clifford Sifton, the talented and effective minister of the interior, the answer was accelerated development of the agricultural west, which would finally give full meaning to the great economic vision of a confederation based on the east-west market. With Laurier's agreement, Sifton took immediate and dramatic action. He reorganized his department, centralized decision-making in Ottawa, simplified regulations, and made land more accessible. Most important, he mounted a recruiting campaign of a kind not seen since confederation. Blacks, city folk, and a few other groups were excepted; everyone else was invited to come and build the west. (Immigration to Canada would reach 55,747 in 1901.) Among the new settlers were members of some minorities persecuted in their own countries, such as the Doukhobors and the Mennonites. A different region gradually came into being, more individualistic, competitive, and cosmopolitan than the rest. There were Canadians, of course, who worried about the lack of French-speaking immigrants, or the difficulty of integrating the new arrivals into Canadian life, or Sifton's somewhat hasty methods. Along with this policy, the Laurier government introduced others aimed at developing communications and stimulating production. Some, such as the Crowsnest Pass agreement of 1897, were very important to farmers. Thus the government conveyed the impression that it had sparked what was considered a most promising Canadian reawakening.

Internationally, matters were becoming more complex. External relations preoccupied Laurier more than any of his predecessors, often much against his own wishes. Here too, the Liberal leader hoped to show his country to advantage and to build it in security by gaining recognition for what it was becoming. The basic challenge for him was to establish Canada's position in relation to Great Britain and to the United States, the powerful, overly aggressive neighbour that considered it a mere appendage to the mother country. The issues between Canada and the United States had to do with trade, fishing rights, and, most serious, the determination of the Alaska boundary. It had to be established who owned the posts at the end of the Lynn Canal and thereby controlled maritime access to the Yukon. In the winter of 1897–98 Laurier secured an agreement with President William McKinley to set up a joint Anglo-American commission that would study their outstanding differences. The negotiations ground to a painful halt on 20 Feb. 1899 because of the inflexible American stand on Alaska. In the face of this set-back and the ensuing criticism, Laurier stood firm and let it be understood that Canada would make no more concessions to the major partners of the North Atlantic Triangle. It was a popular stand with Canadians, and one that had implications for the future.

The situation with regard to the mother country was much more complex. Britain was trundling out a new imperialism centred on the incomparable virtues of the 'Anglo-Saxon race' and its duty to convert as many peoples as possible to its brilliant civilization. The preservation of Britain's security and of its supremacy over the United States and Germany was now all-important. With this object in mind, Colonial Secretary Joseph Chamberlain wanted to bring the colonies into his proposed imperial federation, a military, economic, and political structure. The plan split Canadians into two camps. Many English Canadians who considered themselves nationalists accepted this imperialism and believed that the imperial framework would be an engine driving the advance from the status of colony to that of fully sovereign nation. On the other hand, many French Canadians rejected imperialism because it could lead to involvement in foreign wars and to the sacrifice of the country's interests.

Laurier was reluctant to take a clear public stand on such a delicate matter, but two events would force his hand. The first was the celebration of Queen Victoria's diamond jubilee in the summer of 1897, to which the colonial secretary attached a conference where the dominions and the mother country could discuss the role of the self-governing colonies within the empire. Laurier made his first visit to England, where he was showered with honours, honorary degrees, and medals, and on 22 June was even knighted. With Zoé at his side, he paraded in splendour through the streets of London immediately behind the queen and at the head of all the representatives of the dominions. At the beginning of his visit he often said what the imperialists wanted to hear. In London on 18 June, for instance, he stated, 'If a day were ever to come when England was in danger, let the bugle sound, and ... though we might not be able to do much, whatever we can do shall be done by the colonies to help her.'

At the colonial conference, however, the wily Laurier held his ground on essential points, even drafting and winning approval for the very important resolution stating that the current political relationship between Great Britain and the colonies was acceptable. Hopes of an imperial federation vanished at this point, much to Chamberlain's disappointment. In fact, there was nothing else Laurier could do, given the differences of opinion in Canada itself and his own views on imperial relations. He did not believe that such an all-encompassing federation was feasible. Above all, he knew he had to protect constitutional gains in anticipation of the day when a stronger and more united Canada could become independent.

The second event nearly proved fatal to the prime minister. On 12 Oct. 1899 London declared war on the Boers in South Africa, and the delicate question of military aid to Britain arose. After various stormy consultations, Laurier, true to form, arrived at a policy based on a compromise that came close to the wishes of the English Canadian majority. On 13 October, without convening parliament but after taking pains to emphasize that his action was not to be considered a precedent, he agreed to arm and send 1,000 Canadian volunteers to South Africa, where Britain was to assume full responsibility for their maintenance. There was great consternation on the part of many French Canadians; Liberal MP Henri Bourassa, who resigned his seat in the commons on 18 October, argued it indeed was a precedent that reduced Canada to the status of a dependent colony. Laurier held firm against Bourassa and against the imperialists who accused him of not doing enough. His middle-of-the-road position had to do with staying in power, but in his view there were also other factors. He was certain that his nation was not giving up its status, he recognized the justice of the British cause, and he was conscious of the need to preserve national unity and accommodate the sentimental attachment of English Canadians to the mother country. He won in the end, but he realized that the South African War had introduced imperialism into Canadian politics. He also saw that Bourassa, re-elected in Labelle on 18 Jan. 1900, was only beginning to make a name for himself. Canadian voters ratified Laurier's decision on 7 November by giving him a majority of 53 seats despite the disdain shown by Ontario, whose interests he had none the less served so well. Even Quebec overlooked his latest compromise, giving him 57 seats.

At the outset of Laurier's second term, political clarification was the order of the day. In imperial relations, he decided to remove ambiguities, keeping a close eye on his electoral base in Quebec where Bourassa's impassioned speeches were stirring more and more unrest. At a colonial conference in the summer of 1902, he rejected proposals for an imperial council, the creation of an imperial navy, and commercial union. On 13 March 1903 he gave this clear summary of his views to the House of Commons: 'The British empire is composed of a galaxy of free nations all owing the same allegiance to the same sovereign, but all owing paramount allegiance ... to their respective peoples.'

Sir Wilfrid Laurier, as photographed by F. W. Lyonde of Toronto in the early 1900s.

These words met with a rather cool reception from many imperialists, but Bourassa was overjoyed. He made peace with the prime minister, even though at the same time he became the mentor of the militant Ligue Nationaliste Canadienne, to which imperialism was anathema.

There were clarifications in Canadian–American relations. This time Laurier pressed for an arrangement dealing exclusively with the Alaska boundary, which was to be settled by a judicial commission of six impartial jurists. However, the Americans, upheld by Great Britain, selected three men well known for their partiality in the case, while the choice of the British side, two Canadians and one Englishman, respected the spirit of the agreement. On 20 Oct. 1903 the commission by a majority including the British representative rejected the Canadian claims, and Canada was awarded only two islands at the mouth of the Portland Canal, on the southern boundary of Alaska. This decision immediately set off a wave of anti-American and even anti-British sentiment in the country, which

Laurier, to conceal some mistakes of his own, temporarily encouraged. Canadians eventually calmed down, of course, but they did not forget.

There was also a need to clarify his authority over his cabinet colleagues: specifically, he had to bring into line Joseph-Israël Tarte, his right-hand man in Quebec and the vaunted representative of the moderate Conservatives in the ministry. While Laurier was travelling in Europe in the summer of 1902, Tarte had campaigned publicly for stronger protectionism. This behaviour was a direct affront to the prime minister, and on his return to Canada in mid October he took swift and vigorous action. Despite Tarte's importance in Quebec, he demanded his resignation.

In this trying year Laurier was also afflicted with illness. He had come back from Europe exhausted, so broken in health that he was afraid he had cancer and so tormented by the fear of death that he considered resigning. In Ottawa, work went on in slow motion, much to the displeasure of the busiest ministers. But in November and December a trip to bask in the warmth of Florida gradually restored him to health, and in January 1903, in his usual easygoing way, he began working on a quite special series of immense projects.

First, with Sifton as his indispensable coordinator, Laurier pursued the great challenge of developing the west, which would soon be the most dynamic element in the country's economic growth. Canadians witnessed what has been called the wheat boom. With its ever-increasing population of immigrants, the west produced up to 80 per cent of the entire Canadian output of wheat, which was being exported in unprecedented quantities. This wheat-based economy attracted capital into the region, encouraging a degree of industrialization. Because of the need it created for manufactured goods of all kinds, it even accelerated the industrialization of eastern Canada. Naturally, criticisms resurfaced, keeping pace with the success of the endeavour. Thanks to the Conservatives under their new leader, Robert Laird Borden, the work of parliament was interrupted by cries about shameless corruption, the difficulty of integrating newcomers into Canadian society, and the social problems connected with immigration. Even Bourassa, who had once been supportive, was increasingly concerned about the French Canadians' relative loss of importance in confederation. Although there was some basis for these criticisms, most Canadians were too optimistic to be affected by them. This optimism would lead Laurier to design another gigantic project: the construction of a second transcontinental railway. An extravagant undertaking, it would elevate him for the moment to the rank of the Fathers of Confederation.

The need for such a transcontinental line seemed urgent to many people, for the Canadian Pacific Railway was clearly showing its limitations. In the west, it could not transport everything produced by the farmers, while in the east it did not reach into northern Ontario or northern Quebec. Two companies in particular had shown an interest in building a new transcontinental line: the Canadian Northern Railway and the Grand Trunk. The former, headed by William Mackenzie and Donald Mann, had lines mainly in Manitoba and between Winnipeg and Port Arthur (Thunder Bay), Ont. The latter, headed in North America by Charles Melville Hays, had a network in the eastern part of the country. In 1903 Laurier personally took almost complete control of the huge project, as if he wanted to be associated with a specific venture in the way his sector-based ministers were. Although Blair was minister of railways and canals, he was pushed aside. Guided far more by his emotions and by the optimism sweeping the country than by economic realism, Laurier opted for a transcontinental line built entirely on Canadian territory by private enterprise. Unable to bring about an agreement between the two railways, he awarded the project to the Grand Trunk, in which he had more confidence. Left to its own devices, the Canadian Northern made plans for a transcontinental of its own. The Grand Trunk proved to be a difficult partner when the time came to discuss the general terms of the undertaking. Moreover, Laurier had to deal with all kinds of pressures, from every direction: his cabinet, itself divided on the subject; members of his caucus eager for a route guaranteeing their riding a station; and numerous pressure groups anxious not to miss out on this windfall. On 30 July 1903 the prime minister officially introduced in the house a catch-all bill calculated to satisfy everyone. The new transcontinental would be divided into two parts. The western section, from Winnipeg to the Pacific, would be built by the Grand Trunk Pacific Railway Company with financial assistance from the federal government, while the eastern, from Winnipeg to Moncton, N.B., would be built by the federal government and named the National Transcontinental Railway. On completion, the eastern section would be leased to the Grand Trunk

Pacific. Laurier carried the day both in the house and in the country at large, despite the lack of realism in some aspects of the project. On 3 Nov. 1904 the voters returned him to office with a comfortable majority of 64 seats. It was his most decisive victory to date.

At the height of his glory, Laurier wanted to enhance the reputation he enjoyed as the builder of modern Canada. He undertook to fulfil his most important promise of the day: to transform part of the North-West Territories into one or more autonomous provinces. The proposal threatened to touch off bitter debates. Frederick William Gordon Haultain, the president of the territories' Executive Council, wanted a single province covering the vast expanse of land between Manitoba and the Rockies, with provincial ownership of public lands and complete jurisdiction over education. Laurier favoured the creation of two provinces which, given the government's desire to pursue its immigration policy, would receive generous financial compensation in lieu of ownership of public lands. Most important, he devised an education clause designed to give as much protection as possible to the separate schools of the Roman Catholic minority, who made up only one-seventh of the population. He wanted to go back to the federal statute of 1875, which granted Catholics the full right to separate schools and the necessary financial assistance. It was not his intention, then, to preserve the status quo created by the 1892 and 1901 ordinances of the territorial government, which had severely limited the possibility for separate schools even to exist. Laurier stubbornly persisted in seeking the whole loaf. This time he would ignore the lofty principle of protecting provincial rights and put the emphasis on article 93 of the British North America Act, which he interpreted as stipulating that separate schools were to be protected if they already existed in a province requesting admission into confederation. This position, as he knew only too well, would ruffle many feathers. The danger of confrontation was real.

On this basis Laurier began negotiations on 5 Jan. 1905, and then manœuvred with Haultain, with Sifton, who was eager to maintain the status quo, and with his caucus, while at the same time scheming with those who shared his views to draft an article (which would become the famous article 16) in line with his intentions. On 21 February he suddenly presented everyone with a *fait accompli* by tabling his formal decisions in the house. Haultain was disappointed; the Catholic minority and their leaders were overjoyed. Sifton, who believed the west should be Canadianized in the English Canadian way, with non-denominational schools, was so bitter he resigned and helped fan the flames of public protest in English-speaking Canada. The disconcerted Laurier was now forced to work with Sifton in redrafting article 16 to reflect his views. He lost the battle of the education clause. He had miscalculated. With his eyes firmly fixed on retaining power, the prime minister became once more the skilful politician he had been before. From 22 March and for nearly four long months, he retreated to the status quo, proposing only minor amendments which the minority leaders referred to as crumbs. Some were satisfied, but not Henri Bourassa, who finally broke with Laurier and began stirring up Quebec. Bourassa rightly considered that the episode of the western schools was the culmination of a series of ordeals endured by Catholic and French minorities outside Quebec. Even worse, the country had probably lost its last chance of finding the concrete means to become a truly bilingual and bicultural nation.

In spite of Laurier's spectacular coup in creating the provinces of Alberta and Saskatchewan, this set-back foreshadowed the difficulty of consolidating the work he had accomplished since 1896, a task that would epitomize his third term. Indeed he and his Liberals now appeared less imaginative, and the cabinet, weakened by the departure of Tarte, Sifton, Mills, Sir Louis Henry Davies, Blair, Charles Fitzpatrick, and Mulock, fell into an attitude of complete docility towards an increasingly unenterprising leader, imprisoned in a 19th-century liberalism that progressive Liberals, less wedded to laissez-faire theory and less focused on the individual, were beginning to question. To make matters worse, though divided and weak, Borden and his Conservatives in 1906 undertook systematically to destroy this enfeebled cabinet. They waged a relentless campaign against the gross corruption of ministers and their departments, harping on the slogan, 'wine, women, and influence peddling,' in a campaign that reached fever pitch in 1908. Laurier was not affected personally by the Tory offensive, but he did not let it go unanswered. He made two of his ministers resign, appointed commissions of inquiry that identified a number of irregularities, and put through remedial laws such as the one on the civil service and the one on elections, which cleaned up party financing. On the whole, however, his reaction seemed rather belated, even timid. The leader and his demoralized party saw their star fading because of this unpleasant situation which left many Canadians perplexed.

They were still more perplexed in these years by the government's failure to propose measures adequately taking into account the changes in society that had occurred. A new Canada had been built since 1896, more industrialized, more urban, and more diversified in its ethnic composition and in the values of various interest groups. For instance, the Lord's Day Act, introduced in the house on 12 March 1906, did not satisfy the Lord's Day Alliance, and aroused anxiety among French Canadians in the province of Quebec which was stirred up by the Nationaliste movement of Bourassa and La Vergne. The timid tariff reform presented to the commons on 29 November was a disappointment to both manufacturers and farmers. Measures such as the Industrial Disputes Investigation Bill, which was introduced on 17 December, had the long-term effect of antagonizing the working class. It made conciliation mandatory for employers and workers before any strike or lockout in public utilities or mines, but did not require the parties to accept the conciliators' report. From the workers' point of view, this process favoured the employers. Imbued with his own brand of liberalism and too much a product of his own rural background, Laurier kept the state in its role of arbiter in the employer-labour conflicts that would become more frequent in an industrial society and would not give it a more active part in labour relations. The prime minister's failure to comprehend the demands of the new society was fraught with risks and even more with disappointments.

The country continued to develop economically, however, during Laurier's third term. Moreover, positive results in other areas, such as the federal–provincial conference of 1906 and the imperial conference of 1907, mitigated the difficulties of these strenuous years. But let there be no mistake. The empty slogan of the general election of 26 Oct. 1908, 'Let Laurier finish his work,' in itself revealed the spirit of the times. Canadians gave it their approval with a majority of 50 seats, but they sent disturbing signals to Laurier. He lost 14 seats, his lead over the Conservatives in the vote was only 42,136, and outside Quebec he had a tiny majority of 7.

The 66-year-old Laurier emerged from the election exhausted and ill. In mid November he gave serious thought to resigning in favour of

Fielding but was persuaded to stay. Realizing that his future was insepar-
able from that of the country and the party he had contributed so much
to shaping, he stayed on, although he confided to Ernest Pacaud's wife,
Marie-Louise, on 25 Dec. 1909: 'I carry my advancing years lightly, but
I no longer have the same zest for battle. I undertake today from a sense
of duty, because I must, what used to be "the joy of strife."' In spite of
everything, he went back to work. One feather in his cap was the creation
in 1909 of the Conservation Commission to advise the government about
avoiding the wasteful use of natural resources. Next he tried to mend a
few fences with the working class. On 2 June 1909 he appointed a full-
time minister of labour, the talented William Lyon Mackenzie King, and
a little later he acknowledged in the commons the increasing power of
working people in Canadian society. However, his rather timid law on
the investigation of combines, monopolies, and mergers, passed in 1910,
and his lukewarm support for labour during major strikes, intensified the
growing distrust that many workers felt for him.

Two issues would contribute to the final destruction of Laurier's
political power. The first, the creation of a navy, brought imperial relations crashing back into Canadian politics. In the background was Britain's
visceral fear of losing her naval supremacy and, as a corollary, the deep
and opposing emotions this apprehension aroused in both English and
French Canadians. In the house on 29 March 1909 anglophone and
francophone MPs alike gave unanimous approval to a resolution calling
for the establishment of Laurier's long-promised naval service 'in close
relation to the imperial navy.' But Laurier's attempt to translate it into a
bill shattered the fine unanimity of a house divided between the imperial
nationalism of English Canadians and the Canada-centred nationalism
of French Canadians. His Naval Service Bill, introduced in the house on
12 Jan. 1910, did attempt to steer a middle course. It created, under the
authority of the Canadian government, a navy of five cruisers and six
destroyers which would be able to fight where Britain was involved in
conflict. The force would consist entirely of volunteers and could also,
in critical circumstances and with the approval of parliament, operate
under imperial command. There was a fierce debate in the house. Borden,
the spokesman for the imperialists, demanded that a subsidy be voted
immediately to Britain so it could purchase two Dreadnoughts and that,
when the time came, the people should be consulted on any permanent

Prestige ou Prestigitation?

Sarah W. Laurier :—Pour moi c'est tout un ! ! !

Sir Wilfrid Laurier's handling of the naval question is portrayed as a juggler's trick in *Le Nationaliste* (Montreal), 9 Oct. 1910.

naval policy. His colleague Frederick Debartzch Monk, with the support of the other French Canadian Conservative MPs, distanced himself from Borden, rejecting the idea of an emergency contribution. Fearing the prospect of conscription and the enormous cost of this useless navy, he demanded an immediate plebiscite. Laurier's reply did not convince either extreme, but with a united party behind him he won in the house on 20 April. He still had to parry attacks from outside parliament. They were vicious in English-speaking Canada, but in Quebec they became disastrous under Bourassa's leadership. Bourassa, who had just begun publishing his daily *Le Devoir*, formed an alliance with Monk in the summer of 1910 and organized meeting after meeting to heap scorn on Laurier and his accursed navy. On 3 November the alliance even defeated Laurier's candidate in a by-election in the Liberal stronghold of Drummond and Arthabaska. The prime minister suddenly realized that his hold on Quebec was slipping.

Commercial reciprocity with the United States, which Laurier put back on his agenda after his triumphant visit to the west in the summer of 1910, was a still more disastrous policy, even though this time Laurier could count on the Americans since they had approached him on the subject the previous spring. Negotiations conducted by Fielding and William Paterson, the minister of customs, got under way on 5 November. Laurier sought an arrangement that would satisfy farmers without penalizing manufacturers. The Americans quickly understood the Canadian position. On 26 Jan. 1911 Fielding triumphantly announced to a stunned house the details of an agreement that would permit free trade between the two countries in most so-called natural products but only a small number of manufactured goods. Borden's crestfallen Conservatives were convinced they would languish in opposition for a long time to come. Laurier's beautiful dream soon faded, however. A couple of weeks were enough to reinvigorate the Conservatives and arouse opposition outside parliament. In February financiers and manufacturers, along with a few Liberal MPs, began a savage attack on the bill as destructive of Canadian prosperity and identity. They formed an alliance with the Conservatives and raised the spectre of annexation to the United States and disloyalty to the empire. Sifton, who was still an MP, and 18 Liberal businessmen and financiers in Toronto made a private pact with Borden to defeat Laurier. Thus strengthened, the Conservatives dragged out the debates in the house. Laurier disputed every one of the dangers enumerated, but he had been caught off balance and remained on the defensive. He committed the blunder of suspending the proceedings of the house from 19 May to 18 July in order to attend the coronation of King George V and the imperial conference in London, and he thereby enabled his opponents to consolidate their forces. On 29 July, unable to regain control of a turbulent house, the prime minister decided to ask for the dissolution of parliament.

The election of 21 Sept. 1911 was a total disaster for Laurier. The two central issues – both major – were reciprocity and the navy, and they

Sir Wilfrid Laurier
speaking in favour
of Liberal candidate
Georges Parent
at Sainte-Anne-
de-Beaupré, Que.,
20 Sept. 1911.

underpinned two concepts of the nation, one more continentalist and the
other more closely linked to the British empire. Proud of his accomplishments in the previous 15 years, Laurier underestimated from the very
outset the extent of his regime's exhaustion. In addition to discontent in
the Maritimes and among social classes to whom the country's prosperity
had brought too little benefit, he was hindered by the ossification of his
cabinet and of his party, which was poorly organized in Ontario, and by
his own inability to adapt his liberalism to the needs of a new society.
Laurier undoubtedly had recognized these weaknesses, but he made no
basic changes, as if he were too sure of his own power. Because of the
issues involved, he became the target for furious opponents whose accusations, informed by nationalist ideology, all began and ended with the
word 'traitor.' To Bourassa's Nationalistes, joined in an outrageous alliance

with Borden's imperialists, he was a traitor to his country. To the imperial-ists and the foes of reciprocity, he was a traitor to Canada and the empire. The evening of 21 September saw the Liberals with only 87 seats to the Conservatives' 134. The politics of compromise had had its day.

Laurier at the age of 69 once more became leader of the opposition. Instead of quitting politics and going back to rest in Arthabaska as he had so often wished to do, he decided to stay on and play his full role to the limit of his strength. His aim was to drive out the Conservatives as quickly as possible, since their program, with its reformist and imper-ialistic tendencies, threatened to destroy what he had achieved. To the surprise of many, he immediately made a splendid start by redoubling his efforts, and he soon restored life to his party. He first revitalized its parliamentary wing, bringing defeated ministers back into either the house or the party's councils. Then he provided a permanent structure to coordinate action and strengthen ties with party workers. In 1912, for example, he set up the Liberal information office under King, which published the *Canadian Liberal Monthly*. Although he made no basic changes to the 1911 program, partly to avoid reopening divisions within his caucus, he kept in regular touch with all the regional leaders. From 1912 to 1914 he held some 30 meetings and political banquets in Quebec and Ontario. But above all, he worked feverishly in the house, angrily baring his claws and relentlessly attacking Borden's bills, even using the Liberal majority in the Senate to defeat them or amend them beyond recognition. The best example of this approach is undoubtedly the extremely bitter debate that began in December 1912 on Borden's pro-posed emergency contribution of $35 million to Great Britain, which again felt threatened by the German naval program. In the name of Canadian autonomy Laurier waged a ruthless parliamentary battle for six long months, a battle that the Liberal senators brought to an end by defeating the Naval Aid Bill on 29 May 1913. Borden was weakened by all these attacks. He lost Monk from his cabinet and he lost the support of Bourassa's Nationalistes. Although he suffered a few reverses, Laurier saw an increase in his own popularity and that of his party. Once again the golden stairway to power appeared on the horizon.

World War I soon crushed these fine hopes and shattered the two most important foundation-stones of Laurier's career: national unity and the unity of the Liberal party. From 1914 to 1918 he lived through the worst ordeals of his life. At the outset of this terrible war there was no hint of such results. Throughout the country English- and French-speaking Canadians alike, under stress and in a highly emotional state, agreed on almost everything, from voluntary service in the armed forces to the dispatch of material assistance to embattled Britain. In tune with his fellow Canadians, Laurier renounced partisan politics and even proposed a truce between the parties. He loyally supported Borden in the commons and participated in a series of recruiting meetings to stimulate the war effort. People rallied around their leaders, one of whom, the 72-year-old Laurier, displayed a sense of duty and a boundless energy that were a constant source of astonishment.

In just three years these fine sentiments were transmuted into tragedy. As the war dragged on, with its enormous demand for human and material resources and with voluntary recruitment declining, Borden imposed military conscription in the summer of 1917. This decision went against the country's military and political traditions and broke the promises previously made by politicians. Some workers and farmers, and the vast majority of French Canadians, were stunned. Entrenched in their traditional way of thinking and swayed by the stinging speeches of Bourassa's Nationalistes, French Canadians vigorously demonstrated their opposition. Borden held his ground, sustained by his principles, the necessities of war, and the repeated calls to stand fast from numerous English-speaking Canadians, both Liberal and Conservative. Believing that Canada was fighting as a nation and that the war would put the country on the world map, inspired by the ideology of service, filled with notions of honour, and, in some cases, with progressive social thinking, many English-speaking Canadians saw themselves as engaged in a moral crusade that had to be supported by all-out effort. They never understood the French Canadians, whom they wrongly characterized as traitors to the nation. In 1917 cultural and partisan differences reached new heights in Canada.

Laurier was utterly opposed to conscription. Because of his principled liberal resistance to coercion of any kind, his past promises, and the inevitable divisions conscription would create, he rejected it unless it was approved by the Canada-wide referendum for which he called. He explained his decision to the house on 18 June 1917, but to no avail. His choice immediately drew almost all the francophones to his side, but it cut him off dramatically from the majority of anglophones, including the English Canadian parliamentary wing of his party. All but seven of his English-speaking MPs abandoned him, demonstrating even more pointedly than they had done in the thorny Ontario school question their disapproval of his support for the French Canadian minority. Like the country itself, the Liberal party was now split on the issue of conscription. Laurier was heartsick. On 24 July in the house he pathetically poured out his distress at the collapse of his political *raison d'être*. But that was not all. Still to come was the formation of a coalition whose main objective would be the enforcement of conscription. The Liberal leader again declined to cooperate in this arrangement. He had already flatly rejected it on 6 June when Borden had made him a specific offer. Despite Laurier's heroic efforts to repair his party and offset the effects of two congresses organized in Toronto and Winnipeg by Liberals who favoured a coalition, Borden on 12 October triumphantly presented his Union government, which included nine Liberals. The Liberal party of Canada disintegrated. From that time also dates the quasi-isolation of Quebec, which was becoming increasingly desperate, wrongly believing itself the sole target of the actions being taken. In the autumn of 1917 Laurier again, and more fully, plumbed the failure of his political career.

The disaster was confirmed by the election of 17 Dec. 1917. Had the vote been held a year earlier, Laurier would have had a chance of winning, but not in 1917. By now, conscription had broken up his team and Borden, already well supplied with funds and supporters, had enacted legislation disenfranchising many immigrants from enemy countries, giving the vote to female relatives of enlisted soldiers, and allowing the soldiers' vote to be shamelessly manipulated. Aged 76 and broken in both body and spirit, Laurier fought his hardest, presenting himself as a saviour in a Quebec fervently united behind him, and in English-speaking Canada as a leader abandoned by his friends, a victim of general misunderstanding and condemnation. How often the word 'traitor' sounded harshly in his ears or brought tears to his eyes! He endured a time of indescribable tension, undisguised hatred, and virtual electoral robbery. With 82 seats to Borden's 153, Laurier was crushed, winning only 20 seats and 34.6 per cent of the popular vote outside Quebec.

The old man felt the end coming. With a final burst of energy, he harnessed himself once more to his party in order to rebuild it. He issued one directive: forget the past. Certain that the Union government would be defeated before long, he made a discreet and friendly approach to influential Liberals who had gone over to Borden. Almost paternally, he advised William Lyon Mackenzie King to stay close to Ottawa. Even though weakened by illness from the summer of 1918, he resumed his correspondence with regional leaders. The armistice of 11 November restored his enthusiasm. He began to set in motion a great congress that would define the structures and program of his party, the better to reunify it. Would it also choose a new leader? No one knew for sure, because Laurier continued to be evasive on the subject. On 14 Jan. 1919 he issued a public invitation to the Unionist Liberals to return to the fold. He was in the midst of a promising reconstruction of his party when on 16 February he was suddenly struck down by a cerebral haemorrhage and paralysis. To the tearful Zoé he said simply, 'This is the end.' The next afternoon death opened wide for him the doors to the history of his country.

Following a magnificent state funeral on 22 February, Sir Wilfrid Laurier's body was escorted to Notre-Dame cemetery in Ottawa by more than 100,000 people. Whatever reservations they had about the man's achievements, on that day the vast majority of Canadians knew that a significant chapter of history had come to an end, taking with it a part of their souls. The entire country was in mourning. Despite disappointments and often justified criticisms, Laurier was already a legend; he had gradually achieved the stature of a giant, a symbol personified. And what an engaging personality! Few people at the turn of the century could resist his charm and courtesy. When necessary, Laurier was able to abandon his prime ministerial ways for a simplicity that won over the most obdurate hearts. His disarming frankness despite his subterfuges, his exceptional honesty in a rather lax environment, his respect for others regardless of differences of opinion, his unshakeable loyalty to the Liberal cause and to his friends, his determination and firmness despite moments of discouragement and the limits already mentioned, all aroused the admiration of many Canadians. Even his opponents were captivated. To be sure, his personality also drew less favourable comments. It was said, for instance, that Laurier was so full of contradictions that he resembled Machiavelli as well as Sir Galahad; that he often wore a mask and played a game, feigning both joy and sadness; that he set his sights on immediate successes with no concern for long-term results; that he was incapable of taking great risks. Laurier indeed was not of a piece. He did not see things in black and white, and no doubt he had developed a personality that enabled him to face the complexity and harshness of his milieu at any time. He was nevertheless a man of honour, generous, enamoured of liberty, and able to confer nobility on the causes he supported. A humanist, he found arrogance, bigotry, and intolerance repugnant. Lord Minto once said of him that he was 'far the biggest man in Canada.' He was right. And this was the portrait of Sir Wilfrid Laurier that in the end has remained in the collective memory.

RÉAL BÉLANGER

Further reading

Réal Bélanger, *Wilfrid Laurier; quand la politique devient passion* (2ᵉ éd., Québec, 2007) and 'Le libéralisme de Wilfrid Laurier: évolution et contenu (1841–1919),' in *Combats libéraux au tournant du XXᵉ siècle*, sous la direction d'Yvan Lamonde (Montréal, 1995).

H. B. Neatby, *Laurier and a Liberal Quebec; a study in political management*, ed. R. T. Clippingdale (Toronto, 1973).

Joseph Schull, *Laurier: the first Canadian* (Toronto, 1965).

O. D. Skelton, *Life and letters of Sir Wilfrid Laurier* (2v., Toronto, 1921; abridged ed., 2v., ed. D. M. L. Farr, 1965).

Sir Wilfrid Laurier: une bibliographie choisie et annotée/an annotated and selected bibliography, Sylvie Arend et Julianna Drexler, compil. (Toronto, 2002).

Sir ROBERT LAIRD BORDEN,

lawyer and politician; b. 26 June 1854 in Grand Pré, N.S., first child of Andrew Borden and Eunice Jane Laird; m. 25 Sept. 1889 Laura Bond (d. 8 Sept. 1940) in Halifax; they had no children; d. 10 June 1937 in Ottawa.

Robert Laird Borden's paternal ancestor Richard Borden left Headcorn, England, in 1638 to settle in Portsmouth, R.I. More than a century later, after the Acadians had been expelled from Nova Scotia in 1755, Richard's great-grandson Samuel Borden, a landowner and surveyor in New Bedford, Mass., was commissioned by the Nova Scotia government to survey the vacated lands and lay out plots for New Englanders intending to settle there. In 1764 Samuel received a parcel of land in Cornwallis for his work, but he returned to New Bedford. His son Perry, Robert's great-grandfather, took up the grant, beginning the establishment of Borden families in the Annapolis valley bordering on the Bay of Fundy.

The Bordens were farmers, tilling the rich tidelands rescued from the sea generations earlier by the expelled Acadians. Robert's father, Andrew, who was born in 1816, owned a substantial farm at Grand Pré. He first married Catherine Sophia Fuller, and they had a son, Thomas Andrew, and a daughter, Sophia Amelia, before her death in 1847. Three years later Andrew married Eunice Jane Laird, the daughter of John Laird, the village schoolmaster and a classical scholar and mathematician of local repute. Robert was born in 1854 and was followed by a brother, John William, a sister, Julia Rebecca, and another brother, Henry Clifford, born in 1870. John William would become a senior civil servant in the Department of Militia and Defence in Ottawa; Julia remained in Grand Pré, unmarried and living with her parents; Henry Clifford, known as Hal and Robert's favourite among the siblings, graduated from Dalhousie law school in Halifax and practised as a lawyer.

Of all the members of the family it was Eunice, Robert's mother, who had the strongest influence on his upbringing and development. He later wrote that she was of 'a highly-wrought nervous temperament,' 'passionate but wholly just and considerate upon reflection,' and totally devoted to the welfare of her four children. Borden admired her 'very strong character, remarkable energy, high ambition and unusual ability' – traits that marked his own emerging personality. Borden's reflections on his father were much more restrained. Andrew did not take to agricultural pursuits and left management of the farm to Eunice and the children. He dabbled and failed in small business ventures and in time found a comfortable sinecure as stationmaster at Grand Pré for the Windsor and Annapolis Railway. Though 'a man of good ability and excellent judgment,' Robert wrote, Andrew 'lacked energy and had no great aptitude for affairs.'

Robert's education began in the village's Presbyterian Sunday school, where he was initiated into the mysteries of the Shorter Catechism, and at home, where he learned reading with his mother from the pages of John Bunyan's *Pilgrim's progress*. In due course, lessons with the village schoolmistress were interspersed with visits from his uncles, who introduced him to the poets Horace and Virgil. When he was nine, in 1863, his parents sent him as a day student to the local private academy, Acacia Villa School, presided over by Arthur McNutt Patterson. Patterson's mission was to 'fit boys physically, morally, and intellectually, for the responsibilities of life.' Each morning began with Patterson reading a chapter of Proverbs to his charges, who then moved on to exercises in grammar, mathematics, literature, and natural philosophy. Borden excelled at Greek and Latin. Soon his instructor, James Henry Hamilton, also had him studying Hebrew. The classical poetry and literature stayed with Borden all his life. A volume in Latin or Greek, perhaps one of each, was on his bedside table until the day of his death. In 1869, when Hamilton suddenly left Acacia Villa to join a private school in New Jersey, Robert, at age 14, found himself promoted to 'assistant master,' charged with taking Hamilton's place in classical studies.

The contrast with his chores at home was sharp and telling. He later recalled that he never had mastered 'the mysteries of building a load of hay,' and found hoeing vegetables 'extremely disagreeable' and sawing cordwood for winter fires 'unpleasurable.' Even on the rich bottomlands and upland fields of 'the Valley' the rewards of agriculture were hard won. He never forgot that 'throughout the year labour was severe and hours long.' As attached as he was to his family, Borden resolved not to spend his life as a farmer in Grand Pré. Teaching at Acacia Villa had more than its share of routine, and his failure to complete his schooling precluded study at university. Still, teaching hinted at a better way of life. Self-education, he discovered, had its own satisfactions. One learned the value of time: 'To waste it seems like wasting one's future.' Discipline, hard work, persistence, patience, and a sense of humour were common enough virtues but essential to shape the ambitions of a young man determined to succeed. Borden taught at the academy for four years and then accepted Hamilton's invitation to join him at the Glenwood Institute in Matawan, N.J.

It was the first time he had ever been away from home and he was desperately lonely in the fall of 1873. But he was not alone. A ferry ride away in the great metropolis of New York his half-brother, Thomas, a sailor, and his wife lived. Other Nova Scotia friends resided in Brooklyn and he and a fellow boarder named Horner, a public-school teacher, often went to the city on weekends to visit its parks, museums, galleries, and libraries and to listen to temperance lectures. At the Glenwood Institute, he was a 19-year-old professor of classics and mathematics. Borden found the work demanding. He kept a short-lived diary and frequently recorded entries like 'I worked too hard this afternoon at reports &c. I was somewhat ill this evening about 7 o'clock.' He had nine different classes, most with fewer than a dozen students, and none of them particularly challenging.

In the spring of 1874, as the school year was drawing to a close, Borden surveyed his prospects. They were not encouraging; without completion of his formal education in school and college, a career in teaching would likely mean working in second-rate academies trying to inspire dull, uninterested students. Casting about, he wrote to an uncle who was a barrister in Ontario, asking for information on studying law in that province. The reply was enough to convince him that he should give the profession a try. But his mother would have nothing to do with his going to Ontario. She told him he could do just as well at home in Nova Scotia. He applied to and was accepted by the prominent Halifax firm of Robert Linton Weatherbe and Wallace Nesbit Graham. As the fall of 1874 began, Borden, always punctilious, recorded: 'Commenced the study of the law by reading a small portion of [Robert Malcolm Napier] Kerr's 1873 edition of the Student's Blackstone on Saturday evening, Sept. 19 at 8.45 o'clock.'

He was apprenticed to Weatherbe and Graham as an articled clerk for four years, 'entitled to be instructed in the knowledge and practice of the Law.' In truth, he learned by doing. He was expected to prepare briefs for his masters and watch over the ordinary office affairs of their clients. Formal instruction depended upon his after-hours initiative. A diversion from the routine of the office was enlisting in the 63rd (Halifax Volunteer) Battalion of Rifles. There, in three yearly terms, he earned a meagre but welcome six dollars for twelve days of service and a fifty dollar bonus when he qualified for commission. Other companions were found at the St Andrew's Lodge of British Templars and the debating society of the Young Men's Christian Association. In September 1877 he joined Charles Hibbert Tupper, who had a law degree from Harvard, and 23 others to sit the provincial bar examinations. Borden topped the class. He still had a year of apprenticeship before admittance to the bar and during the winter of 1877–78 also attended the School of Military Instruction in Halifax.

Borden and a classmate briefly had a practice in Halifax before he went to Kentville as the junior partner of Conservative lawyer John Pryor Chipman. Then, in 1882, Wallace Graham called him back to Halifax. John Sparrow David Thompson, a partner in the firm since Weatherbe's promotion to the bench in 1878, had himself been made a judge. Graham and Tupper, who had become a partner in 1881, needed help, especially so because Tupper had just been elected to the House of Commons. Borden had hardly settled in when Graham assigned him a long list of cases before the provincial Supreme Court. Other work came from the firm's Conservative friends in Sir John A. Macdonald's government in Ottawa. Borden helped prepare the government's cases in the seizure of two American fishing vessels in 1886 during the long-standing Canadian–American dispute over fishing rights in the North Atlantic. Then, early in 1888, Thompson, now Macdonald's minister of justice, invited Borden to work with him in Ottawa as deputy minister. Borden was tempted but declined, preferring to remain in practice in Halifax.

Robert L. and Laura
Borden around
the time of their
marriage in 1889.

In September 1889 Robert Borden married Laura Bond, a daughter
of the late Thomas Henry Bond, who had been a successful hardware
merchant in Halifax. How they first met is not known, though it may
have been at St Paul's Anglican Church, where she was an organist and
he a regular attendant. Their courtship had begun in the summer of 1886.
When they were married he was 35 and she 28. Laura was a lively,
attractive, and strong-willed young woman whose interest in music and
theatre complemented his in literature. Both enjoyed tennis, water sports,
and especially golf. At first the Bordens rented rooms in downtown Halifax
but in 1894 Borden bought a large home, Pinehurst, on Quinpool Road
in the western suburbs of the city. He was now very successful in his
career, and he and Laura spent several weeks in the summers of 1891
and 1893 touring in England and Europe. There were no children of the
marriage but Borden's brother Hal was often with them at Pinehurst while
studying at Dalhousie.

By the mid 1890s the Borden firm, now including William Bruce
Almon Ritchie and others, was among the largest in the province. The
Bank of Nova Scotia, Canada Atlantic Steamship, Nova Scotia Telephone,
and the bread and confectionery business of William Church Moir were
among its prominent clients. Most of Borden's work was on referral of

appeals to the Supreme Court in Halifax or in Ottawa, and in 1893 he appeared for the first time before the Judicial Committee of the Privy Council in London. He had several cases each year in Ottawa. While there he frequently visited Sir John Thompson, who had become prime minister, and other Nova Scotia acquaintances. His closest friends were the Tuppers, Charles Hibbert and his family. In the early nineties Borden and Tupper took up the new fad of bicycling and were often seen on the roads in and about Ottawa and Hull. At home in Halifax, Borden's reputation and influence in the bar steadily grew. He was elected vice-president of the Nova Scotia Barristers' Society in 1895 and became its president a year later. While he was serving in that office he and his colleague Charles Sidney Harrington played leading roles in organizing the founding meeting of the Canadian Bar Association in Montreal in 1896.

That spring, on 27 April, Borden was in Ottawa arguing cases and went to dinner at Sir Charles Tupper's home. It was the day that Sir Mackenzie Bowell resigned as Conservative prime minister and Tupper was about to succeed him. It was clear that there would be an election before the year was out. Tupper asked Borden to stand for Halifax with the veteran Catholic MP Thomas Edward Kenny. John Fitzwilliam Stairs, Halifax businessman and Protestant colleague of Kenny in the House of Commons, was stepping down and Tupper wanted Borden to replace him. Before Borden left the dinner party, he accepted.

It was an abrupt change in Borden's life and opponents would later charge that he had suddenly switched sides. What political interests he had had in his earlier years were certainly on the Liberal side – the Valley was a Liberal stronghold – and he had spoken once on behalf of his cousin the Liberal politician Frederick William Borden in 1882. In 1886, however, he had abandoned the Liberal cause in disagreement with Nova Scotia premier William Stevens Fielding's campaign against confederation. Several of his legal partners in Graham's firm were prominent Conservatives and when Borden took over the firm all the new associates he chose had Conservative leanings. Yet Borden himself had never before expressed any interest in running for public office. Nor was he deeply moved by the big issue in the 1896 election, the Manitoba school question. After winning the nomination he campaigned on the hardy staple of Macdonald-era Tory politics, the National Policy. This, after all, was the plank in the Conservative platform that captured the interest and support of most of his clients. On election day, 23 June, Halifax voters, for only the second time since confederation, split their ticket. Both the Conservative and the Liberal Catholic candidates were defeated. Borden and Liberal Benjamin Russell, another prominent lawyer and Protestant, were elected. Borden took his place in the commons as a member of the opposition party: Tupper and his Tory colleagues had been soundly defeated by Wilfrid Laurier's Liberals.

For the next four years Borden was a backbencher, practising law in Halifax and politics in Ottawa. He disliked being away from Laura. 'It is a miserable irregular life one has to lead,' he complained early in the 1896 session, 'and I am more than sick of it, I can assure you.' As always, the duties of the backbencher revolved around attending to the wishes and complaints of his constituents and defending the interests of his riding when occasion demanded. Borden became involved in his work on house committees and, over time, grew more confident to speak on broader, national issues. As one of the few 'new men' in the party, he was steadfast in his loyalty to his leader, Tupper, and distanced himself from the incessant bickering that characterized the Conservatives in opposition. By 1899 he had been moved to the front bench and had begun to be noticed as an emerging figure in the party.

On 7 Nov. 1900 the Conservatives were soundly defeated in another general election and Tupper was ready to give up the leadership at year's end. The more obvious candidates were veteran warriors such as George Eulas Foster and Sir Charles Hibbert Tupper. But they had acquired as many rivals and enemies as friends during their long careers, and their prospects of beating Laurier in a future election were dismal. The party needed a fresh face and the Tuppers, father and son, turned to Borden. He had no enemies in the caucus and had been an able and conscientious worker in parliament. Charles Hibbert approached him in mid November, well before his father's formal resignation was announced in February. 'I have not either the experience or the qualifications which would enable me to successfully lead the party,' Borden replied. 'It would be an absurdity for the party and madness for me.' The Tuppers persisted and when the disheartened Tory MPs and senators met in February 1901, they rallied support for their candidate. On 6 February the members, many sceptically, chose Borden as their leader. Borden played out the formalities of surprise and set two conditions. He would, he said, accept for only one year and he demanded that the party appoint a committee to search for a permanent leader. The committee was quickly forgotten and the commitment to one year was never made public.

Borden led the party in opposition for a decade. Previous leaders, Macdonald, Thompson, Tupper, and the others, had had years of parliamentary experience before assuming the position. Borden, in his late forties, had spent his adult life as a lawyer and had had only a brief apprenticeship in politics. Though he applied himself to his new duties with the same earnestness and ambition that he had devoted to his legal career, he regarded politics with a sense of detachment unknown to the career politicians who preceded him. Political life, he believed, was a responsibility, something a successful man should take on in the public interest. While he had long since conquered his anxieties about arguing the law in the highest courts of his country and the empire, Borden never enjoyed public speaking and debate. He found it both physically and emotionally demanding.

Leading his colleagues was even more challenging. They were a fractious lot in parliament and the constituencies, cursed with long-standing rivalries and deep divisions between Catholic and Protestant, French and English, and, reflecting changing times, urban and rural factions. Though ultimately the leader had the authority to decide, party organization and party policy had evolved as prerogatives of the MPs, which they jealously guarded. They chafed at Borden's tendency, throughout the opposition years, to bypass them and seek advice from outsiders, Conservative provincial premiers and prominent business leaders sympathetic to the Tory cause. One veteran of party warfare, Samuel Hughes, developed a strong affection for his leader but shared his long-serving colleagues' doubts about Borden's political skills. Borden, he observed in 1911, was 'a most lovely fellow; very capable, but not a very good judge of men or tactics; and is gentle hearted as a girl.' Many MPs found Borden reserved, distant, and occasionally imperious. Once, in 1913, Borden had to reprimand a colleague and then regretted it. 'Wrote [John Allister] Currie a consoling letter,' he wrote in his diary. 'He wept. Geo[rges] Lafontaine also wept today when I spoke kindly to him.'

Borden's most difficult problem was with his French Canadian MPs. Once the backbone of the Conservative Party, the Quebec membership in caucus had been reduced to a tiny rump. Borden often thought their ideas were parochial but never went out of his way to try to understand them. Following a practice of Macdonald, he chose a lieutenant from their ranks, Frederick Debartzch Monk. Monk, like Borden, was a lawyer who had first been elected in 1896 and, again like his chief, he was serious, earnest, and moody. Neither man got on easily with the other. Monk was a champion of growing nationalist sentiment in Quebec. Borden, who spoke competent French, was frequently impatient with his lieutenant and failed to grasp the significance of French Canadians' views on national issues that threatened their sense of identity. Nor was he able to curb the sometimes virulent antagonism of his more ardent Ontario Protestant colleagues to the Quebec Conservatives' aspirations. Monk, feeling isolated and unsupported by his leader, resigned his position in January 1904. A year later he and Borden clashed over the schools issue in Alberta and Saskatchewan. Monk wanted Borden to stand up for establishing separate schools in the new provinces while Borden, knowing they were opposed by local officials, backed the arguments for provincial autonomy. Monk, angered, said that his leader had set back the Conservative cause in Quebec by 15 years.

Borden was influenced by the progressive ideas about democratizing political parties and using state power in the public interest that were being debated in the United States. An example was his opposition to the extravagant plans of Laurier's government, in 1903, to support the building of two more transcontinental railways, the Grand Trunk Pacific and the Canadian Northern. Borden agreed that the rapid expansion of the prairie region required new transportation routes. But the two railways, which would run for miles within a carriage ride's distance of each other, were wasteful and irresponsible. He countered with a proposal for a government-owned and -operated transcontinental railway, controlled not by private corporations but by the people of Canada. Though the Liberals easily carried the day in parliament, Borden said that in the forthcoming general election the people would have a choice, 'a government-owned railway or a railway-owned government.'

It did not work. Laurier's Liberals, at the peak of their power, humiliated the Tories in the election of November 1904. They took every seat in Nova Scotia, including Borden's, swept British Columbia, and increased their majority to 64. Borden talked of resigning. But the attractions of public life had begun to grow on him: he enjoyed the recognition a party leader received and the continual association with men of affairs that political life demanded. His confidence in his performance as leader had grown and his job was unfinished. 'For a long time I more than hesitated' about staying on, he would tell his friend John Stephen Willison. But just before Christmas 1904 he decided to remain as party leader. 'I have put all the hesitation and doubt behind me and I shall endeavour to do my full duty.' A vacancy was hastily found in Carleton constituency in Ontario and Laurier graciously arranged that Borden be acclaimed on 4 Feb. 1905.

Shortly after his election it was clear that Borden's commitment to national politics was complete: he told Laura on 9 February that he was house hunting in Ottawa. The couple moved into their new home, Glensmere, on Wurtemburg Street and backing onto the Rideau River, in the summer of 1906. Borden spent much of his second term as leader developing a new platform for his party. A scheme to hold a policy

In 1906 Robert L. and Laura Borden moved into their new house in Ottawa, Glensmere, shown here in the 1920s.

convention was mooted and then shelved when Quebec Conservatives declined to attend. He turned for advice to the Conservative provincial premiers, Richard McBride in British Columbia, Rodmond Palen Roblin in Manitoba, and James Pliny Whitney in Ontario, to some of the new members of his caucus who shared his views, and to businessmen such as Joseph Wesley Flavelle and Sir Thomas George Shaughnessy. He announced his Halifax Platform – in his words, 'the most advanced and progressive policy ever put forward in Federal affairs' – in his home city on 20 Aug. 1907. It called, among other things, for reform of the Senate and the civil service, a more selective immigration policy, free rural mail delivery, and government regulation of telegraphs, telephones, and railways and eventually national ownership of telegraphs and telephones. The proposals received a cool reception from his parliamentary colleagues who had not been consulted and a mixed public reception among businessmen who were concerned by Borden's unorthodox ideas about state intervention in business affairs. Though he spent more than a year promoting the platform in speeches across the nation, the effort was not enough to prevent another victory by the Liberals in October 1908.

Borden had now lost two general elections and his party four in a row. But in 1908 the Conservatives gained 14 seats, reducing Laurier's majority to 50. Borden was more determined than ever to carry on. Many of his parliamentary colleagues had other ideas. They resented having been ignored in the planning of the Halifax Platform. They feared his ideas for developing party structures that would lessen their influence. And he had now led them to another painful defeat. They carried their discontent into the new parliament, a parliament soon dominated by two issues that challenged Canadians' views of their relationship with the United Kingdom and the United States and that triggered successive revolts against Borden's leadership within his caucus. The struggle appeared to be over Borden's determination to break the MPs' dominance of party affairs by holding a national convention and establishing a counterweight of democratically controlled local organizations. But what sparked the revolts was Borden's stand on the naval question in 1909–10 and on reciprocity with the United States in 1911.

In February 1909 the Conservatives placed upon the order paper of the House of Commons notice of a resolution recommending that Canada provide for its own coastal defence, something Laurier had promised in 1902 but never acted upon. Early in March, before the resolution could be debated, a short-lived crisis in Great Britain over the relative strengths of the imperial and German navies shocked and surprised both parties. In English-speaking Canada public figures and many of the large urban dailies demanded a Canadian contribution to the sudden apparent shortfall in British Dreadnoughts. Neither Laurier nor Borden was sympathetic to this clamour. Laurier proposed an amendment to the Conservative resolution, recommending that the house approve any necessary expenditure designed to promote the organization of a Canadian naval service which would work in close cooperation with the imperial navy. It was quickly accepted by the Conservatives and the revised resolution passed unanimously at the end of March. By then, however, the demand for a contribution of Dreadnoughts had been embraced by Borden's three strongest allies, premiers McBride, Roblin, and Whitney.

In January 1910 Laurier introduced a bill to create a Canadian naval service, with ships stationed on both the Atlantic and the Pacific coasts. If required, they could be put at the service of the imperial navy in time of war. The Conservatives were deeply divided. Monk, whom Borden had reappointed as his Quebec lieutenant a year earlier, was demanding a plebiscite on the issue. Borden continued to support the concept of a Canadian naval service – though not necessarily the one proposed by the Liberals – but now also favoured immediate aid. Many other Tory members wanted a simple, outright contribution to the imperial navy. Before the session was over Laurier's proposal would be carried by his party's large majority and soon become law. In early April the *Toronto Daily Star* broke the story of seething discontent in the Tory caucus, claiming as many as seven different factions at war with each other. That was not true but there were three groups, the French Canadians and two small cliques of English Canadians, who were challenging Borden's authority and calling for McBride to abandon Victoria and rescue the national party in Ottawa. Borden responded by handing his resignation as party leader to the chief whip on 6 April. He had no intention of leaving. Instead, he was challenging his caucus. He addressed it for an hour on the 12th and left knowing that his allies would beat back the revolt. Shortly after noon a motion reaffirming support for him was passed by all.

In November 1910, responding to an invitation from the United States, Laurier sent his ministers of finance and customs to Washington to discuss a new Canadian–American trade arrangement. After another session there in January, the finance minister, William Fielding, announced the agreement in the house on the 26th. It was staggering in its breadth. The two nations undertook to eliminate customs duties on a long list of natural products. Then there was another long list of reduced duties on many manufactured goods. The arrangement concluded with two further lists, one Canadian and one American, of lower duties on yet more processed products of the other nation. To avoid the possibility of the agreement being defeated in the United States Senate if it was styled a treaty, it had been decided to bring it into effect by reciprocal legislation. The Conservatives, to a man, were stunned. There had never been such a challenge to their National Policy; there had never been a proposal so calculated to win the support of the vast majority of Canada's farmers, fishermen, lumbermen, and industrial workers. Laurier's party, though old, tired, and slipping badly in its organizational prowess, seemed assured of another sweeping victory; Borden's men faced a fifth deeply humiliating defeat.

It was the Tory premiers who initially rallied the troops. For them the issue was not a cheaper cost of living for ordinary Canadians, it was a betrayal by Laurier of Canada's cherished ties to the empire. Robert Rogers, Roblin's minister of public works in Winnipeg, told Borden the reciprocity agreement was a 'departure from Imperialism to continentalism.' Then the manufacturers, who had prospered under the protection of National Policy tariffs sustained by both Conservative and Liberal governments since 1879, took up the cause. The Canadian Manufacturers' Association quickly developed a shadowy subordinate, the Canadian Home Market Association, to carry on a propaganda war against reciprocity. Soon important business spokesmen who had long supported Laurier's party, Zebulon Aiton Lash and Lloyd Harris, joined Clifford Sifton, a former minister in the Liberal cabinet, and John Willison, the Conservative editor of the Toronto *News*, to propose an alliance with Borden's party. Their delegation met him on 1 March, anticipating that the reciprocity issue would force a new election. What would Borden do if he won? They asked that he consult their spokesmen before appointing his cabinet and that its membership include 'men of outstanding national reputation and influence' who would appeal to the 'progressive elements' of the electorate. In short, they wanted representation of the anti-reciprocity Liberals in his cabinet. Borden quickly agreed and a curious coalition against the trade agreement began to emerge under his leadership.

A large majority of his caucus, led by its more recent members from the business class such as Herbert Brown Ames, George Halsey Perley, and Albert Edward Kemp, supported Borden's developing strategy. But a group of veteran Tories, including Monk and his friends, were appalled by Borden's pact with Sifton and the anti-reciprocity Liberals and denounced it in a stormy March caucus. Borden again threatened to resign, triggering a petition asking him to carry on. Sixty-five members signed; twenty did not. For a second time in a year opposition in his caucus had been crushed just as the prospects for eventual electoral victory looked better than they had in 15 years. In the House of Commons the party obstructed progress on the reciprocity bill. After a two-month adjournment to allow Laurier to attend an imperial conference, the Liberals lost control of the commons, abandoned their bill, and dissolved the house on 29 July. Borden and his coalition allies campaigned across English-speaking Canada on the slogan 'Canadianism or Continentalism.' Their appearances in Quebec, Laurier's fortress, were few. In a tacit understanding the fight there was left to Monk, his Nationaliste friend Henri Bourassa (a roommate of Borden years before), and Monk's parliamentary colleagues. For them the issue was not reciprocity, it was Laurier: Laurier and his Naval Service Act, Laurier and his capitulations to English Canadian interests through the years, Laurier and his alleged corrupt dominance of politics in Quebec.

The strategy worked brilliantly. On 21 Sept. 1911 the Conservatives took all seven seats in British Columbia, eight of ten in Manitoba, and seventy-three of eighty-six in Ontario. In Quebec their representation jumped from eleven to twenty-seven. Borden's Tories had won 134 seats in the House of Commons; Laurier's Liberals were returned in 87 constituencies. Borden was the new prime minister of Canada.

Borden's cabinet mirrored the groups that had won the election under the Conservative banner. All the Conservative premiers, McBride, Roblin, Whitney, and John Douglas Hazen of New Brunswick, were offered places but only Hazen accepted, becoming minister of marine and fisheries and minister of the naval service. The other three chose to have their interests protected by surrogates. Martin Burrell, an MP and a friend of McBride, became minister of agriculture; Robert Rogers from Manitoba accepted the Department of the Interior; and Francis Cochrane from Ontario took Railways and Canals. William Thomas White, a talented young financier and vice-president of the National Trust Company, was the nominee of the anti-reciprocity Liberal interests. Though he had no political experience, he was appointed minister of finance and quickly became a close friend and trusted colleague of Borden. There was no shortage of veteran Tories waiting to be called. George Foster, deeply hurt that he did not get Finance, took Trade and Commerce. Sam Hughes unblushingly wrote to Borden celebrating his credentials – 'I get the name of bringing success and good luck to a cause' – and was rewarded with the patronage-rich Department of Militia and Defence. John Dowsley (Doc) Reid, who had been a leader in the caucus revolts against Borden, was named minister of customs. From Quebec, Monk represented the Nationaliste forces as minister of public works and Louis-Philippe Pelletier and Wilfrid-Bruno Nantel were selected from the more traditional Bleu wing of Conservative support. English Quebec was recognized by Charles Joseph Doherty's appointment as minister of justice.

The new government began with high hopes for a mildly progressive legislative program. From the Halifax Platform, Borden promised further reform of the civil service – Laurier had begun the process with the establishment of the Civil Service Commission in 1908 – but sidestepped the more controversial ideas of government regulation or public owner-ship of national franchises such as the telegraph and telephone systems. The farmers, who were the principal victims of the defeat of reciprocity, needed attention. The Canada Grain Act of 1912 established a board of grain commissioners to supervise grain inspection and regulate the grain trade, and enabled the federal government to build or acquire and operate terminal elevators at key points in the grain marketing and export system. By 1916 the government would have elevators in operation at Port Arthur (Thunder Bay), Ont., Moose Jaw, Sask., Calgary, Saskatoon, and Vancouver. A second measure provided financial support to the provinces for the purpose of encouraging agriculture. Another proposal had the backing of many manufacturers and businessmen. The government introduced a bill in 1912 to establish a tariff commission, an innovation that had been mooted in the Halifax Platform; it was to apply 'scientific principles' to management of the tariff, which accounted for more than 80 percent of the government's revenue, and remove it from partisan influences. Yet another measure that year called for financial assistance to the provinces to build or improve provincial highways and begin the construction of a national highway system. All of these initiatives seemed promising and a distinct departure from the Laurier era. Then, on 18 March 1912, Borden announced that he was halting the Liberals' naval program and preparing a permanent program of his own. It was a major tactical error, enraging the opposition and leaving Canada's naval service in limbo. The Liberals, who had a huge majority in the Senate, retaliated. Borden's tariff commission was rejected in 1912 and his highways bill in 1912 and again in 1913.

The same day that Borden suspended the naval plan Winston Churchill, Britain's first lord of the Admiralty, announced a new construction program for the Royal Navy to counter a growing threat from Germany. Once again the contribution-minded Tories in English-speaking Canada demanded action, and Borden, Hazen, Doherty, and Pelletier soon left for consultations in London; Monk refused to go. In the fall of 1912 Borden told his colleagues that his permanent naval plan was postponed and he was going to make a contribution of Dreadnoughts. The debate among them dragged on for some weeks, with Monk again insisting that there must first be a plebiscite. On 18 October, realizing his position was hopeless, he resigned from cabinet. On 5 December Borden introduced his Naval Aid Bill, which was to provide $35 million for the construction of three Dreadnoughts to be placed 'at the disposal of His Majesty the King for the common defence of the Empire.' Borden expected something significant in return. He was convinced that support for the imperial cause had to be recognized by Canada having a voice in the determination of imperial foreign policy. Following his conversations in London he believed he had received that concession and announced to the house that 'no important step in foreign policy would be undertaken without consultation with … a representative of Canada.'

The debate in the house also went on for weeks, becoming ever more acrimonious. After an all-night session in March, Borden recorded, 'Our men angry at end and both sides wanted a physical conflict. Primeval passions.' Then, on 9 April, for the first time in the Canadian parliament, the government introduced closure and a month later the bill passed. But the 'gagged' opponents had their revenge. The Senate rejected the Naval Aid Bill at the end of May. Canada's naval service was in suspension, its emergency contribution to the Royal Navy dead. The impasse would continue in June 1914, when the Senate rejected a bill, unanimously passed in the commons, to increase its numbers so as to give adequate representation to the western provinces. With partisan bitterness at a peak and good portions of its legislative program crippled, the Tories called out the battalions for a snap general election. Borden had one plank to put to the people: a pledge to amend the constitution and have an elected Senate. However, the weakness of the party in Quebec and in Manitoba, where Roblin won only the barest of majorities in July, combined with the illness of Whitney in Ontario, caused him to draw back.

On 22 June 1914 the king had awarded Borden the GCMG. Late in July, he and Laura escaped Ottawa's summer heat for a vacation in Muskoka. It was short-lived. On Friday morning, 31 July, Borden was on a train rushing for Toronto. The next day he was in his Ottawa office and on Tuesday evening, 4 Aug. 1914, at 8:55 a cable from London arrived during an emergency cabinet meeting. Canada was at war.

The war was greeted with enthusiasm. Prominent men of affairs competed for recognition of their contributions to the war effort. Robert Rogers guaranteed to support the dependants of members of the Fort Garry Horse who joined up. Clifford Sifton donated a battery of armoured cars, and Andrew Hamilton Gault raised a battalion of ex-soldiers, the Princess Patricia's Canadian Light Infantry, that were the first Canadian troops to land in France. The Imperial Order Daughters of the Empire solicited funds for a hospital ship. And Sir Richard McBride surprised both the Admiralty and Ottawa when he used provincial funds to purchase two submarines being built for the Chilean navy in Seattle and had his operatives slip them over the border just as the United States neutrality laws were coming into effect.

In Ottawa, the government was unprepared for war. So was the nation. The only member of cabinet with any military experience, and it was chequered, was Sam Hughes. Key departments of the public service, Finance, Justice, Trade and Commerce, and Labour each had fewer than one hundred employees as late as March 1915. Small arms – the Ross rifle – were manufactured in Canada but there was no capacity, or manpower, to produce heavy armaments. A much-touted war book, quickly implemented, barely hinted at what a government at war needed to do. But by Sunday, 9 August, the basic orders in council had been proclaimed, and a war session of parliament opened just two weeks after the conflict began. Legislation was quickly passed to secure the nation's financial institutions and raise tariff duties on some high-demand consumer items. The War Measures Bill, giving the government extraordinary powers of coercion over Canadians, was rushed through three readings. Finally, the Canadian Patriotic Fund was set up to assume responsibility for assistance to the families of soldiers. With complete support from Laurier and his party, the government's war legislation was in place in just five days.

The centrepiece of the effort was recruiting the force that Canada would send to the front. Hughes abandoned a mobilization plan that had been drawn up by the chief of the general staff, Colonel Willoughby Garnons Gwatkin, and turned recruiting over to the more than 200 local militia commanders. Chaos reigned while Hughes went on to contract businessman William Price to build a training site from scratch at Valcartier, near Quebec City. In less than three weeks the camp had been established and thousands of troops had arrived. A division had been offered as Canada's contribution; many more men were at Valcartier and, while Hughes strutted and dithered, Borden decided late in September to send them all to England. The men were not trained and would spend months on Salisbury Plain in winter learning the rudiments of warfare. The fear in the government, and the country, was that the Canadians would not get to the front in time: it was widely anticipated that the war would be over by Christmas. On 18 Dec. 1914 Borden told the Halifax Canadian Club that 'there has not been, there will not be, compulsion or conscription.'

The eagerly awaited 'decisive battle' that would crush the Germans never happened. Almost immediately the Western Front settled into years of ghastly skirmishes and inconclusive trench warfare. In April 1915, when the 1st Division fought its first major battle, at second Ypres, Canadians became acquainted with the growing casualty lists that appeared in urban dailies and rural weeklies from Nova Scotia to British

Columbia. Recruiting for a second division had begun as the first was crossing the Atlantic. The authorized force level of the Canadian army rose again and again: 150,000 in July 1915; 250,000 in October 1915; and finally 500,000 in January 1916. Throughout, Hughes left the responsibility decentralized in the local units and military districts: his department remained on the sidelines. The recruits, very largely from Canada's towns and cities, came by the thousands – until mid 1916. By then the war effort in factory and field was running at full capacity and labour shortages were appearing on production lines and farmsteads alike. By then, too, the reality of a war of attrition had been grasped. Potential recruits had a choice not open to many in 1914 and early 1915 when unemployment had reached serious levels: there was a very dangerous job available at $1.10 a day in France and another at unprecedented wages in the home-front war economy. By July 1916 the seemingly endless flow of recruits had become a mere trickle: 8,389 men. In April and May 1917, especially in the aftermath of Vimy Ridge, just over 11,000 men enlisted. The days of volunteerism were over.

The government's approach to the war effort at home paralleled the volunteerism of military recruiting. Worried that an already troubled economy might collapse because of 'uncertain conditions,' Borden and White had opted for 'business as usual.' In 1915 White rejected calls for direct taxation. It would cost too much to implement, he said, and would intrude upon a tax field traditionally used by the provinces. After the London market closed at the end of 1914, White, reluctantly and complaining about the high rates charged, turned to New York for bond issues in 1915, 1916, and 1917. He did not believe that the Canadian market was big enough to sell major issues. But a very tentative offering of $50 million in 1915, spurred by the escalating costs of the war, was doubly subscribed. Much larger issues in 1916 and 1917 were equally successful and a Victory Loan of $300 million in 1918 brought in $660 million. In the manufacturing sector Sam Hughes's hastily appointed Shell Committee vied for munitions orders from the Allied governments. The Canadian government's contracts for the many needs of its soldiers were dispersed by Militia and Defence and other departments in the partisan ways that had been practised for decades. Then minor scandals in early 1915 persuaded Borden to set up the War Purchasing Commission under Edward Kemp, now minister without portfolio. It took over the contracting for Canada's military expenditures and for all British and Allied orders for war supplies except munitions. Scandals also struck the Shell Committee, and in November 1915 it was shut down and replaced, as contractor for munitions, by the Imperial Munitions Board under the leadership of Joseph Flavelle.

These were the first manifestations of change. Others followed as war production in the factories and on the farms of Canada began to grow. In response to an urgent need for foodstuffs in Europe, Borden's government commandeered the 1915 wheat crop. In 1917 skyrocketing prices led to the establishment of the Board of Grain Supervisors of Canada under Robert Magill, which took marketing of the crops of 1917 and 1918 away from the private grain companies. It was succeeded by the Canadian Wheat Board with the same mandate for the 1919 crop. Also in 1917, a food controller, William John Hanna, was appointed to regulate the production and distribution of Canada's food supplies and a fuel controller, Charles Alexander Magrath, was given the power to regulate the distribution and price of fuels and the wages of coalminers in Alberta and Nova Scotia. A year earlier, responding to increasing concern about war profiteering by Canada's businesses, Borden and White had reversed themselves on the tax issue and imposed the nation's first direct impost, the business profits war tax. It was politically motivated. So too was the income war tax, grudgingly introduced by White in 1917 as a companion to the Military Service Act, ostensibly to conscript the excesses of the nation's wealth to match the forced enlistment for military service. The rates were deliberately low and affected only a minority of people, and the impact of the two direct taxes on the government's revenue was insignificant. Both, as well, were temporary, intended to end with the end of the war. The profits tax expired in 1920 but was revived in World War II and the income tax would become the federal government's largest permanent source of revenue. In 1916 the deep and long-lasting problems of the new transcontinental railways were temporarily alleviated through government loans; the crisis was finally resolved the following year with the takeover of the Canadian Northern Railway and the initial steps toward nationalization of the Grand Trunk–Grand Trunk Pacific system. The Canadian National Railways, government-owned and operated by an arm's-length board, would incorporate both lines with other government railways. In short, by 1917 precedent and tradition had been abandoned; business as usual had given way to remarkable government intervention in the economy.

Dramatic and unanticipated changes also took place in policy towards military manpower and in imperial relations. Borden made his first wartime visit to Britain and France in 1915. In Paris he visited President Raymond Poincaré and received the grand cross of the Legion of Honour. In London the government of Herbert Henry Asquith was welcoming and cordial but refused to concede any possibility of consultation on war policy. That was true also in 1916 as Borden wrestled with the chaotic administration of military manpower in Canada and Britain under Hughes. Eventually, in the fall of 1916, Hughes, in London, deliberately defied Borden's instructions for management of the overseas forces. Borden stripped him of his responsibilities and, in response to Hughes's bitter reaction, fired him in November. Hughes was replaced in Ottawa by Edward Kemp, and in London a new ministry of overseas military forces was established with George Perley, Canada's acting high commissioner, as its minister.

In December the new British prime minister, David Lloyd George, initiated a revolutionary change in the United Kingdom's relations with its dominions. He desperately needed more fighting men but realized that the time had come to give the dominions and India some say in the direction of the war. 'They are fighting not *for* us,' he was reported as saying, 'but *with* us.' In the spring of 1917 Borden, the leader of the senior dominion, attended the first imperial war cabinet and conference. Between regular visits to Canada's soldiers in military hospitals, Borden participated in war-cabinet discussions of a wide range of matters including possible peace terms. At meetings of the conference he and his brilliant young legal adviser, Loring Cheney Christie, led the passage of Resolution IX, which called for a post-war constitutional conference to 'provide effective arrangements for continuous consultation in all important matters of common Imperial concern, and for such necessary concerted action, founded on consultation, as the several Governments may determine.'

Back in Canada, Borden met his cabinet on 17 May and told them that he was ready to introduce conscription. The pressure to impose compulsory service had been building for more than a year, especially among more well-to-do English Canadians convinced that Quebecers were slackers who refused to do their part. In 1916 the Toronto-based

Bonne Entente movement, organized by John Milton Godfrey and Arthur Hawkes, sought but failed to win Quebecers over to a greater military contribution to the war effort. The more strident Win-the-War movement in 1917 openly agitated for conscription and a coalition government to enforce it. Quebecers were not impressed. They were angered that Borden's government had failed to support their demands for redress of the grievance felt by Franco-Ontarians as a result of the Whitney government's imposition of Regulation 17 on their schools. This 1912 regulation had abolished the use of French as a language of instruction beyond form one (the first two years of instruction). In Ottawa the dispute was particularly heated as resistance to the regulation grew year by year, leading the government of William Howard Hearst to put the Ottawa school board in trusteeship in 1915. In February 1916, nearly five thousand angry French Canadians marched in protest to Borden's office and demanded federal intervention in the dispute. Borden said he would 'see what could be done.' He did nothing, firmly convinced that the dispute was strictly a provincial matter. Then in April his three French Canadian ministers, Pierre-Édouard Blondin, Thomas Chase-Casgrain, and Esioff-Léon Patenaude, pleaded to have the dispute referred to the Privy Council in Britain. He refused, calling their request 'foolish.' In May Liberal MP Ernest Lapointe's resolution in the commons recommending to the Ontario legislature 'the wisdom of making it clear that the privilege of the children of French parentage of being taught in their mother tongue be not interfered with' was soundly defeated with 'loud cheers' by the Tory majority. Ominously, five of Borden's members voted for the resolution and eleven of Laurier's caucus voted with the majority. Borden's view that intervention was unconstitutional was sound, but his insensitivity to French Canadians' concerns and to the pleas of his Quebec colleagues, and his adamant refusal to intervene with the Conservative government in Toronto, all but eroded what limited support his government had in Quebec. The increasingly strident clamour for conscription made matters even worse and sharpened the growing division between French and English in Canada.

For months Borden had resisted the conscription agitation, fearing large-scale unrest if it was imposed. 'That might mean civil war in Quebec,' as he told one of the Bonne Ententists. In May 1917, when cabinet was informed there would be conscription, Blondin and Patenaude warned that it would 'kill them politically and the party [in Quebec] for 25 years.' Borden's participation in the imperial war cabinet and his keen awareness that voluntary recruiting had fallen well behind battlefield casualties had been decisive in changing his mind. Casualties in the spring of 1917 were double the number of new recruits. Being taken into the imperial government's council, participating in discussions of war and peace policy at the centre of the empire, Borden believed, heightened Canada's responsibility to do everything possible to support its soldiers. Even more important was the bond he had established with 'his boys' at the front and in the long rows of hospital beds in England. When he introduced the Military Service Bill on 11 June, he asked a hushed and sombre House of Commons, 'If we do not pass this measure, if we do not provide reinforcements, if we do not keep our plighted faith, with what countenance shall we meet them on their return?'

At that same cabinet meeting in May, Borden announced that he was going to ask Laurier to join him in a coalition government to support conscription. He did so a week later. Laurier hesitated, opposed to compulsion but aware that several of his English-speaking colleagues strongly supported it. Finally, on 6 June, he refused. Several members of Borden's cabinet were vastly relieved. They abhorred the idea of cooperating with the Liberals and believed that they could easily win the forthcoming election on a conscription platform without them. But Borden persisted and worked for months to achieve a coalition of his party with conscriptionist Liberals. Along the way his men rammed through two bills to rig the franchise for the coming election. The Military Voters Act made it possible to manipulate the counting of votes at the front, and the War-time Elections Act, which finally passed in late September, disenfranchised enemy aliens who had come to Canada after 1902 and extended the vote to the immediate female relatives of soldiers. This raw display of partisan determination finally tipped the scales for coalition. Dithering conscriptionist Liberals such as Arthur Lewis Watkins Sifton, Newton Wesley Rowell, and Frank Broadstreet Carvell knew that this was their last chance and quickly signed up. The Union government was announced on Saturday, 13 October. There were seven Liberals in the new cabinet, and one more would be added before the end of the month. Doc Reid, who like dozens in the Tory caucus had thought the coalition would never happen, reportedly quipped that he would 'back Borden against Job in a patience contest.'

The angry debates that accompanied passage of the Military Service Act, the accusations and recriminations in both parties over coalition, were but preludes to the bitterness of the election campaign that began in November. The *Manitoba Free Press* (Winnipeg) declared that 'a vote for Laurier is a vote for the Kaiser.' Sir John Willison's paper, now the *Toronto Daily News*, published a front-page map of Canada: English-speaking Canada was coloured in red, Quebec in black. In Quebec, Albert Sévigny, Borden's minister of inland revenue, was driven from a platform amidst revolver shots and flying stones. After he took refuge in a hotel, the building's windows were smashed and Sévigny had to escape by sneaking out the back door. The campaign of insinuation, intimidation, and violence came to an end on voting day, 17 December. The Unionists won a huge majority of 114 Conservative and 39 Liberal members. Laurier's Liberals won 82 seats, 62 of them in Quebec and only 2 in western Canada. The disgraceful attempts to fix the vote were a price Borden had been willing to pay. So was the fact that both the great national parties had split – the Grits over conscription, the Tories over the necessity of coalition. For Borden the election of 1917 was a confirmation of 'a solemn covenant and a pledge' he, and Canada, had made to the soldiers at the front.

The Union government moved quickly to implement its most important undertakings. Foremost was support for the war effort. The first men called up under the Military Service Act had been required in October to register for service, though in keeping with Borden's promise not to introduce conscription until an election had been held, they were not to be sent for training until January 1918. The continuing process resulted in hundreds of thousands of petitions across Canada for exemptions and Easter-weekend riots in Quebec City in 1918. In due course just under 100,000 single men, aged 20 to 22, would be conscripted. In parliament the War Appropriation Act, for a half-billion dollars, was approved. The enfranchisement of women, partially granted in 1917 as a partisan political ploy, was extended to include all eligible females for the purposes of national elections. A new Civil Service Act quickly passed to start the process of removing the outside service – federal government employees serving beyond the nation's capital – from appointment by patronage. The Dominion Bureau of Statistics was organized to provide the kinds of systematic information about the nation's population, social structure, and economy that had been so deficient during the early years of the war. The government also established daylight saving time. The parliamentary session ended in May with a heated debate, initiated by William Folger Nickle, over the abolition of hereditary titles in Canada. Borden was in agreement: 'They are very unpopular and entirely incompatible with our institutions,' he observed. In fact, a March order in council, then under consideration by the British government, had prescribed not only that hereditary titles be abolished but that, except for military distinctions, honours not be conferred on residents of Canada without the approval or the advice of the Canadian prime minister. Later, in mid July, the government belatedly announced a war labour policy which forbade strikes and lockouts for the duration while assuring employees of the right to organize and guaranteeing female workers equal pay for equal work.

Sir Robert L. Borden decorating members of the Canadian Army Medical Corps in France, 1 July 1918, with Lieutenant-General Sir Arthur W. Currie in the background to the right of the recipient.

In June 1918 Borden and several colleagues had returned to London for the second set of meetings of the imperial war cabinet and conference. He was angry that he had not been consulted before the Canadian Corps had suffered huge losses at Passchendaele and threatened Lloyd George that he would send no more troops to the front if such a situation arose again. More serious still, he had received reports throughout the war critical of the performance of the British high command and of British military planning, reports that reached a peak in his consultations with Lieutenant-General Sir Arthur William Currie, commander of the Canadian Corps. At the second meeting of the war cabinet Borden gave an impassioned speech detailing the faults of the high command. It resulted in appointment of a prime ministers' committee which held intensive hearings with officials and senior commanders about the war effort. Its draft report, completed in mid August, gloomily forecast that the war could go on until at least 1920, perhaps longer. It reinforced the commitment to participation by the dominions in war policy and highlighted the need for the civil authorities to exert control over their military commanders. But the report was outdated before it was discussed. Allied forces, spearheaded by Canadian and Australian troops, had attacked at Amiens, launching the final offensive that carried on as Borden returned to Canada.

On 27 October Lloyd George summoned him back to Britain to prepare for possible peace talks. Two days later Borden replied that 'the press and the people of this country take it for granted that Canada will be represented at the Peace Conference.' Lloyd George was sympathetic but predicted 'difficult problems.' When Borden arrived in London, the British prime minister proposed that Borden, as the leader of the senior dominion, represent all the dominions at any conference that took place. Borden refused. In December it was agreed that dominion and Indian representatives would be present when questions directly relating to their interests were at stake and that one of the five members of the British delegation at the peace talks would always be from the dominions or India. A month later, after the conference had assembled at Paris, Lloyd George persuaded American president Woodrow Wilson and French premier Georges Clemenceau that Canada, Australia, South Africa, and India would have two delegates and New Zealand one at its plenary meetings. Borden recognized that these were more matters of form than substance and that representation was 'largely a question of sentiment.' But, he told Laura, 'Canada got nothing out of the war except recognition.' It was a point worth pressing to its logical conclusion: formal acknowledgement of Canada's international status. On 6 May 1919, as discussions on the membership of the League of Nations were drawing to a close, a memorandum by Borden argued that Canada, as a member, should have the right to be elected to the League's council. Lloyd George, Wilson, and Clemenceau agreed and added that Canada should also be eligible for election to the governing body of the International Labour Organization. Five days later he was on his way home. It was Charles J. Doherty and Arthur L. Sifton who signed the Treaty of Versailles on Canada's behalf.

His colleagues in Ottawa were in trouble. The Liberal and Conservative Unionists were squabbling over White's 1919 budget and arguing over how to deal with the Winnipeg General Strike. The strikers were put down with force on 'Bloody Saturday,' 21 June. When White's budget had come to a vote two days earlier, 12 Liberal Unionists joined the opposition. Then White, exhausted by the incessant demands of the war, resigned on 1 August. The next day Liberal Unionist Frank Carvell left. His fellow Liberal Thomas Alexander Crerar had quit in June over the budget. Conservatives Doherty, Foster, and Burrell also talked of leaving. Other members of the coalition hoped to transform the Union government into a new political party and looked to Borden to lead them. But the prime minister had also had enough. Since 1914 he had responded to the challenges of leadership with an energy and zest that contrasted with his more detached approach to governing in the pre-war years. His soldiers, his country, and the Allied cause had been worth every ounce of effort he could summon. After seeing his government through ratification of the Treaty of Versailles in a short fall session of parliament, and after making provision for the appointment of a Canadian to deal with Canadian affairs at the British embassy in Washington, he was done. 'At the end,' he recorded, 'I was very tired.'

His doctors advised that he should leave politics immediately. On 16 Dec. 1919 he told his cabinet he was going to resign. Led by Newton Rowell, they pleaded with him the next day to stay in office but take a vacation for a year. Unwisely, he agreed. It did not work. Even on vacation in the south, he was, after all, the leader of the government and could not dismiss the responsibilities of his office. Nor could his colleagues leave him alone. He returned to Ottawa in May and finally announced his retirement to his caucus on Dominion Day, 1920. Caucus then asked him to choose his own successor. It was an unusual request. Both national parties had procedures for changes in leadership. The Tories

Sir Robert L. Borden (right) and Liberal house leader Daniel Duncan McKenzie greet each other on Parliament Hill, Ottawa, 29 Aug. 1919.

were long accustomed to selecting a leader in their caucus. In the Liberal Party Laurier's death in February 1919 had led to the calling of a national convention, which elected William Lyon Mackenzie King as leader. But the Union government was of neither party and of both. It had no procedure and was as dependent on Borden in leaving as it had been upon him when he formed it. Borden asked each member to indicate to him their three choices for leader. He then recommended White, who adamantly refused. In due course Arthur Meighen, deeply troubled that he had not been the first choice, was persuaded by Borden to lead the coalition and assume the prime ministership on 10 July 1920.

Sir Robert Borden lived another 17 years. He and Laura remained at Glensmere, where they entertained friends and he took great pleasure in working in his wildflower garden on the bank of the Rideau. In season the couple regularly played golf. There were frequent dinner parties, evenings of bridge, and, in the twenties, the novelty of radio broadcasts. Laura continued her work with various volunteer associations while Borden read and wrote in his library. Two valuable constitutional studies were published: his 1921 Marfleet lectures at the University of Toronto, *Canadian constitutional studies* (Toronto, 1922), and his 1927 Rhodes lectures at Oxford, *Canada in the Commonwealth: from conflict to cooperation* (Oxford, 1929). In 1928 he began his memoirs, a manuscript that was nearly finished when he died; it would be published in a hefty two volumes by his nephew, Henry Borden, shortly after his death. Henry would also edit and publish a series of Borden's *Letters to limbo* (Toronto, 1971), his reflections on politics, literature, friends, and a host of other subjects which he had written in the 1930s.

Borden was very well off and the couple's life in Ottawa was as comfortable as it was quiet and understated. In 1901, when he had become party leader, he had had a substantial income from his law firm. That continued until 1905 and was the foundation for a broad range of premium securities in his portfolio. In 1922 he had assets of $800,000, a large sum for the time, and an average annual income of about $30,000; all his expenses, including considerable support for family members and annual trips to the south in late winter, were about $17,000. His fee for a 1922 arbitration of a dispute between Britain and Peru supplemented his income as did his acceptance of the presidency of the Crown Life Insurance Company and Barclays Bank (Canada) in 1928. In 1932 he became the chairman of Canada's first mutual fund, the Canadian Investment Fund. 'There is nothing that oppresses me,' he reported to Lloyd George. 'Books, some business avocation, my wild garden, the birds and the flowers, a little golf, and a great deal of life in the open – these together make up the fullness of my days.'

Sir Robert Laird Borden died in early Thursday morning of 10 June 1937. A thousand Great War veterans in mufti lined the procession route from Glensmere to All Saints' Church for a funeral on Saturday afternoon. He was buried in Beechwood Cemetery in Ottawa.

It was fitting that the veterans, all members of the 1st Division, played a prominent role in Borden's funeral. World War I had been his greatest political challenge. In 1896 he had been unprepared when Sir Charles Tupper had asked him to run for parliament. Once he had been elected, Tupper and his son Charles Hibbert had guided and encouraged him as he moved from the back to the front benches of opposition. In 1901 he had been unprepared for party leadership. His career as opposition leader was long and conducted against formidable odds with Sir Wilfrid Laurier at the height of his powers and veteran members of his own caucus frustrating his attempts at party reform and challenging his position. In 1911 he had been unprepared for government leadership, and his first years, as a peacetime prime minister, were marked by controversy with both the Liberal-dominated Senate and his own Nationaliste followers and cabinet colleagues from Quebec. In the middle of 1914 Borden was preparing for an election, not war.

After the initial excitement of August 1914 passed, Borden and his colleagues were worried that Canada's soldiers would not get to the front in time and hurried them to a winter of training on Salisbury Plain. At home his government proceeded with caution and reserve, attempting, as far as possible, to maintain the stance of business as usual. The War Measures Act gave the administration extraordinary powers but it used them sparingly. It tinkered with tariff rates to raise badly needed revenue; it distributed the largesse of hundreds of contracts for war supplies by the tried and true methods of patronage and favouritism; and Borden tried, and failed, to gain access to imperial war planning. What success the government had was in recruiting; young men continued to volunteer in huge numbers throughout most of 1915.

It was clear by 1916 that the war was not going to end any time soon: Canada's soldiers, now two divisions, were bogged down with their Allies in the dirty trenches of the Western Front. Their casualty rates were appalling and the first cries for conscription were heard on the home front. Borden resisted, fearing compulsion would divide the war effort there, which was producing the goods of war, from food to wagons to munitions, at an unprecedented pace. But the first steps away from business as usual had begun. The domestic market for war bonds had been tapped and had surpassed all expectations. The government introduced the first measure of direct taxation at the federal level in Canada's history. It also took the first modest steps toward resolving the long-standing fiscal problems of the new transcontinental railways.

By 1917 the last vestiges of hesitation in Borden's leadership were gone, displaced by a firm and at times stubborn resolve to commit his government and his nation to whatever contributions of men and machines were needed to win the war. In the aftermath of the Canadian victory at Vimy Ridge on Easter Monday 1917, Borden abandoned his promise of no conscription and led the effort to pass the Military Service Act. With his Quebec support nearly exhausted that spring, he sought, and failed, to persuade Sir Wilfrid Laurier to join him in a coalition to enforce con-scription. He persisted, much to the dismay of a sizeable portion of his caucus, and eventually crafted a coalition of Conservatives and Liberal Unionists which crushed the Liberal Party in the bitter election of December 1917. The political cost was enormous: the Conservative Party's support in Quebec was destroyed and would not be recovered for decades to come. Moreover, Unionist support in western Canada was ephemeral and vanished at the first hints of peace.

Compulsion for overseas service was echoed by vigorous use of the powers of the state at home. The nationalization of the transcontinental railways was begun. Borden's government regulated food and fuel dis-tribution and controlled fuel prices and miners' wages. It imposed a 'temporary' direct tax on incomes, both personal and business. It forbade both strikes and lockouts. And, with the support it enjoyed from the Liberal Unionists, it reformed the federal civil service. Compared with the exercise of state power during World War II, the actions of Borden's government in World War I were almost amateurish. In the context of the time, however, they were breathtakingly bold.

Borden's most lasting contribution grew out of his deep commitment to the war effort and his long-standing belief that Canada had the cap-acity and was entitled to control its own external affairs in both peace and war. Dominion autonomy and the transformation of the empire into the new British Commonwealth of Nations was born of the Great War. Lloyd George provided the opportunity. Borden and his legal adviser,

Loring Christie, seized it. Canada's soldiers, Borden believed, had earned it. His duty, his responsibility to them and to Canada, was to achieve it. Recognition of Canada's right to craft its own external policy, to have its own diplomatic representation in foreign capitals, to have full membership in the League of Nations, and to play a leading role in development of the Commonwealth were the rewards of Borden's persistent campaign for equal status. General Jan Christiaan Smuts of South Africa, a strong supporter in London and Paris, told Borden in 1927, 'You were no doubt the main protagonist for Dominion Status.'

Sir Robert Borden had not the magnetism of Laurier, the daring flair of Macdonald. He was an uncommonly reserved person for a national political leader, a man who believed that his often stodgy public persona was the country's business but his private life belonged to his very close friends and family. He was, throughout his political career, less interested in politics than in policy. He was devoted more to his nation than to his party. His determination and commitment to lead Canada through the Great War made him the only Allied leader to stay in office throughout the conflict, an accomplishment of which he was very proud. Lloyd George called him 'a sagacious and helpful counsellor' who was 'always the quintessence of common sense.' Borden would have liked that.

ROBERT CRAIG BROWN

Further reading

R. C. Brown, *Robert Laird Borden: a biography* (2v., Toronto, 1975–80).

R. L. Borden, *Letters to limbo*, ed. Henry Borden (Toronto and Buffalo, N.Y., 1971) and *Robert Laird Borden: his memoirs*, ed. Henry Borden (2v., Toronto, 1938).

John English, *Borden: his life and world* (Toronto, 1977) and *The decline of politics: the Conservatives and the party system, 1901–20* (Toronto, 1977).

ARTHUR MEIGHEN,

teacher, lawyer, politician, businessman, and office holder;
b. 16 June 1874 near Anderson, Ont., second child and eldest son
of Joseph Meighen and Mary Jane Bell; m. 24 June 1904 Jessie
Isabel Cox in Birtle, Man., and they had two sons and a daughter;
d. 5 Aug. 1960 in Toronto and was buried in St Marys, Ont.

Arthur Meighen's paternal grandfather, Gordon, was a Presbyterian Ulsterman who left Londonderry (Northen Ireland) in 1839 for Upper Canada. Five years later he acquired a farm lot in the southwest part of the province, near St Marys, where he became the local schoolmaster. At his death in 1859 his 13-year-old son, Joseph, left school to run the farm. Marriage in 1871 and six children followed in orderly progression. The oldest boy, Arthur, showed more aptitude for book learning than farm work. Accordingly, his parents moved to the outskirts of St Marys so he could attend high school without the expense of boarding. Arthur did his share of chores on the family's dairy farm; at the same time he read voraciously, maintained first-class honours, and took part in the debating activities of the school's Literary Society. His home environment, he later recollected, instilled in him 'the immeasurable value of sound education and the equally limitless and permanent importance of habits of industry and thrift.' Upon graduation in 1892, he enrolled at the University of Toronto, majoring in mathematics. Unlike his more worldly contemporary William Lyon Mackenzie King, Meighen did not cut a broad swath on campus, limiting his scope to his courses, wide reading in English, history, and science, and enthusiastic participation in the mock parliament. In 1896 he received his BA with honours in mathematics; the next year he returned to Toronto to earn teaching qualifications at the Ontario Normal College.

Having obtained an interim specialist's certificate, Meighen was hired in 1897 by the high school board of Caledonia, east of Brantford, to teach mathematics, English, and commercial subjects. The year started well, but by spring he had become embroiled in a bitter dispute with the chairman of the board, who resented his strict discipline of his daughter. Meighen resigned and moved west to Manitoba, where he found work heading the commercial department of the Winnipeg Business College. In the summer of 1899 he applied unsuccessfully for the post of principal at a high school in Lethbridge (Alta). In January 1900 the transplanted Ontarian commenced legal studies and was articled in a Winnipeg firm; by 1902 he was attached to a small law office in Portage la Prairie. On 2 Feb. 1903 he was called to the bar of Manitoba. He set up his own practice in Portage la Prairie, where he handled a mix of business, including wills, estates, real estate transactions, and minor criminal cases. About this time he met Isabel Cox from Granby, Que., who was then a schoolteacher in Birtle, and they married in June 1904. While Meighen built up his practice, he dabbled in the hot real-estate market, joined the Young Men's Conservative Club, and in 1904 was an enthusiastic worker in the unsuccessful campaign of the local Tory MP, Nathaniel Boyd.

In the federal election four years later, Meighen himself carried the Conservative colours in Portage la Prairie. His nomination was uncontested, it being assumed that the Liberal incumbent, John Crawford, was a lock to hold the constituency. Meighen jumped into the campaign with vigour, travelling to the four corners of the riding by wagon or buggy. He proved to be an effective speaker. His opponent anticipated an easy ride on the coat-tails of Prime Minister Sir Wilfrid Laurier. On polling day, 26 Oct. 1908, Meighen won by a narrow margin of 250 votes and he went to Ottawa, where he sat in the backbenches of the opposition led by Robert Laird Borden. He made but two brief speeches in his first session of parliament, though they did catch Borden's attention, and scarcely more in 1910. His one significant oration that year, in connection with a proposed railway investigation, even earned the praise of Laurier, who remarked to a colleague, 'Borden has found a man at last.' In 1911 Meighen burnished his credentials as a progressive prairie Conservative with speeches advocating a reduction in tariffs on farm implements and stricter limits on business trusts. He took no part in the Conservatives' obstruction in 1911 of Laurier's reciprocity bill, but he campaigned hard for his party's traditional National Policy of protection in the general election in September. Nationally, Borden led his Conservative forces to victory; in Portage la Prairie, Meighen upped his winning margin to 675 votes.

He was not, nor did he expect to be, appointed to the new cabinet as a representative of Manitoba. Dr William James Roche, the MP for Marquette since 1896, and Robert Rogers, the master of the province's Conservative machine and a member of Premier Rodmond Palen Roblin's cabinet, stood ahead of him, and both became ministers. Meighen's growing command of parliamentary procedure soon found an outlet, however. When the Liberals held up the government's Naval Aid Bill, Borden turned to his young Manitoba protégé to find a way out. Meighen urged the adoption of a form of closure that was already operating in the British parliament, and suggested an ingenious ploy by which the rule could be implemented in the Canadian House of Commons without sparking an even more protracted debate. Borden introduced the motion for closure on 9 April 1913; although the enraged Liberals fought it tooth and nail, their efforts were in vain. Closure was passed after two weeks of heated debate, followed three weeks later by the bill (which was defeated in the Senate). Meighen's role behind the scenes soon became known, for it was he who explained the procedural details in the commons. Opposition MPs mockingly saluted him as the 'Arthur' of the rule. Borden too was impressed. On 26 June Meighen was sworn in to the vacant position of solicitor general, which was then not part of cabinet.

While still a backbencher Meighen had acquired a reputation as a progressive Conservative. Just prior to his appointment, he, Richard Bedford Bennett, William Folger Nickle, and others had voted against amendments to the Bank Act that they considered harmful to prairie farmers. In his new post, Meighen found himself defending the govern-ment from his erstwhile maverick allies. Borden assigned him the task of negotiating a financial arrangement with the Canadian Northern Railway, which was teetering on the edge of bankruptcy and threatening to bring down several provincial governments and a major chartered bank with it. After several weeks of investigation and hard bargaining, Meighen and his small team of government officials presented the cabinet with a proposal: a $45 million government guarantee of Canadian Northern bonds in return for a mortgage and a significant share of common stock. The cabinet was pleased, and Meighen was asked to pilot the resulting bill through the commons. Here, in May 1914, he encountered his fiercest opposition from his fellow western Tory, Bennett, who branded him 'the gram[o]phone' of Sir William Mackenzie and Sir Donald Mann, the entrepreneurs who had created the Canadian Northern. The bill nonetheless became law, and Meighen continued to impress Borden as a troubleshooter. On 2 Oct. 1915 the prime minister would elevate his solicitor general to cabinet rank.

Canada entered World War I united, in parliament and across the country, but the unity did not last. By 1915 partisan divisions were apparent. Chief among the contentious issues were the conduct of the war, continuing railway deficits, and the lingering question of French-language schooling. In 1912 the Ontario government under Sir James Pliny Whitney had imposed Regulation 17, which severely limited the scope of French as a language of instruction. By 1915 this issue was poisoning federal politics, pitting English against French and draining Quebec support for the war. The government preferred to leave the matter alone – it involved provincial jurisdiction – but in April 1916 three cabinet members from Quebec, Thomas Chase-Casgrain, Esioff-Léon Patenaude, and Pierre-Édouard Blondin, urged Borden to refer it to the King's Privy Council in Britain. No such action was taken. Feelings in Quebec remained strong and influential politicians there may have known of Meighen's role in drafting Borden's refusal. Meanwhile, military casualties in a war of attrition were threatening the viability of Borden's commitment in 1916 that Canada would field half a million men. Meighen favoured a selective draft, and the prime minister came to support conscription after a tour of the Western Front. Meighen was given the job of drafting the Military Service Bill, which Borden introduced in June 1917, and then shepherding it through parliament. He performed brilliantly, even clashing with the revered Laurier. 'We must not be afraid to lead,' the Manitoba MP declared. Victory in the commons blinded him to Patenaude's prediction that conscription would 'kill ... the party for 25 years' in Quebec.

The government's solution to the crisis over railway finance was, first, to appoint a commission of inquiry and, second, to use its ambiguous report as justification for nationalizing the Canadian Northern. The Liberals, who opposed the nationalization bill strenuously, charged the Conservatives with compensating shareholders for worthless stock, as a political payoff. Sir William Thomas White, the finance minister, led the government forces in the debate, but Meighen was prominent in fending off opposition charges of cronyism and corruption. The solicitor general took the lead in navigating an even more controversial bill through the commons in September 1917. The War-time Elections Bill was a highly partisan measure, branded a cynical gerrymander by the Liberals and defended as a noble act of patriotism by the Conservatives. This measure disenfranchised citizens of enemy alien birth who had been naturalized since 1902; at the same time it enfranchised the immediate female relatives – wives, widows, mothers, sisters, and daughters – of Canadian servicemen overseas. At one stroke, thousands of probable Liberal voters were removed from the rolls and replaced by women likely to vote Conservative. 'War service should be the basis of war franchise,' Meighen declared in parliament. It was not the principle of the partial franchise for women but rather the reality of votes for the government that motivated him. He would take no part in the Borden government's extension of voting rights to all females in 1918.

Borden led a Conservative government committed to a maximum war effort, but also a party whose electoral fortunes appeared grim, based on the results of recent provincial elections. The Military Service Act not only promised a solution to lagging military enlistment, it also split the opposition, with most English-speaking Liberals favouring conscription and francophone Quebecers rallying around Laurier, who stood opposed. Partisan Tories such as Robert Rogers urged a quick election, but Borden feared two things: national disunity and Laurier's campaign magic. All through the summer of 1917, with much tense negotiation, Borden had sought a coalition with pro-conscription Liberals. Meighen was by this time one of his closest confidants. Borden made him secretary of state and minister of mines in August, and Meighen and cabinet colleague John Dowsley Reid worked closely with the prime minister on the make-up of the Union government formed in October. Both Meighen and Reid were firm on Borden continuing as leader. Meighen moved to Interior, traditionally the key western portfolio, but his status was somewhat diminished as a result of the prime minister's inclusion of three prominent western Liberals: Arthur Lewis Watkins Sifton, Thomas Alexander Crerar, and James Alexander Calder. Meighen gained from the exclusion of his Tory rival, Rogers, but he had to share administrative and political influence with immigration minister Calder. The alternative, an anti-conscription Liberal win in the election called for December, would be worse, he decided.

Initially leery of Calder, the master of the Saskatchewan Liberal machine, Meighen was assigned by Borden to work with him to organize the Union government's campaign in the four western provinces. Meighen took charge of Manitoba, Calder had Saskatchewan, and Alberta was left to Sifton. In British Columbia, Calder saw to the organization while Meighen supplied the oratory. The two kicked off the Unionist campaign at Winnipeg on 22 October; they shared the platform with Crerar, whose background as president of the United Grain Growers was used to solidify farm support. Meighen quoted statistics to show that voluntary enlistments had fallen far below the Canadian Expeditionary Force's casualty rate. The three heavyweights reprised their pitch for bipartisan support the next night in Regina. Meighen shared several platforms with the Liberal premier of Manitoba, Tobias Crawford Norris. He barely needed to lift a finger in his own riding of Portage la Prairie, where a farmers' candidate stepped aside so he could easily defeat F. Shirtliff. On election night, Meighen was in Vancouver. 'The conscience of the nation triumphed,' he declared confidently at news of the Union government's victory. He gave little thought to one ominous development: the total absence of Unionist MPs from Quebec, which had voted overwhelmingly Liberal.

Borden decided to focus on two priorities: a full war effort and preparations for post-war demobilization. He had already established, in October, a coordinating committee of cabinet for each area; Meighen sat on the reconstruction and development committee. In May 1918, Borden brought Meighen and Calder with him to England to attend the Imperial War Conference, where matters of demobilization, reconstruction, and immigration were slated for discussion. Even in wartime, there was a full schedule of pomp and circumstance. Meighen found time to meet Canadian troops at the front, and at a meeting of the Royal Geographical Society he proclaimed that 'Canada is British – never more British than now.' His main job in England, however, was to strike a deal with the Grand Trunk Railway, by which its assets would be brought into a national transcontinental system that included the Canadian Northern. No great fan of public ownership, he nonetheless believed there was no alternative. The head of the Grand Trunk, Alfred Waldron Smithers, held out for better terms, but within a year the Grand Trunk Pacific went into receivership. Meighen concluded the final negotiations in Ottawa in October 1919 and then piloted the Grand Trunk Railway acquisition bill through parliament.

Following the Allied victory in Europe, the government had turned its attention to the demobilization of half a million Canadian troops. Meighen oversaw one of the government's main initiatives: a program to assist financially those veterans who wished to become farmers. This measure received all-party support, but another of Meighen's high-profile actions did not. When a labour dispute in Winnipeg in May 1919 escalated to a general strike involving more than 30,000 workers, including sympathetic postal employees, Meighen and labour minister Gideon Decker Robertson were dispatched to the west. Their immediate objective was to restart the postal system. On 25 May an ultimatum was issued to the sympathy strikers: return to work or lose your jobs. The majority of postal workers rejected the ultimatum though, with the hiring of new workers, deliveries soon resumed. Meighen held no brief for the strikers, most of whom he considered 'revolutionists' intent on overthrowing duly constituted authority. He approved the arrest of the strike leaders, and urged that any foreign-born among them be summarily deported. Shortly after the strike ended, he brought forth amendments to the Criminal Code, collectively known as section 98, to ban association with organizations deemed seditious. This section effectively inverted the normal presumption of innocence. Meighen was unrepentant; for him, preserving 'the foundation of law and order' took precedence.

The government's aggressive stance at Winnipeg earned it the enmity of the more radical union members in Canada, one more addition to the growing list of groups with a grudge against it. The list included French Canadians angered over conscription, farmers irked by tariffs, Montreal businessmen alienated by railway nationalization, and citizens disenfranchised by the War-time Elections Act. Meighen was among those in cabinet who favoured a vigorous program of organization and propaganda to firm up a new unionist party that would cement the ties so recently formed between the Liberal and Conservative supporters of the coalition government. Preoccupied with national and international affairs of state, Borden deferred action on party matters until his health gave out. In early July 1920 he announced his intention to resign. Press rumours mentioned Meighen and the wartime minister of finance, Thomas White, as his likeliest successors. The caucus authorized Borden to choose. After input from over 100 MPs, he ascertained that Meighen was the backbenchers' favourite, while White was preferred by the ministers. Borden first approached White, who declined, and then he anointed Meighen. The new government took office on 10 July under the name of the National Liberal and Conservative Party.

As prime minister, Meighen faced a new opposition leader. Laurier had died in 1919 and been replaced at a Liberal convention by Mackenzie King. There were several parallels in the lives and careers of the two leaders. Both had been born in 1874 in southern Ontario and raised in Presbyterian homes. Both were undergraduates at the University of Toronto in the 1890s. Meighen went west and became a lawyer, while King pursued postgraduate studies. Their paths linked up again in 1908, when each was sent to the House of Commons, but whereas Meighen was re-elected in 1911 and 1917 and rose through Conservative and Unionist ranks, King was defeated both times. Having stood by Laurier, his reward was solid Quebec support in the Liberal leadership race. For his role in shaping the Military Service Act and the Union government, Meighen was vilified by Conservatives in Quebec, who had favoured White. On the personal level, the leaders provided a study in contrast. Meighen was a dogged logician and orator who believed in straight talk. His opponent was given to wordy platitudes and endless consultations. Their temperaments clashed, and so did their ambitions.

Meighen's first priority was to pull together a functioning party organization behind his government. The Unionist caucus meeting in July, besides choosing a leader and a name, had also hammered together a platform. Key planks included support for a moderately protective tariff, opposition to class-based or sectional appeals harmful to national unity, and firm support for the British connection, accompanied by full Canadian autonomy. By this time, several prominent Liberal Unionists had retired from the cabinet, but the government continued to rely on the voting support of 25 to 30 Liberal Unionist backbenchers. Meighen's challenge was to build a fighting force out of disparate elements. Such traditional Tories as Robert Rogers openly advocated a return to pre-war party lines, but Meighen refused to drop his new allies. Proud of the Union government's record, he was committed to broadening the base of the old Conservative Party, much as John A. Macdonald had done in 1854 and 1867 and Borden in 1911 and 1917. Accordingly, a national organizer (William John Black) was appointed in August 1920 and a publicity bureau was established. Meighen launched a countrywide speaking tour that summer and fall, accompanied through the western provinces by Calder, the ranking Liberal Unionist. The crowds were large and seemingly receptive. Less encouraging were his efforts to rejuvenate his party in Quebec. Its organization was weak and divided, and he himself was reviled as the architect of conscription.

In the commons Meighen faced not one but two new leaders. In addition to King, there was Thomas Crerar, the former Unionist minister of agriculture, who now headed a recently coalesced grouping of agrarian MPs calling themselves the Progressive Party. This situation made for a highly competitive atmosphere during the 1921 session, though the government was able to sustain its position in key votes by margins of 20 to 30. In the debates over the throne speech and the budget, the Liberals challenged the government's right to continue holding office in the face of by-election defeats, but Meighen held fast. With an eye to the upcoming election, he made moderate but consistent tariff protection his constant theme. Significant legislation included bills to ratify a trade treaty with France and to complete the takeover of the Grand Trunk Railway. The severity of the post-war recession increased public discontent, while paradoxically convincing the government of the need for budgetary retrenchment. In April a royal commission was established to investigate the grain trade, a partial response to farmers' demands for the reinstitution of the post-war wheat board.

At the close of the session in June 1921, Meighen travelled with his wife to attend the Imperial Conference in London. Faced with the problem of reconciling the dominions' growing autonomy with the need for a common imperial foreign policy, the British government had decided to convene a 'Peace Cabinet' meeting for the purposes of informing and consulting the senior colonies. Although defence and constitutional adjustments were discussed, the chief topic proved to be the Anglo-Japanese alliance. For almost 20 years a pact of understanding and assistance had linked the two empires. Westminster, strongly supported by Australia and New Zealand, favoured the retention of the treaty. Meighen feared its renewal would alienate the United States. As early as February 1921, supported by a prescient memorandum from Loring Cheney Christie of the Department of External Affairs, Meighen (its ex officio minister) had recommended to the British government the termination of the alliance, followed by an international conference of Pacific powers. Supported in London by Jan Christiaan Smuts of South Africa, he carried the day. At the ensuing Washington Conference on disarmament, the alliance was replaced by a multilateral agreement.

Despite this success, in August Meighen returned to a deteriorating political situation in Canada. The economy languished in recession. The accumulated resentments of four divisive wartime years had not abated. Voters with a grudge against the intrusive Union government awaited the next general election. A different leader might have evaded responsibility for the Borden record, but Arthur Meighen was not that kind of man. He was proud of the Conservative and Unionist achievements, to many of which he had personally contributed. If the ship of the National Liberal and Conservative Party were to go down, it would be with all guns blazing. Meighen renewed his call for the protectionist National Policy of Macdonald and Borden, and prepared to wage war against his Liberal and Progressive adversaries. 'The one unpardonable sin in politics is lack of courage,' he had written to a supporter in 1920. 'As a Government we are in an impregnable position, in point both of policy and of record, and I do not propose to make apology either by act [or] word.'

To face the electorate, Meighen needed first to reconstruct his cabinet. The government was especially vulnerable in Quebec and the prairies, precisely the areas of the country where promising ministerial recruits were scarce. The resounding western majorities of 1917 had melted away. Some Liberal Unionists had returned to King; others had followed Crerar into the Progressive Party. Arthur Sifton had died and in September 1921 James Calder left the cabinet for the Senate. Meighen did bring in his old backbench sparring partner, R. B. Bennett of Calgary, to be minister of justice, but Saskatchewan was left unrepresented. Prairie weakness in cabinet was mirrored at the constituency level; in many cases there was no organization at all for the government party. If anything, the situation was bleaker in Quebec, where traditional Bleus had had to share the spotlight with the nationalists in 1911, and had vanished in the disastrous conscription election of 1917. Meighen appointed four French Canadians in the reorganization of September 1921 but not one carried any weight with the public. His sincere attempts to recruit E.-L. Patenaude, who had resigned from Borden's cabinet over conscription, were unsuccessful.

By the time Meighen had formally launched his campaign for re-election, with a major speech in London, Ont., on 1 September, political observers were unanimous. The National Liberal and Conservative Party was doomed to ignominious defeat in the contest set for December. Quebec was solidly Liberal and the Progressives were set to sweep the prairies. Ontario promised a three-way fight, with the Progressives bene-fiting from the friendly United Farmers government elected in 1919. Even the coastal regions seemed unpromising. Still, Meighen conceded nothing. For three months he stumped the country, travelling by rail, automobile, and boat to deliver some 250 speeches. He preached tariff protection in the west, defended conscription in Quebec, and championed public ownership of railways in the heart of Montreal, where the press, the Canadian Pacific Railway, and the Bank of Montreal were all bitterly hostile towards him. Although he lacked female candidates – few women ran altogether and only one, Agnes Campbell Macphail, a Progressive, was elected – Meighen appealed to the million-plus female voters, reminding them it was the Union government that had legislated votes for all women. He denounced King's ambiguity on the tariff and railway issues, and attacked the class basis of the Progressives. Hecklers he handled with ease, and everywhere the crowds cheered. Even *L'Action catholique* (Québec), which opposed the government, conceded on 9 November that he was 'a man of intellect and a leader.' The campaign was a personal triumph, but voting day was a disaster.

The National Liberal and Conservative Party was reduced to 50 seats, representing just three provinces (Ontario, New Brunswick, and British Columbia) and the Yukon. Meighen and nine cabinet colleagues were defeated in their own ridings. The Liberals, with 116 MPs, would form the new government, though they fell just short of a parliamentary majority. The Progressives, with 65 members, earned official opposition status but declined the role. Some of them hoped to ally themselves with a reformed Liberal Party; others rejected party government on principle. Meighen moved quickly to position himself to face King's minority government and exploit the ambivalence among the Progressives. While

An official photograph of Arthur
Meighen in the 1920s, stiff
and formal like the man himself.

King deliberated over cabinet selections, Meighen arranged for his return
in January 1922 in Grenville, a safe seat in eastern Ontario. When parliament convened in March, he was seated across from King, ready to do
battle. Knowing that some in his party would blame him for the defeat,
he had called a meeting of MPs, senators, and defeated candidates just
prior to the session. This meeting unanimously endorsed his leadership
and officially reclaimed the traditional party name of Macdonald and
Sir George-Étienne Cartier: Liberal-Conservative. Thus fortified, Meighen
undertook to undermine the new government and its sometime Progressive allies, while reviving his own party's fortunes.

During the session of 1922 he reviewed King's campaign promises,
wondering aloud where the promised tariff reductions were. Meighen
still favoured protection; he simply wished to place Liberal hypocrisy on
the record. The major issue of the year blew up in September, long after
parliament had recessed. A press release from the British government had
invited the dominions to join it in defending the Dardanelles strait

(Çanakkale Boğazi) from possible Turkish attack. The conflict was a left-over from the post-war peace settlement between the Allies and Ottoman Turkey. A new revolutionary government in Turkey had repudiated it and now threatened British troops. King, annoyed at the lack of consultation and alarmed at the potential for national and party disunity, played for time. Parliament would decide, but parliament was not in session. In a speech in Toronto on 22 September, Meighen publicly criticized the government's inaction by quoting Laurier in 1914. 'When Britain's message came,' Meighen thundered, 'then Canada should have said: "Ready, aye ready; we stand by you."' His remarks went over well in Toronto, but poorly in Quebec and the prairies.

The Çanak crisis underscored a serious political dilemma: the incompatibility of some of Meighen's deepest beliefs with the prevailing views of French-speaking Quebecers. On 9 July 1920 Henri Bourassa had condemned the new leader in *Le Devoir* (Montréal): 'Mr. Meighen represents, in person and temperament, in his attitudes and his past declarations, the utmost that Anglo-Saxon jingoism has to offer that is most brutal, most exclusive, most anti-Canadian.' Through 1923 and 1924 there was little reason to think that Quebecers had changed their minds. The encouraging results of provincial elections and federal by-elections indicated clearly that the pendulum was swinging back to Meighen's Tories in Ontario, British Columbia, and the Maritimes, but not in Quebec. The party could not even win a by-election fought on the tariff issue in September 1924 in the once Tory riding of St Antoine, in the heart of protectionist Montreal. The Liberals retained the seat and many, including the influential *Montreal Daily Star* and *Gazette*, blamed Meighen for the debacle.

Undaunted, in parliament and on the public platform the Conservative leader continued to stress tariff protection, which he coupled with the promise of freight rate adjustments to make the package more attractive to Maritime and prairie voters. King, encouraged by a decisive Liberal win in Saskatchewan in 1922 under Charles Avery Dunning, announced a federal election for 29 Oct. 1925. The prime minister asked for a mandate to deal with four issues: the railway deficit, immigration, the tariff question, and Senate reform. Meighen immediately placed King on the defensive by demanding what solutions the Liberals proposed and by reminding voters the government had done little in four years in office. The Progressives, now led by Manitoban Robert Forke, were a much diminished force compared to 1921, and they limited their focus to the prairies. Aided by four newly elected provincial premiers, Meighen struck a solid chord all across English Canada. In Quebec he secretly delegated control of the Conservative effort to a former colleague from pre-conscription days, E.-L. Patenaude, who campaigned at the head of a slate of Quebec Conservatives loyal to the Macdonald–Cartier tradition, but independently of the controversial Meighen. Among those in Patenaude's following was the prominent nationalist Armand La Vergne.

The result was a stunning victory for the Conservatives, just seven seats short of a majority. In Ontario, the Maritimes, and British Columbia, they made a near sweep. Even on the prairies, where Meighen was returned in Portage la Prairie, they picked up ridings in Manitoba and urban Alberta. Quebec was a disappointment – just four anglophone Tory MPs were returned – but Patenaude's presence had doubled the Conservatives' share of the popular vote. When King determined to carry on with Pro-gressive support, despite losing his own seat, Meighen decided on a bold move to win back needed Quebec support. The death of the Liberal MP for Bagot opened a by-election there in December. The Conservative candidate was Guillaume-André Fauteux, one of Meighen's francophone ministers from 1921. To boost his candidacy, Meighen announced a dramatic shift in policy. In the event of a future war, his government would seek electoral endorsement before sending troops overseas. The venue for his speech was not Bagot, but Hamilton, Ont., though he repeated the pledge in person and in French while campaigning for Fauteux. Unfortunately, the gambit was not only insufficient to win Bagot, it also upset a number of imperialist Conservatives, notably Ontario premier George Howard Ferguson.

Meighen nonetheless approached the parliamentary session of 1926 aggressively. The decisive round with his Liberal nemesis was about to begin. King sought to win the support of the Progressive and Labour MPs with policy concessions, but Meighen intended to hold firm to the prin-ciples of Conservatism, confident that the Liberal government would stumble. He was ready to assume office immediately, and bent all his efforts to winning a no-confidence vote in the commons. If a new election was

Shortly before the federal general election, Quebecers are reminded by cartoonist Arthur Lemay in *Le Soleil* (Quebec City), 23 Oct. 1925, that a vote for Conservative Esioff-Léon Patenaude is a vote for Arthur Meighen, the imperialist ready to sacrifice Canadian soldiers.

required, he did not doubt the outcome. Interestingly, both he and King faced whispers of insurrection, with R. B. Bennett, the Tory MP for Calgary West, and Liberal premier C. A. Dunning waiting in the wings. In the first few divisions of the session, the Liberals secured sufficient third-party support to establish their right to retain office. Promises to ease rural credit, investigate Maritime rights, and reform the tariff were secured respectively by legislation, a royal commission, and a tariff advisory board. Finance minister James Alexander Robb presented a prosperity budget with tax cuts and a surplus. However, Progressive support splintered when a special commons committee reported flagrant abuses in the Department of Customs and Excise under Jacques Bureau. A motion on this maladministration by Henry Herbert Stevens in late June 1926 threatened to bring down the government.

To avoid censure, King decided that parliament should be dissolved and an election called. Governor General Lord Byng, the thoroughly honourable soldier who had commanded the Canadian Corps in France, refused his request. A surprised King abruptly resigned, leaving the country without a government. When Byng offered Meighen the chance to form a ministry, he accepted, though not without misgivings. His brief administration (Canada's shortest until the 1980s) would run from 29 June to 25 September. By the rules of the day, MPs who accepted cabinet appointment had to resign their seats and seek re-election. In a session where divisions were routinely decided by a handful of votes, the resignation of a dozen frontbenchers would be self-defeating. As a temporary measure, Meighen decided upon the legal, though unusual, ploy of appointing acting ministers. To become prime minister, however, he could not avoid resigning his own seat. Leadership of the Conservative forces in the commons fell to less skilled hands. The new government survived three key votes, but a motion in July by J. A. Robb, questioning the constitutional validity of Meighen's acting ministry, killed it. Citing dubious constitutional precedents, and alleging British interference, King persuaded a handful of Progressives, who only days earlier had voted to censure his government, to switch their allegiance. The Robb motion carried by a single vote, the decisive margin provided by a Progressive who broke his pairing agreement.

Meighen had no choice but to request a dissolution, and an election was set for 14 Sept. 1926. After one indecisive victory each, the rubber

match between King and Meighen was finally under way. Both entered
the campaign brimming with confidence. King felt sure the country would
rally behind his clarion call to assert Canadian autonomy in the face of
obvious collusion between a British-appointed governor general and the
Tory party. Meighen was just as certain that Canadians would see through
the Liberals' constitutional hue and cry, and punish them for the customs
scandal. This time he would have a respected Quebec lieutenant at his
side. His Hamilton speech may have ruffled imperialist feathers in Ontario,
but it persuaded E.-L. Patenaude to campaign openly as a Meighen Conservative. Meanwhile the Progressives, sensing their ebb, scrambled to
save their seats by arranging saw-offs with the Liberals. King used Robb's
prosperity budget to good effect, and he turned the untimely death of
former Liberal customs minister Georges-Henri Boivin to advantage with
a symbolic pilgrimage to his grave. (Boivin, appointed to clean up the
mess left by Bureau, had come under fire by the opposition.) When the
votes were counted, it was King who emerged victorious. Quebec stood
firm, and the Liberal–Progressive alliance produced victories in two dozen
Ontario and Manitoba seats. Meighen lost his own riding.

And there it was. In the decisive battle, Arthur Meighen had come
second best. He immediately tendered his resignation to the governor
general, agreeing to stay on as prime minister until King had constructed
a cabinet. Without a seat for the second time in five years, he decided to
relinquish the party leadership as well. He summoned a special meeting
in Ottawa of Conservative MPs, senators, and defeated candidates on
11 October. They accepted his resignation, and selected Hugh Guthrie,
a prominent Unionist Liberal who had stayed with the Tories, as their
parliamentary leader for the next year. At the same meeting a committee
was struck to organize a leadership convention; for the venue it settled
on Winnipeg in October 1927. Press speculation centred on Meighen
and Ontario premier Howard Ferguson as the prime contenders, though
each firmly denied any aspiration. When Meighen, from the convention
platform, launched into an eloquent defence of his controversial Hamilton
speech of 1925, Ferguson offered a spirited rebuttal. Most delegates
cheered for Meighen and hooted at Ferguson, but the net result was the
elimination of both from consideration. R. B. Bennett carried the convention on the second ballot.

Now in his early fifties, Meighen launched himself into a new career in the business world. It was not an entirely novel departure: years ago, in Portage la Prairie, he had branched out from law into land speculation and directorships in local companies. The business world intrigued him. Of the many offers that had come his way, he had accepted an invitation in 1926 to become a vice-president and general counsel for Canadian General Securities Limited, a Winnipeg investment brokerage firm that was looking to expand into Toronto. In November 1926 he moved with his wife and daughter to the Ontario capital – their two sons were then at university. The next September they purchased a home at 57 Castle Frank Crescent in the affluent Rosedale neighbourhood. For three years Canadian General Securities prospered, but the stock-market crash of 1929 nearly bankrupted it. Meighen suffered great anxiety, in particular because many modest investors had entrusted their funds to the company out of regard for him. Long hours and prudent management paid off and within two years the worst was over. He began to accept non-political speaking engagements in Toronto and as far away as Washington. He even took on a few legal cases. In June 1931 he was appointed to the Hydro-Electric Power Commission of Ontario on the recommendation of Ferguson's successor as premier, George Stewart Henry.

Life in Toronto for the Meighens differed considerably from their years in Ottawa. Almost from the time he had entered Borden's cabinet in 1915, politics and government had consumed his life. It was his wife, whom he affectionately called Nan in private, and more formally referred to as Mrs Meighen in public, who had largely raised their three children: Theodore Roosevelt O'Neil, Maxwell Charles Gordon, and Lillian Mary Laura. He was a loving but reserved father, given to delivering admonitions, to his sons in particular, on the virtues of thrift, perseverance, and hard work. He had never sought the social or ceremonial frills of public life, so he did not miss them when he left politics. His wife enjoyed social gatherings more than he did, but neither of them was in the least bit pretentious. In Toronto, he insisted on walking to work, a distance of some three miles from Rosedale to his Bay Street office. One advantage of his career change was that he found more time to indulge his lifelong interest in reading, as well as games of bridge and golf with close friends. And once the financial crisis of 1929 was overcome, he began to accumulate a substantial fortune from various astute investments. Meighen had largely missed his children's formative years, but he was determined to provide for them and his future grandchildren whatever material support they might need as they made their own way into responsible adulthood. In the meantime, he was avoiding involvement in partisan politics. That part of his life, it seemed, was over.

Since the convention of 1927, R. B. Bennett had completely ignored him. Meighen was not asked to help in the slightest way during the victorious Conservative campaign of 1930. The obvious snub wounded a proud man. When at last an offer came to head the federal Board of Railway Commissioners, Meighen declined, but he did not refuse Bennett's next proposal: appointment to the Senate and the position of government leader there. Meighen accepted, effective 3 Feb. 1932, on condition that he would be expected in Ottawa only while the Senate was sitting. Though technically a member of cabinet as a minister without portfolio, he did not attend meetings on a regular basis. One of his first responsibilities was to press the Conservative case in the consideration of three Liberal senators implicated in the Beauharnois Scandal. Meighen was at his eloquent best in the climactic debate, though he took little pleasure in the outcome: censure of senators Wilfrid Laurier McDougald and Andrew Haydon. He was more at home in expediting the refinement of complex pieces of legislation. For example, in 1932 he introduced the Canadian National–Canadian Pacific Bill, to facilitate the coordination of the railways' operations, before it moved through the commons.

Meighen was himself the target of conflict-of-interest allegations by Ontario's Liberals, who charged that trust funds he administered had benefited from decisions made by the Hydro-Electric Power Commission, on which he sat. The newly elected government of Mitchell Frederick Hepburn established an inquiry in 1934 to investigate the charges, but its report was inconclusive and the issue died down. The country's attention shifted to Ottawa when Bennett, in a series of five nationwide radio broadcasts early in 1935, denounced the old order and advocated fundamental reforms, a Canadian version of President Franklin Delano Roosevelt's New Deal in the United States. Meighen was not impressed by the prime minister's radical oratory, but as chief lieutenant in the upper house, he loyally shepherded the reform legislation through the Red Chamber. Typically, the Senate would make a series of amendments to each bill, numbering 51 in the case of the Employment and Social Insurance Act. At the end of the session Meighen was satisfied with the result. Later, in the presence of Bennett himself, he would denounce 'not the legislation, which was enlightened, but the [radio] speeches, which frightened.' Despite their parliamentary collaboration, Meighen declined Bennett's request to campaign in the election of 1935. He still remembered the snub of 1930.

As the two Tory titans watched their common foe, King, comfortably take back power, they finally discarded their old animosities. Meighen in the Senate and Bennett in the commons were still Canada's outstanding Conservative parliamentarians. When Bennett decided in March 1938 that his health would not permit him to carry on, he hoped Meighen would be his successor. The latter had no desire to reassume the leadership – it was clear to him that the west and Quebec would not accept him – but he did share Bennett's misgivings about the apparent front runner, Robert James Manion. Though defeated in his riding in 1935, 'Fighting Bob' had parlayed marriage to a French Canadian woman and his congenial personality into a formidable candidacy. Meighen tested the waters for Sidney Earle Smith, president of the University of Manitoba, but there was little interest, even in Winnipeg. When Bennett asked Meighen to give the keynote address to the national party convention in July 1938 and suggested Commonwealth defence as a topic, he readily agreed. With war threatening to break out in Europe, and Canada ill-prepared, it was a subject near to his heart. He delivered another barnburner reminiscent of his Winnipeg address of 1927, except this time Bennett and Ferguson applauded while the Quebec delegates sat on their hands, bitterly opposed to his call for Canadian–British solidarity. The convention confirmed the change of the party's name, from Liberal-Conservative to National Conservative. On the leadership vote, Manion won on the second ballot, but neither Meighen nor Bennett was present to congratulate him.

Although Meighen sought to avoid open conflict with the new leader, he was singularly unimpressed with Manion's performance. Where Meighen would have harassed the Liberals mercilessly for their tepid preparations for war, Manion simply echoed the government's pledge to avoid conscription in any conflict. On the question of railway deficits,

Meighen reversed his long-standing opposition to the amalgamation of the Canadian National Railways and the CPR, and supported a Senate motion that advocated unified management. This volte-face angered Manion, who was publicly opposed to such a step. When the 1940 election campaign began, Meighen stayed out of the fray, as he had in 1935. He was not surprised at the drubbing administered to his party by the Liberals, though he regarded the King ministry with barely concealed contempt. When some Conservatives urged him to leave the Senate and reassume the leadership, however, he declined. Manion, who had lost his own seat, was replaced by Richard Burpee Hanson of New Brunswick, who provided competent if unexciting parliamentary direction. The stiffest opposition criticism still came from Meighen, whose public and Senate speeches deplored government hypocrisy and inaction on preparations for war. 'I cannot agree that we are doing our part,' he thundered in the Senate on 13 Nov. 1940.

Sensing the growing demand that he take the Conservative helm, in 1941 Meighen approached John Bracken, the Liberal-Progressive premier of Manitoba, to see if he could be persuaded to come to Ottawa and take on the job. Though flattered, Bracken remained on the sidelines as the pressure on Meighen mounted. He despised King and despaired of ever seeing the Liberals mobilize a full war effort, but he still resisted the call, feeling himself too old at 68 to accept the challenge. King certainly did not want him back in the commons. Meighen's debating skills and grasp of administrative detail and parliamentary procedure were exceptional. King understandably regarded the possibility of his old foe's return with foreboding, as he revealed in his diary on 6 Nov. 1941: 'I am getting past the time when I can fight in public with a man of Meighen's type who is sarcastic, vitriolic and the meanest type of politician.' At a party meeting in Ottawa that month, Meighen launched another blistering assault on the Liberal government's faltering war effort. Subsequently, the delegates voted by a margin of 37–13 to offer the vacant party leadership to Meighen. Citing the lack of unanimity and noting that the meeting was called for other purposes, he declined the honour. The delegates persisted and, in a subsequent motion, they unanimously requested that he accept. Reluctantly, Meighen agreed and he assumed control on 12 November, but on the condition that the Conservative Party would commit itself to 'compulsory selective service over the whole field of war.' No longer would the party follow public opinion, as it had under Manion and Hanson. With Meighen back at the helm, the Conservatives would attempt to lead it.

Meighen could not forget his own two boys in uniform: Ted was in the Royal Canadian Artillery while Max served in the Royal Canadian Ordnance Corps. 'I never knew what human longing was until separated by war from the sons I love so much,' he had written in March 1941. 'I sit in my office just gazing on the folder with its two photos.' Such fatherly devotion gave a harder edge to his attacks on the Liberals. It was not just that he had warned of impending disaster through the 1930s. Now, his own kin were putting their lives on the line, yet the country was still not on a full war footing. Not surprisingly, he fought the by-election of 9 Feb. 1942 in York South on the issue of compulsory service. Occasioned by his need as party leader to obtain a seat – he had left the Senate on 19 January – the battle took on a decidedly nasty tone. The Co-operative Commonwealth Federation attacked him as yesterday's man and a tool of big financial interests. Officially, the Liberals stayed out of the contest but most of their foot soldiers supported Joseph William Noseworthy, the CCF standard-bearer. King played his part by announcing a national plebiscite on the issue of conscription, thus spiking the Conservative guns. Moreover, the CCF, in an appeal to working-class voters, called not just for a full war effort but for social justice after the war. Meighen met humiliating defeat in a traditional Tory riding.

Meighen's first instinct was to resign but he felt obligated to the party. Rather than contest another by-election, he allowed Hanson to continue as Conservative house leader. The arrangement did not work well. They clashed over tactics and policy. Meighen still believed Canada's lacklustre war effort was the central issue, while Hanson emphasized social and economic reforms. A semi-official policy conference at Port Hope, Ont., in September 1942 developed a platform significantly more progressive in tone than Meighen would have preferred. It advocated the adjustment of farm debt, a national labour relations board, federal aid for low-cost housing, comprehensive social security, and a national contributory system of health care. Meighen was wary of the state providing such a range of social services, but his attention was directed elsewhere. On his initiative, an organizing committee was established that same month to arrange a leadership convention for December in Winnipeg. He worked relentlessly behind the scenes to persuade John Bracken to stand for the leadership, and he used his party contacts to advocate the Manitoba premier as the best choice to succeed him. Both Bracken and the party were reluctant, but Meighen prevailed. The party left Winnipeg with a new name (Progressive Conservative), a new leader (Bracken), and new policies (the Port Hope platform). As for Meighen, he informed the delegates he was retiring for good, leaving his words and deeds as leader 'unrevised and unrepented.'

Inevitably, Bracken's failure to defeat the weary Liberals in the election of 1945 reflected nearly as much on Meighen's judgement as it did on Bracken's modest gifts. Still, the Progressive Conservative Party was alive and would eventually triumph under another westerner, John George Diefenbaker. Meighen took little part in politics after 1945. A collection of his major speeches going back to 1911 was published as *Unrevised and unrepented* … (Toronto, 1949). To his delight it garnered favourable reviews, even from Liberals. A few years later, a recording of one of those speeches, 'The greatest Englishman of history,' was made into a vinyl LP and circulated to every Canadian university and every Ontario high school, courtesy of an anonymous benefactor. This speech, a tribute to William Shakespeare, had been first delivered in 1936. Meighen's speech-making declined with his advancing years, as did his attention to his investment business in Toronto. He continued to enjoy reading, golf, bridge, and lunches at the Albany Club until well into his eighties. After a short illness, he died in his sleep on 5 Aug. 1960. He was given a state funeral in Toronto and then driven slowly across Ontario to St Marys, the town of his childhood years, for burial.

On any list of Canadian prime ministers ranked according to their achievements while in office, Arthur Meighen would not place very high. Taken together, his two stints as first minister total less than half a normal four-year term. In 1920–21 he was preoccupied with post-war reconstruction and a severe economic recession. Although his performance was competent, it was not exciting. Only at the imperial prime ministers' conference did he shine, loyally but effectively prodding Britain to transform the Anglo-Japanese alliance into a multilateral agreement that properly included the United States. In 1926 he had time only to carry out the most necessary administrative functions, while fighting the ultimately decisive campaign against King's Liberals. Therein lay the rub. In three contests between King and Meighen, the Grits won in 1921, the Tories placed first in 1925, but in the winner-take-all third match, he was beaten by his hated rival. This period in Canadian history became the Age of King, not the Age of Meighen. Tellingly, Meighen himself would not have accepted such an assessment as either fair or just. In our dominion, he stated in a farewell tribute to R. B. Bennett in January 1939, 'there are times when no Prime Minister can be true to his trust to the nation he has sworn to serve, save at the temporary sacrifice of the party he is appointed to lead.' In the same speech he took aim at the indecisive ambiguity of their mutual foe, King. 'Loyalty to the ballot box is not necessarily loyalty to the nation,' he pointedly declared. 'Political captains in Canada must have courage to lead rather than servility to follow.'

Arthur Meighen had courage in abundance. His instinct was to confront an issue, an opponent, or a situation. Early in his career, he benefited from this quality. Utilizing his prodigious memory, crystal-clear logic, and gift for oratory, he rose rapidly through the Conservative ranks. Once he was face to face with a master tactician like King, however, his advance faltered. From Meighen's perspective, the Liberal leader did not play fairly. He dodged issues, avoided accountability, and elevated hypocrisy to new heights. What Meighen could not see was that his own early successes as a minister in the Union government of Sir Robert Borden exacted a price on his later career. Before he even assumed prime ministerial office, he had seriously alienated French Canadians by advocating conscription, new Canadians by passing the War-time Elections Act, Montreal businessmen by nationalizing railways, labourers by suppressing the Winnipeg General Strike, and farmers by sticking to the protective tariff. Given his personality, he would not recant any of these policies. They would remain 'unrevised and unrepented.'

The record must also show Meighen's accomplishments, however. As a rising minister in the wartime government, he did much of Borden's heavy lifting, particularly after 1915. As leader of the opposition in the 1920s, he rallied Conservative forces in the House of Commons, held a vacillating Liberal government accountable for a wretched customs scandal, and came close to reclaiming power. During the 1930s he served capably as Conservative leader in the Senate, and his speeches decrying

isolationism helped to rally public opinion away from a dangerous neutralism. Late in his sixties, he heeded a party draft and did what he could
to lead his beloved Conservatives back from oblivion. His final act was
to hand over leadership of a renewed party to a competent, if not mag-
netic, successor. These achievements were not all that he set out to do in
1908, but his performance in politics was certainly well above average.
His most fitting epitaph came from a bitter opponent, the Liberal *Manitoba
Free Press*. Upon his first retirement, in 1926, its legendary editor, John
Wesley Dafoe, lamented Meighen's loss to Canadian public life: 'To fight
his way to the charmed government ranks in six years; ... to attain and
hold against all comers the position of the first swordsman of Parliament
– these are achievements which will survive the disaster of to-day.'

LARRY A. GLASSFORD

Further reading

Roger Graham, *Arthur Meighen: a biography* (3v., Toronto, 1960–65).

Arthur Meighen, *Unrevised and unrepented: debating speeches and others*
(Toronto, 1949).

J. B. Brebner, 'Canada, the Anglo-Japanese alliance and the Washington
conference,' *Political Science Quarterly* (New York), 50 (1935): 45–58.

J. L. Granatstein, 'The York South by-election of February 9, 1942: a
turning point in Canadian politics,' *Canadian Historical Review* (Toronto),
48 (1967): 142–58.

E. [A.] Forsey, *A life on the fringe: the memoirs of Eugene Forsey* (Toronto,
1990).

WILLIAM LYON MACKENZIE KING,

journalist, civil servant, author, labour conciliator, and politician;
b. 17 Dec. 1874 in Berlin (Kitchener), Ont., son of John King
and Isabel Grace Mackenzie; d. unmarried 22 July 1950
at Kingsmere, Que.

William Lyon Mackenzie King had a long political career. He was leader of the Liberal Party for 29 eventful years through the buoyant expansion of the 1920s, the depression of the 1930s, the shock of World War II, and then the post-war reconstruction, and for 21 of these years he was Canada's prime minister. His decisions during this time contributed significantly to the shaping of Canada and to its development as an influential middle power in world affairs. During his lifetime his achievements were sometimes obscured by a style notable for its compromises. After his death his political career was sometimes overshadowed by the revelation of his unsuspected personal idiosyncrasies.

King's father, who had spent time in Berlin as a youth, met his future wife in Toronto when he was a university student there. Isabel Mackenzie, a daughter of William Lyon Mackenzie, was born in the United States while he was in exile, and her early years were marked by poverty and insecurity. Matters did not greatly improve after the family returned to Toronto; Mackenzie lived as a gentleman but never earned enough money to sustain his lifestyle. For Isabel, marriage to John King, who went into law, held out some promise of financial security. King, however, decided to give up his prospects in Toronto and to return to Berlin in 1869 to practise law and it was there that Willie, as he was called, spent his childhood. Willie and his two sisters and a brother had happy memories of their early years. Woodside, the home the family rented from 1886 on the outskirts of Berlin, was an attractive brick house surrounded by a large garden. As a child Willie was healthy and active, with a self-assurance that sometimes got him into trouble and a ready smile, which often minimized his punishments. He was a good student, active in debates and sports, popular among his peers, and trusted by his elders. His family was close-knit and in later years King looked back with nostalgia to memories of family games and hymn singing with his mother at the piano.

These years were less idyllic for his parents, whose serious financial problems would plague them for the rest of their lives. John King was not a success as a lawyer. He lacked the aggressiveness to build up his practice, the conflicts and scandals of one of his uncles (a local news-paperman) negatively affected the family, and the German community in Berlin patronized German-speaking lawyers. His income was not enough to pay for the servants and keep up appearances, and the family was soon in debt. He became withdrawn and Isabel became frustrated and shrewish. A move back to Toronto in 1893, after Willie had started university, changed little. A lectureship at Osgoode Hall brought in some money but John King failed to get a professorship and his practice produced little income. Willie knew nothing of this situation as a child, but he was marked by the experience. He absorbed his parents' social values and came to be embarrassed by their shabby gentility; he learned as well to sense the moods of his parents and to avoid confrontation. More signifi-cantly, his mother gradually came to think of him as the person who might be able to give her the status and security her husband could never provide. It was a burden from which the young Mackenzie King would not be able to escape.

King enrolled at the University of Toronto in 1891, taking the hon-ours program in political science. A disciplined and well-organized student with the advantage of a good memory, he graduated with first-class honours, standing second in his class. He was not an academic grinder, however, and found time for sports, contributed to the *Varsity*, and spent many hours discussing the purpose of life and its moral obligations with other serious-minded students. He stood out among his classmates, was elected president of his class in his first year, and in 1895 was a leader of a student strike to protest the arbitrary dismissal of a popular professor, William Dale. He was still known as Willie to his family but at university he adopted W. L. Mackenzie King as his signature and was called Mackenzie by other students. Though the name suggests a more formal self-image, it also reflects King's closer identification with his grandfather, who even then he saw as an early champion of responsible government and political liberty. In later years a few close friends in England, including John Buchan, called him Rex, but there would be none of this easy familiarity with his colleagues or acquaintances in Canada.

As a young man King was a practising Presbyterian and, indeed, he would attend church regularly throughout his life. His correspondence and diary from his student years refer constantly to spiritual values and his personal dedication to Christian duty. If his religious views seemed sentimental and sometimes self-justifying, they were nonetheless influential. He might have been priggish but his faith also led to good works. In addition to his student activities, he participated in a men's reading club in a working class district in Toronto and he regularly visited patients at the Hospital for Sick Children. He even made a few attempts to reform prostitutes, although on these occasions his Christian motives were likely supplemented by the prurience of a repressed young man. More noteworthy was the influence on him of Arnold Toynbee's work on the Industrial Revolution, which led King to the conclusion that industrialism was the pre-eminent challenge to Christianity at the end of the 19th century. This theory attracted him to social reform but not to socialism. He saw no distinction between his religious faith and a liberal commitment to build a better society on earth, but his emphasis was on conversion, not coercion.

King's sense of Christian obligation was combined with a strong personal ambition. He nonetheless remained undecided about what profession to pursue. His father encouraged him to become a lawyer and after completing his BA at Toronto in 1895, he did take a one-year LLB there. He was not interested in practising law, however. He talked of a possible career in the church or in politics, and between 1895 and 1897 he wrote for a number of Toronto newspapers, but MAs at Toronto and Harvard and fellowships in political economy at the University of Chicago and Harvard seemed more likely to lead to an academic future. After a summer stint as a journalist, writing articles for the Toronto *Globe* on local sweatshops, he began work at Harvard on a doctoral thesis on labour conditions in the clothing industry. This scholastic pattern was interrupted by a telegram in June 1900 from William Mulock, Canada's postmaster general who was also responsible for the newly formed Department of Labour. King had already drawn Mulock's attention to the link between sweatshops and federal contracts for postbags and Mulock now offered him the editorship of the proposed *Labour Gazette*. King yielded to family pressure, to the attractions of financial security, and to what he saw as an opportunity for public service, and he accepted the job. He arrived in Ottawa in late July. The following month Mulock also offered him the position of deputy minister of labour, which he formally took up on 15 September.

He joined the department at a crucial time in the development of industrial relations. In the early years of the 20th century the conflict between labour and capital seemed irrepressible. Trade unions offered some possibility of collective action by workers but employers could frustrate organizers and break strikes by forcing their way across picket lines through the use of injunctions, the police, or the militia. Violence seemed to be the only effective response. King saw the *Labour Gazette* as an important contribution to labour relations. It would publish tables of strikes and lockouts, summaries of court decisions, and regional accounts of working conditions, wage settlements, and costs of living. He knew the importance of earning a reputation for being non-partisan and with the help of his university friend Henry Albert Harper, whom he appointed assistant editor, the *Gazette* soon became a respected reference, though as early as 1901 it came under attack from the Canadian Manufacturers' Association.

King's ambitions did not stop with the *Gazette*. He was soon writing speeches for his minister that associated Mulock and the Liberal government of Sir Wilfrid Laurier with a policy of fair wages for its employees; he also took the initiative to offer his services to employers and workers in the settlement of strikes and lockouts. King quickly showed a remarkable talent for conciliation. Exceptionally patient, he regularly won the confidence of leaders on both sides by listening carefully to their concerns, and he was remarkably sensitive to their unspoken hopes and fears. On many occasions he was able to devise compromises which both sides could accept. One dispute with important consequences was the coal strike in Lethbridge, Alta, in 1906, which threatened to leave westerners vulnerable to the rigours of a prairie winter. Sent west by his new minister, Rodolphe Lemieux, King negotiated a settlement and then went on to draft legislation to establish formal procedures to defuse similar strikes. The Industrial Disputes Investigation Act of 1907 postponed any strikes in a public utility or a mine until a conciliation board had resolved the conflict or, failing that, had published a report on the facts and suggested terms for a settlement. The act did not prohibit a strike but its original feature was to enforce a cooling-off period and to expose the disputants to the pressure of public opinion to encourage a resolution.

King's success in conciliation led the government to call on him to troubleshoot a wide range of problems. He served on royal commissions dealing with industrial conflicts in British Columbia (1903), at Bell Telephone in Toronto (1907), and in the cotton industry in Quebec (1908), and with the problem of compensation to Japanese and Chinese residents arising out of riots in Vancouver (1907–8). He even undertook a quasi-diplomatic mission to London, England, to convey the concerns of American president Theodore Roosevelt and the Canadian government on the issue of Japanese immigration to North America. These were major responsibilities for a civil servant, but King still found it frustrating not to be in a position to make political decisions. Consequently, on 21 Sept. 1908, he resigned as deputy minister to devote his talents to active politics.

He was now 33 years of age. His career in the civil service had been remarkably successful but he had also found time to lead an active social life. In Ottawa he was seen by many, including Governor General Lord Grey, as a man to watch. He was a regular guest at the dinners and balls of Ottawa's elite. He enjoyed the company of women and expected to get married eventually – as a graduate student in Chicago he had proposed to a nurse – but his caution, his obligations to his family, and his reluctance to accept any fetters on his ambition probably account for his avoidance of the commitments of married life. He paid off his father's debts and regularly responded to his mother's appeals for money for clothes or housekeeping expenses. In the Gatineau hills of Quebec, north of Ottawa, he and Bert Harper had long walks, were enchanted by the area around Lac Kingsmere, read uplifting literature, and shared their spiritual concerns. Their friendship ended in December 1901 when Harper died trying to save a young woman from drowning. King wrote a touching memoir, *The secret of heroism*, but he never again gave himself over to a close friendship. Before Harper's death, he had acquired property at Kingsmere and built a small cottage as a refuge from the pressures of Ottawa. More and more, however, his career would overshadow his private life.

In the federal election of October 1908 King presented himself as the Liberal candidate in the riding of Waterloo North, which included Berlin. The riding had been held by a Conservative but King won it by a small margin. On 2 June 1909, soon after the first session of parliament had ended, Laurier appointed him minister of labour. King proceeded cautiously, aware that his senior colleagues saw him as an upstart and were dubious about his progressive views. On the labour front the new minister's intervention in 1910 in the Grand Trunk Railway strike, which led to the blacklisting of workers and the loss of pensions, hurt the government. At the same time, he introduced the Combines Investigation Act of 1910, which established machinery to investigate alleged restraints of trade or price manipulation and authorized fines for those operating contrary to the public interest. He also spoke of the need for a bill for an eight-hour day but his legislative activity was interrupted by the reciprocity agreement and the federal election of September 1911. The government was defeated and, more serious for King, he lost his seat because reciprocity proved to be unpopular among the industrialists and factory workers of Berlin.

King's defeat was a setback but he remained committed to a political career. To earn his living he gave speeches, wrote political articles and pamphlets, and ran the Liberal Party's new central information office in Ottawa, a job that included editing the *Canadian Liberal Monthly*. Then, in 1914, he received an unexpected offer. John Davison Rockefeller Jr had found himself harshly criticized for a bitter miners' strike in Colorado; he knew nothing about it but was blamed because the mine belonged to his family. His response was to ask King to direct a study for the Rockefeller Foundation on industrial relations. When the two men met, they were mutually impressed. King saw a man who was naive about the obligations of employers but who seemed receptive and sincerely committed to reform, while Rockefeller saw a mentor who could guide him through this industrial quagmire. King agreed to conduct the study using the Colorado strike as a test case, and he was given permission to remain politically active in Canada. He first went to Colorado to meet the management and workers and then involved the young industrialist in negotiating a settlement, which resolved the conflicts over wages and working conditions and arranged for the election of workers to grievance committees. This negotiated plan was open to the objection that it

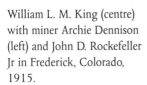

William L. M. King (centre)
with miner Archie Dennison
(left) and John D. Rockefeller
Jr in Frederick, Colorado,
1915.

provided for a 'company union' instead of an independent union that could be less easily intimidated by management. King saw the arrangement as a necessary first step, however, and he received some credit for insisting on inclusion of the miners' right to join a union and the right of organizers to campaign for members.

Published in 1918, *Industry and humanity: a study in the principles underlying industrial reconstruction* (Toronto) was King's report to the Rockefeller Foundation. The book had little impact because its analysis was laboured and abstract; his arguments drew on Toynbee, James Mavor at the University of Toronto, and other theorists. His thesis, however, was a serious attempt to put industrial relations in a broader social context. A reformer but not a radical, King rejected the ideas of an inevitable class struggle. Labour, management, and capital were partners, not rivals, and conflict happened when there were grievances that the other partners did not fully appreciate. Industrial peace could be restored only if the partners recognized they had common interests and if there were structures wherein interests could be explained and understood. King broadened the debate further by arguing that the community was a fourth partner and its interests must also be considered. *Industry and humanity* never adequately clarified how the community's voice could be expressed in negotiations but King's theory could be used to justify government intervention if the community's interests were ignored.

Even if the book attracted minimal attention, it is important for the light it throws on his subsequent success as a politician. In politics, more interest groups were involved and the issues were often more complex, but for King the basic assumption of common good was the same. Leadership did not mean imposing policies or adopting ones because they were popular. It meant a cautious and incremental approach: discussions in cabinet and caucus, which could be heated and protracted, with the leader ensuring that all points of view were presented and that a consensus would be reached.

King could derive some satisfaction from his work for the Rockefeller Foundation, which he left in February 1918, and from subsequent contracts as an industrial consultant in the United States. Back in Canada, however, his political career had not been going well. He had gained the Liberal nomination for York North in Ontario in 1913 but had spent little time in the riding. Then in 1917, in the midst of World War I, Sir Robert Laird Borden, the Conservative prime minister, opted for a policy of conscription for overseas service and proposed a coalition of Conservative and Liberal MPs to form a government to introduce this policy. Many French Canadians saw it as an attempt by the English Canadian majority to force them to fight in a primarily European war. King tried to avoid taking a position but when Laurier insisted on opposing conscription, he accepted the party line. In the federal election of 1917 the newly formed Union government, which included Conservatives and conscriptionist Liberals, won a sweeping majority, with the opposition Liberals taking most of their seats in Quebec. In York North, King once again failed to get elected.

King's private life was also disrupted during these years. He had been an eligible bachelor for many years but his emotions became more and more centred on his family. The family, however, was narrowing. One of his sisters died in 1915, followed by his father the next year. His mother became more demanding, but King idealized her; he thought of her as the only person who appreciated him and believed in his political future. By this time she was an invalid; King installed her in his Ottawa apartment in late 1916 and nursed her through a series of crises. She passed away the day after his defeat in York North, before he could get back to Ottawa. With her death King felt painfully alone. Not surprisingly, he often thought of her and felt her presence. His interest in a world beyond the material world, which had its roots in his Christian faith, was heightened by this loneliness.

Politics soon filled the void. Laurier died in February 1919, shortly after the war and before the Liberal Party had recovered from its split over conscription and crushing electoral defeat. In August, for the first time in Canada, a federal party opted for a leadership convention instead of allowing the caucus to select a new leader. William Stevens Fielding, Laurier's long-serving finance minister, would have been the obvious successor in spite of his 70 years, but he had supported the Unionists and many Liberals, especially French Canadian Liberals, would not forgive this disloyalty. King had the advantage of being young and energetic as well as a recognized expert on the disturbing social and industrial questions of the day. It was a close contest but King's loyalty to Laurier gave him the advantage. On 7 August he had the support of most of the Quebec bloc and enough backing from delegates from other regions to be chosen leader on the third ballot.

King won the leadership at a time when Canadian politics had never been more volatile. The Union government had no future now that the war was over. Arthur Meighen, who succeeded Borden as prime minister in 1920, tried to prepare for the next election by reorganizing the Conservative Party and campaigning on its customary platform of tariff protection. Many Canadians, however, had lost confidence in traditional politics. Wartime inflation and post-war industrial unrest led many workers to look to radical solutions, including socialism, militant action, changed forms of union organization, and new visions of social and political order. The year 1919 was one of strikes, most notably the Winnipeg General Strike, with leaders often using the rhetoric of class struggle to justify their demands. Almost as dramatic was the radicalization of farmers, who saw the prices for their products drop and who blamed transportation costs and tariffs for their financial difficulties. In Ontario and on the prairies many farmers who had supported the Union government now rejected the Conservatives and the Liberals in favour of the Progressive Party, which would be formed on the national level in 1920 when members of the Canadian Council of Agriculture united with dissident Liberals led by Thomas Alexander Crerar.

Politicians would also have to come to terms with an unstable world beyond Canada's borders. For most Canadians this adjustment meant redefining the country's relations with Britain. Canada had entered the Great War as a colony but its experience during the war had many convinced that a subservient colonial status was no longer acceptable. At the same time few wanted total independence. The options ranged from a more centralized British empire, in which Canada would have an influential role, to a loosely associated commonwealth of nations in which the emphasis would be on Canadian autonomy. The implications for Canada were far from clear but change was in the air.

The Liberal Party that had chosen King as its leader was itself deeply divided. King would have to win back the Liberals who had supported the Union government and conscription without alienating the French Canadians. At the same time he would have to make the party more hospitable to the new labour and farm groups, which meant reducing tariffs and giving more social assistance to the less privileged while retaining the support of the industrialists. The Liberal convention of 1919 did propose a forward-looking platform that favoured lower tariffs without opting for free trade and approved of unions, better working conditions, and public insurance for the sick, the aged, and the unemployed. This platform was more an aspiration than a commitment, however, one to be adopted 'in so far as the special circumstances of the country will permit.' King too was cautious; in his acceptance speech he was careful to describe the platform as a 'chart' and not a contract. The new leader needed to construct a majority party in a divided country but he clearly intended to move slowly.

King wanted to get into the House of Commons as soon as possible. He had a choice of ridings but in most cases he would have had to run against a farmers' party candidate. To avoid any confrontation he picked Prince, in Prince Edward Island, where he was acclaimed in October 1919. Once in the house he was careful to give W. S. Fielding a major role in the debates, a move that both reassured the conscriptionist Liberals and gave King time to familiarize himself with the current issues. He took the opportunity in 1920 to tour Ontario and the west, making a point of expressing sympathy for the farmers' problems and meeting with Progressive leaders to suggest some collaboration against the common

Conservative enemy in the next election. The Progressives, who were riding a political crest, showed little interest. At the provincial level organized farmers won elections in Ontario (1919) and Alberta (1921), and were so strong in Manitoba and Saskatchewan that the Liberals there had to distance themselves from their federal counterparts in an effort to survive. It was revealing that after King was nominated in his old riding of York North for the next election, Ralph W. E. Burnaby, president of the United Farmers of Ontario, was nominated to run against him. It would not be easy to convince farmers that the Liberal Party had changed its ways.

The election of December 1921 – the first in which all women would vote – was a graphic illustration of how fragmented the country had become. Meighen was burdened with the unpopularity of the Union government and his role in guiding the conscription legislation through the house. His defence of the tariff was largely ignored in Quebec, where conscription was still vividly remembered, and attracted little support in the west or the Maritimes. Only 50 Conservatives were elected, 37 of them from Ontario. The Progressives were surprisingly successful, taking 38 of the 43 prairie seats and 24 in Ontario; among their number was Agnes Campbell Macphail, Canada's first female MP. The Liberals achieved victory with 116 seats, a bare majority; enjoying representation from every province except Alberta, they could claim to be the only national party. With 65 of their seats from Quebec, however, the Liberals' dependence on French Canadian voters was a major concern. King had won the election and thus became prime minister (and ex officio secretary of state for external affairs); in due course, on 3 June 1922, he would be sworn to the British Privy Council, an honorific appointment he valued most because he felt it vindicated his grandfather's 'great purpose & aim.'

King was still on trial. He would need to broaden the basis of Liberal support without alienating his own supporters and he would have little margin for error. His first decision was crucial. King knew that the Liberal Party had to retain the support of French Canada. He could read French but spoke it haltingly; the larger problem was more cultural than linguistic. To ensure that his government would not ignore the French Canadian point of view, he resolved that his closest colleague would come from Quebec. His choice was Ernest Lapointe, a backbencher and lawyer who had earned a reputation as a moderate Liberal and a champion of French

Canadian rights. King called him to Ottawa immediately after the election, explained the role he would be expected to play, and offered him the justice portfolio to confirm his position. The most prominent figure among the French Canadians elected from Quebec was Sir Lomer Gouin, a former premier of the province, but King was suspicious of his liberalism because of his protectionist leanings and close ties with Montreal's business community. King eventually yielded to the political pressure to give justice to Gouin – Lapointe got marine and fisheries – but he made it clear that Lapointe was his chief lieutenant. This status was publicly corroborated in 1924 when Gouin resigned and Lapointe became minister of justice. King and Lapointe would work closely together for almost 20 years, until Lapointe's death in 1941.

The next issue for King was the cabinet representation from the west. This was important because he saw the cabinet as the central institution of government. Policy was expected to emerge from debates there, with ministers defending the interests of their region and King playing the role of mediator. In 1921 his task, as he understood it, was to consolidate the anti-Conservative forces, a seemingly simple undertaking. The Liberal and Progressive parties were both opposed to the high-tariff policies of the Conservatives and they both favoured greater autonomy in Canada's relations with Britain. If Progressive leaders entered cabinet, the farmers' point of view would be effectively presented and the emerging consensus would more adequately reflect a balanced national perspective. The difficulty was that the Liberal and Progressive parties both had deep internal divisions, which left their leaders with little room to manoeuvre. T. A. Crerar, the Progressive leader and MP for Marquette, Man., was tempted by the offer of a cabinet post; when he asked King for policy commitments on tariffs and railways, however, he got sympathy and understanding but no specific promises. The more radical Progressives made it clear that if he did enter the government he would not have their support. King eventually had to concede defeat and turn to elected Liberals to form his cabinet.

For the next few years the Progressives were never far from King's mind. The farmers' concerns continued to be his preoccupation and in cabinet he represented, as best he could, the interests of those who were absent. The Crowsnest Pass agreement, which gave preferential freight rates on grain moving eastward from the prairies on the railways and some commodities westward, had been suspended in 1919 in response to wartime inflation but it was restored by the government in 1922. The government also committed itself to creating a railway system out of the bankrupt lines it had acquired during the war and agreed to complete the Hudson Bay Railway to placate the farmers who wanted a shorter link to salt water. For most farmers, however, the real test would be tariff changes and here the government's record was ambivalent. Although King argued in cabinet for some dramatic gesture, he had little support and Fielding, once again minister of finance, included few tariff reductions in his budgets of March 1922 and May 1923. Some Progressives split with their party to support the first budget but it was a sign of the farmers' frustrations that all of the Progressives voted with the Conservatives against the second.

King's effort to unite the anti-Conservative forces fared better in international affairs. As prime minister, Meighen had continued Borden's policy of preserving the diplomatic unity of the empire, though at the Imperial Conference of 1921 he had opposed the renewal of Britain's alliance with Japan, recognizing that the United States had interests in the Pacific and wanting to maintain good Canadian–American relations. King too understood that imperial affairs abroad could have profound consequences for Canada. Within months the difficulties of maintaining imperial diplomatic unity were again exposed, dramatically, by the Çanak crisis. In September 1922 the Turkish government, in repudiation of a treaty it had signed with the allied powers, threatened to reoccupy the neutral zone of Çanak on the Dardanelles strait (Çanakkale Boğazi). Britain was determined to block this action, by force if necessary. With no prior consultation it appealed to the prime ministers of the dominions to provide military support and then released a statement to the press. King, who had not received the official message, first heard of the crisis from a journalist. His response, after meeting with the cabinet, was to refuse any participation without the consent of parliament. This assertion of autonomy was in sharp contrast to Meighen's statement, in a speech in Toronto on 22 September, that Canada should have replied to Britain 'Ready, aye ready; we stand by you.' King was careful to keep Crerar informed during the crisis and the Progressives openly supported his position. The Turks fortunately backed down, but the implications of

Çanak could not be ignored. There would be no common imperial foreign policy if each dominion decided its own course of action.

The Imperial Conference of 1923 could not disregard this challenge. The British government, with support from Australia and New Zealand, hoped that the conference would approve a broad statement on foreign policy. King was convinced that any attempt to make binding decisions for the dominions would be an encroachment on their autonomy. The conference, as he envisaged it, was an important way to exchange information and foster understanding but it had no authority; decisions would have to be made by the parliaments. The conference's final report, which affirmed King's belief, marked a decisive step in the evolution of the British Commonwealth of Nations (a term that had received imperial statutory recognition in the Anglo-Irish treaty of 1921). The affirmation was an admission that there would be no centralized empire. It left undecided how the unity of the Commonwealth might be achieved or if, indeed, the Commonwealth would survive. King had no misgivings. He believed that self-governing members of the Commonwealth shared profound social and political values and so would agree on major issues if there was no coercion. His analogy was the family: the dominions, like children, would grow up but they would not be tempted to slam doors or leave home if their autonomy was acknowledged. For him the recognition of the self-governing powers of the dominions would strengthen rather than weaken Commonwealth unity.

Among the advisers who accompanied King to the 1923 conference was Oscar Douglas Skelton, a political scientist at Queen's University in Kingston and a biographer of Laurier. He attracted King's attention by his lucid comments on Canadian autonomy and, after the conference, was persuaded by King to become a departmental counsellor in 1924 and then under-secretary of state for external affairs in 1925. The appointments confirmed King's sound judgement. Skelton had a phenomenal capacity for work and a talent for organizing material and producing memoranda or speeches of remarkable brevity and clarity. He soon became King's most trusted official. Skelton did not always agree with King – he was, for example, more sceptical about the benefits to Canada of membership in the Commonwealth – but he expressed his opinions frankly and then loyally accepted King's decisions.

External affairs, however, and King's crucial role at the Imperial Conference attracted little attention in Canada. Fortunately the political situation at home was promising. It was becoming easier to make concessions to the farmers because economic conditions were improving and because the protectionist wing of the Liberal Party had been weakened by the resignations of Fielding and Gouin for health reasons. At the same time the divisions within the Progressive Party were deepening. In 1924 the government was able to reduce some tariffs and still promise the first surplus since before the war. A few high-tariff Liberals voted against the budget but, more significantly, the moderate Progressives voted for it. King was now confident that the voters would reward his efforts and he dissolved parliament the next year.

King was wrong. He had pushed his party as far as he had dared in the direction of lower tariffs and had defended Canadian autonomy within the empire, but electoral results in October 1925 constituted a major setback. The Liberals did increase their representation in the west by 18 seats; however, this gain was offset by the loss of 10 seats in Ontario and 19 in the Maritimes, where King's courting of the Progressives was resented. The Liberals ended up with 99 seats, of which 59 were from Quebec. The Conservatives, on the other hand, gained seats in every region for a total of 116, just short of a majority. The Progressives fell dramatically to 24, although they could find some consolation in the fact that they would hold the balance of power in the new parliament.

Not only had King led the Liberal Party to defeat but, along with eight other cabinet ministers, he had lost his own seat. Many observers, including Governor General Lord Byng, assumed that he would resign and allow Meighen to take over. But King would not concede. He insisted on meeting the house, convinced that the Progressives would support his government rather than see it replaced by the Conservatives. For a few tense months King proved to be right. The Progressives voted for the throne speech of 8 Jan. 1926 and then for the Liberal budget in April. King also won the support of the two Labour MPs (James Shaver Woodsworth and Abraham Albert Heaps, both from Winnipeg) by introducing a bill for old-age pensions, though it would be defeated in the Senate. King himself was back in the commons after a by-election in Prince

Albert, Sask., on 15 February and the Liberal government seemed likely to survive the session. It even seemed possible that it could survive one or two more.

King's plans were upset by a scandal in the Department of Customs and Excise. There had been collusion between smugglers and members of the department to run goods into Canada from the United States. King had known for some time that there were problems and had moved the minister, Jacques Bureau, to the Senate in September 1925 and appointed a successor, Georges-Henri Boivin, to reorganize the department. The Conservatives, however, were not impressed and saw the corruption there as an opportunity to defeat the Liberals, knowing that the Progressives, who had identified their party with honest government, would find it difficult to support the administration. King avoided any debate on the scandal as long as possible but in June 1926 the house had to deal with the report of a parliamentary committee on the scandal. When the Conservatives moved a vote of censure, King arranged a series of delaying amendments but it was clear that the Progressives were divided and that the government would likely be defeated on the final vote.

King's response was to avoid the vote by asking the governor general to dissolve the house and force another election. Byng refused on the grounds that Arthur Meighen should be given a chance to form a government. Meighen was prepared to try. On 27 June King speculated in his diary on his opponent's prospects. 'Meighen too will fall heir to some difficult situations – Western provinces. ... If he seeks to carry on I believe he will not go far. Our chances of winning out in a general election are good. I feel I am right, and so am happy may God guide me in every step.' The following day King resigned. Meighen succeeded in forming a government and in passing a vote of censure but his hopes of ending the session quickly were frustrated by King's refusal to cooperate. King arranged for a series of resolutions criticizing the new government. Enough Progressives, embarrassed at having to support Meighen, backed the Liberals in a vote of no-confidence on 2 July that narrowly defeated the new government. Byng then accepted Meighen's advice and dissolved parliament.

The election of September 1926 was decisive for King's career. Support for the Liberals had declined under his leadership and now the party had the additional handicap of fighting under the cloud of the customs scandal. King, however, fought an aggressive campaign, nationally and in Prince Albert. He argued that the constitution had been violated when Byng had refused him a dissolution but granted one to Meighen. In constitutional terms, Byng was right and King was wrong. Politically, however, King was the winner. He had focused attention on Byng's decision even though many Liberals doubted whether the electorate would be interested. The outcome seemed to confirm his judgement. The constitutional issue distracted voters from the customs scandal, with King posing as the champion of Canadian autonomy against an interfering governor general. The decisive factor was the cumulative effect of King's sustained efforts over five years to regain the confidence of the dissident farmers. The moderate Progressives had concluded that they preferred a Liberal to a Conservative government and in a number of ridings had agreed to nominate a Liberal-Progressive candidate. The Liberals won 116 seats and, with the support of 10 Liberal-Progressives, would have a clear majority. King himself retained his seat for Prince Albert.

The next few years were good ones to be in office. The Canadian economy expanded as post-war recovery in Europe and prosperity in the United States increased the market for Canadian cereals, minerals, and wood products and as domestic demand grew for Canadian automobiles and other manufactured goods. The federal government could cut taxes and still reduce its debt and have a modest surplus. The provincial governments wanted financial concessions but these claims were nothing new and King's skill as a negotiator would stand him in good stead. Late in the decade there were signs of economic trouble, including weakening newsprint and grain markets and excessive stock-market speculation, but optimism proved hardy. King continued to believe that his government was performing well and that the voters would show their gratitude.

The Imperial Conference of 1926 came only two weeks after King had returned to office in September. This conference was important because it attempted to define the nature of the British Commonwealth of Nations. King did not initiate the discussions. He was prepared to live with an undefined relationship with Britain, confident that he could defend Canadian autonomy when necessary. James Barry Munnik Hertzog, the prime minister of South Africa, was more impatient: he threatened to leave the Commonwealth if the conference refused to draft a declaration that would affirm the independent status of the dominions. He had the support of Ireland but not the prime ministers of Australia or New Zealand. King played an important role as a mediator. He favoured the middle ground of a declaration of autonomy but not of independence. After two weeks of negotiations the conference agreed on a definition of Britain and the dominions: 'They are autonomous Communities within the British Empire, equal in status, in no way subordinate one to another in any aspect of their domestic or external affairs, though united by a common allegiance to the Crown, and freely associated as members of the British Commonwealth of Nations.'

This definition did not end the debate. Hertzog interpreted 'freely associated' to mean that South Africa could leave the Commonwealth if it chose to; the British did not agree. The definition was significant, however. Equal status meant that Britain could no longer assume that its foreign policy should be the policy of the Commonwealth. It also meant that Canada, like the other dominions, could develop a diplomatic service and a foreign policy of its own. The Imperial Conference of 1926 and the Statute of Westminster of 1931, which would give this new status legal definition, confirmed that the British Commonwealth of Nations would be a voluntary association, with its strength to be determined by the decisions of its respective members. Canada's diplomatic service quickly took shape. Charles Vincent Massey, the first representative to be appointed abroad with full diplomatic status, was named envoy to the United States in November 1926. This assignment was followed by the appointment of Philippe Roy to France in 1928 and Herbert Meredith Marler to Tokyo in 1929.

King had no misgivings about the new imperial arrangement put in place in 1926. He assumed that Canada would have to continue to defend itself vigilantly against British predilection for centralization but any defence would be easier now that the autonomy of the dominions had been formally conceded. As before, King was not concerned that the Commonwealth might not survive. He believed that ethnic ties and a common political heritage were powerful bonds. Independence was not an option he considered, presumably because membership in the Commonwealth would not encroach on Canadian autonomy and would give Canada a status and a security it would not have as an independent country.

Back in Canada, King had to deal with continuing regional dissatisfaction. The Maritimes were aggrieved because they were not sharing in the prosperity of the rest of the country and were convinced that federal tariffs and railway freight rates were to blame. The prairie premiers complained that federal reluctance to relinquish control of their natural resources was discriminatory. The premiers of Ontario and Quebec objected to the limitations placed on their authority to develop hydroelectric power by federal jurisdiction over navigable streams. At the Dominion-Provincial Conference of 1927 King used his conciliatory skills and held out concessions to each region if they raised no objections to the offers made to the other regions. And so the Maritimes got higher subsidies and lower freight rates, the prairie provinces got control of their natural resources without losing a compensatory subsidy, and Ontario and Quebec got the right to distribute water power developed on navigable streams. For the moment King's approach had appeased the regional demands.

This relative political harmony was linked to the prosperity of the mid 1920s but it can also be seen as the end of a long era of nation building. The three-pronged National Policy of Canada's first prime minister, Sir John A. Macdonald, had achieved its objectives. Most of the arable land offered to homesteaders on the prairies was now occupied and for the first time in half a century the federal policy of assistance to agricultural immigrants was questioned. Railway policy was also being modified. The government-owned Canadian National Railways, under the aggressive management of Sir Henry Worth Thornton, had spent federal funds to develop an integrated railway system. The success of this investment seemed confirmed by 1928 when the operating revenues of the system exceeded the interest payments on the railways' bonds. The third prong, the tariffs, was a major subject of political debate – farmers still deemed them too high – but they were no longer a dynamic factor in the Canadian economy.

King had no new policy to substitute for the old National Policy. He did reintroduce old-age pensions after the 1926 election but he did not follow up with other measures of social security for individuals in an increasingly urban and industrial Canada. Instead of spending the increased revenue which prosperity provided, the government used its annual surplus to reduce its debt and in 1927–28 it lowered the sales and income taxes. King saw no reason to question this frugality. By reducing taxes and so reducing the costs of production, his government, he was sure, deserved credit for Canada's economic growth and he expected to be rewarded at the polls.

The Republican victory south of the border in 1928 introduced a possible complication because President Herbert Clark Hoover was committed to raising the American tariffs on farm products. King used what influence he could to change Hoover's mind. He agreed to help American agencies enforce Prohibition by making it more difficult to smuggle Canadian liquor into the United States. He also tried to take advantage of Hoover's interest in a St Lawrence River seaway by suggesting that Canada was ready to negotiate an agreement. Hoover would not change his mind. The King government responded in the federal budget of 1930 by promising countervailing rates if the American government did increase its tariffs.

By then the good times were over, though not all Canadians realized this at the time. In Canada the onset of the world-wide depression of the 1930s differed by region and by industry. The Maritimes had already entered into severe economic decline. The overproduction of pulp and paper had meant lay-offs in northern communities as early as 1927. The price of western wheat dropped in 1928. In other regions, even in 1930, there might be some concern for the future but the factories were still operating. Richard Bedford Bennett, the leader of the opposition in parliament since 1927, argued that there was a crisis and demanded that the government do something. King was not impressed. It is revealing that there is no reference in his diary to the famous stock-market crash in October 1929; it would take two more years to push the government financially to the wall. King's own investments were in government bonds and gilt-edged securities and it was easy for him in 1929 to assume that only speculators had been hurt. He also found the talk of unemployment exaggerated – in 1930 the Dominion Bureau of Statistics was only starting to register a drop – and surely next spring would bring higher prices and more jobs. It was, King believed, a temporary recession and just patience was needed.

The prime minister spent the early part of 1930 mulling over the timing of the next election and related budgetary options. What scant attention he paid to the appointment in February of Canada's first female senator, Cairine Reay Wilson, was of a partisan nature. On the economic front his optimism led to an uncharacteristic slip in a debate on unemployment on 3 April 1930. The Conservatives argued that the crisis was so severe that Ottawa should offer financial assistance to the provincial governments, which were responsible for unemployment relief. King pointed out that no premier had asked for help and that, in Ontario, George Howard Ferguson had even denied his province had an unemployment problem. The federal Tories, according to King, were playing partisan politics, asking him to subsidize provincial Tory governments for no good reason, and he 'would not give them a five-cent piece.' He did not often deliver such an unguarded statement and the opposition would make much of 'the five-cent speech' in the election called for July.

King was still confident that voters would appreciate his frugal financial policy. In the campaign he did not ignore the economic downturn but he offered caution and sound government as the appropriate response. On the other hand, Bennett, who used radio with telling effect, talked of an economic crisis and promised dramatic measures, including the use of tariffs 'to blast a way into the markets that have been closed.' On the prairies, where wheat prices had dropped sharply, and in Quebec, where dairy farmers wanted protection against New Zealand butter, Bennett's appeal swung enough votes to give the Conservatives a majority. Returned in Prince Albert, King would spend the next five years in opposition.

His lifestyle was now well established. At 55, he was a confirmed bachelor with few interests outside of politics. Laurier House, the Ottawa residence he had inherited from Lady Laurier and occupied since 1923, was a comfortable, yellow-brick abode maintained by a staff that included a valet, a cook, a chauffeur, and a gardener. Peter Charles Larkin, a loyal Liberal businessman, had collected private funds to renovate it and pay for its upkeep. An elevator was installed. It took King and sometimes his invited guests to the third-floor library, where a portrait of his mother was prominently displayed. King occasionally had people for dinner but these were usually formal occasions. He was not a gregarious man and none of his colleagues and friends would visit him without an invitation. His closest friend was Mary Joan Patteson, wife of Godfroy Barkworth

Laurier House in Ottawa, shown here in 1902, was bequeathed by Lady Laurier to William L. M. King, who moved into his new residence in January 1923.

Patteson, a local banker with limited interests. Joan was a discreet and sympathetic woman who listened to King with patience and understanding and who rarely intruded her own problems into the discussions. King regularly talked to her over the telephone or dropped in for a visit to recount the difficulties or good fortunes of the day. The friendship was never a secret and it was a tribute to Joan's discretion and transparent dignity that no scandalous rumours about the nature of the relationship were ever taken seriously.

King's summer residence at Kingsmere was even more of a refuge than Laurier House. He expanded the property in the 1920s and 1930s and spent his summer months there to escape the sultry heat and social pressures of Ottawa. He rented a cottage on his property to the Pattesons and sometimes entertained foreign guests for lunch, but if he saw his colleagues or secretaries there it was only because he had asked them to make the trip to conduct business. King's interest in erecting artificial ruins at Kingsmere – still one of its most fascinating features – emerged in 1934, when his grandfather's house in Toronto was threatened with demolition. The Kingsmere collection actually began the following year, with a stone window frame from the Ottawa residence of the late Simon-Napoléon Parent.

William L. M. King (right) at his Kingsmere estate in Quebec during the summer perhaps of 1932 or 1934, with Ottawa friends Godfroy B. and M. Joan Patteson and Mrs Etta Wreidt (second from left), a noted medium from Detroit.

If King seemed settled in his ways, he was still a lonely man and politics was not enough to fill his life completely. He had no close family ties by this time; his surviving sibling, Janet (Jennie) Lindsey Lay, lived in Barrie, Ont., but they were not intimate. As leader of the Liberal Party he kept himself at arm's length from his colleagues, who might try to presume on his friendship and might have to be jettisoned if the political winds changed. He did continue to correspond with acquaintances outside Ottawa and to talk to Joan Patteson, but this was not enough for a man who constantly needed the reassurance that he was loved. Pat, his Irish terrier, was important because Pat showed affection without making too many demands on his time. King, however, also found emotional support in more unusual ways. In 1916, after visiting the graves of his sister Isabel Christina Grace and father in Toronto, he had noted in his diary, 'To me the spiritual presence of both Bell & himself was far more real than their graves which my eyes were witnessing.' His faith that his family (especially his mother) and others were somehow still watching over him became more important as time passed; he regularly saw coincidences as a sign of their presence and interpreted his dreams as evidence of their affection and support. This faith in itself did not make King unique but the need for signs of approval from the spirit world gradually led him to seek confirmation in more eccentric ways. He was intrigued by forecasts of the future based on tea leaves and his horoscope, consulted a fortune-teller, and during his years in opposition, when he had more leisure time, tried to make contact with the spirit world through other means, including the Ouija board and sessions with a medium. King occasionally expressed scepticism about the messages he received – he justified his interest by calling it psychic research – but he was still fascinated by the apparent contacts with the departed. He did not seek their political advice; his political decisions were based as always on his own analysis of situations. The content of the messages was less important than the evidence that the spirits were present and watching over him. This reassurance gave him the strength to deal with the stresses and strains and with the isola-tion of politics. In a paradoxical way, his eccentric links with this other world made it more possible for him to cope with the normal pressures of a political career.

The normal pressures were intensified after the 1930 election by allegations of corruption. What became known as the Beauharnois Scandal had its roots in a scheme to divert water from the St Lawrence into the Beauharnois Canal near Montreal to develop hydroelectric power. In March 1929 the King government had authorized a diversion after confirming that it would not interfere with navigability on the river. The Beauharnois Light, Heat and Power Company, however, saw this approval as only the beginning. It looked forward to a seaway with most of the St Lawrence diverted into its canal. The potential profits were enormous. The corporation, apparently concluding that it was necessary to keep the Liberals in power, funnelled more than half a million dollars into their campaign fund in 1930. This contribution proved awkward for the party when it became public knowledge after the Liberal defeat. Even more embarrassing for King was the disclosure that he had gone on a holiday to Bermuda with Wilfrid Laurier McDougald, the chairman of the Beau-harnois board, and that McDougald had paid King's hotel bill and submitted it to Beauharnois on his expense account. Between June 1931 and April 1932 committees of the commons and the Senate investigated the many related allegations.

King managed to have his name cleared. McDougald explained that he had submitted his bill by mistake; nobody seemed concerned that King's acceptance of McDougald's generosity might be interpreted as a conflict of interest. The donation to the Liberal campaign was more difficult to deal with. King could argue that his government had protected the public interest when it allowed the diversion of water and had made no further commitments to the corporation, but he knew that many Canadians would remain unconvinced. Though the scandal did no long-term damage – nor did it lead to any major reforms in the financing of the party – it put the Liberals, King conceded in parliament on 30 July 1931, 'in the valley of humiliation.' His solution was to isolate himself from party finances. Liberal bagmen would continue to collect and distribute campaign funds. As leader, King would not be told who the contributors were, so his political decisions would not be affected by their identity. This solution left him with a clear conscience but it still left the party largely dependent on undisclosed donations from private corporations.

In the meantime Bennett had begun his administration actively, as he had promised. In a special session of parliament he offered $20 million as a palliative measure for emergency relief, an unprecedented amount for a federal government that had no direct constitutional responsibility for relief. To solve the larger economic crisis, his response fell into the traditional pattern of a Canadian Conservative: he raised the tariff rates sharply on manufactured imports to encourage domestic production and create jobs. Unfortunately exports dwindled, the prices for Canadian goods continued to decline, and unemployment rose. By 1932 Bennett had shifted his hopes to the Imperial Economic Conference in Ottawa, where a number of trade agreements with Britain and other dominions were worked out. An effective negotiator, he won some preferences, especially in the British market, without making major concessions. Though Bennett trumpeted his achievements and promised Canadians that economic recovery was on the way, the trade preferences unfortunately still left Canadians with unsold goods and deflated world prices.

Bennett, who initially acted as his own minister of finance, had to face declining revenues as well as ever stronger demands for federal aid. He raised taxes slightly but revenues declined with the economic slowdown. Further tariff increases would have little effect because the existing structure already excluded most foreign competition. Bennett's only choice seemed to be the reduction of expenditures, especially relief costs. He tried to keep aid to the provinces to a minimum by hard bargaining; in the unemployment and farm relief acts of 1931–32 he even refused to disclose the amount of federal funds available in order to negotiate more effectively. At the same time he showed his frustration with the depression by stressing law and order, denouncing strikes and demonstrations, and insisting that his administration was doing everything possible.

After King had dealt with the Beauharnois problems, he proved to be an effective opposition leader. The depression of the 1930s was of unprecedented severity in Canada. The dependence on exports of raw materials and farm products meant that Canadian providers were especially vulnerable in a world where nations raised tariffs to protect their producers. Western farmers were doubly unfortunate because not only did prices reach historic lows, but in many regions drought, rust, and grasshoppers also meant crop failures. In cities, factories closed because consumers could no longer buy. Desperate Canadians had to turn to governments when they had no other place to turn, first for food and shelter and then for any means to restore their hope. The depression brought regions and classes into conflict and encouraged demagogues to propose radical and unorthodox policies. King seemed an unlikely leader for this troubled time. He had earned a reputation for being cautious, a man of compromises and half measures. In a world where the battle seemed to be between left and right, with communism and fascism at the extremes, King looked indecisive, even colourless. Yet within five years he would be back in office, at the head of the largest majority enjoyed by any party up to that time. He kept the Liberals together while the Conservative Party disintegrated and new political parties emerged to compete for votes. It was no mean achievement. As he had explained in 1929 to a correspondent, 'The supreme effort of my leadership of the party has been to keep its aims and purposes so broad that it might be possible to unite at times of crisis under one banner those parties, which for one reason or another, have come to be separated from the Liberal party.' By 1923 most Progressives would have rejoined it. In 1931–32, however, unity seemed a distant goal: the party was torn between high and low tariff factions, and on the front benches of opposition King had few strong supporters at his side.

Like Bennett, King was slow to recognize that politics would be transformed by the depression. He had begun his years in opposition convinced that his administration had not deserved defeat. The economy had flourished, he believed, because of his government's financial caution. The recession, if it was a recession, could be blamed on the speculative excesses of businessmen and on the weather cycle. The worst mistake Canada – and the rest of the world – could make was to react by raising tariffs and restricting international trade. Bennett, from King's perspective, had won election by exaggerating the threats to the Canadian economy and by rashly promising that he could somehow use the tariff to counteract international and climatic constraints. Voters, King believed, would soon learn that they had been deceived and would come to appreciate the Liberal years of frugal administration and freer trade.

King thus saw little need to reconsider or revise his political assumptions. The Conservative government was clearly in political trouble and King was content to draw attention to its difficulties. He repeatedly reminded the house of Bennett's election promises. He denounced the federal deficits as irresponsible without suggesting how budgets could be balanced. He did not object to aid to the provinces – the need was too apparent – but he did denounce the 'blank cheques' parliament was asked to approve for relief, and delayed the passage of these bills over the objections of caucus members who feared constituents might conclude that the Liberals had no sympathy for those in distress. And each year, after the throne speech and the budget, he introduced amendments that blamed the depression on Bennett's high-tariff policy.

He was still responding as a traditional Canadian Liberal, convinced that the depression would end only with the restoration of international trade, when Canadian producers would once more have markets. Sure that high tariffs had made matters worse, he was encouraged too by the fact that Bennett and his government were being widely blamed and would surely be defeated. It was enough to focus attention on trade and tariffs until voters had the opportunity to remedy their mistake. King, however, gradually realized that for many Canadians, including some long-time Liberals, waiting was not good enough. Talk of tariffs had little relevance for parents who could not feed their children or for farmers who could not buy seed or hay. For them, the capitalist system seemed to have failed and tinkering with tariffs would accomplish nothing. It was also significant that voters would have more choice in the next election. The more radical Progressives and the Labour members in the commons had founded a new political party in 1932 – the Co-operative Commonwealth Federation – which offered the socialist alternative of government planning and public ownership. That same year, in Alberta, evangelist William Aberhart became a convert to monetary reform in the shape of social credit, a doctrine that advocated the distribution of money for purchases by consumers. Within two years he had transformed it into a political platform. By 1935 Social Credit candidates would come forward federally, and dissident Conservatives would form a new party. Many Liberals in the west, where the impact of the depression was most severe, were convinced that their party would have to adopt more radical measures to be relevant; more traditional Liberals rejected such policies as irresponsible.

King's response reflected his fundamental commitment to finding a consensus among 'liberally-minded' Canadians. He did not expect to convert the Tories, whom he believed were wedded to big business, or the socialists, who wanted a monopoly of power for the workers. Criticism from his own caucus members, however, he took seriously. He might regret their impatience but he would not ignore them. His role was to keep the party united. By 1933 he had reluctantly concluded that traditional Liberal preconceptions were not enough. If the party was to survive, it would have to face the challenge of the depression more directly. Here his talents as a conciliator would be crucial. Although lower tariffs would be part of a new Liberal platform, the most controversial issue would be inflation. King and his more conservative followers still equated inflation with theft, but, for indebted producers especially, inflation seemed the only way to meet their financial obligations. King's compromise was a government-controlled 'central bank' that could modify the money supply on the basis of 'public need.' He was proposing an institution, not a policy. He succeeded because the moderates saw the bank as an agency that could protect sound money and the radicals saw it as an agency that could introduce a policy of controlled inflation. The significance of this compromise should not be minimized. It recognized that the state should play a positive role in determining fiscal policy. It certainly implied more intervention than did the Bank of Canada legislated by Bennett in 1934, which was to be an agency of the chartered banks.

This new platform was quite satisfactory to King. It placed the party in the centre of the political spectrum, more open than the Conservatives to regulating business without resorting to the socialist panacea of government ownership. It was also important to King that the platform had been approved in 1933 by both the conservatives and the radicals in the Liberal caucus. Some, among them Vincent Massey, wanted to take Liberalism in different directions, and not necessarily with King at the helm. With party unity assured, King eagerly awaited the next election. Late in the 1934 session he denounced Bennett for holding on to office when he no longer had popular support and promised that if he insisted on meeting the house for a fifth session, the Liberals would obstruct and force an election. In January 1935 the political situation changed when Bennett made five radio speeches known as the New Deal broadcasts. 'The old order is gone,' he told a startled audience, and he announced that he was for radical reform through government intervention. In the next session, he promised, he would introduce appropriate legislation. There was more rhetoric than substance to these broadcasts and Bennett, in contrast to King's approach to leadership, had not consulted his colleagues. Confident that it had the jurisdictional authority, the government nonetheless passed the Employment and Social Insurance Act early in 1935. Bennett certainly won the attention of Canadians who, after five years of depression, wanted to believe that a political leader could end the crisis.

King quickly revised his strategy. There would be no obstruction when the House of Commons met. He persuaded his caucus that the New Deal broadcasts were not about reform but were really the first phase of the election campaign. The Liberals must not appear to be opposed to reform. It would be wiser to seem cooperative and encourage the government to introduce the promised laws immediately. The embarrassed government had none prepared and when measures were introduced, they were less radical than the broadcasts had suggested. The New Deal, however, did mean an expansion of the federal role in marketing farm products, regulating business, and supervising working conditions. In constitutional terms it meant federal intervention in assumed provincial jurisdictions. King avoided any direct challenges. He persuaded caucus that the party should express its constitutional reservations and then vote for the legislation.

The changed strategy worked. The Liberals remained united, at least in public, but the Conservatives became deeply divided. By the end of the session the government's claim to be the party of reform was discredited and in July 1935 some dissident Conservatives led by Henry Herbert Stevens had even formed a separate Reconstruction Party. In the federal election of October the Liberals were returned with 173 seats, the largest majority on record, with members from every province, while the Conservatives were reduced to a rump of 40 members. The popular vote, however, told a different story. The Liberals received only 45 per cent, almost unchanged from the previous election. The dramatic change was the drop for the Conservatives and the support of 20 per cent for the new parties: the CCF and its socialism, Reconstruction and its emphasis on regulating business, and Social Credit and its panacea of inflation. If the choice was between 'King or chaos,' as the Liberal slogan put it, a good many Canadian voters were prepared to risk chaos.

The next four years would be a difficult time for the country. For its new prime minister it would be a stern test of his political skills. His experience and confidence showed in his cabinet. King again took on external affairs. Ernest Lapointe, still his closest colleague, returned to justice. The financially conservative Charles Avery Dunning was persuaded to become minister of finance, and from among the new MPs King appointed Clarence Decatur Howe, who had business experience, to the newly created portfolio of transport. The cabinet was recognized as an able group, and King would give his ministers a good deal of autonomy in the administration of their departments, but King, more than ever, was in charge. He set the government's agenda and chaired the cabinet discussions. After some slow improvement in economic conditions, 1937 saw another downturn, especially on the prairies, where the summer was the driest on record. Regional grievances fed on the frustrations of deferred recovery, and the government again became a popular target. The divisions within the Liberal Party, which reflected regional rivalries, were compounded by a series of international crises that threatened to involve Canada in a European war.

The new government, as one of its first problems, had to decide on its international obligations as a member of the League of Nations. King had supported membership – it enhanced Canada's status as a nation and provided evidence that Canada favoured the peaceful settlement of international disputes – but he had shown little interest in the debates at League headquarters in Geneva. Canada's foreign policy had been mainly confined to relations with Britain and the United States, and King expected to deal with these countries directly. Shortly after the election, however, his government was faced with a request from the League to impose economic sanctions on Italy because it had invaded Ethiopia. The cabinet agreed to apply sanctions but the discussion made it clear to King that if the League went on to propose military intervention, the cabinet and the country would be deeply divided. The request for military sanctions never came because Britain and France backed away from any confrontation with Italy's Fascist leader, Benito Mussolini. King nevertheless learned an important lesson: membership in the League might have serious political consequences for Canada. He took steps to minimize the risk. Though he affirmed, in the commons and later in Geneva, his support for the League as a necessary institution for the resolution of disputes, he bluntly rejected the idea of the League as a military alliance against aggressors. Canada, he told the League's Assembly in 1936, did not support 'automatic commitments to the use of force.' Editorials in much of the Canadian press applauded. King's political faith in non-intervention, and his fear of domestic division, can be seen too in his decision to distance Canada from the Spanish Civil War in 1937 and his refusal to modify Canadian immigration regulations to admit European Jewish refugees.

For King, Canada's economic problems had higher priority than international relations, but he had no simple solution to the complex challenges of the depression. Although he had shown a willingness to consider extending the role of government when party unity seemed to require it, he was still reluctant to take new initiatives. His caution meant that his government's honeymoon was brief. King's only specific election promise had been to negotiate a trade treaty with the United States. Bennett had already begun the discussions but political interests on both sides of the border had delayed matters. In November 1935, within two weeks of taking office, King was in Washington to make the best deal possible. He wisely enlisted the support of Cordell Hull, the American secretary of state and an evangelist for expanding international trade. President Franklin Delano Roosevelt, however, was the key. King and Roosevelt found it easy to discuss their political concerns. Roosevelt had a talent for putting visiting heads of state at ease and King could talk knowledgeably about United States politics and politicians. In the trade details King was well prepared and he returned to Canada with a treaty, which, modest in scope, gave Canadian farm products some welcome access to the American market.

He was also encouraged by a conference with the provincial premiers, in December 1935 shortly after the election. He was confident that a change in governing style would make a difference, that his emphasis on consultation would smooth relations. The premiers faced declining revenues and higher welfare costs and needed federal grants and loans to reduce their deficits. The national government had deficits of its own and hoped that provincial demands could be limited through the elimination of extravagances or duplications of welfare payments. At the conference King pleased the premiers by increasing the federal grants until the spring of 1936; his talk of a federal commission to supervise welfare payments and the possibility of constitutional amendments affecting provincial jurisdiction over social policy did not attract much attention. He had already referred Bennett's Employment and Social Insurance Act to the courts, which would strike it down as exceeding federal jurisdiction. King's objective at this stage was a federal system in which each level of government would be able to pay for its programs out of its own tax sources. He was no more precise because he had no concrete measures in mind and assumed that any new distribution of powers would emerge from discussions with the provinces.

King, however, soon found that confrontation was unavoidable because, without more federal aid, some provinces faced bankruptcy. William Aberhart, Alberta's Social Credit premier since August 1935, was a populist with little concern for convention. In 1936 he could not refinance an issue of maturing provincial bonds without a federal guarantee of the interest payments. When C. A. Dunning suggested some federal supervision of provincial finances in return, Aberhart refused and extended the term for the bonds while halving the interest rates. Then, in 1937, under pressure from his backbenchers, he passed legislation to compel chartered banks to lend money to Albertans. When the newspapers criticized this measure Aberhart retaliated with a bill that obliged them to publish press releases giving the government's side of the story.

King's response was to disallow the bank legislation and to refer the newspaper bill to the Supreme Court of Canada, which nullified it as unconstitutional.

King could claim to be standing up for civil rights in Alberta by defending the banks and the newspapers but he was less forthright in Quebec. In 1937 Maurice Le Noblet Duplessis, the Union Nationale premier, passed the Act Respecting Communistic Propaganda (the so-called Padlock Law) to intimidate labour leaders and 'agitators' by threatening to lock up their offices for any alleged communist activities. King's government, which had already repealed the section of the Criminal Code prohibiting unlawful associations, considered disallowing this act but Ernest Lapointe believed such a move would be politically disastrous for the Liberal Party in Quebec. King and his English-Canadian colleagues did not question Lapointe's political judgement and so, as King recorded in his diary in July 1938, 'we were prepared to accept what really should not, in the name of liberalism, be tolerated for one moment.'

Aberhart and Duplessis might show little respect for civil rights but the rift between the federal and provincial governments had a more basic cause. The provinces, dependent as they were on revenues from direct taxes, could not provide even essential social services without subsidies or loans from Ottawa. Thomas Dufferin Pattullo, the Liberal premier of British Columbia, whose concept of liberalism embraced the provision of work and wages, committed his government to construction projects for which it had no funds. When King refused to provide money for a bridge across the Fraser River, Pattullo was furious. Ontario's Liberal premier, Mitchell Frederick Hepburn, was critical for quite different reasons. He objected to federal grants to western provinces to finance relief measures because most of the money came originally from Ontario taxpayers. In 1937 he announced that he was no longer a 'Mackenzie King Liberal.' Other premiers might be less outspoken but all of them were facing demands for social services they could not afford. If there was to be effective coordination, the onus would have to be on Ottawa. Privately King resented Hepburn and Duplessis's narrow regionalism, but it was, he reasoned in his diary in December 1937, 'just as well to have these two incipient dictators out in the open. The public will soon discover who is protecting their interests and freedom. ... We will win in a "united Canada" cry.'

King was still not prepared to risk constitutional changes that might overextend federal finances. He focused instead on defending the fiscal stability of his government, convinced that a more efficient administration of relief by the provinces would reduce costs. When the National Employment Commission, formed in 1936, recommended a constitutional amendment to shift relief to the federal government, King remained dubious. The next year he postponed any decision on constitutional change by appointing a royal commission on dominion–provincial relations, known after its chairmen as the Rowell–Sirois commission. His liberal views, which still associated government planning with socialist coercion, were reinforced by his concern to balance the budget.

The prime minister did agree to some extension of the economic role of government when he felt the political pressures could not be safely ignored. He had objected to Bennett's Canadian Wheat Board in 1935 but had accepted its operation while it disposed of the wheat it had bought up to support prices. By 1938, however, the board had sold its holdings and King proposed a return to the open market. Western farmers were incensed. They wanted a board that would give them a guaranteed minimum price, with the federal government covering any losses, and they organized a public campaign that could not be ignored. King and agriculture minister James Garfield Gardiner reluctantly agreed to extend the board's life and to offer a minimum price that would protect the farmers from further declines.

There was one other significant increase in federal expenditures that King agreed to with reluctance. He and Dunning had initially planned a balanced budget for 1938, sure that voters would reward a financially responsible government, but some colleagues, to King's surprise, were not convinced. They wanted to create jobs to stimulate the economy. Their argument was reinforced by the theory of influential British economist John Maynard Keynes that governments could increase employment by spending when private investment was low. King, however, was swayed more by political than by economic arguments. To placate his colleagues he agreed to budget for a deficit in 1938 and again in 1939. This acceptance of contra-cyclical financing was hesitant but for King it was a major step towards using the budget more to craft fiscal policy than to balance accounts.

Lowering trade barriers still seemed a surer way of stimulating the economy. King saw a great opportunity when Cordell Hull asked him to use the Imperial Conference of 1937 as an opportunity to encourage British prime minister Arthur Neville Chamberlain to negotiate a trade agreement with the United States. King responded with enthusiasm because he firmly believed that such an agreement would strengthen the economies of Canada's closest friends and improve their relations. But he also knew that Canada would have to be involved in any negotiations because Britain could not reduce its tariffs on such American goods as apples and lumber without asking Canada to forgo some of the preference that the 1932 Ottawa agreements had guaranteed. When talks began King insisted on compensation for Canadian concessions. He drove a hard bargain. In 1938, after prolonged triangular negotiations, a treaty was signed that had some tangible benefits for each region of Canada. Both Hull and Chamberlain learned to be more sceptical about King's altruism.

By then the economic situation, frustrating as it might be, was overshadowed by the threat of a European war. As a liberal, King still favoured resolving international disputes by negotiation and he shared the widespread hostility to the 'merchants of death' who profited from the arms trade. He had tried to limit expenditures on the armed forces, but by 1937 he had decided that his government could no longer ignore its obligation to defend Canada 'in a mad world.' Though the British Royal Navy and the United States' Monroe Doctrine might mean that the dominion was in no immediate danger of attack, Canadian autonomy required it to take some responsibility for its own defence. Most Canadians would recognize the duty to protect their coasts, but what of the argument that Britain was Canada's first line of defence? Many Canadians, including King, accepted it; to many French Canadians it was a reminder of the coercive behaviour of the majority in the Great War. King decided to almost double the defence budget in 1937. Some Liberals were strongly opposed but they yielded to his insistence that the additional money would be spent on the navy and air force for coastal defence and not on an expeditionary force for Europe. He was not being dishonest; he was merely keeping his options open. Coastal defence was needed but he knew that augmentation of the navy and the air force would be useful as well in a European war. In 1939, with war even more likely, he again overrode opposition in the party to double the defence estimates. Canada was still unprepared for war in September of that year but King had shown more forethought than most of his followers.

By this time he had reluctantly concluded that he could not isolate Canada from a European crisis. The League of Nations had never recovered from Ethiopia and so membership no longer threatened to involve Canada in war. Membership in the Commonwealth, however, carried risks that were not so easily dealt with. King saw the danger: the country – and the Liberal Party – might again be divided. His first response was to persuade the British government to avoid entangling alliances. Germany might provoke a war, but if Britain was not drawn in Canada would not be involved. At the Imperial Conference of 1937, therefore, King encouraged the British to resist confrontations and to resolve disputes with Germany through peaceful negotiations. Though appeasement would later be denounced as yielding to an aggressor, at the time it was seen as a legitimate response to legitimate grievances. King himself visited Adolf Hitler after the conference. He warned the Führer that Canada would be at Britain's side if Britain was drawn into war, but King was optimistic. Hitler, he reported to Chamberlain, seemed to be a reasonable man.

In 1938, however, King was forced to realize that Britain would not be able to isolate itself from events. The crucial event for him was the Munich Agreement of late September, when Chamberlain helped to negotiate the cession of Czechoslovakian territory to Germany. Had negotiations failed and war ensued, King and most of his government would have been at Britain's side, though some members would have resigned. Much relieved when the agreement ended the crisis, he nevertheless recognized that war was likely and that Britain would be engaged. He was sure that most Canadians would want to be, and should be, involved. The political problem, as he saw it, was to have this decision accepted without serious divisions. In the commons on 20 March 1939, King explained his position. His government had made no commitments. If war came, parliament would decide what to do, based on Canadian interests. Here was reassurance for those who suspected the malign influence of London, but King did not stop there. 'If there were a prospect of an aggressor launching an attack on Britain, with bombers raining death on London, I have no doubt what the decision of the Canadian people and parliament would be. We would regard it as an act of aggression, menacing freedom in all parts of the British Commonwealth.' Ten days later he returned to the subject of involvement, to reiterate the understanding that his government would never introduce conscription for overseas service. French Canada acquiesced. His position convinced many other Canadians too, but it did make it difficult to plan for war. In 1936, for example, Britain had proposed a joint venture to manufacture Bren machine-guns in Canada. King procrastinated because, if Britain went to war and Canada was committed to supplying the guns, it would be considered a belligerent. King eventually yielded to British pressure, however, and the contracts were signed in 1938. A British proposal to train pilots in Canada was even more controversial. King's rejection of the project in 1936 and 1938, and then his insistence on Canadian control, meant that no decision was reached before Germany invaded Poland and war was declared. There could be no effective joint planning with its Commonwealth allies if Canada made no commitments in advance.

King's strategy also meant that Canada played no part in shaping British foreign policy. King was shocked in March 1939 when Chamberlain reversed Munich and promised to defend Poland's borders, but he expressed no objections. Again there was no consultation when Britain declared war on 3 September, though this time at least King and his government were united in their support. Canada's own declaration of war was delayed because King had to assemble parliament to keep his promise that it would decide. When the Liberal-dominated commons met in emergency session, starting on the 7th, the decision that had seemed so controversial a year before was accepted on the 9th almost unanimously. King repeated the pledge he had made in parliament in March not to introduce conscription for overseas service. His strategy had disadvantages, but it did help to bring Canada into the war without irreparable division.

Now in his mid 60s, King was conscious of his age. The pressures of the depression and the international situation had exhausted him. Politics had become an endless effort to avoid disasters; in his diary King talked of retiring after winning one more election. Then came the war, which provided an overriding sense of purpose. Leadership now meant more than staying in power. For the next five years King would face political decisions that were more demanding and in many ways more important, but there was no further talk of retirement. He might be exhausted or frustrated at times, but he never questioned the importance of what he was doing. And King was still a decisive political opportunist. In 1940, when Hepburn and Conservative leader George Alexander Drew combined in the Ontario legislature to condemn Ottawa's war effort, he seized the occasion to call an election before any spring offensive in Europe and so renewed the Liberals' federal majority for another five years.

The Canada led by King would play a significant role in the war. Convoy duty by the Royal Canadian Navy had begun immediately, in September 1939, and in December the 1st Canadian Division of the army went overseas. Isolated after the fall of France in June 1940, Britain would depend on the industrial and military might of North America for its survival. In its darkest days, Canada was a major source of troops and supplies. The United States would provide a lend-lease arrangement for materials in 1941 and then become an active ally, but Canada, in proportion to its size, made a larger contribution. Industrial production expanded rapidly and the government's generous financial arrangements made it possible for Britain to purchase Canadian food and munitions. The effort was remarkable by any standards.

King's role should not be exaggerated. The depression meant that Canada had land, resources, and workers that were underutilized and available for an initial restructuring of its economy. Canada also had the advantage of being close to Europe but far enough away not to risk invasion. With its close cultural and economic ties to Britain, it could have been a valuable ally under a number of leaders. King's political talents and experience nonetheless gave him an influence that, directly or indirectly, would shape the wartime decisions of his government. There was nothing dramatic about his leadership. He produced no Churchillian phrases to rally Canadians and none of Roosevelt's fireside chats to involve them in the issues of the day. Initially, through its focus on coastal defence, Canada was committed only to a qualified participation in the war. Canada still felt remote from Europe in geographic terms and it still harboured deep regional and cultural divisions. King's political sensitivity, made acute by decades of experience, and his skills as a conciliator were well suited to this wartime Canada.

As minister of external affairs, King had direct responsibility for maintaining the delicate balance between Canadian autonomy and commitment as Britain's ally. After war began, for example, Canada was a logical place to train aircrew; it was safe, had space for airfields and a tradition of flying, and could draw on the industrial and technical resources of North America. But how was a Commonwealth training plan to be organized and financed? King again insisted that any training be conducted under Canadian control, and here the British government was obliged to give way, though the standards and overall policy were set by the Royal Air Force. The Canadian government eventually took over most of the costs because Britain was short of dollars. The British Commonwealth Air Training Plan, under an agreement of 17 Dec. 1939 that initially involved Canada, Britain, Australia, and New Zealand, was an unquestioned success. Most of the Commonwealth's aircrew learned their skills here, making the scheme one of Canada's distinctive contributions to the war.

Canada's relations with the United States were more anomalous, especially because the United States was not at war until the Japanese attack on Pearl Harbor in December 1941. King's personal relations with Roosevelt helped to circumvent some of the diplomatic barriers imposed by neutrality. In early September 1939, for instance, Canada was allowed to purchase American airplanes because King had reassured Roosevelt, in a telephone conversation, that Canada was not technically at war until parliament had approved an official declaration. After the fall of France in 1940 an invitation to King from Roosevelt led to the Ogdensburg Agreement for a joint board to study continental defence. The Hyde Park Agreement in April 1941 was initiated by a telephone call from King. He explained that Canada was facing a financial crisis because it was supplying Britain on credit and so had no cash to pay for the American imports needed by Canadian manufacturers. Roosevelt agreed to ease the crisis by including, in the lend-lease agreement, exports to Canada that could be identified as components of Canada's munitions production.

At times during the first two years of the war King acted as an intermediary between the United States and Britain. When Roosevelt worried about the fate of the Royal Navy, if Britain was conquered, he asked an embarrassed King to urge British prime minister Winston Churchill to announce that it would seek refuge in North America. King complied. Churchill, for his part, asked him on occasion to use his influence with Roosevelt to try to increase American aid to a beleaguered Britain. After Pearl Harbor, Churchill and Roosevelt no longer needed an intermediary and King found himself excluded from most of the strategic planning for the war. Even at the Quebec conferences of August 1943 and September 1944, where King hosted the two leaders, he recognized that he was not expected to join in their discussions.

King's personal contacts with Churchill and Roosevelt were nonetheless of some importance. The British and Americans were inclined to make decisions and to expect their smaller allies to accept them. Much of the planning for the production and distribution of war supplies was done by joint Anglo-American boards. The Canadian government regularly asked to be represented on boards that allocated supplies produced by Canada. Requests for representation on the Combined Food Board, to name one, were ignored. King eventually appealed directly to both Churchill and Roosevelt, and Canada was finally given a place. For other bodies, however, his appeals were not effective.

His wartime leadership in domestic affairs is less easily assessed because, although he might question his ministers' decisions, he rarely reversed them. Much therefore depended on his relations with his cabinet. In the late 1930s he had known that some of his ministers were weak or thinking of retirement, but he had hesitated to take action until the war provided the needed incentive to strengthen his government. He lured James Layton Ralston, a prominent Nova Scotia Liberal, back into politics, first as minister of finance (to replace Dunning) and then as minister of national defence, where his presence and his concern for enlisted men, dating back to the Great War, were reassuring to Canadian servicemen. King's choice for Ralston's successor in finance was James Lorimer Ilsley, who could be a stubborn colleague but whose integrity and determination to control expenditures shaped Canada's wartime finances. Moved from transport in 1940, C. D. Howe was the central figure in munitions and supply, where his contacts with Canadian businessmen and his aggressive reliance on tax incentives and public investment stimulated a dramatic expansion of production. And when Ernest Lapointe died in 1941, King persuaded Louis-Stephen St-Laurent, an eminent

Quebec City lawyer, to become minister of justice and his new Quebec lieutenant. St-Laurent had no political experience but he did have sound judgement and a gentlemanly respect for his colleagues, even when he disagreed with them. He quickly emerged as the most influential minister in the government and King's closest associate. These and the other members of the cabinet grew accustomed, under King's leadership, to discuss issues openly and to take decisions collegially. As a wartime administration they earned a reputation for competence and efficiency.

King, as *primus inter pares*, did more than choose his colleagues and chair their discussions. He constantly sought measures or half measures they could agree on. Occasionally, when he found himself in disagreement, he might give way or more rarely exercise an implicit veto. His interventions in financial decisions provide examples. The government and its financial advisers had agreed from the beginning to avoid inflation of the sort that had followed the first war by paying as much of the war costs as possible out of current taxes. One possibility was for the federal government to take over the personal and corporate income-tax fields from the provincial governments and raise the rates sharply. A conference in 1941 showed that the provincial premiers would not agree to a constitutional amendment to this effect. J. L. Ilsley therefore proposed that he should tell the premiers the federal government would invoke the War Measures Act to take over these tax sources, with compensation. King expressed his uneasiness about this authoritarian approach but agreed that the government had no option. The tax increases would be effective but inflation was still a threat, so Ilsley next proposed wage and price controls. Again King had reservations about such drastic intervention, but again he yielded. Later, when miners argued that their wages had been frozen at an unfairly low level and demanded wage increases in spite of the controls, King stepped in. Ilsley argued that concession would encourage other appeals, but King insisted that the program would not survive if it was too inflexible and eventually Ilsley gave way. King also intervened when Howe wanted anti-strike legislation to keep steelworkers on the job, producing munitions. King, recognizing that arbitrary measures would be self-defeating in the long run, insisted on the right of collective bargaining. These interventions were exceptional and were related to labour relations, where King considered himself an expert, but his interpositions do illustrate his formidable role in the government.

King's authority would be most seriously tested by the issue of conscription. He was determined that the split it had caused in 1917, in his party and in the country, would never happen again. From the beginning of World War II he had promised that only voluntary recruits would be sent overseas. The other party leaders had supported this policy in the election campaign of March 1940 but the fall of France a few months later posed a threat to Britain's survival. Leading Conservatives now demanded conscription, arguing with some effect that it would be fairer and more efficient than voluntary enlistment. Few French Canadians, however, were impressed by this reasoning. King resolved the controversy, for the moment, by passing the National Resources Mobilization Act, which imposed conscription only for the defence of Canadian territory. This act placated those who favoured conscription without alienating those who objected to compulsory service overseas. King did increase the size of Canada's overseas contingent but only after his military advisers assured him that voluntary recruitment would provide the necessary strength.

The next crisis came in 1942. Allied defeats in Europe and in the Pacific, including the grievous loss of two Canadian battalions in the fall of Hong Kong, had convinced many more Canadians that a full commitment to the war required conscription for overseas service. Predictably most French Canadians believed it would be a betrayal of King's promise. He found a face-saving compromise. In January he announced a national plebiscite on releasing the government from its pledge. The outcome of the vote, held on 27 April, was disturbing. Strong support in English Canada meant that a majority of Canadians voted yes but in Quebec over 70 per cent were opposed. On conscription Canada was a country of two distinct cultures. Nevertheless, King moved quickly to repeal, through Bill 80, the section of the NRMA that restricted conscription to home defence. The resulting policy, King explained in the commons on 10 June, 'may be described as not necessarily conscription but conscription if necessary.' The bill passed third reading in July.

The plebiscite had a sobering effect on responsible politicians, and conscription received little attention until heavy Canadian casualties were sustained after the invasion of Normandy, France, in 1944. Defence minister J. L. Ralston then decided that only conscription could provide the needed reinforcements. King did not believe conscription was necessary to win the war and desperately tried to find a compromise. When Ralston remained obdurate, King replaced him abruptly in November with Andrew George Latta McNaughton, a retired general who King hoped would be able to attract sufficient volunteers. Only when McNaughton admitted failure a few weeks later did King, with the support of Louis St-Laurent, decide to send overseas some of the men conscripted for home defence. An order in council signed on 23 November authorized the transfer of 16,000 NRMA men, but only 2,463 would actually be posted to the 1st Canadian Army. The deliberations within cabinet over the switch to conscription had been extremely hard on King, particularly the real possibility of ministerial resignations on the 21st. That night he wrote in his diary: 'I mentioned to St. Laurent ... how very difficult it was for me all alone at Laurier House with no one to talk to and by myself to face over too long a period the kind of situation I am faced with today. He was very helpful.'

Remarkably, most French Canadians accepted in 1944 what they had bitterly opposed two years before. What had happened? King deserves much of the credit. It was clear that he had opposed conscription for as long as he dared. Now it was easier to believe that conscription for overseas service was at least politically necessary. He had won the confidence of St-Laurent and most of his French Canadian colleagues and this support helped reassure Quebec. Though French Canadians were not enthusiastic, most at least conceded that King was more sensitive to their point of view than the leaders of the other federal parties. It had been a close thing, but King had held the party and the country together.

The end of the war in Europe in May 1945 and in the Pacific in August brought new concerns. King and his government had already begun to plan for the post-war world. Planning was needed because the closure of munitions plants and the return of almost a million members of the armed services to civilian life would be enormously disruptive and because memories of the depression were still vivid. The government was credited with efficient administration during the war and many Canadians looked to it to provide economic security during the transition to a peacetime economy.

King's response was an accelerated shift to the left. In a reversal of his court reference of 1935, in 1940 the government, with provincial

A relieved William L. M. King manoeuvring out of the dangerous waters created by the 1944 conscription crisis, as depicted by *Halifax Herald* cartoonist Robert W. Chambers.

approval, had introduced unemployment insurance, a move strenuously opposed by Ralston on grounds of cost in wartime. In 1945 the government's financial advisers, converts to Keynesian policies, favoured increased public expenditures to create jobs and recommended family allowances and other social measures to boost consumer demand. King had misgivings about an expanded role – he still felt uneasy about government deficits – but he was sure these measures were consistent with his concern for the less fortunate. There were partisan motives too, although the self-righteous King would never have admitted it. The political pressure on the Liberal Party to compete with the CCF for votes could not be ignored. The prime minister might worry about an interventionist government encroaching on individual liberties but a Liberal government was clearly a lesser evil than a coercive socialist one. King introduced family allowances and for the election of June 1945 he campaigned on a broad program of social security. His government was handicapped by the legacy of conscription, which for different reasons had been unpopular in many parts of the country. The social program, however, was enough to redress the electoral balance and produce a narrow Liberal victory. Defeated in Prince Albert, King was returned in a by-election in Glengarry, Ont., in August.

King did not adapt easily to the post-war world. He had attended the founding conference of the United Nations at San Francisco in April–June 1945 but played only a minor role. He realistically conceded that the major powers would dominate the UN although he did argue for a 'functional principle' that would give such middle powers as Canada an influence based on their contributions to the settlement of disputes. Later that year he had to face the implications of a divided world more directly when Igor Sergeievich Gouzenko, a cipher clerk in the Soviet embassy in Ottawa, revealed Soviet spying in Canada. King was too realistic to believe that Canada could isolate itself from the Cold War, but he continued to be ill at ease with the demands made on Canada for the defence of North America and western Europe. He was also dubious about the international commitments favoured by Canadian diplomats; foreign entanglements would limit Canadian autonomy. Even closer relations with the United States left King concerned at the risk of falling into a new imperial orbit. Feeling overwhelmed with external affairs, in September 1946 he transferred the portfolio to Louis St-Laurent.

King was no more at ease in domestic politics. He admitted the need for fiscal planning and therefore the need for the federal government to retain jurisdiction over income and corporate taxes. He worried, however, about a system in which provincial governments depended heavily on federal subsidies or, as King saw it, spent money that Ottawa had collected. His skills as a conciliator were still valuable but policy initiatives came from his ministers and, more commonly, from the bureaucracy. Fortunately the expected post-war depression never arrived; the pent-up demands for housing and consumer goods facilitated a quick transition to a peacetime economy and full employment.

The burden of politics affected King's health. Tired out, he told St-Laurent in May 1948 that he could not face another campaign. He resigned as party leader in August and as prime minister on 15 November, to be succeeded by St-Laurent. King had planned to write his memoirs but he found it exhausting to recall the stresses of his political career. His papers were still being organized when he died at Kingsmere on 22 July 1950; he was buried in the family plot at Mount Pleasant Cemetery in Toronto.

The Canada of that year bore little resemblance to the Canada of 1919, when King had started out as Liberal leader. It had become prosperous and united, proud of its domestic stability and leadership in international affairs. King's political direction had facilitated Canada's development by avoiding or minimizing confrontations and by providing political steadiness in tumultuous times. This was no mean achievement.

W. L. Mackenzie King was essentially a party leader. He operated through cabinet and caucus, relying on his political judgement and his skills as a conciliator to shape policy. He provided national leadership by creating a Liberal Party that reflected the diverse regional, economic, and ethnic interests of the country. His modus operandi meant choosing colleagues who would represent and defend these interests while accepting collegial compromises. If some groups or regions were not adequately represented within the party, it was up to King to ensure that their interests were not overlooked. The respect for consensus required patience and produced policies that were cautious and incremental. King's form of leadership also tended to ignore grievances which had no effective political podiums – he paid little attention to the plight of aboriginals or the rights of women because in his day these groups posed no threat to the party. More positively, if King's approach meant that Liberal policies might not be popular, they were at least likely to be acceptable in all parts of the country. King was not a dynamic figure but he did have the qualities needed for this form of leadership. His liberalism, his political sensitivity, his skills as a conciliator, and his driving ambition for office had kept the party and country united during three decades of dramatic challenges. It was a credit to his leadership that, even after his retirement, his party, led by former colleagues, continued in office for almost nine more years.

H. BLAIR NEATBY

Further reading

R. MacG. Dawson and H. B. Neatby, *William Lyon Mackenzie King: a political biography* (3v., Toronto, 1958–76).

W. L. M. King, 'The diaries of William Lyon Mackenzie King': *king .collectionscanada.ca* (database created by Library and Archives Canada).

R. C. Brown and Ramsay Cook, *Canada, 1896–1921: a nation transformed* (Toronto, 1974).

J. H. Thompson and Allen Seager, *Canada, 1922–1939: decades of discord* (Toronto, 1985).

J. L. Granatstein, *Canada's war: the politics of the Mackenzie King government, 1939–1945* (Toronto, 1975).

RICHARD BEDFORD BENNETT,
1st Viscount Bennett,

lawyer, businessman, and politician; b. 3 July 1870 in Hopewell
Hill, N.B., eldest of the six children of Henry John Bennett
and Henrietta Stiles; d. unmarried during the night
of 26–27 June 1947 near Mickleham, England.

T he Bennett family came from England to Connecticut in the early
17th century. In 1761 they migrated eastward, part of a movement of New Englanders to take up old Acadian lands in Nova
Scotia. The family settled first near present-day Wolfville and then moved
across the Bay of Fundy to the estuary of the Petitcodiac in southeastern
New Brunswick. There Nathan Murray Bennett, Richard Bedford
Bennett's grandfather, established a shipbuilding yard at Hopewell Cape.
Henry Bennett, R. B.'s father, was apprenticed at age 20 to a relative to
learn the shipping business. By 1868 he was a partner in the Bennett
firm. On 22 Sept. 1869 he married Henrietta Stiles of Hopewell Hill,
some eight miles west of the Cape.

Henrietta was a staunch Wesleyan Methodist, her husband an easygoing, occasionally bibulous, Baptist. Her stern teetotal Methodism
became in her family the law supreme, its emphasis on work, diligence,
and self-denial. Make sure, John Wesley had said, not to waste time on
'silly unprofitable diversions': 'Gain all you can. … Save all you can. …
Give all you can.' Bourgeois to the core, those lessons that Henrietta urged
upon her first-born inculcated a way of life austere, sober, and hard-
working. Charitable to the outer world, they could be exacting to the
inner person. Self-indulgence was sin.

His mother also imbued him with ambition. Her aspirations for Dick,
as the family called him, came probably from hopes frustrated by her
husband and the difficulties of their shipyard. There were four children
born between 1870 and 1876, just at the time when it was finding trouble.
With increasing competition from iron hulls and steam engines, the ship-
yards of New Brunswick and Nova Scotia were being outclassed. Yards

like the Bennett one had to content themselves with building schooners for the coastal trade. Those schooners would be around for many a year yet, but in the depression of the 1870s Henry Bennett's shipbuilding was not enough to support his growing family; there were hints that he was an ineffective businessman. He had to turn himself into a general merchant, blacksmith, and farmer. R. B.'s penury started early. In 1934 he reportedly remarked to a friend, 'I'll always remember the pit from which I was [dug] & the long uphill road I had to travel. I'll never forget one step.'

A small legacy his mother received allowed him at age 16 to attend Normal School in Fredericton, and he eked out a living as teacher at Irishtown, north of Moncton. He raised his licence to first class in 1888 and that autumn was appointed at age 18 as principal of the school at Douglastown, on the north bank of the Miramichi six miles downriver from Newcastle. Alma Marjorie Russell, then a schoolgirl, described him on his arrival, six feet tall, slim, freckled, sitting bolt upright on the wagon seat under a bowler hat too large for him, looking even younger than his age. He was a good teacher, able, firm, and fair. He liked to have his students memorize poetry, as he himself did all his life. His examinations were stiff going, but he was also prepared to criticize even the school authorities. His report of June 1890 noted that in his two years at Douglastown 'I have not been favoured by a visit from one of the trustees.'

In his spare time he worked at Lemuel John Tweedie's law office across the Miramichi at Chatham. By the autumn of 1890 he had saved enough to go to law school at Dalhousie University, Halifax. R. B.'s notes that first term include a poem, 'The crossing paths,' that seems to have been of his own making.

> As passing ships whose wide-flung sails
> Are for an instant furled
> We hail, and banter words of cheer,
> Brought from the other world,
> With eager question, quick reply
> Across the deck we lean,
> Then part and put the Silences
> Of ocean wastes between.

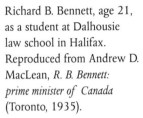

Richard B. Bennett, age 21,
as a student at Dalhousie
law school in Halifax.
Reproduced from Andrew D.
MacLean, *R. B. Bennett:
prime minister of Canada*
(Toronto, 1935).

At Dalhousie he plunged into work. His fellow students never saw him at rugby games; his interests were in the library, the moot court, debating. His record was sufficiently remarkable that when the dean of law, Richard Chapman Weldon, was later asked by Senator James Alexander Lougheed, a fellow Conservative, to recommend a good junior for his law office in Calgary, Weldon suggested Bennett.

After graduating in 1893, Bennett was back in Chatham in the law office now called Tweedie and Bennett. About 1895 there was a new office boy, William Maxwell Aitken (the future Lord Beaverbook), at the age of 15 getting an early start on assorted mischief. In 1896 he persuaded a hesitant Bennett to run as alderman in the new municipality of Chatham; with Max for publicity on the Bennett bicycle, Bennett squeaked in by 19 votes out of 691. He received Lougheed's invitation that same year, but he did not jump at it. Calgary was smaller than Chatham; Calgary was new, raw, untried; Alberta was not yet a province. There was the call of western opportunity to be sure, but there were also risks. In his mind, however, were (and would remain) Robert Browning's lines 'Ah, but a man's reach should exceed his grasp, / Or what's a heaven for?'

Bennett, tall, lean, and 26 years old, got off the train at Calgary in late January 1897. It was not an inviting place, -40°F with a hard wind, a skiff of snow holding down the dust of unpaved streets. The station had no cabs; Bennett lugged his bags over to the Alberta Hotel a block or two away. He was something of an outsider from the very first. Never one to follow the crowd, he neither smoked nor drank and he dressed formally at all times. He could work like a horse, long hours with no play. When some years later a friend sent him, along with New Year's wishes, hopes for 'a quiet mind,' Bennett replied, 'Just why you should contemplate such a disaster I cannot understand.' Bennett's was not a quiet mind: if amazingly retentive, it was an intensely restless one, his thought translated into action with enormous energy and by quick decisions.

The Lougheed–Bennett practice went slowly at first but by 1900 Calgary was growing and by 1905, when Alberta became a province, growing rapidly. Bennett was now buying and selling land, and with the firm's retainer from the Canadian Pacific Railway, making a good thing of it. Calgary had become the centre of a large farming and ranching community. There were soon oil leases and oil companies as well. Bennett invested in William Stewart Herron's Calgary Petroleum Products Company, of which he became director and solicitor. Under manager Archibald Wayne Dingman it struck oil in the Turner valley. Bennett also became involved with Aitken in the successful promotions that produced the Alberta Pacific Grain Company, Canada Cement, and Calgary Power. His reputation grew throughout, as an honest, versatile, clever, persistent lawyer. By 1914 he had an extremely busy and profitable practice. And R. B.'s teetotal principles would never obstruct legitimate legal business; among his clients was Alfred Ernest Cross's Calgary Brewing and Malting.

He was then well into Conservative politics. He had first been elected in 1898, as the member for West Calgary in the Legislative Assembly of the North-West Territories at Regina. There he challenged the view of the premier, Frederick William Gordon Haultain, a Conservative, that party politics had no place in the territories. After Alberta's creation as a province in 1905, its capital at Edmonton, he was put forward by friends for the new Legislative Assembly. He lost, but was elected in 1909. In that contest the Liberals took 37 seats; there were 3 Conservatives and 1 Socialist. Of this unpromising opposition, Bennett was soon the spokesman, giving the government little quarter, especially in the matter of the Alberta and Great Waterways Railway contract. He was a vigorous debater, not afraid of challenges, confident, perhaps too confident, of his own knowledge. In the subsequent litigation deriving from this issue that pitted the province against the Royal Bank of Canada, he acted for the bank and would ultimately be successful in 1913 on appeal to the Judicial Committee of the Privy Council.

Bennett was that rare being, a successful Alberta Conservative, and was elected to the House of Commons for Calgary in 1911. His leader, Prime Minister Robert Laird Borden, gave him the honour of moving the address in reply to the speech from the throne. R. B.'s red Toryism was a little ahead of Borden's, embracing workmen's compensation, trade unions, government grain elevators, and government control of freight rates. As he put it in his maiden speech in the commons, 20 Nov. 1911, 'The great struggle of the future will be between human rights and property interests; and it is the duty and the function of government to provide that there shall be no undue regard for the latter that limits or lessens the other.'

He had come to Ottawa feeling, however, that the party owed him more than just the address in reply. He had given up his CPR retainer of $10,000 a year the day after he was elected and there seemed to be few compensations. He could not be appointed to cabinet because Lougheed was government leader in the Senate. Three weeks after his commons speech he wrote to Aitken impatiently: 'I am sick of it here. There is little or nothing to do & what there is to do is that of a party hack or departmental clerk or messenger.' But he believed in Borden's Naval Aid Bill of 1912–13 and made a four-hour speech supporting it. He thought that the self-governing nations within the empire should be federated, that there must be recognition, as he had written to Aitken in 1910, 'of common interests, common traditions, & above all common responsibilities and obligations.' 'I hold out to this House' he said in the commons in 1913, 'the vision of a wider hope, the hope that one day this Dominion will be the dominant factor in that great federation.' The Naval Aid Bill nevertheless foundered in the Liberal-dominated Senate.

As a new MP, Bennett was a maverick, his views on Canadian railways, tariffs, and Canada's position within the empire not always conforming to party policy. His independence was starkly revealed in his opposition to the Canadian Northern Railway Guarantee Bill of 1914. His speech against his government's financial support of this line was buttressed by wide experience and knowledge of railways. His targets included not only the railway and its principals, Sir William Mackenzie and Sir Donald Mann, but Arthur Meighen, the solicitor general. Meighen was Borden's bully boy whom the prime minister had given the job of piloting this complicated legislation. Meighen kept interrupting Bennett's speech. Bennett did not like it: he was not going to have his argument broken up by 'the gram[o]phone of Mackenzie and Mann.' Borden was uneasy about Bennett's independence, but both he and Meighen recognized that Bennett's long denunciation of the Canadian Northern was condemnation in detail of the most dubious of former Liberal prime minister Sir Wilfrid Laurier's railway adventures.

When World War I came late that summer, Bennett tried to enlist, but he was turned down as not medically fit, for reasons that he never revealed. Then the sudden death of his mother, whom he had visited in New Brunswick each Christmas, supervened in October. His father had died in 1905, probably without much insurance, and it is reasonably certain that Dick supported his mother and Mildred Mariann, the younger of his two sisters. The other sister, Evelyn Read, was about to be married to Horace Weldon Coates, a physician. They soon moved to Vancouver, where Dick bought them a house. Mildred followed them, and Dick's next Christmases, 1915–27, would be spent on the west coast.

In July 1915 Borden invited Bennett as his assistant to London, to ascertain how Canada might help British military and civilian needs. The following year he was made director general of the National Service Board, charged with determining the number of prospective recruits in Canada. The war seriously affected his practice in Calgary, enlistments taking his political organizer, George Robinson, and several others from his office. The loss of these men, he told Max in London, 'leaves me absolutely without assistance and heartbroken.' He then added a strange qualification: 'so far as it is possible for a man of my type & temperment [sic] to be heartbroken about anything.'

What did that signify? He had been a devoted son, a dutiful and loving brother. Benevolence was an obsession; he was giving money to deserving students, needy widows, and a host of charities, altogether ten per cent of his gross income. What then were the springs of his nature? He loved hard work for the sheer satisfaction of mastery, in finance, accounting, law. He was a wizard with legal precedents and uncanny with errors in a balance sheet. At the same time he was a sublime egotist, clever, irascible, unsparing of himself or others. Forgiveness was one of the Christian virtues he found difficult to practise. He had a volatile temper, explosive while it lasted. Wound up in the coils of his own nature he seems rarely to have considered the effects of his words and actions. His receiving antennae were weak; sometimes they did not appear even to be deployed. R. B.'s limited receiving capacity was often the source of his strength and courage. His future rival William Lyon Mackenzie King's sensitive antennae made him timid, his hypocrisy more crafty as he got older. Bennett scorned hypocrisy. He had the dangerous habit of saying what he really thought. What drove Bennett was his own mind, not what others might think of him.

Bennett supported the Military Service Act of July 1917, which was guided through the house by Meighen and which brought in conscription, but he opposed Borden's idea of the Union government. He thought an alliance between Conservatives and Liberals, even for purposes of war, would end in disaster for his party. It did. Thus while in the election of December 1917 R. B. campaigned for the Conservatives, he did not run himself. In February 1918 he was further alienated by Borden's failure to honour a promise Bennett believed the prime minister had made, to appoint him to the Senate. Borden chose instead an obscure Alberta Liberal, William James Harmer, to satisfy coalition arrangements. Bennett was furious. As for being senator, Bennett needed neither position nor money; his object was to put his knowledge and experience at the service of his country. He wrote Borden an aggrieved 20-page letter. There was no reply.

By 1918 Bennett had acquired a growing commitment to the E. B. Eddy Company of Hull, Que. This had developed from his long friendship with Jennie Grahl Hunter Eddy, whom he had met in New Brunswick. After her husband, Ezra Butler Eddy, died in 1906, leaving her a controlling interest in his lumber company, she called on Bennett to help her manage her financial affairs. When she herself died in 1921, her will left 500 shares to Bennett and 1,009 to her younger brother, Joseph Thompson (Harry) Shirreff. Harry died suddenly in 1926, bequeathing all his shares to Bennett. They were now being assessed at $1,500 each, a valuation that made Bennett's holdings worth $2,263,500. He thus became the principal director of the company. He kept watch on the firm but claimed an arm's-length relationship, which most of the time it was. After Bennett had been given Mrs Eddy's shares, there were rumours that there had been a romance between them. Some said that Mildred Bennett, born in 1889, was really their daughter. There was no truth in it. Bennett replied that when Mildred was born he had not even met Jennie Shirreff. As to romance, he said, Jennie was almost eight years older than he was, as if that were an impediment.

On 1 July 1920 Sir Robert Borden resigned, worn out with the war, Versailles, and politics. When the Unionist caucus chose Arthur Meighen as successor, many Liberals in it were already feeling the tug of ancient loyalties. Laurier had died in 1919 and the Liberals had chosen Mackenzie King as leader. In 1921 Meighen, with his majority crumbling, called an election for 6 December. To strengthen his government he asked Bennett to be minister of justice. Canada was in disarray socially and politically: a post-war recession, rising unemployment, continued labour unrest following upon the Winnipeg General Strike in 1919, industrial decline and discontent in the Maritimes, and an agrarian revolt on the prairies that had led to the formation at the national level in 1920 of the Progressive Party under Thomas Alexander Crerar. Bennett decided to put his influence 'on the side of law, order and constituted authority.' He was sworn in on 21 Sept. 1921. Soon enough he knew that there was little hope for the Meighen government. Bennett and his friends were also too confident of his own seat in Calgary West; the contest was so close that the outcome of a judicial recount depended on the way the X on the ballots was made. Bennett lost by 16 votes.

By March 1922 he was spending much time with the Eddy firm in Hull. He was thinking of giving up his 25-year-old partnership with Lougheed. Sir James was 67 years old, was doing little work, and had been hiring juniors whose quality Bennett distrusted. He was seeing Lougheed about dissolving the partnership when a Privy Council appeal called him to England. Arrangements with Lougheed were left in suspense, but Sir James was persuaded that he could proceed with dissolution. His unilateral action set off irascible cables from Bennett, who indignantly bounced back to Canada. Thus began a messy litigation. The old Lougheed–Bennett firm split three ways, Bennett's group, Bennett,

Hannah, and Sanford, retaining most of the important clients, including A. E. Cross and fellow businessmen William Charles James Roper Hull and Patrick Burns.

By the mid twenties Bennett was extremely well off. His total income in 1924 was $76,897. Only 25 per cent came from his legal practice. His 1924 director's fees, from E. B. Eddy and Alberta Pacific Grain mostly, totalled 7 per cent. The bulk of his income, 62 per cent, derived from dividends. Half of these came from Alberta Pacific Grain, of which he was president; he sold this firm to Spillers Milling of England late in 1924. Two other firms, E. B. Eddy and Canada Cement, represented 16 and 13 per cent of dividend income. The dividend portion kept growing. In 1930 he made $262,176, of which 85 per cent was dividends. That was the high point until 1937. Bennett was also a director of Metropolitan Life Insurance of New York and by the mid 1920s was on the board of the Royal Bank of Canada.

At the same time Bennett was being urged by Meighen to get back into politics. Going into the election of 1925 Meighen offered the justice portfolio should he be prime minister. Bennett threw himself into the campaign. He won Calgary West with a comfortable majority, and in Alberta his party gained three seats and 32 per cent of the vote. (The 1921 election had resulted in no seats and 20 per cent of the vote.) Across Canada the Conservatives took 116 seats, the Liberals 99. King was personally defeated in York North. It looked like a Liberal defeat, but King did not resign; he believed that with 24 Progressive MPs he could carry on. It was dangerous going. Then came the customs scandal, an unholy mixture of rum, money, and bribery that began to unhinge King's precarious coalition.

A select committee was set up to inquire into the administration of the Department of Customs and Excise, with Bennett and Henry Herbert Stevens as the leading Conservatives. Its report, tabled in the commons on 18 June 1926, sharply criticized the former minister, Jacques Bureau; Stevens, dissatisfied, moved for censure of King's government. By this time Progressive loyalty to the Liberals was nearly gone. King, who had been returned to the commons at a by-election in Prince Albert, Sask., in February, managed to adjourn the house at 5:00 A.M. on 26 June by only one vote. That was when, to avoid the defeat of his government, he asked Governor General Lord Byng for a dissolution. Byng refused, King resigned, and the King–Byng crisis was on.

Bennett had promised to go to Calgary to help provincial Conservative leader Alexander Andrew McGillivray in an election. He tried to renege, but his Alberta friends held him to it. While he was gone, the new Meighen government was defeated by one vote, 2 July 1926, on an ingenious but spurious attack by King and James Alexander Robb on the legality of the acting ministers that Meighen had quickly appointed. Meighen did not, as yet, have a seat; Bennett was paired and in Calgary. Had Bennett been in the house, he would have been able to face down King, and Meighen almost certainly would not have been defeated. Meighen got the dissolution he had to ask for, with the election set for 14 Sept. 1926.

Immediately upon Bennett's return to Ottawa he was sworn in to a clutch of portfolios: minister of finance, acting minister of mines, acting minister of the interior, and acting superintendent general of Indian affairs. Meighen expected to win the 1926 election with the customs scandal; King won it with an obscure constitutional issue made vital by the throb of Canadian nationalism that King put into it. Meighen was devastated. He resigned the Conservative leadership and caucus selected as temporary leader Hugh Guthrie, a former Liberal who had joined Borden in 1917. It then called a convention to elect a new leader, to be held after the 1927 session of parliament.

One of the principal issues in 1927 was old age pensions, which Bennett strongly favoured. King had been hesitating about them for many reasons, not the least of which was the fact that existing war pensions, introduced by Borden's government in 1919, ate up over 14 per cent of government expenditure in 1926. King had tried to bring in old age pensions that year, but the legislation had been killed in the Conservative-dominated Senate. In 1927 he reintroduced it, revised but still with weaknesses that Bennett thought unfortunate. The cost was still to be shared 50–50 with the provinces, though the provinces had not been consulted about the plan. 'We are imposing our will upon the provincial legislatures,' Bennett said. He thought old age pensions should be funded wholly by Ottawa. He believed as well that the pensions should, like Britain's, be contributory. Thrift in the form of pension contributions would thus earn its own reward. Those who could not afford such contributions would have them paid by Ottawa. In March, however, the bill as King presented it passed both the commons and the Senate, the upper house having apparently decided that the Canadian people had endorsed the scheme in the election.

Bennett was also an advocate of unemployment insurance and supported proposals put forward in the house that session by labour politician Abraham Albert Heaps, though with conditions. Unemployment insurance should be funded by premiums paid by both the person concerned and the government, he argued. The subscription principle would encourage economy and industry. But Heaps's proposals were voted down. Another major debate in 1927 arose over the administration of war pensions, mainly the narrow way entitlement was being viewed by the Board of Pension Commissioners. Bennett said the Pension Act was being handled too harshly, putting on the applicant the onus of proving his case. Bennett's amendment won Progressive and Labour support; the government had to defeat it, which it did 95–78, but promised the act would be revised. Bennett's contributions to the 1927 session well illustrate the forward thrust of his mind. 'Shall we be statesmen or politicians?' he asked in one debate.

The Conservative convention opened in Winnipeg on 10 Oct. 1927. Various candidates were mooted. As late as the end of August, Bennett seems not to have entirely made up his mind whether he wanted to be leader. Some friends were trying to dissuade him, one contrasting 'prestige, liberty, ease ... delights, leisure' with 'abuse, ingratitude, selfishness and slavish work.' Bennett was but 57 years of age, brimming with energy and ambition. Except for Robert James Manion, he was the youngest candidate. He was not concerned about ease or delights or prestige. There was such a thing as duty. Canada had been good to him. But as late as the day of the convention he may not have been fully decided. Then on the 13th he had a plurality on the first ballot and a majority on the second, rather to his surprise. His acceptance speech was sincerity and sentiment. He admitted being rich, but stressed that he had made his money from hard work. As elected leader, he would resign his company directorships. 'No man may serve you as he should if he has over his shoulder always the shadow of pecuniary obligations.' Service to Canada would be his motto; out of Mark 9:35 he would be 'servant of all.'

Bennett's leadership of the party, prospective or real, induced offers to buy E. B. Eddy, all or part. Immediately after the convention he and Mildred went to New York and London. The Eddy match business, which had always been a headache, was sold to Bryant and May of London in December 1927, with a new entity called Eddy Match Company Limited established at Pembroke, Ont. Bennett retained a considerable block of Eddy Match stock. Eddy Pulp and Paper at Hull was more awkward to unload; Bennett would not accept any fire-sale price, and it was only in 1943 that it was sold to Willard Garfield Weston. Bennett returned to Calgary late in 1927 to a flood of congratulations. He baled out of his many directorships as he had promised. 'Must you?' asked Haley Fiske, president of Metropolitan Life, noting that Premier Louis-Alexandre Taschereau of Quebec had kept his directorship in the company. Bennett insisted.

He had more pressing work now on hand. The state of the party was not promising. In Ottawa its national office was the back rooms of senior Conservative MPs. It had no money; moreover, Bennett discovered that after what had happened in 1926, 'it is exceedingly difficult to obtain money.' Newspaper support was unreliable. Across Canada there were only 11 dailies that could be called Conservative. Quebec Conservative papers had been devastated, as the party had been, by Borden's and Meighen's war policies. R. B. had been given authority by the Conservative convention to establish a central office in Ottawa. By February 1930, under national director Alexander Duncan McRae, there would be 27 full-time employees using modern office equipment to spread the Conservative word across the provinces. The money for this enterprise, and some provincial ones, came from Bennett and senior party members; they each put up $2,500 a month. More would be needed and by April 1929 Bennett had added a considerable chunk of his capital. By May 1930 he had contributed $500,000 since becoming party leader. About one-fifth went to Quebec.

In that province the Conservatives, French and English, were riven by faction, both communities apt to have more generals than soldiers. Bennett was urged to appoint a Quebec leader, but with so many groups he hesitated. He made a major speech in Montreal at a party banquet in October 1928, mostly in English, but with Quebec Conservative leader

Arthur Sauvé, long estranged from Borden and Meighen, on the platform giving him warm praise. The party that in 1927 was described as 'utterly helpless' was by the end of 1929 looking distinctly better. Some of the credit was owing to Conservative Ontario premier George Howard Ferguson's repeal of repressive rules against bilingual schools, some to Sauvé's successor, Camillien Houde, and some to Bennett. In English-speaking Canada the situation was also fairly optimistic, with the Conservatives in power in five provinces.

The party's fortunes had also been bolstered by Bennett's considerable success as leader of the opposition. He went cautiously, Borden congratulating him on his excellent judgement and good results. After the session of 1928 ended he dutifully and energetically toured the constituencies, as he did again in 1929. He was not, however, without rueful reflections about his role: 'Sometimes I wonder why I ever undertook this work at my time of life, after all my years of toil and effort.' In parliament his speeches were seldom marked with partisan venom. Bennett seemed rather to disarm enmity. The cheerfulness and charm with which the 16th parliament ended in May 1930 owed something to him. At dissolution, he and King shared a joke; MPs flocked across the floor shaking hands. King remarked how pleasant it all was. And so the campaign of 1930 started.

Bennett left Ottawa at 2:10 A.M. on Sunday, 8 June 1930, in a private railway car attached to the Winnipeg train. He was glad to go; campaigning was hard work but in the capital that last week he had, as he told a friend, 'been driven to death' by party demands of all kinds on the eve of a general election. Private railway cars were the way much electioneering was done. Radio was the big change from 1926. Bennett's first campaign speech, out of Winnipeg on 9 June, was heard by Mackenzie King in Ottawa and by perhaps a million others. Bennett came over well on radio, having a resonant voice that carried better than King's wheeziness. In 1926 there had been 134,000 radios in Canada; in 1930 they numbered close to half a million. Most operated by battery and did not require power lines, so the isolation of rural areas began to change. Radio also meant politicians did not need so many meetings. Nevertheless, from 9 June until 26 July Bennett travelled some 14,000 miles, delivering as many as five speeches a day.

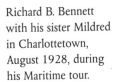

Richard B. Bennett
with his sister Mildred
in Charlottetown,
August 1928, during
his Maritime tour.

There were not sufficient women candidates. Liberals were running women in hopeless constituencies simply to attract the female vote. Bennett wanted them in safe seats but was unable to persuade the constituencies. His sister Mildred campaigned with him. She had a remarkably deft political sense, as well as style, charm, empathy, and a sense of humour that often made up for her brother's occasionally strident bluntness. She was a political asset in her own right and party officials were well aware of it. There were plenty of issues. After some years of steadily increasing prosperity, the stock market crash of 1929 and a collapse in the price of natural products had begun to undermine the Canadian economy. Wheat prices were down from $1.75 a bushel in July 1929 to below $1 a year later, causing great hardship in western Canada where the situation was worsened by drought and crop failure. Other agricultural areas contended with a flood of New Zealand butter. The malaise spread to the transportation and construction sectors and to the manufacturing industry, which began to experience lower prices and a decline in production and investment. Unemployment was greatly on the rise, and there was no security net. King's angry assertion in April 1930 that he would not give any Tory provincial government even a five-cent piece to help with joblessness was exploited by the Conservatives in cartoons and speeches. Bennett promised employment, through tariff protection for Canadian industries and a large program of public works. It was the issue that won him the election.

'The Grand Panjandrum Comes to Ottawa' – the day after Canada's general election of 28 July 1930, *Manitoba Free Press* cartoonist Archibald Dale depicted Prime Minister Bennett's triumphal arrival in the capital. Reproduced from *Five years of R. B. Bennett* (Winnipeg, 1935), courtesy of the *Winnipeg Free Press.*

The result on 28 July 1930 was that the Conservative Party won 137 seats against 91 for the Liberals and 17 others and a majority of seats in five of the nine provinces. During the election Joseph-Hormisdas Rainville, the party's organizer in Quebec, had provided some funding for Adrien Arcand, leader of an anti-Semitic movement there, in return for support from his three small newspapers. The Conservatives greatly improved their Quebec representation, from 4 to 24 MPs, though they fell well short of a majority of the province's 65 seats. (Subsequently Arcand made several trips to Ottawa to get further funding. Bennett was distinctly unhelpful; in effect, Arcand got the cold shoulder. His papers would collapse early in 1933, a clear indication that prominent Tories in Quebec were by then fighting shy of any public association with what would become a Fascist and Nazi party.)

The cabinet that Bennett formed, 19 members in all, sworn in on 7 August, had able people, Guthrie, Stevens, Charles Hazlitt Cahan, Edgar Nelson Rhodes, and Edward Baird Ryckman, but it was thin on similar French Canadians. Bennett himself took on Finance besides the portfolio usual to the prime minister, External Affairs (which he almost single-handedly saved from extinction, his caucus wanting to abolish it).

There would be a lot of cabinet meetings, proportionately almost double the number held by King. The oft-repeated story that Bennett was a tyrant in cabinet is, as Manion recalled, 'just so much balderdash.' Most of Bennett's ministers handled their departments without either his direction or his interference. In caucus it was much the same. Where Bennett did fail was in thanking cabinet colleagues in parliament or in public for things well done. In 1932 Manion would say to him, 'My first ambition is that some day I may make a speech that will meet with your approval.' Bennett fairly fumed at this remark. But he telephoned the next day to make amends, though not apologies. R. B. hated to apologize. He was a critical taskmaster. He knew so much and hated to see questions incompetently handled; he found it difficult to praise those who did not meet his standards.

Bennett took office with action on his mind. Action he had promised and action Canada got. A special session of parliament was called for 8 September. He believed that tariffs were necessary not only to keep Canada independent of the United States but to create markets for Canadian producers, so tariff revision, steeply upward on a range of manufactured goods, was instituted. The emergency Unemployment Relief Act, providing $20 million for public works at the federal and local levels, was also passed. Parliament prorogued in two weeks. Then it was organization for the Imperial Conference in London, which was to start on 30 September and which Bennett hoped would provide a solution to Canada's economic difficulties through the establishment of a reciprocal preference in trade. The conference was mostly a Canadian idea but Canadians would be a day late for it.

The composition of the Canadian delegation was a question in itself. Oscar Douglas Skelton, under-secretary of state for external affairs, came to Bennett about it. At first Bennett distrusted Skelton; he was too anti-British. 'I'm not going to have you monkeying with this business,' Bennett was reported to have said. 'It is for the Prime Minister's office, not for External Affairs.' Skelton explained the role of External Affairs in imperial conferences under Borden and King, and a compromise was reached whereby John Erskine Read, a legal adviser at External, was put on Bennett's delegation.

At the second plenary conference at the Foreign Office in London on 8 October, Bennett came to the point. 'I offer to the Mother Country and to all the other parts of the Empire, a preference in the Canadian market in exchange for a like preference in theirs.' The proposal was bold, blunt, and frank. It left the British government, committed to free trade, in shock. By that weekend the British papers were full of Bennett and Canada. 'Empire or not?' asked the *Observer* (London). When the conference ended on 14 November there was still no answer. The real response came late that month in the British House of Commons when the rough-spoken James Henry Thomas, the dominions secretary, simply said that Bennett's proposal was 'humbug.' Nevertheless, when Bennett left London for Canada, Thomas was at Euston Station to bid him farewell. 'On to Ottawa!' said Bennett as they shook hands. The conference would be renewed in the Canadian capital.

Bennett returned to an economic situation that was far more intractable than he had thought. Wheat prices had continued to drop and drought on the prairies was in its third year. Another series of tariff increases was instituted in 1931, and the Unemployment and Farm Relief Act was passed to provide funds for further public works as well as direct relief (more than $28 million would be spent and similar acts would be passed in 1932, 1933, 1934, and 1935). Bennett also began to try to find ways to help market the wheat crop, efforts that would culminate in the establishment of the Canadian Wheat Board in 1935.

In the later 1920s and early 1930s the Ontario school primers had a colour picture of the Union Jack under which was printed, 'One Flag, One Fleet, One Throne.' By 1931 that neat logic was no longer quite tenable. 'We no longer live in a political Empire,' Bennett declared after the adoption that year of the Statute of Westminster, which gave Canada and the other dominions autonomy in external relations. But he still hoped to construct 'a new economic Empire.' He knew, however, that the 'Empire Free Trade' being promoted by Beaverbrook in London was a chimera. His ideal continued to be an imperial preferential trade arrangement in which Canada would 'play a part of ever-increasing importance.' The Imperial Economic Conference was supposed to have been held in Ottawa in 1931, but impediments had arisen and it had been put off until July 1932. Meantime Britain introduced a general tariff of 10 per cent, a development that gave some encouragement to Bennett's hopes.

By the time of the conference Bennett had acquired much-needed help in Finance. He appointed Edgar Rhodes as minister on 3 Feb. 1932. That spring he hired William Clifford Clark, professor of commerce at Queen's University in Kingston, Ont., to prepare position papers. They were so useful that in October Bennett asked Clark to be deputy minister of finance. It was a brilliant appointment; Bennett was unerring in his judgement of able financial men. Nevertheless the Canadian civil service was weak to mount such an important conference. When the British were running them, the agenda had been circulated six months ahead. The Canadian agenda was ready only on 7 July, after the antipodean delegates had already sailed. The delay was also because, as Sir William Henry Clark, the British high commissioner in Ottawa, explained, 'the Prime Minister is waiting as usual until he can find time to deal with matters himself.' During the conference Arthur Neville Chamberlain, Britain's chancellor of the exchequer, would come to think 'that the reason for Bennett's difficulties is really inadequate preparation on his side. He has no professional civil service & no minister whom he trusts.'

When the conference opened in the Parliament Buildings on 21 July, Bennett was chosen to chair it. His opening speech suggested that Britain might have free entry into Canada for any products that would 'not injuriously affect Canadian enterprise.' Only on 4 August, however, did the British get a list of Canadian concessions and it was much less than they expected. Bennett was subjected to many political pressures: his cabinet was deeply divided; he no longer quite trusted Stevens, his minister of trade and commerce; and there was intense lobbying by Canadian industrialists on cotton, coal, iron, and steel. Bennett did not want to wreck his own conference, but he and his cabinet colleagues believed that Britain was offering very little. Among the British representatives his reputation declined sharply. Walter Runciman, the president of the Board of Trade, became so annoyed with Bennett's bullying manner that in mid August he warned him privately the conference was heading straight for failure and 'the world would put the failure down to him.' Bennett had an aggressive style, he admitted it himself.

What emerged from the Ottawa conference was not any great imperial economic principle but hard-fought bilateral treaties. The British–Canadian one, as it turned out, benefited Canada more than it did Britain.

Canadian wheat, apples, and other natural products got British preferences; the British got Canadian preferences for certain metal products and textiles not made in Canada. In a few years, Canadian exports to Britain were up 60 per cent; Britain's to Canada were up 5.

One of Bennett's constant advisers that summer was Major William Duncan Herridge. A lawyer and a former Liberal, he had broken with his party in 1926 and joined Bennett's election campaign in June 1930. Mildred Bennett's marriage to Herridge, now minister to Washington, took place on 14 April 1931. As she was packing up her things in the Château Laurier suite where she and R. B. had lived for nearly four years, she wrote a heartfelt note to 'Dick, my dear dear brother.' It says much about them both: 'If I could only say all that is in my heart but I can't ... in the midst of my most sacred and divine love you have never for a moment been out of my mind. ... I sometimes think that loving Bill as I do – I've loved and valued you even more.' After Mildred had gone, R. B. seems to have become sharply aware of the huge interior space she had left vacant. 'We're the bumpers on his car,' Mildred had once remarked to Bennett's long-time secretary, Alice Millar. 'We save him from a lot of damage.'

On 21 Aug. 1932, as the *Empress of Britain* was sailing down the St Lawrence with exhausted British delegates aboard, Bennett was on his way to a restored 18th-century seigneurial house at Mascouche, Que. It was owned by Hazel Beatrice Colville of Montreal, the twice-widowed daughter of Sir Albert Edward Kemp, an old colleague of Bennett's from the 1921 cabinet. Hazel, attractive, intelligent, and wealthy, was 43 years old, and her romance with R. B. had begun in April. Bennett went to Mascouche that summer whenever he could. Perhaps it was this intimacy that J. H. Thomas meant when he described Bennett's private life as 'very disreputable.'

Bennett's relations with women have a strange history. He liked them, they liked him; he was tall, well-made, and rich. Why had he not married? The problem, according to one contemporary account, was phimosis, a tight foreskin that could be very painful at erection. That may well have been corrected by surgery during one of R. B.'s visits to London in 1905 or 1910. A more intractable difficulty seems to have developed by 1914, and may be the reason Canadian army doctors rejected him: Peyronie's disease, a fibrous thickening of the penile shaft creating a distinct bend and at erection discomfort. It is a rare chronic condition of middle age and is sometimes related to incipient diabetes. What the effect of this was on Bennett's affair with Hazel is guesswork. Certain it is that R. B. at age 62 was overwhelmed by the affair – 'I miss you beyond all words & I am lonesome beyond cure without your presence,' he wrote. Then by 1933, certainly by 1934, it was over, ended by Hazel. She liked her life as a society woman, not least bridge, cocktails, cigarettes; Bennett disliked all three. There seemed to be lots of men; she did not need an exigent husband, however in love he might be.

Hazel may have been one reason why Bennett lacked time to prepare for the 1932 conference, but the House of Commons was another. The most urgent question there was radio. Canada was being inundated with American programs, hence American values. In December 1928 the King government had appointed a bipartisan royal commission, under chairman Sir John Aird, to inquire into radio broadcasting. Its report the following September was a model of concision and decision. The text was nine pages. Radio, it maintained, had to be Canadian, English *and* French, but Canadian. Existing radio offered too much entertainment and not enough education. To these conclusions the leaders in the commons all subscribed, King, Bennett, and James Shaver Woodsworth, who headed the Labour group. The problem was how to put them into effect. Where lay the constitutional authority to regulate radio? Quebec claimed it fell within provincial jurisdiction. King had shied away from the question; Bennett acted as soon as he returned from London in December 1930. A reference was made to the Supreme Court of Canada and on 30 June 1931 it decided for the federal government. Quebec appealed to the Judicial Committee of the Privy Council, supported by Ontario. Judgement was given in London on 9 Feb. 1932 in favour of Ottawa.

Within a week Bennett proposed a special committee of the commons. Everyone agreed, he said, that the present system was unsatisfactory. Radio was of surpassing importance, essential in nation building, and with a high educational value. The special committee reported on 9 May 1932 and the bill setting up the Canadian Radio Broadcasting Commission, to regulate all broadcasting in Canada and establish a nationally owned radio system, was presented a week later. In Bennett's speech to the house on 18 May there was more than a touch of his red Toryism. Only public ownership could ensure to all Canadians the service of radio; no Canadian government was justified in leaving the airwaves to private exploitation. The House of Commons approved overwhelmingly the act setting up the CRBC.

The following year the country was facing even graver difficulties. Unemployment had reached 27 per cent of the workforce, as high as in the United States. On the prairies, drought, crop failures, and soil erosion continued, turning especially southern Saskatchewan into a dust bowl. The government's budgetary deficit stood at $150 million and more than a million and a half Canadians were dependent on direct relief. The work camps for unemployed single men that had been set up in 1932 under the aegis of the Department of National Defence were becoming hotbeds of discontent. Everywhere established institutions seemed to be under threat. Bennett was doing the best he could to weather the economic storm; the problem was, as he told Sir Robert Borden, 'that we are subject to the play of forces which we did not create and which we cannot either regulate or control.' People demanded action, but 'any action at this time except to maintain the ship of state on an even keel … involves possible consequences about which I hesitate even to think.'

The pervasive feel of the depression was of this very helplessness. The lack of any vestige of hope exacerbated the climate of fear: fear induced by watching the old and familiar crumbling; fear that next month,

The desperate faces of the Great Depression: the Deynaka family leaving Edmonton's Market Square for High Prairie, Alta, 6 May 1933.

especially next winter, there would not be enough to eat or the where-withal to keep warm. Even for those on fixed incomes it was a distressing time, having to cope with tramps at the kitchen door and watching the freight trains going by with men riding to unknown destinations and for unknown purposes. Roots were drying up like the prairies. Borden told Bennett he and his wife fed everyone who came to the door at their Ottawa home. Two thirds of them, Borden said, were genuinely down on their luck, battered and bruised by economic forces over which they had no control.

By 4 March 1933, the day Franklin Delano Roosevelt was sworn in as president, almost every bank in the United States had locked its doors. The Canadian banking system had stood up well – there had not been a Canadian bank failure since 1923 – but there was urgent need of a central bank to regulate credit. Bennett had seen first-hand what the Bank of England could do to help Britain's depression. On 21 March 1933 E. N. Rhodes announced there would be a royal commission on banking and currency in Canada. The commission reported in September, recom-mending three to two in favour of a central bank, the two dissenters being Canadian bankers. The legislation passed almost unanimously in 1934 and the Bank of Canada was established the following year with Graham Ford Towers as its first governor. The chartered banks did not like it; they had to give up their profitable issue of bank notes in favour of a national currency, and they were required to transfer their gold reserves to the Bank of Canada. For the gold, they sought a much higher price than they had paid, a demand Bennett thought iniquitous. R. B. said to James Herbert Stitt, MP for Selkirk, who asked about it, 'his eye-brows bristling like quills … "Jimmie Stitt, you quit worrying. We are going to get that gold and it is just about time for us to find out whether the banks or this government is running this country."'

There was other legislation in 1934. The Farmers' Creditors Arrange-ment Act was designed to allow families to remain on their farms rather than lose them to foreclosure. The Natural Products Marketing Act estab-lished a federal board with powers to arrange more orderly marketing in the hope of obtaining better prices. The Public Works Construction Act launched a federal building program, worth $40 million, aimed at getting the unemployed back to work. A special committee (which later became a royal commission) headed by H. H. Stevens was set up to investigate mass buying by large businesses and the difference between the prices received by producers and the prices consumers were being charged. But Bennett considered the Bank of Canada his best domestic achievement.

Nevertheless, his government found the going difficult. 'It may be too late,' Manion had reflected as early as 9 Dec. 1933, 'to save the party from deluge.' In 1934 Conservatives lost provincial elections in both Ontario and Saskatchewan; they also lost four of five federal by-elections in September 1934. There were increasing doubts within the party that they could win a general election. Then in October the popular Stevens, having in the eyes of many in the cabinet overstepped the mark in his criticism of Canadian capitalists, was forced to resign his portfolio.

The Bennett New Deal of 1935, promising federal government intervention to achieve social and economic reform, arose from that political anguish. It was also genuine Bennett, policies he had espoused for many years, with roots in his own political instincts. He had long believed in old age pensions, unemployment insurance, and labour unions. What was new was the strong rhetoric devised by William Herridge and Bennett's executive assistant Roderick K. Finlayson and delivered by Bennett in incisive radio speeches. 'The old order is gone,' Bennett announced. 'If you believe things should be left as they are you and I hold irreconcilable views. I am for reform. And, in my mind, reform means Government intervention. … It means the end of laissez-faire.' According to Manion, the New Deal speeches had not been discussed in cabinet. The centrepiece of Bennett's program was the Employment and Social Insurance Act. It was followed by bills introducing a minimum wage, an eight-hour day, and a 48-hour work week. There were doubts about the constitutionality of these measures, but with elections due in a few months that was worth risking.

Herridge's plan seems to have been to call parliament for mid January, goad the Liberals into denouncing New Deal legislation, and then dissolve late in February and go to elections. The strategy was thwarted by two things: King's clever tactic of saying very little and, more to the point, Bennett's illness. In February it was just a bad cold, but on 7 March atrial fibrillation of the heart was diagnosed. The doctors said he needed to rest for a month. His health was excuse sufficient that, had he chosen to retire then, it might have been managed. But the party would have had to select a new leader. The temporary house leader was Sir George Halsey Perley, 77 years old, in voice and physique wasted and feeble; the leadership would probably have then devolved on H. H. Stevens, whom Bennett would not have had at any price. In Bennett's absence more New Deal legislation was passed, especially the important Prairie Farm Rehabilitation Act, which set in motion a mighty enterprise that would eventually teach 100,000 farmers how to handle and restore the dust bowl in southern Saskatchewan. The house then adjourned in April.

Bennett went to England on 18 April to consult doctors and to take in George V's silver jubilee. He returned to Ottawa a month later not much invigorated. The Canadian Wheat Board Act was then passed, as was a supplementary public works bill providing another $18 million for construction projects. Legislation was also approved to implement some of the recommendations of the price spreads commission, including the establishment of the Dominion Trade and Industry Commission to regulate business activity.

Bennett also had to deal with the On-to-Ottawa trekkers, a small army of the unemployed from the relief camps set up in 1932. The trek, begun in Vancouver, had been stopped by police in Regina. Delegates led by Arthur Herbert (Slim) Evans came on to Ottawa and met with Bennett on 22 June. It was not an amicable meeting. If Bennett was hard with the bankers of 1934, he was much more so with the trekkers of 1935, who threatened to disrupt law and order. The trek did not need to end the way it did, with a Dominion Day riot in Regina, the killing of a policeman, and many injuries, one case leading to the death of

A jovial Richard B. Bennett chatting with friends at Waterloo Station in London, England. Reproduced from Andrew D. MacLean, *R. B. Bennett: prime minister of Canada* (Toronto, 1935).

a trekker three months later; better communications between Ottawa and the Saskatchewan government might have avoided it. Bennett with his back up could be a chalcenterous animal.

Like many lawyers, Bennett distrusted public disorder. Strikes when legitimate he accepted, as disagreements inevitable over work or wages. But public law and order were to him fundamental. He hated the Communists with their too clever tactics at undermining the state. He himself was fearless and outspoken, able to face down and even convert a hostile crowd. There are many worse things in the world, Bennett would have said, than 'Peace, Order, and good Government.' In his mind that was what Canada was all about.

Parliament prorogued on 5 July; Stevens, restless and dissatisfied, now quite at odds with Bennett, formed the Reconstruction Party two days later; parliament was dissolved on 15 August. Spurred by Stevens's defection, and with desperate support from MPs, his sister, and Herridge, Bennett fought a stirring campaign. But he was not sanguine, believing that Stevens had 'crucified' the party. Bennett was indeed defeated on 14 Oct. 1935, but in terms of the popular vote it was not a massive defeat. From 1930 to 1935 the percentage of the Liberal Party's popular vote actually decreased slightly. In 1935 the Conservatives still took 30 per cent. The Liberals really had no policy; they expected the depression would defeat Bennett and the depression did exactly that.

Seats in the House of Commons were quite another matter: the Liberals took 173, the Conservatives 40, and the other parties 32. The Reconstruction Party won only one, Stevens being elected, but their 8.7 per cent of the popular vote had cut deeply into Conservative seats. Stevens's defection owed not a little to Bennett himself. Stevens and the wide sympathy that his price spreads commission evoked ought not to have been allowed to get away. The most popular politician nationally that the Conservatives had, Stevens should have been tolerated, even cosseted. Bennett was incapable of it. The Toronto *Evening Telegram* remarked about Bennett the day after the election, a 'great statesman [was] defeated by a poor politician.'

For the next three years Bennett was a model opposition leader; indeed, government legislation was often improved by his interventions. In 1936 he was in the house almost every day, the most faithful of his party in his duty to parliament. Ostensibly he bore no grudges; he seemed to have accepted that the Canadian people who had suffered so much in the depression would want to punish the government. But he had given so greatly of himself, his energy, his health, and his fortune to captain the Canadian ship through that storm, he was hurt that so few Canadians seemed to be cognizant of his sacrifices. His charities, which were private, had become a huge burden. The requests he received in a single week 'make life almost unbearable.' He estimated that in the years 1927–37 he had spent $2.3 million. His benevolence was in fact outrunning his income.

During the summer and autumn of 1936 he travelled to New Zealand, Australia, and South Africa. Back in Canada, he was introduced to a lively and likeable reporter from the *Victoria Daily Times*, William Bruce Hutchison. Hutchison had seen Bennett at the fag end of the 1935 election campaign, backstage at a Victoria theatre, slumped, tired, a boisterous crowd ready to get at him. When Bennett came to speak he was transformed: his moral force, his booming voice, his sheer bravura triumphed over hecklers, over everybody. Hutchison had never seen anything like it. Bennett did the same with an even noisier Vancouver crowd the next night. Now in the spring of 1937 there seemed to be a newer Bennett, relaxed, his leg thrown casually over the arm of a chair in his office, talking almost continually about politics, Alexander the Great, Ming pottery, and the military geography of the South African War.

After the abdication of Edward VIII in December 1936 ('... speak / Of one that lov'd not wisely but too well,' Bennett quoted Othello in the House of Commons) Bennett and Mildred went to London for the coronation of George VI and then to a spa in Germany. He checked in at 228 pounds. Even for a man six feet tall, he was heavy; maple sugar and chocolates had taken their toll. His English doctor told him to lose at least 10 pounds to ease the strain on his heart. That autumn of 1937 Bennett discussed retirement, but the party persuaded him to carry on. By March 1938 he knew he could not continue. King could call an election any time and Bennett was now incapable of taking his party through it. He resigned on 6 March 1938, but stayed on until a new leader was chosen in July. There came a flood of appreciations for his work, including one from King; Bennett's replies suggested that the compliments would have meant a great deal more to him had they come three to four years earlier, when the going was really difficult.

Then suddenly, on 11 May, Mildred, who was being treated for breast cancer in a New York hospital, died. Her death devastated Bennett; he shut himself up in her old room in their Château suite, consumed with grief, reading the Book of Ruth ('aught but death shall part thee and me'). She was only 49 years old.

The Conservative Party convention was held in Ottawa early in July. There was talk that Bennett wanted to be asked to carry on, but there is little firm evidence of it. There is strong evidence, however, that members of the party wanted him to make peace with Stevens and shake hands with him in public. Bennett was not having it. Robert Manion was chosen as leader; Bennett was not there.

Bennett had decided to live in England. In Canada he could have had positions from president of a university to president of a bank, but in Canada there were huge public pressures on his time and on his purse. He did not want to live in the United States; in London he was almost as much at home as in Canada. He went to England in August 1938 and on 1 November took over Beaverbrook's option on Juniper Hill, a 94-acre property near Box Hill in Surrey. He proceeded to order those Canadian essentials, efficient plumbing and central heating. He then returned to Canada to take his leave. That proved to be much more difficult than he had imagined. His last farewell was aboard the *Montclare* in Halifax Harbour, on Saturday, 28 Jan. 1939. There was a luncheon aboard for 292; there were toasts and tears and Byron: 'Fare thee well! and if for ever, / Still for ever, fare thee well.' He resigned his seat as MP for Calgary West that day. The *Montclare* sailed in the evening.

Bennett came to love Juniper Hill. It was the only home he had ever had, and he acquired a devoted staff. He joined a host of organizations in England and was a popular speaker wherever he went. He seemed to be able to chair any meeting with grace and aplomb. As reward for his work as trouble-shooter at Beaverbrook's Ministry of Aircraft Production, Winston Churchill offered him a viscountcy. Thus he headed the list of birthday honours for June 1941. He enjoyed the House of Lords and faithfully attended. He had had extensive first-hand experience of the

British Commonwealth of Nations, and his presence in the Lords was felt and appreciated.

Lonely he was not. Garfield Weston in 1943 reported him 'happy as a clam.' Most of the evidence runs that way. Two people, Beaverbrook and Thomas Clement Douglas, thought him lonely, but their judgements were made perhaps after R. B.'s two nephews in the Canadian army were killed in Normandy in 1944. R. B. did find that hard. He was diagnosed with diabetes in 1944 too. But even in June 1947, Janice Amery had him to dinner at Eaton Square in London and declared him older 'but happy and … so charming and interesting.'

He liked hot baths. He was warned to be careful, but late on Thursday evening, 26 June 1947, he neglected the warning; he died in his bath of a heart attack and was found there the following morning. The Mickleham church was crowded for his funeral, and there was a crowd too at the memorial service in Westminster Abbey on 4 July. He was buried in the Mickleham churchyard. Perhaps the best eulogy is the April 1938 letter from Harold Adams Innis, professor of economics at the University of Toronto, when Bennett resigned the Conservative leadership: 'Your leadership of the party especially during the years when you were Prime Minister was marked by a distinction which has not been surpassed. … No one has ever been asked to carry the burdens of unprecedented depression such as you assumed and no one could have shouldered them with such ability. I am confident that we shall look to those years as landmarks in Canadian history because of your energy and direction.'

Bennett lacked the common touch; he was too often in thrall to his own deeply held convictions. Although his charity was vast, his capacity for mercy was limited. Moral transgression he found difficult to forgive, whether in his brother George Horace, the ne'er-do-well father of an illegitimate daughter, or in H. H. Stevens, who had in Bennett's view betrayed the Conservative Party. His inability to receive and absorb other people's opinions and ideas made him strong and self-reliant but could also make him seem overbearing and self-righteous. His sense of humour was lively enough, but it never prevented him from taking himself too seriously. He was unable to laugh at himself. Though a statesman of note, he was a poor politician. But once out of politics, in England as the squire of Juniper Hill, he rose to an elegant maturity, hard-working, well liked, and respected.

No Canadian prime minister served Canada at greater personal cost, cost to his health and well-being, his own fortune, and even, be it said, his historical reputation. No Canadian prime minister deserved less the obloquy he received. He took Canada through the hardest years of the depression, and he did it with courage and determination. He put in place institutions and social policies that Canadians still have and still cherish. Despite his failings, perhaps he should be cherished too.

P. B. WAITE

Further reading

L. A. Glassford, *Reaction and reform: the politics of the Conservative Party under R. B. Bennett, 1927–1938* (Toronto, 1992).

J. H. Gray, *R. B. Bennett: the Calgary years* (Toronto, 1991).

P. B. Waite, *The loner: three sketches of the personal life and ideas of R. B. Bennett, 1870–1947* (Toronto, 1992).

Ernest Watkins, *R. B. Bennett: a biography* (Toronto, 1963).

LOUIS-STEPHEN ST-LAURENT
(baptized Louis-Étienne),

lawyer, professor, and politician; b. 1 Feb. 1882 in Compton, Que., son of Jean-Baptiste-Moïse St-Laurent and Mary Anne Broderick; m. 19 May 1908 Jeanne Renault in Beauceville, Que., and they had two sons and three daughters; d. 25 July 1973 at Quebec, and was buried in Compton.

Nicolas Huot Saint-Laurent had arrived in New France around 1660. Starting in the Quebec City region, the family gradually moved west along the St Lawrence River, settling in Nicolet in the early 19th century. Though Huot Saint-Laurent was a man of some learning – he served as a sheriff at Quebec – most of his descendants were illiterate farmers. Jean-Baptiste-Moïse St-Laurent, the first family member in 150 years to attend school, abandoned farming for commerce. He moved with his father from Trois-Rivières to Sherbrooke in the Eastern Townships to set up shop and then to the nearby village of Compton, where he opened a general store and married the local schoolteacher, Mary Anne Broderick, the child of Irish immigrants. Jean-Baptiste learned English because she refused to speak French. The Brodericks and the St-Laurents were Roman Catholics. Mary Anne, for her part, had some passing acquaintance with Protestants, having been raised for a time in her childhood in a Protestant family. Louis-Stephen St-Laurent was the first of their seven children.

At the time of his birth, Compton was mainly English speaking. It and the surrounding township of Compton would become majority French at some point between 1901 and 1911. The St-Laurents' home, next to their store, served as a social centre for the village. In a political riding long dominated federally by the Conservative John Henry Pope, Jean-Baptiste was a faithful Liberal and would run in a provincial by-election in 1894. The couple's children spoke French with their father, but because of their mother they were equally at home in English. Educated in French in the local separate school, Louis had learned to read and write English first, he was exposed throughout his childhood to English literature, and he spoke the tongue with no accent. He was a talented and studious child, and his family were encouraged to seek further education for him. He left Compton in 1896 to enter the Séminaire Saint-Charles-Borromée in Sherbrooke. Attendance was an expensive proposition for the son of a country storekeeper, but Louis was buoyed by Compton's curé, Joseph-Eugène-Édouard Choquette, who had persuaded the college authorities to waive the customary tuition fees. At the seminary, which was a bilingual institution, its staff a mixture of French and Irish priests, St-Laurent distinguished himself; he developed a writing style in both French and English and played an active role in student life. Although his parents hoped he would become a priest, he opted instead for law on graduation in 1902.

Financial and cultural considerations led him to the Université Laval at Quebec rather than McGill University in Montreal. At Laval's law school, the Liberal St-Laurent studied under some of the city's most prominent Conservative lawyers, who made up much of the faculty. Despite taking time out to assist his father in another unsuccessful run for the provincial legislature, in 1904, St-Laurent graduated at the top of his class in 1905 and won the Governor General's Medal. He was also offered Laval's first Rhodes scholarship, but refused it in order to turn to a (presumably lucrative) legal career. It started modestly. St-Laurent accepted a berth in the office of a prominent Quebec City lawyer, Louis-Philippe Pelletier, at $50 a month. He found time as well to court

Louis-S. St-Laurent and Jeanne Renault pose cheerfully on their wedding day, 19 May 1908, in Beauceville, Que.

Jeanne Renault, the daughter of a prosperous merchant in Beauceville; they had met at a party in Quebec in 1906 and married two years later. She was accustomed to a comfortable life, and the marriage forced St-Laurent's departure from Pelletier's firm and his meagre salary there. Instead, at the beginning of 1909, he formed a partnership with Antonin Galipeault, a young lawyer with political – reliably Liberal – prospects. Galipeault found St-Laurent's easy English a distinct advantage. Equally important, St-Laurent was a notoriously hard worker, with a reputation for painstaking preparation. When Galipeault was elected to the legislature in February 1909, St-Laurent took over much of the firm's ordinary business; eventually he found himself specializing in commercial law. The firm expanded – the partners soon included Liberal senator Philippe-Auguste Choquette – and in 1914 they moved to impressive quarters in the Imperial Bank Building on Rue Saint-Pierre. The same year St-Laurent joined his mentor, L.-P. Pelletier, as a professor of law at Laval. In 1915 he was made a provincial KC and received an honorary LLD from Laval. By this time he was earning $10,000 a year; though comfortable, he would never be rich.

The St-Laurent family grew steadily, numbering five children by 1917. In 1913 he had built a 15-room house on the Grande Allée, Quebec City's most fashionable street. This house, servants, and an automobile (acquired in 1916) were easily within his means, which depended on his reputation for steady, reliable intelligence in his practice. By the 1920s his work extended to cases before the Supreme Court of Canada. St-Laurent, according to a contemporary at the Quebec bar, Warwick Fielding Chipman, 'was solid, sound, pleasing to his courts, and established an intimacy with them. He had a human touch despite his technical detail and thoroughness.'

St-Laurent's interests diverged from those of Galipeault, whose political career took more and more of his attention. They went their separate ways, amicably, in 1923. By this time St-Laurent was being frequently retained by the governments of both Canada and Quebec, sometimes on constitutional cases. In an important test case before the Supreme Court in 1926, he argued for minority rights: the Jewish demand for representation on Montreal's Protestant Board of School Commissioners or for a separate Jewish system of schools. In the event, representation was refused but provincial authority to establish separate schools for non-Christians was recognized. It cannot be said that St-Laurent consistently took a provincial or a federal position in his cases, nor was he always successful. He was, however, successful enough to join the select and highly remunerated elite who pleaded before Canada's highest court of appeals, the Judicial Committee of the Privy Council in London, England. As biographer Dale Cairns Thomson has observed, St-Laurent's quiet, scholarly arguments matched the style of the British law lords. In 1928 the JCPC, which rarely gave compliments, praised his illuminating and able argument on behalf of Ottawa in a conflict between the Quebec Civil Code and the federal Bankruptcy Act.

St-Laurent, though known as a Liberal supporter, was not much involved in partisan activity in the 1910s and 1920s. His one appearance on a platform, in support of Charles Gavan Power in Quebec South in 1926, was unremarkable. He was not indifferent, however, to the larger political currents swirling around him, and his national reputation and interest in national affairs grew apace. During World War I he had been a prominent participant in the Bonne Entente movement that sought to reconcile the divergent perspectives of English and French Canadians, strained by the conscription issue and the bilingual schools question in Ontario. Within legal circles, he served as *bâtonnier* of the Quebec bar in 1929 and as president of the Canadian Bar Association in 1930–32. St-Laurent became a well-known speaker in English Canada, especially on the theme of national unity, and in opposition to such French Canadian nationalists as Abbé Lionel Groulx who blamed others – the English and the Jews – for the inequities of the Quebec economy and the perceived subordination of French Canadians in society.

The Great Depression of the 1930s severely tried Canada's political and economic institutions. Some provinces struggled financially; only the federal government appeared to have the resources to deal with the burden of welfare and reconstruction. In 1935 the Conservatives under Richard Bedford Bennett passed New Deal legislation that included employment and social insurance and regulations governing minimum wages and hours of labour, fields that many legal authorities felt were provincial responsibilities. In January 1936 the new Liberal government of William Lyon Mackenzie King submitted this legislation to the JCPC for its opinion and hired St-Laurent as counsel. He founded his argument on section 132 of the British North America Act, which gave the federal government authority to implement imperial treaties, in this case the labour aspects of the 1919 Treaty of Versailles. It was at best a difficult proposition, and to no one's great surprise St-Laurent lost on the main issues, the labour conventions and the Employment and Social Insurance Act.

The crisis, economic and constitutional, endured and King's next expedient, in 1937, was to appoint a royal commission on dominion–provincial relations chaired by Ontario's chief justice, Newton Wesley Rowell. James McGregor Stewart of Halifax and St-Laurent were named commission counsel. No end of a lesson, the experience exposed St-Laurent for the first time to a Canadian reality outside the business centres of the east. It corrected his impression, based on magazine stories, that western wheat farmers enjoyed winter vacations in California and were a source of unlimited revenue. The depression-bound west, in fact, was a sink-hole of misery, with no markets for its products and no means to support its people. St-Laurent saw a need for stronger federal authority. 'It seems likely that our constitution will have to be amended if Confederation is to survive,' he told a French-speaking audience in Winnipeg in January 1938. Events soon overtook the royal commission. Before it could report under its new chairman, Joseph Sirois (Rowell having resigned because of illness), World War II broke out. In 1940 it did recommend constitutional adjustments, mainly in the direction of greater federal activity in the field of social security, but by this time Ottawa had already assumed the power to direct the war effort, subordinating provincial authority to this greater cause.

King and his Quebec lieutenant, justice minister Ernest Lapointe, tried to appease opinion in Quebec on the volatile issue of conscription. Their promise of no conscription, first made in the spring of 1939, was repeated in the provincial election of October and again in the federal contest of March 1940. The Quebec ministers in King's cabinet, led by Lapointe, pledged to resign if conscription was imposed, but, like everyone else, King and Lapointe underestimated the problems the war would bring. When Germany defeated France in June, Britain and its empire, including Canada, were left to fight on alone. Fearing the worst, King and Lapointe agreed to impose conscription after all, but only for home defence. Canadians sent overseas would be volunteers. When Lapointe died in November 1941, a large gap opened in the prime minister's carefully balanced political structure. King consulted several Quebec notables, including those in his cabinet as well as Archbishop Jean-Marie-Rodrigue Cardinal Villeneuve. King's first thought was to recruit Liberal premier Adélard Godbout, but he did not wish to be translated to Ottawa. It was on the suggestion of Villeneuve and Pierre-Joseph-Arthur Cardin, the minister of transport, that King began to consider St-Laurent, who earlier that year had co-chaired the Victory Loans committee in Quebec. He knew him 'only as a distant and rather chilly lawyer,' while St-Laurent knew King hardly at all.

On 4 December, King telephoned St-Laurent, asking him to be in Ottawa the next day. Though he did not give a reason, it was obvious. After lunch on the 5th, he proposed that St-Laurent succeed Lapointe as minister of justice and MP for Quebec East. Anticipating that St-Laurent might be reluctant to leave his home, and an income in excess of $50,000 a year, for the relatively ill-paid and insecure life of a minister and politician, King appealed to his sense of duty. The war was a national crisis, and Canada (and King) needed somebody who could 'interpret the Quebec point of view' to the rest of the country. St-Laurent asked for time to consult; the answers were mixed from his family but affirmative from most of his friends, the cardinal, and the premier. On 10 December he was back in Ottawa, to be sworn in as minister of justice. Soon after, the Liberals of Quebec East adopted him as their candidate in a by-election set for 9 Feb. 1942.

St-Laurent entered the cabinet just as the war expanded to include the United States, a fact that put pressure on King to implement a policy of total war, which would include a commitment to conscription not just for home defence but also for overseas. The problem was the government's promise of 1939–40. The prime minister and his cabinet worried over this question through Christmas, and in January 1942 they agreed on a possible solution. There would be a plebiscite, in April, to ask voters to release the government from its pledge. St-Laurent was cooperative; he had made no promise and would not be bound by commitments made by others. He took this line in the by-election, running against a nationalist candidate, and won. The plebiscite was another matter. Outside Quebec, the electorate went along with King's purpose. Inside Quebec, voters opted against the government by a heavy margin. In the aftermath, in May, as King prepared to push through parliament a bill (Bill 80) that would repeal the legislative provision against conscription, Arthur Cardin quit the cabinet.

Cardin's departure confirmed St-Laurent's position as the senior Quebec minister. He had already succeeded Lapointe on cabinet's War Committee, becoming Quebec's voice in the higher direction of the conflict. St-Laurent spoke effectively on behalf of the government's conscription policy in the House of Commons on 16 June, arguing against the contention of Quebec nationalists that Canada was at war merely in the service of the British empire. The dominion was engaged in its own interests, not those of Britain, and he urged English Canadians to accept French Canadians 'as full partners and full citizens.' King warmly shook St-Laurent's hand on the conclusion of the speech, and he recorded in his diary that the occasion was of great symbolic significance. With passage of Bill 80 in July, the conscription issue was defused. Conscription for overseas service was now legally possible, but it need not be implemented until the military ran short of men. With the Canadian army in England in anticipation of an eventual invasion of the European mainland, that day was not at hand. King and his colleagues fervently hoped it would never come.

In Ottawa, St-Laurent was now accepted as King's Quebec lieutenant. He gave frequent speeches there on the war effort and national unity; in addresses that October he foresaw the need for policies on social security and to consolidate the levels of employment security made possible by the war. In Quebec the church was divided on his support for social welfare. Right-wing clergy opposed it, but he was indifferent to their arguments. From time to time, as a senior minister, St-Laurent assisted King directly, including a spell as acting minister of external affairs (a post traditionally held by the prime minister) during King's visit to London in the spring of 1944. The same year St-Laurent attended the conference at Bretton Woods, N.H., that led to the creation of the International Monetary Fund, and in April–May 1945 he participated with King in the founding conference of the United Nations in San Francisco. His presence meant that Quebec's interests were represented, but St-Laurent also viewed these occasions as an affirmation of the larger national interest apart from regional or linguistic considerations. During these two years he also carried out his duties as minister of justice, including the appointment of judges and advice to his colleagues on the constitutionality of proposed legislation.

St-Laurent took a broad view of the federal spending power, which he held could justify such programs as family allowances; the legislation for family allowances emanated from his department in 1944. In March 1945 he supported a sweeping program of economic reconstruction and more social welfare, including federal–provincial cost-sharing schemes for old-age pensions and hospital and medical insurance, and the federal assumption of responsibility for the unemployed. He brushed aside warnings that these proposals would 'precipitate acrimonious disputes with the provinces,' though it was over revenue-sharing differences that the program would run aground. Disagreement should not deter his colleagues from supporting good policy, the minister of justice argued. 'Acrimonious dispute was inevitable with Quebec in any case,' and he did not believe the people would automatically support the provinces over Ottawa. Canadians identified with provincial programs, he reasoned, because they 'were constantly made aware of the services which provincial governments render while they tended to think of the central government as one imposing burdens such as taxation and conscription.' Sound federal initiatives, including family allowances, would correct and even reverse this situation.

The principal issue confronting the government in 1944–45, however, was conscription, not social welfare. Heavy casualties suffered during the Normandy Invasion of 6 June 1944 and afterwards caused the military's pool of manpower to run dry. The minister of national defence, James Layton Ralston, told the prime minister in October that conscript reinforcements must be sent immediately. King manoeuvred to secure the backing of colleagues who were, he knew, deeply divided on the issue. At each stage, he turned to St-Laurent, keeping him apprised and firming up his support. Content with the policy adopted in July 1942, St-Laurent saw no need for conscription with the war's end in sight and other means for securing reinforcements untried. Still, he watched King's policy sympathetically. Realizing that the prime minister had done everything in his power to avoid offending Quebec, the justice minister moved from a position on 30 October where he 'could not possibly support introduction of conscription' to resigned acceptance a month later. St-Laurent's attitude was crucial to King: no other Quebec minister had as much prestige or authority. In the end, conscripts reached Europe in early 1945.

The government survived the conscription crisis but its political future was most uncertain. An election was due in 1945, and King's Liberals were beset by an assortment of Quebec nationalists, Ontario conscriptionists, and prairie socialists. As much as anything, fortune favoured the Liberals. The European phase of the war came to an end in May 1945, a month before the election. King and St-Laurent marked the occasion with radio broadcasts in English and French; the choice of St-Laurent as oratorical partner underlined his primacy among the Quebec ministers. The Liberals won the election, though narrowly. 'Independent Liberals' elected in Quebec could cause trouble in the future by tending towards Quebec nationalism and the provincialist policies of Union Nationale premier Maurice Le Noblet Duplessis. The election was, in a sense, King's last hurrah. Aged 70, he understood it was time to give thought to a successor.

Fortunately, there was one at hand, though St-Laurent's decision to run in the election had been a surprise to many. Perhaps it was based on the timing of the campaign, before the war was truly finished; perhaps he sensed that national unity, a fragile flower, demanded his continuing attention. There were problems of policy as well, not least dominion–provincial relations, which the war left unresolved. In the summer of 1945 St-Laurent participated, along with the minister of finance, James Lorimer Ilsley, and the minister of reconstruction, Clarence Decatur Howe, in a dominion–provincial conference on reconstruction. The federal government proposed nothing less than a redistribution of responsibilities, with Ottawa taking the lead in the comprehensive social welfare scheme that St-Laurent had supported the previous spring. Duplessis and Ontario premier George Alexander Drew objected, and their objections prevailed. Duplessis presented the episode as an ambitious power grab by Ottawa, but he could not present it in strictly ethnic terms because of St-Laurent's prominent presence in the federal delegation.

The King government had an ambitious external agenda as well, and here too St-Laurent's role was crucial. The government believed that trade should to be restored to pre-war levels. A surplus in trade with Britain had usually helped to pay for a trade deficit with the United States, but the war had devastated British commerce and it would take time for exports to recover. To help the British return to their role as purchasers of Canadian wheat, apples, and cheese, Canada proposed a loan of $1.25 billion (roughly a tenth of Canada's annual gross national product) spread over a number of years. The advance was to be made in conjunction with an American loan of $3.75 billion, the terms of which set the pattern for the Canadian loan. To Quebec nationalists it was more evidence of Canada's objectionable subordination to the empire. It was essential, then, to the political credibility of the government's case that St-Laurent accept the desirability, even the necessity, of the loan. Persuading him that it was in Canada's interest, not just Britain's, was a tall hurdle for government economists to surmount, but once convinced, St-Laurent took the lead in defending the loan in parliament in April 1946 and in Quebec against the vitriolic abuse heaped on him by the nationalists, some of them nominal Liberals.

St-Laurent's career now stood at a turning point. When King returned exhausted from a trip to Europe in August, St-Laurent, as acting prime minister, met him in Montreal. King used the occasion to raise the question of succession. St-Laurent was the logical leader and future prime minister, and King asked him to accept the possibility. He hesitated. Life as a minister had drained his savings. His law practice had suffered, and his sons, though qualified as lawyers, were too inexperienced to take his place. Eventually, however, he accepted King's proposition, and with it an immediate change in assignment. King broke with tradition and separated the office of secretary of state for external affairs from that of prime minister. St-Laurent thus became minister of external affairs on 4 Sept. 1946 as part of a major cabinet shuffle. He did not see the appointment as definitive. There was still a chance for him to return to private life, or so he assured his colleagues, but these same colleagues, especially Howe, were beginning to think of him for the longer term; it was clear that King's departure could be postponed no further. On the same day King made another important commitment: he appointed a new under-secretary for external affairs, Lester Bowles Pearson, the former Canadian ambassador in Washington. It was the beginning of a long and advantageous collaboration.

St-Laurent was aware that the international scene was not promising. The Soviet Union, the world centre of communism, was expanding its influence in eastern Europe, already occupied by the Red Army. Soviet policy alarmed the British in particular and they passed their fears on to King during his several visits to London. He hardly needed to be reminded: a Soviet spy ring had been uncovered in Ottawa in September 1945, when a defector, Igor Sergeievich Gouzenko, arrived unexpectedly at St-Laurent's office. As minister of justice, he followed the subsequent police investigation and the revelations of a royal commission on espionage. He did not need to be told the Soviet Union represented a clash of ideologies that transcended national boundaries. Yet foreign affairs were never an easy issue in Canada because of what were thought to be differing opinions on the subject between English and French Canadians – the latter were assumed to be disengaged and isolationist – and to have them re-emerge as a major question only a year after the war posed a challenge to the King government. Certainly King bore this risk in mind when he appointed a French Canadian to the portfolio.

The Department of External Affairs drew from the Canadian academic elite. Most of its officers were educated abroad, and the department tried to recruit French as well as English Canadians. It might be thought that St-Laurent, who had travelled little until well on into middle age, and the sophisticated members of the foreign service were ill-matched, but that did not prove to be the case. The diplomatic staff appreciated his logical and quick habits of thought and his powers of concentration. They appreciated him even more because they had endured King's fussiness. St-Laurent was the opposite: courteous and easy to brief, he relied on them to present him with clear recommendations that he would consider on the spot, and then accept or reject. Unlike King, he was accessible and attended his office regularly. Best of all, as senior diplomat Escott Meredith Reid explained, St-Laurent backed up his staff when they were in difficulty. 'I knew,' Reid wrote, 'that here was a man who deserved loyalty because he was loyal.' In a cabinet of strong ministers, St-Laurent distinguished himself by his unusual executive capacity.

The two most important items on St-Laurent's plate were the confrontation with the Soviet Union – what was coming to be called the Cold War – and a proposal for union with the British colony of Newfoundland. On the Cold War, there was little to be done: its development was beyond Canada's control and in any case Canadians had no hesitation in taking the side of the West. It would have been impossible to do anything else. On Newfoundland, however, there was a choice. It had remained out of confederation in 1867, and had resisted the notion ever since. But the Island's history as an autonomous jurisdiction had been rocky, and by 1946 some Newfoundlanders, notably Joseph Roberts Smallwood, were prepared to reconsider union. St-Laurent found the idea of completing confederation highly attractive, and early on he became Newfoundland's strongest supporter in the King cabinet. He ignored objections from the Quebec government, which had territorial claims against Newfoundland and demanded a right of veto over the admission of any new province. Once again St-Laurent advanced a strong defence of national power, holding that the federal government represented all Canadians. He headed negotiations with Newfoundland in the summer of 1947 and again in the fall of 1948. The discussions bore fruit: on 31 March 1949 it would join Canada, with St-Laurent presiding over the ceremonies in Ottawa as prime minister.

St-Laurent's main duties in 1947 lay outside the country, in explaining the world to Canadians and Canada to the world. Much of his work had been done. The experience of the war, and reflection on the slide to war in the 1930s, had convinced many that their country could take no refuge in isolation or comfort from its geography. St-Laurent searched for an occasion to define Canada's foreign policy. He took advantage of an invitation to inaugurate a lecture series at the University of Toronto in January 1947 (the first Gray Lecture) to give what was probably his most notable speech. It was drafted by one of his officers, Robert Gerald Riddell, a former teacher at the university who was familiar with what a Toronto audience would expect. But there was no doubt that St-Laurent was entirely comfortable with the ideas in the speech, which served to define the bases of Canadian foreign policy for the next generation. Not surprisingly, he placed national unity first among the principles that must underlie this policy. A disunited Canada would be powerless, he reminded his audience. The search for national unity did not mean that Canadians should avoid the subject of foreign policy as too dangerous or contentious. They agreed on other principles – political liberty, Christian values, and 'the acceptance of international responsibility' – and these principles, he argued, justified an active role in international affairs. He prescribed engagement with Britain, the United States, and France, as well as commitment to 'every international organization which contributes to the economic and political stability of the world.' Seen from St-Laurent's perspective, foreign policy should unite rather than divide Canadians.

In 1947 and later St-Laurent repeatedly stressed the ideological gulf between Canada (and the West in general) and totalitarian communism. Like other ministers and most of his diplomatic staff, he did not believe the Soviet Union was out to provoke war, but he did agree that economic and social disorder abroad favoured its cause. Political uncertainty more than anything else was undermining the democracies of western Europe. St-Laurent saw a need for greater international security, and he agreed too that the UN was failing to provide it. In speeches and in the cabinet he promoted the idea of a Western or Atlantic security organization that would supplement the UN. He did not participate directly in the negotiations in Washington that would produce the North Atlantic Treaty Organization in 1949, but he was recognized as one of the first responsible politicians to propose such an institution.

Canada's response to another focal point of clashing ideologies, Korea, was complicated by King's lingering interest in the conduct of his old department. In December 1947 St-Laurent supported American attempts within the UN to establish a stable regime in South Korea through elections, and he recommended to the cabinet the appointment of a Canadian to a UN committee to study the subject. The appointment had actually been approved by J. L. Ilsley, now the minister of justice, who was interim head of the Canadian delegation at the UN in New York City at the time, but St-Laurent and his staff saw no reason to object. This minor event triggered an entirely disproportionate reaction from the prime minister, who dreaded the possibility that UN involvement in a difficult international situation might set off a third world war. King demanded that St-Laurent rescind the appointment. St-Laurent, who believed he would be abandoning his staff and another minister, refused. Only when King understood that his chosen successor, and half his cabinet, might resign did he withdraw his demand. The incident 'marked a watershed in the political lives of King and St. Laurent,' in the estimate of journalist William Bruce Hutchison.

It was clearly time for King to go, but he had one more function to perform – assuring that St-Laurent would in fact be his successor. King

Louis-S. St-Laurent (left, with Jeanne St-Laurent) is congratulated by William L. M. King on becoming Liberal Party leader at the Ottawa Coliseum, 7 Aug. 1948.

scheduled a Liberal convention for 7 Aug. 1948. St-Laurent was nominated, and so were three others: C. G. Power, agriculture minister James Garfield Gardiner, and national health and welfare minister Paul Joseph James Martin. To illustrate the trivial nature of the opposition, King had had the names of half his cabinet placed in nomination, and each named minister then duly withdrew, telling the convention that a better man – St-Laurent – was providentially available. In the background C. D. Howe managed such organization as was needed for St-Laurent. Martin also withdrew, and Power and Gardiner were overwhelmingly beaten. St-Laurent had to wait some months for the prime ministership; on 15 November, King finally resigned and handed over office. St-Laurent had occupied the intervening time as justice minister, making room for Pearson to become secretary of state for external affairs.

St-Laurent was already a known quantity around the country, and his cabinet was almost the same as King's. As prime minister, however, he was very different, though it was a difference best understood in Ottawa. St-Laurent ran the cabinet in his own way. Under him, each minister had his individual responsibility, and he did not intrude unless a subject slopped over departmental boundaries or higher political direction was plainly needed. He shared, however, King's aversion to foreign travel, believing that the prime minister could ill afford time outside the country. Most trips were left to Pearson or to Martin, often as a delegate to the UN. St-Laurent spent most of his time in Ottawa or at his vacation home, bought in 1950, on the shores of the St Lawrence in Saint-Patrice, Que. He did grudgingly consent to the purchase in 1951 of an official prime-ministerial residence at 24 Sussex Drive in Ottawa, though he insisted on paying rent. It was then that Jeanne St-Laurent moved to Ottawa from their home in Quebec City. As a prime minister's wife, she was not a major figure. She would go on tour with her husband, but she refused to fly and, according to his biographer, never became reconciled to living in Ottawa.

One duty did involve travel. As party leader, St-Laurent had to show himself in all parts of the country during elections, and following his elevation as prime minister in November, one was due in 1949. The main opposition, the Progressive Conservatives, had a new leader, former Ontario premier George Drew. Handsome and energetic, he promised a change from the Liberals who, he claimed, were tainted with Red connections in the federal bureaucracy. For the public, however, the more important issue was not the Communist menace, which was being contained overseas by NATO and vigorous diplomacy, but Canada's abounding prosperity. The gross national product had

Louis-S. St-Laurent with two of his grandchildren, Easter 1948, at Quebec City.

been moving up significantly, unemployment was nearly at low wartime levels, and $634 million had been paid out in 1948 in veterans' benefits, health services, family allowances, and old age security. On a western tour in April 1949 St-Laurent recognized this prosperity, unassailably and with a good amount of earnestness. Though in manner he was a shy, rather stiff corporate lawyer (his secretary and later biographer, D. C. Thomson, wrote of his resistance to 'light conversation and exchanges of humour'), he still had a kindly, grandfatherly appearance enhanced by his immaculate attire and white moustache. During the campaign, a journalist dubbed him Uncle Louis, and the nickname stuck. On 27 June everybody's favourite uncle led the Liberals to their greatest majority since confederation: 193 of the 262 seats in the commons and almost 50 per cent of the popular vote.

The government's policy can be summed up as 'managing prosperity,' through regular budgetary surpluses and modest improvements to social welfare programs. The provinces had blocked any progress toward a comprehensive welfare state and St-Laurent had no ambition to go farther for the time being. (His government would institute universal old-age pensions in 1951.) Foreign investment, overwhelmingly from the United States, drove the economy while exports lagged. In a soft-currency world, there were many trade barriers to be overcome, but Canada did not take the lead. Under St-Laurent and his trade and commerce minister since 1948, C. D. Howe, tariffs were still high. On the other hand, taxes remained low, certainly by comparison with Britain, the rest of Europe, and the United States, which in the 1950s had a more extensive social welfare system than Canada as well as greater burdens for defence.

As prime minister, St-Laurent continued to enjoy an unusual rapport, not just with his cabinet, but also with the senior civil service. For cabinet meetings he carefully readied himself by reading every cabinet paper and consulting with the clerk of the Privy Council and cabinet secretary. 'I did my best to prepare myself,' one clerk, Robert Broughton Bryce, later recalled, 'but almost invariably the Prime Minister thought of matters that I had overlooked.' Depending on the same careful groundwork that had served him so well as a lawyer, St-Laurent took the lead in discussions, introducing material, giving 'the pros and cons on each item on the agenda,' outlining 'his own views, and [asking] for comments,' according to Mitchell William Sharp, who as a senior bureaucrat sometimes watched from the sidelines. 'As St. Laurent hated to waste time,' noted another Privy Council clerk, John Whitney Pickersgill, 'cabinet meetings were exceedingly business-like.' Another wrote admiringly that he 'handled his colleagues to a consensus with sure judgment.' Some ministers received preferential treatment, though in meetings all were accorded equal consideration. The seniors at the table were St-Laurent, Howe, and agriculture minister Jimmy Gardiner. In Gardiner's opinion St-Laurent did not fully understand the west's problems, but Gardiner was a loyal minister who ran his own shop and seldom interfered with others, unlike Howe. Other outstanding ministers included Brooke Claxton in National Health and Welfare, and the charming Douglas Charles Abbott and then the intelligent if chilly Walter Edward Harris in Finance. St-Laurent completely trusted Pearson in External Affairs and the confidence was mutual. On the other hand, Pickersgill recalled, 'some ministers were restrained by the fear of appearing ill-informed or ineffective.' St-Laurent was fortunate that his principal English-speaking colleague, Howe, had no leadership ambitions. He admired Howe's single-minded decisiveness, and considered his services to Canada second to none. In 1951 he briefly considered making him governor general; this office was traditionally held by British aristocrats and politicians, but St-Laurent, always a positive nationalist, thought Howe had 'earned' the job. Howe's lack of tact, in reality, made him a poor choice, and the following year St-Laurent chose Charles Vincent Massey, a wealthy Torontonian with a diplomatic background.

St-Laurent had a professional interest in the Canadian constitution, and it was to be expected that he would try to reform some of its inconveniences. The constitution, as it affected federal–provincial jurisdiction, was reserved for amendment by the British parliament under the Statute of Westminster in 1931. In the throne speech of September 1949, rejecting opposition demands that provincial consent be obtained first, St-Laurent had announced the abolition of appeals to the JCPC. There was no point in asking Quebec, he told the commons, because Maurice Duplessis would pointlessly object. At the same time he announced that he would seek an amendment to the British North America Act that would allow the Canadian parliament to change the constitution as it affected federal jurisdiction only. He convened a dominion–provincial conference in January 1950 to find a way to amend it, a goal that had escaped justice minister Ernest Lapointe as far back as 1927. These bold moves expressed a clear and uncompromising view. Still, the constitution did not have to be amended to produce practical change in the balance of power between Ottawa and the provinces. War had concentrated revenues and expenditures in Ottawa, and post-war programs, for veterans for example, had kept the balance there. In 1947 most provinces had begun to 'rent' their tax revenues to Ottawa in return for compensation, a complex exchange that gave rise to agreements in 1947–51 for equalization payments to some underfinanced provinces. These agreements would be renewed with adjustments in 1952. Ontario, which under Drew had abstained from tax rental, later joined the program under St-Laurent and Premier Leslie Miscampbell Frost.

Beginning in 1950 there was even more reason for Ottawa to spend, and spend heavily. The first stage of the Cold War was diplomatic and political, more about confidence than armament. In June 1950 the war became hot, when Communist North Korea invaded anti-Communist South Korea. It was the reaction of the United States that mattered most. President Harry S. Truman surprised the Canadian government – and most of the American government – by intervening in Korea and seeking authorization for his action from the UN. Led by St-Laurent and Pearson, the Canadian government welcomed Truman's action. Early on St-Laurent promised Canadian support, including military support, to the UN in Korea, and he announced that three Canadian destroyers would join its forces in the Far East. He made it clear that UN authority was a sine qua non for Canadian participation, but that said, the cabinet had to decide how much support to give and what its impact would be on national unity. In Quebec, nationalists compared St-Laurent's co-operation with the United States to Canada's old subservience to the British empire. St-Laurent paid no attention. The cabinet brushed aside fears of conscription, and authorized a larger army, an expeditionary force to Korea, a permanent garrison in Europe, and $5 billion for a rearmament program. To launch this program the government created a new department in 1951, Defence Production, and made Howe its minister. He had a reputation for imperiousness, got into trouble in parliamentary debate over the department's establishment, and had to be rescued by the prime minister, who quieted the political waters.

The program was a success. The size of Canada's military rose substantially, but otherwise the war did not impinge greatly on Canadian life. Relations with the United States (the alliance leader in Korea and Europe) remained calm. The American government, under both Democratic and Republican administrations, seems to have accepted Canada's contribution as appropriate. St-Laurent in turn accepted American leadership as desirable and in any case inevitable. As he said in a speech to an American audience in 1949, 'There is only one nation with the wealth and the energy and the knowledge and the skill to give real leadership, and that nation is the United States.' He confined his contacts with its presidents to bilateral issues, and rejected even the appearance of giving advice on matters of world strategy. A reluctant participant in the Canadian–American–Mexican summit in 1956 at White Sulphur Springs, W.Va, the prime minister saw it primarily as an empty photo opportunity.

Canadian–British relations were also close. The British government, which appreciated Canadian economic aid and found that Canada's position on international matters often approximated its own, no longer tried to cast an imperial mantle over its policies. Britain was too weak to take much initiative, preferring on most matters to follow the United States and bask in the position of being its chief ally. Although St-Laurent may have been a Canadian nationalist, he was also a traditionalist; he happily hosted the visit of Princess Elizabeth in the fall of 1951 and shepherded a Canadian delegation to her coronation in June 1953. After returning home, he led the Liberals to triumphant re-election in August.

St-Laurent was 71, and he began to consider whether it might not soon be time to step down. There were loose ends to tie up, and a world tour, the first for any Canadian prime minister, beckoned. Late in 1953 he discussed his situation with Howe. They had an understanding, according to Howe, that they would both leave after a year or two in office, but 'unfortunately, our leader changed his mind about retiring, which was a mistake both for him and for the party.' It did not look as if St-Laurent needed to retire. He set off on his global trip in January 1954, and he made a point of calling on India's prime minister, Jawaharlal Nehru, with whom he felt a special rapport. Though Canadian policy valued India as a link between East and West and the developed North and the underdeveloped South, St-Laurent made no secret of Canada's position in the Cold War, a fact some of his Indian hosts resented. A visit intended to bridge differences may not have done the trick, but he did not notice. He returned triumphantly to snowy Ottawa in March and settled down to business.

Business was not quite the same. The cabinet found St-Laurent had changed: he showed signs of fatigue and, worse, indifference. In debates in the commons, he sat mute, rousing himself only with difficulty to intervene. In the cabinet he sometimes stared out the window, and the meetings drifted. An alarmed Howe asked St-Laurent's daughter in April 1954 to take him along on a vacation in Bermuda. She did, but the improvement, if any, was temporary. An agreement between an ineffectual prime minister and Duplessis in October over taxation quickly turned to the advantage of Quebec and left Liberals there feeling abandoned. Two years later, in a meeting with American president Dwight David Eisenhower, the silent and withdrawn St-Laurent presented 'an almost pathetic spectacle,' Canadian ambassador Arnold Danford Patrick Heeney wrote in his diary. There is not much doubt that he was suffering from a form of depression. What brought it on is unclear, but there were plenty of things for him to worry about, most of them personal. Another daughter was unwell, the family's finances were precarious, and there was some danger that they were spending beyond their income. The family law firm had not prospered under his sons. St-Laurent could not make up his mind what to do, and as problems were postponed, they grew.

The rush of events in 1954 masked St-Laurent's personal issues. The Canadian and American governments concluded an agreement to build a canal and power project, the St Lawrence Seaway, which contributed to the country's apparently unending prosperity. At the same time the seaway underlined St-Laurent's seeming disregard for western Canada, especially the South Saskatchewan water and hydro project, which Jimmy Gardiner had been pushing ceaselessly. Politically, two of the mainstays of St-Laurent's cabinet chose to retire in June, Douglas Abbott to the Supreme Court and Brooke Claxton to business. St-Laurent was grieved at their departures, which unquestionably affected the government's effectiveness. This change in personnel also modified expectations for the eventual succession to the prime ministership, leaving only Pearson from the cabinet's front rank to aspire to the position. (It was well known that Gardiner and Paul Martin also had ambitions in this direction, but their colleagues did not take their prospects seriously.) Suddenly the cabinet took on a patina of age, with half its members near or over 65. Matters drifted. The give-away of wheat by the United States (to subsidize American farmers) undermined exports from western Canada. St-Laurent's protests to the American government were unavailing.

St-Laurent's increasingly indifferent direction placed more of a burden on individual ministers, especially Howe, who was not in the best of health himself. The government's solidarity began to leach away, though the decline was unreflected in public opinion polls, where the Liberals continued to lead, as they had since 1944. Such public projects as the Trans-Canada Highway, the Distant Early Warning Line for air defence, and the Canso Causeway in Nova Scotia drew favourable attention, and Howe was concentrating on a project designed to bring natural gas through a transcontinental pipeline from Alberta to central Canada. It would simultaneously give the country security of energy supply and improve its balance of payments by replacing coal and gas imported from the United States. To do the job, Howe had helped design a private company, Trans-Canada Pipe Lines Limited, incorporated in 1951. Much of the money and most of the technology would come from the United States, but a crucial part of the funding, for the section passing through unpopulated northern Ontario, where there was no supporting market, would have to be provided by Ottawa.

In the spring of 1956 Howe introduced legislation to provide Trans-Canada with the necessary federal cash. St-Laurent had no objection, and left the matter to his colleague. This was a mistake. There was a deadline on assembling the money, in order to start construction that summer, and all the opposition had to do was delay the bill. To get it passed, the government, again with St-Laurent's acquiescence rather than his leadership, used the then unusual parliamentary device of closure to limit discussion. The move was a public-relations disaster. As debate raged in the house, St-Laurent sat abstracted, though when he finally roused himself to speak, he uttered a dignified and authoritative summary of the issue, with reasons why the government had to proceed as it did. The majority as well as the minority, he reminded members, had rights and they included the right to pass legislation. The bill passed, and the pipeline eventually snaked from west to east. The government had had its way, but at some cost to its reputation. Opinion polls held, and attempts by the Conservatives to bring on an election foundered on contradictions within their party. In condemning the pipeline, some of them raised the spectre of too close a relationship between the Liberals and the Americans, symbolized by Howe, an immigrant from Massachusetts. That need not have mattered, but in the fall of 1956 the American issue was linked to the question of Canada's traditional association with the British empire, a subject on which the prime minister now had definite views.

St-Laurent had generally maintained amicable relations with his British counterparts, including the prime minister from 1955 to 1957, the ageing Robert Anthony Eden. Eden tried to rationalize Britain's foreign commitments, to bring them more into balance with his country's reduced economic resources. In particular, he had withdrawn the large garrison around the Suez Canal on Egypt's promise to leave this piece of British property alone. In July 1956, however, the Egyptian government nationalized the canal. Eden's reaction to this intended provocation was entirely disproportionate. He immediately prepared, with the French, to invade Egypt. Objections were brushed aside and knowing that the Canadians were likely to complain, he told his staff not to inform them; the Americans too were kept in the dark as much as possible. By late October, the British and French had arranged an Israeli invasion of Egypt and, using it as an excuse, they proclaimed they were intervening to protect the canal against a war. Eden sent St-Laurent a letter asking for Canadian understanding.

Eden had deliberately deceived him and Pearson had to work to contain his chief's fury, while sharing it himself. Pearson prepared a temperate response, placing Canadian policy within the framework of the UN and declining to support the Anglo-French action. When St-Laurent and Pearson brought the issue before the cabinet, some English-speaking ministers argued that such a stand would offend traditionalist Canadian opinion. At the UN, Pearson introduced a proposal for a peacekeeping force that would replace the British and French troops around the canal and cover Israel's withdrawal. His work drew compliments from around the world, but not in Canada, where the Conservatives, now under John George Diefenbaker, a veteran Saskatchewan MP, made the government's failure to support Britain the issue. This time St-Laurent was not indifferent. Rebutting Conservative arguments, he told the house on 26 Nov. 1956 that he had been scandalized by the big powers, 'who have all too frequently treated the charter of the United Nations as an instrument with which to regiment smaller nations.' In response to the derisive interjection from across the floor, asking why the big powers should not be allowed to veto action by the smaller nations, St-Laurent, according to an eyewitness, squared his shoulders defiantly, reddened, and retorted, 'Because the era when the supermen of Europe could govern the whole world is coming pretty close to an end.' Nothing he said was untrue, but in the heated atmosphere of the nostalgic imperial patriotism that was sweeping through parts of English Canada, he had waved a red flag at a political bull.

The next six months were taken up with housekeeping and anticipation of an election. A Liberal gala in Quebec City to celebrate St-Laurent's 75th birthday featured an eloquent speech by Howe, who boasted that his friend stood 'in the shade of no man.' This was St-Laurent's last hurrah, but no thought was being given to replacing him so close to the election, set for 10 June 1957. The Liberals were ahead in the polls, and St-Laurent was considered to be one of his party's major assets. One minister reportedly said in private that the party would go with St-Laurent if it had to run with him stuffed. The contest was Canada's first televised election. St-Laurent did not make much of an impression on the new medium, though the polls, right up to the end, indicated voters still intended to cast their ballots for the Liberals. For the campaign the party had money, but no workers; few of the ministers had much impact outside their ridings, and many stalwarts were dead. Worse, on a variety of issues the Liberals had offended the electorate, from wheat sales (or the lack of them) to the pipeline to the Suez crisis. No single issue would have been fatal, but the combination, joined to an uninspired campaign and an abstracted leader, proved indigestible. As the prime minister travelled through English Canada, hecklers yelled out 'supermen,' referring not just to his remark about the supermen of Europe but sarcastically to the Liberals as the supermen of Canada. At what should have been the Liberals' climactic rally, in Toronto's Maple Leaf Gardens, St-Laurent looked and sounded out of touch. As Jack Pickersgill later wrote, 'John

Diefenbaker did not win the election of 1957; the Liberal party lost it.'
They won more votes than the Conservatives but fewer seats. Half the
cabinet was defeated, though St-Laurent comfortably took Quebec East.
After a pause, while close races were decided, he determined to leave
office. On 21 June the cabinet resigned, Diefenbaker took over, and St-
Laurent moved into the unaccustomed job of opposition leader.

St-Laurent spent the summer at Saint-Patrice. In August, Pickersgill
visited him there: 'He was obviously deeply depressed, could not be
drawn into conversation, and clearly had no interest in his new role.' St-
Laurent's family now took a hand. They invited two former ministers,
Lionel Chevrier and Pearson, to visit and try to persuade their leader that
he would not be deserting the party if he resigned. The family asked
Pearson to draft a statement of resignation; St-Laurent stared at it, and
then gave his consent. According to Chevrier, he did so only after Pearson,
whom he considered his logical successor, agreed that he would run to
replace him. St-Laurent served as opposition leader for the fall session.
At the Liberal convention of January 1958 Pearson was chosen leader,
but Diefenbaker did not give him much time to adapt. Taking advantage
of some Liberal blunders, he called a new election for 31 March, in which
he trounced the Liberals. St-Laurent, who did not run, returned to Quebec
and the practice of law.

He was not quite starting over, but even with his prestige he had to
cope with the handicap of age. Nevertheless, for some years he practised
as he once had, attempting to restore the family fortunes. Old colleagues
dropped in from time to time, and among the ministers and mandarins of
Ottawa his memory remained green. Apart from them, the ex-prime minister was gradually forgotten. He sometimes attended funerals, including
Howe's in Montreal in January 1961, and was occasionally invited to state
occasions, such as the banquet honouring the visit of French president
Charles de Gaulle in Quebec in 1967. His wife died in 1966. Still, in
some respects his health and mood improved after he left office. He greeted
visitors equably. 'I'm just as bright, just as active as I ever was,' he told
Pickersgill. 'And you know, Jack, I'm like that for an hour every day.' His
firm's fortunes improved, permitting him gradually to fade into the background and let his son Renault-Stephen take the lead. Finally, after years
out of the public eye, Louis St-Laurent died in July 1973.

St-Laurent had many of the best characteristics of a prime minister but few of the best attributes of a politician. In his most productive years in the job, 1948 to 1954, he presided over a cabinet of strong ministers, many of them first-class politicians. His views and theirs generally coincided, though when they did not, it was the prime minister who prevailed. His fundamental commitment was to national unity, which he interpreted broadly in terms of an expansive federal power. At home and abroad he was an activist, which an abundant economy allowed him to be. More than any prime minister since, St-Laurent dominated his cabinet and his party. When he entered the room, Liberal MPs stood up in a sign of respect, if not reverence. He was able to master his cabinet in part because he was the master of the issues before it, an authority derived from intelligence and application. St-Laurent also had that most valuable asset, good luck; he served in good times and undoubtedly reaped political rewards from this prosperity. When he had to confront a difficult opposition, his qualities could no longer be mobilized to the task. As a politician, he alternated between two roles, corporate counsel and paterfamilias, without the dynamism of Diefenbaker, who was a superior campaigner and debater. St-Laurent was at his weakest in dealing with practical politics, and he failed to recruit replacements or alternatives for some of his ageing ministers. Because the Liberals depended on regional leaders to rally local support, this was a serious failure.

It was St-Laurent's misfortune to stay in office too long. Afflicted by a form of depression, he was unable to make the best choices for his party or himself, although, where the country was concerned, even his most controversial policies – the pipeline and opposition over Suez – were arguably the right ones. St-Laurent's time as prime minister passed from public consciousness, remembered if at all as a comfortable era of placid prosperity. Perhaps even the worst prime minister could not have avoided the prosperity, but placidity and comfort are not a bad inheritance to pass to posterity.

ROBERT BOTHWELL

Further reading

J. W. Pickersgill, *My years with Louis St-Laurent: a political memoir* (Toronto and Buffalo, N.Y., 1975).

D. C. Thomson, *Louis St. Laurent: Canadian* (Toronto, 1967).

Robert Bothwell and William Kilbourn, *C. D. Howe: a biography* (Toronto, 1979).

Robert Bothwell *et al.*, *Canada since 1945: power, politics and provincialism* (rev. ed., Toronto, 1989).

JOHN GEORGE DIEFENBAKER,

lawyer and politician; b. 18 Sept. 1895 in Neustadt, Ont.,
elder son of William Thomas Diefenbaker and Mary Florence
Bannerman; m. first 29 June 1929 Edna Mae Brower (d. 1951)
in Toronto; m. there secondly 8 Dec. 1953 Olive Evangeline
Palmer, née Freeman (d. 1976); no children were born of either
marriage; d. 16 Aug. 1979 in Ottawa.

I n his memoirs John Diefenbaker describes his ancestors as 'dispossessed Scottish Highlanders and discontented Palatine Germans.'
His paternal grandfather, George M. Diefenbacker (Diefenbach or
Diefenbacher), was born in the Grand Duchy of Baden (Germany). In
the 1850s he immigrated to Upper Canada, where he married and worked
as a wagon maker. His son William, one of seven children, was born in
April 1868, attended school in Hawkesville and Berlin (Kitchener), Ont.,
and received a teaching certification from the Model School in Ottawa
in 1891. In May 1894 he married Mary Bannerman, whose grandparents
had lost their Scottish tenancies during the land clearances of 1811–12
in Sutherland. They had been members of the third party of immigrants
that Lord Selkirk brought to the Red River settlement (Man.), arriving
via Hudson Bay in June 1814. After one harsh winter they travelled by
canoe brigade to Upper Canada and finally settled in what would become
Bruce County, where their granddaughter Mary was born in 1872.

William and Mary Diefenbaker were living an itinerant life when their
first son, John, was born in 1895. A brother, Elmer Clive, arrived in 1897.
During John's early years, the family followed William from one low-paying teaching job to another, first in Neustadt, then in Greenwood, then
in Todmorden. Young John began his schooling at age four in his father's
classroom. In 1903, suffering from debt and ill health, William sought a
teaching post in the North-West Territories and was offered work in the
Tiefengrund Public School District near the site of Fort Carlton (Sask.),
halfway on the wagon route between Winnipeg and Edmonton. For two
winters the Diefenbakers lived in primitive quarters attached to the rural

schoolroom, supplementing their income with gifts of vegetables, sausages, and firewood from their farming neighbours. In December 1904,
on payment of a $10 registration fee, William took possession of a
quarter-section homestead in nearby Borden, but a lack of capital prevented him from occupying the land until the summer of 1906. In the
interim, the family moved once more, to Hague for the winter of 1905–6,
where William taught school and served as village secretary.

In the summer of 1906 the Diefenbakers took up their property,
built a three-room frame house, a barn, and a shack, planted a garden,
broke ten acres of grassland for crops, and welcomed William's bachelor
brother Edward Lackner to a neighbouring homestead. The two brothers
found teaching jobs at local one-room schools – William at Hoffnungsfeld
and Edward at Halcyonia – and that autumn John entered grade 7 at his
uncle's school. For three harsh winters the family survived on the homestead, but in 1910, after satisfying the minimal residence requirement for
full title to the land, the Diefenbakers departed for Saskatoon, where
William found work as a clerk in the provincial public service. In 1911
he became an inspector in the customs office, where he remained until
his retirement in 1937.

John attended the Saskatoon Collegiate Institute for two years. With
his mother's encouragement he entered the University of Saskatchewan
in Saskatoon in the autumn of 1912 to study arts and law. His early
university record was undistinguished. He already had a political career
in mind; in later years his family recalled that his ambition to be prime
minister had been expressed before he was ten. In the spring of 1914
he took up a contract teaching primary school in the Wheat Heart Public
School District. In October, after teaching for five months of the seven-
month contract, he made an unusual arrangement to delegate completion
of the school term to his uncle Edward in order to return to university.
Subsequently Diefenbaker sought payment of what he claimed was a
deficiency in his salary, a claim rejected by the school board and the
Department of Education.

In the spring of 1915 Diefenbaker received his BA and that autumn
he returned to university for an MA in political science and economics.
Meanwhile, World War I had become a contest of steady slaughter on
the Western Front. In March 1916 he enlisted for officers' training and

was commissioned a lieutenant in the infantry. He received his MA *in absentia* and, after a month of lectures and drill, he undertook three months of articling in a Saskatoon law office before requesting an overseas posting in August. He sailed for England in September as a member of the 196th (Western Universities) Battalion and spent the autumn at camps in Shorncliffe and Crowborough. After a few months he was found medically unfit for service at the front and in February 1917 he returned to Canada. He was demobilized in December and denied a pension sought on grounds of disability. The military records and his own account of this episode are contradictory and were never reconciled during his lifetime; the official records suggest that he was judged unfit because of 'general weakness' without demonstration of any physical disability, while he claimed to have been injured by a falling pickaxe. During the 1920s he showed gastric symptoms consistent with a possible diagnosis of psychosomatic illness in 1916–17. Similar cases of neurasthenia, more or less intense, would be common in both world wars.

After returning to Saskatoon, Diefenbaker articled in three law firms during 1918–19 and attended classes in law at the university. He received one year's credit in law school for his undergraduate courses in law and an additional year's credit as a veteran. In May 1919 he obtained his LLB. At his request, the Law Society of Saskatchewan granted him two years' exemption from articling and in June 1919 he was called to the bar. He opened his first office in Wakaw, 40 miles north of Saskatoon. Wakaw was a thriving market town of 400 in a farming district settled by immigrants from central and eastern Europe. It was on the district court circuit and had easy access by rail and road to high court sessions in Saskatoon, Prince Albert, and Humboldt. The tall, thin young man with deep blue eyes and wavy black hair, dressed soberly in a dark three-piece suit, made an immediate and striking impression in the small town.

Diefenbaker's first court case involved the defence of a client accused of careless wounding with a rifle. The assailant had immediately offered first aid and turned himself in to the police. Diefenbaker argued successfully in October 1919 that the shooting was an error committed in the fading evening light. He was soon busy with other cases and within a year he was able to move to larger offices and buy a Maxwell touring car. In the fall of 1920 he was elected to the Wakaw village council for a three-year term. In his first widely noticed case, he acted on appeal for clients from the French-speaking community in the Ethier Public School District, defending two school trustees against a charge that they had violated the province's School Act by permitting teaching in French. Although the court found that the act had indeed been violated, he won the appeal in May 1922 on the technical ground that trustees could not be held responsible for the internal operations of the school. He became known as a defender of minorities and his legal fees in the case were paid by the Association Catholique Franco-Canadienne de la Saskatchewan.

Although Diefenbaker's civil case list grew, his reputation would be founded on his record as a criminal defence lawyer. In the courtroom he discovered and honed his dramatic genius. He mastered juries with his powerful and edgy voice, his penetrating stare, his waving arm and accusatory finger, his ridicule and sarcasm, and his command of evidence and the law. He identified naturally with the dispossessed and the poor, with all those who lacked the wealth, power, and confidence of the British Canadian mainstream; and he argued his cases with passion. Saskatchewan was fertile ground for these talents. In 1924 he took on a partner, Alexander Ehman, in his Wakaw office and moved his own practice to Prince Albert. Two other partners succeeded Ehman before Diefenbaker closed the Wakaw branch in 1929.

The young lawyer's father had been a supporter of Liberal prime minister Sir Wilfrid Laurier. As a repatriated soldier, Diefenbaker had supported the Union government of Sir Robert Laird Borden in the election of 1917, although he was opposed to the War-time Elections Act, which deprived recently naturalized Canadians of the vote. In 1921 his political affiliation was uncertain. He admired Andrew Knox, the MP for Prince Albert who had successfully shifted his candidacy from the Unionists to the Progressive Party, but he kept his own political views private. He would later say that the Liberal Party, which dominated Saskatchewan politics in the 1920s, hoped to recruit him, but claimed that 'I was never keen.' In 1925 his name was proposed and rejected for nomination as a Liberal in the June provincial election, but on 6 August he was acclaimed as the Conservative candidate for Prince Albert in the forthcoming federal election. 'I haven't spent a lifetime with this party,' he would reflect in 1969. 'I chose it because of certain basic principles and those ... were the empire relationship of the time, the monarchy and the preservation of an independent Canada.' But he distrusted the Ontario-centred policies of the party and disagreed publicly with its leader, Arthur Meighen, who opposed completion of the Hudson Bay Railway and threatened to change the railway freight rates benefiting the movement of the prairie grain crop. On the hustings Diefenbaker campaigned feverishly and responded angrily to the insult that he was a 'Hun.' Despite Conservative gains elsewhere in the election of 29 October, the party won no seats in Saskatchewan. In Prince Albert, Diefenbaker ran third and lost his deposit.

The Liberal victor in Prince Albert, Charles McDonald, almost immediately resigned his seat to make way for Prime Minister William Lyon Mackenzie King, who had lost his own seat in York North. The Conservative Party did not nominate against him, although Diefenbaker privately encouraged the entry of an independent candidate. King won easily. In late June 1926 his government resigned in what became known as the King–Byng affair and was replaced by Meighen's Conservatives, who were defeated at once in the House of Commons. The house was dissolved for a September election. Diefenbaker stood again in Prince Albert, facing the former prime minister in a two-way contest. Once again he was at odds with his own leader, who opposed King's recently established old-age pension scheme and maintained his unpopular views on freight rates and the Hudson Bay Railway. King's Liberal Party was returned to power with an absolute majority, while the Conservatives lost all but one seat in the three prairie provinces.

Despite his electoral losses Diefenbaker was beginning to attract attention elsewhere in the country. When he made his first political journey out of Saskatchewan in 1926 to address a Conservative convention in British Columbia, he was described by the journalist William Bruce Hutchison as 'tall, lean, almost skeletal, his bodily motions jerky and spasmodic, his face pinched and white, his pallor emphasized by metallic black curls and sunken, hypnotic eyes.' Yet from this 'frail, wraithlike person,' continued Hutchison, 'a voice of vehement power and rude health blared like a trombone.'

Diefenbaker attended the 1927 federal leadership convention in Winnipeg that chose Calgary millionaire Richard Bedford Bennett to replace Meighen and became Bennett's admirer as he rebuilt the national party. In Saskatchewan the Conservatives prepared to confront the entrenched provincial Liberal government, whose strength lay in its good relations with the grain growers' associations and the large, mostly Catholic, immigrant communities. The Conservatives turned elsewhere for support. From 1926 to 1928 a ragtag Canadian offshoot of the Ku Klux Klan created more than 100 local branches in the province, appealing to anti-Catholic, anti-French, and anti-immigrant sentiments. Although Diefenbaker was never a member, his party was caught up in this bigoted wave of nativism, reflecting or tolerating support for extremist views at its 1928 convention in Saskatoon and during a by-election in Arm River later that year. During the by-election campaign Diefenbaker shared the platform several times with one of the Klan's promoters, James Fraser Bryant, and at one campaign meeting he challenged Premier James Garfield Gardiner over the 'sectarian influences ... pervading the entire education system.' The Liberal Party won by a narrow margin, but Conservatives drew the lesson that extreme claims could win votes. They carried their anti-Catholic message into the provincial election of 6 June 1929, emphasizing the issues of race, religion, language, and immigration. Diefenbaker was the Conservative candidate in Prince Albert and was promised the attorney generalship in the event of victory. He lost the contest to the sitting Liberal, Thomas Clayton Davis, but Gardiner's Liberals were replaced by a Conservative minority government dependent on Progressive support. The Klan soon disappeared from Saskatchewan.

In the summer of 1928 Diefenbaker had become engaged to Edna Brower, a vivacious Saskatoon schoolteacher. They were married three weeks after the provincial election. Edna was an immediate asset to the aspiring politician, offsetting his dour presence with her warmth and spontaneity. She was resented by Diefenbaker's mother, however, who insisted that she remain first in her son's affections. John maintained close ties with his parents, making frequent visits to Saskatoon at their call. He also played a protective and dominating role towards his brother, Elmer, who now occupied part of the Diefenbaker law office in Prince Albert as an insurance broker and minor entrepreneur. Edna was closely involved in Diefenbaker's legal life, watching and commenting on his courtroom behaviour, observing the reactions of judges and juries, and offering support and reassurance to his clients.

In the late 1920s Diefenbaker defended four men on charges of murder. In the first case, *The King* v. *Bourdon* in 1927, he appeared as junior counsel, but afterwards always acted as lead. The defendant was found not guilty. The following year, in *The King* v. *Olson*, Diefenbaker requested on appeal that a conviction for murder be quashed on the ground that the trial judge had improperly directed the jury. The judgement was sustained, but on the court's recommendation Diefenbaker petitioned for mercy, claiming that the defendant had been mentally incapable of standing trial. The federal cabinet commuted the sentence to life imprisonment. He was similarly successful in *The King* v. *Pasowesty* in having a death sentence commuted to life imprisonment. In *The King* v. *Wysochan* he defended his client by arguing that the murder had been committed by the victim's husband. The defendant was convicted, the appeal was dismissed, the federal cabinet denied a reprieve, and Alex Wysochan was hanged in the Prince Albert jail in June 1930.

During this trial, Diefenbaker suffered a recurrence of his gastric illness and afterwards took leave from his law practice to recuperate. He was not a candidate in the federal election of 28 July 1930 which resulted in a Conservative majority government under Bennett and eight seats for the party in Saskatchewan. As a result of the provincial Conservative victory of 1929, however, he had been named a KC on 1 Jan. 1930. Later in 1930 he served as junior counsel to the provincial royal commission known as the Bryant charges commission, investigating Conservative claims that the previous government had interfered with the operations of the provincial police force for partisan advantage. The commission wound up inconclusively in early 1931.

As the Great Depression deepened on the prairies into a descending spiral of drought, crop failure, debt, and unemployment, the new provincial government lost its revenues and its sense of direction. Diefenbaker's law practice in Prince Albert contracted modestly, but he was able to maintain a comfortable income throughout the 1930s. In 1932 his law partner, William G. Elder, departed in conflict, he claimed, over finances and ethics. The following year Diefenbaker recruited John Marcel Cuelenaere as an articling student. Cuelenaere would stay on as his partner until 1957 and, as a Liberal partisan, would later serve as mayor of Prince Albert, an MLA, and a provincial cabinet minister.

In October 1933 Diefenbaker was elected vice-president of the Saskatchewan Conservative Party and in November he put himself forward as a last-minute candidate for mayor of Prince Albert on a platform of interest reduction on the civic debt. He lost by only 48 votes in a record poll. Diefenbaker was not a candidate in the June 1934 provincial election, but he campaigned for the Conservatives in a hopeless cause. The party lost all its seats to the Liberals under Gardiner, who faced a small Farmer–Labour opposition.

Meanwhile, Diefenbaker continued to admire Bennett's leadership. After the prime minister announced his New Deal in January 1935, Diefenbaker wrote that Bennett's radical proposals 'have given our rank and file something to enthuse over – a new hope and a new spirit.' But the federal government was divided and demoralized by the continuing depression. In July 1935 Diefenbaker turned down an offer of the federal nomination in Prince Albert. He campaigned for the party during the October election, only to see its prospects shattered once more in a national Liberal landslide. In Saskatchewan the Conservatives elected only one member in the province's 21 seats. Bennett led the opposition for another three years while King returned to the prime ministership.

After its electoral defeat in 1934, the Saskatchewan Conservative Party had led a ghostly existence with no more than a handful of activists. In August 1935 Diefenbaker inherited the post of acting president of the provincial party. He hesitated in calling a leadership convention until October 1936. One week before the convention he presented his candidacy and on 28 October he was acclaimed party leader, promising a platform that would be 'radical in the sense that the reform program of the Honourable R. B. Bennett was radical.' The *Leader-Post* (Regina) commented that he 'thunders forth his convictions and ideas in resonant tones of purposeful youth.'

For 18 months Diefenbaker ran the party from his law office while Cuelenaere carried the firm's legal work. Diefenbaker appealed fruitlessly to the national party for financial aid and travelled the province seeking potential candidates. When a general election was called for June 1938 he was nominated in Arm River and took a personal loan to pay the nomination deposits for 21 other candidates. The party's moderately progressive program called for refinancing the provincial debt, an adjustment of farm debts, a study of crop insurance or acreage payments, and a commitment in principle to public health insurance. The Conservatives were barely visible in a campaign dominated by the incumbent Liberals, the Co-operative Commonwealth Federation (CCF), and the Social Credit. The Liberal government was re-elected with 38 seats against 14 opponents, none of them Conservative. The Conservative Party's vote fell to 12 per cent, but no one blamed the leader for the result. When the party met in convention four months later, Diefenbaker's resignation was unanimously refused and he remained leader by default for two more years.

During the 1930s Diefenbaker served as defence counsel in four well-publicized murder trials. In *The King* v. *Bajer* his client, a destitute young woman with two children, was found not guilty of suffocating her newborn child. He was unsuccessful in *The King* v. *Bohun*, his client being found guilty of murdering a storekeeper. The jury's recommendation for clemency was rejected and Steve Bohun was hanged in the Prince Albert jail in March 1934. After a raucous preliminary hearing in *The King* v. *Fouquette*, the crown stayed charges through lack of evidence and the murder remained unsolved. In *The King* v. *Harms* Diefenbaker called for a verdict of manslaughter in an unwitnessed alcoholic killing. John Harms was convicted of murder, but Diefenbaker successfully appealed on the ground of an improper charge to the jury. At the second trial he presented meticulous evidence of Harms's intoxication and won conviction on the reduced charge. Harms was sentenced to a prison term of 15 years.

Diefenbaker's political ambitions remained focused on national rather than provincial politics. By the spring of 1939 he was making tentative plans for a nomination in Lake Centre, the federal counterpart of his provincial constituency. On 15 June he was acclaimed the Conservative candidate and began intensive preparations for an election the following year. When Germany invaded Poland in September, the Conservative Party declared its solidarity with the King government's declaration of war. Arrangements for the election campaign were suspended, and commenced again only when the house was dissolved in January 1940. King campaigned confidently as a wartime incumbent, while the Conservatives under Robert James Manion were divided and disorganized. In Lake Centre, Diefenbaker called for a statutory floor price for wheat, asserted his own loyal service in World War I, and attacked the King government for its 'marked tendency towards dictatorship.' The Liberal Party won an overwhelming majority on 26 March. Manion was defeated, but Diefenbaker gained a narrow victory as one of two successful Conservatives from Saskatchewan. After five successive electoral defeats, he would never suffer another.

As one of 40 Conservatives in the new house, Diefenbaker was appointed to the house committee on the defence of Canada regulations, reviewing wartime emergency measures. He made his maiden speech on this subject with a strong declaration of patriotism, supporting wartime restriction of liberty and calling for national registration of adult males. Under the War Measures Act, the cabinet governed for the next five years by decree, while the role of the house was reduced to approval of the annual budget and spending estimates and modest questioning of the war effort within the self-imposed limits of general loyalty. Diefenbaker quickly established himself as one of the opposition's most effective critics, emphasizing the need for conscription for overseas military service and criticizing the cabinet's contempt for the role of parliament.

In the autumn of 1941 a meeting of the national party association chose the former leader, Senator Arthur Meighen, as Conservative chief. Meighen declared that he would pursue a program of coalition and resigned his senatorship to run in York South. The Liberal Party did not contest the by-election, but covertly aided the CCF candidate, who emerged victorious. This defeat – and the Liberal government's political shrewdness – left the Conservatives in confusion. While Meighen pondered a leadership convention, a group of party activists met in Port Hope, Ont., in September 1942 to draft a progressive and internationalist program that might counter the growing challenge of the CCF. The conference reaffirmed the party's belief in private enterprise and individual initiative, but also called for a wide range of social benefits and limited state intervention. When the leadership convention was scheduled for December, the chief organizers of the Port Hope conference were given prominent roles. Meanwhile, Meighen set out to arrange the draft of the Liberal-Progressive premier of Manitoba, John Bracken, as party leader. When the convention opened in Winnipeg, four western candidates, including Diefenbaker, had declared themselves. Bracken joined the race at the last possible moment and won easily on the second ballot.

Diefenbaker ran a respectable third. His nomination speech had incorporated the progressive vision of the Port Hope resolutions, together with a plea for the 'preservation of Canada within the British Empire' and 'the security of the common man.' He came out of the meeting with his reputation and friendships enhanced. The party had adopted a socially progressive platform satisfying to him and, at Bracken's insistence, it would henceforth be known as the Progressive Conservative Party.

Since Bracken decided not to enter the commons, the Conservative caucus met to elect a new parliamentary leader when the house reconvened. Diefenbaker remained in the contest against Ontario MP Gordon Graydon through several ballots; but on the final one Diefenbaker announced that he would support Graydon, who won by a single vote.

The King government began its preparations for the post-war period when it declared in January 1944 that it was committed to a national program aimed at full employment, price stability, and a range of welfare measures. The first of these, a family allowance plan, was introduced in legislation that summer. Diefenbaker took the lead in persuading a reluctant Conservative caucus to support the proposal and led the party in debate on the bill, which was adopted unanimously in July. In the autumn the Liberal government confronted a crisis over the reinforcement of Canadian troops in Europe, reversing its policy and committing 16,000 home service conscripts for duty overseas. Diefenbaker and the Conservatives risked the loss of votes in Quebec by arguing unsuccessfully for full overseas conscription.

While King fought the general election of June 1945 on a forward-looking platform of welfare, national unity, and international cooperation, the Conservative Party under Bracken looked backwards in criticism of the Liberal war effort. As in 1940, Diefenbaker campaigned in Lake Centre on a personal platform. King lost seats to the Conservatives in Ontario and to the CCF in the west, returning to power with a bare majority of 125 seats. In Saskatchewan the only survivors of the CCF sweep were Gardiner for the Liberals, one independent Liberal, and Diefenbaker for the Tories.

Bracken led the party listlessly for three more years. Meanwhile, Diefenbaker solidified his reputation as an MP, supporting progressive causes and criticizing the government for maintaining wartime regulations in peacetime and ignoring the rights of individuals. In 1946 he proposed a bill of rights 'under which freedom of religion, of speech, of association … freedom from capricious arrest and freedom under the rule of law' would be guaranteed. He told the house that his goal was to see 'an unhyphenated nation' in which citizens of many origins and religions would be regarded and treated equally. The call for a Canadian bill of rights became his leitmotif.

Despite (and partly because of) his growing public reputation, Diefenbaker remained an outsider in the Conservative caucus, regarded by other members as aloof, temperamental, and too much the showman. In Ontario, party barons viewed him as erratic and unreliable. When he contested the leadership for the second time at the convention in the autumn of 1948, it was no surprise that he lost on the first ballot to the premier of Ontario, George Alexander Drew. On 27 June 1949 the Liberal government went to

John G. Diefenbaker at his combative best in the House of Commons, Ottawa, 1948.

the polls under its new prime minister, Louis-Stephen St-Laurent, who campaigned on a bland program of prosperity and growth. The government's majority increased and Conservative seats fell from 67 to 41, but in Saskatchewan Diefenbaker added almost 2,000 votes to his majority and remained the sole Conservative member.

During 1945–46 Edna Diefenbaker had suffered several months of illness, identified as severe depression, but she returned to good health in 1947. In the fall of 1950, however, she was diagnosed with acute leukaemia and she died in February 1951. In the House of Commons,

John G. and Olive E. Diefenbaker relaxing at the prime minister's residence, 24 Sussex Drive in Ottawa, October 1962.

three MPs – Arthur Laing, Howard Charles Green, and Gardiner – offered unprecedented eulogies to a colleague's wife. For months Diefenbaker was overwhelmed by this loss. Two years later he married a childhood friend, the widowed Olive Freeman Palmer, a senior civil servant in Ontario's Department of Education. For the rest of his political career, Olive gave John her loyal support, discreetly encouraging his ambitions and reinforcing his beliefs. Her regal presence on platforms at his side gave him strength and reassurance.

In the late 1940s and early 1950s Diefenbaker was uncertain about continuing his political career in the opposition. But his combative instincts were challenged by a brazenly partisan redistribution of parliamentary seats in 1952, which added potential Liberal and CCF voters to his Lake Centre constituency. With his private cooperation, an all-party committee arranged for his nomination in Prince Albert for the federal election of 10 Aug. 1953. In that campaign he made appearances for the Conservatives in four other provinces, but in Prince Albert he stood without party identification. He was returned again as the sole

Conservative from Saskatchewan, while the party made slim inroads into what seemed to be a perpetual Liberal majority.

Public dissatisfaction over the long Liberal incumbency was gradually demonstrated over the next few years as Conservatives took power in New Brunswick under Hugh John Flemming in 1952 and in Nova Scotia under Robert Lorne Stanfield in 1956. In the summer of 1955 the St-Laurent government had stumbled and retreated in face of a Conservative filibuster over its attempted extension of emergency powers under the Defence Production Act, and in 1956 it confronted combined Conservative–CCF opposition in five weeks of parliamentary tumult over public financial assistance for construction of a natural gas pipeline. Diefenbaker, who was doubtful about the tactics of the filibuster, played a curiously low-key role in this struggle. In September 1956 Drew was unexpectedly forced by illness to resign from the party leadership. A convention was called for early December 1956.

Diefenbaker's candidacy was taken for granted. It was boosted by support from vigorous provincial parties in Ontario, New Brunswick, Nova Scotia, and Manitoba. Despite brief efforts to create a 'Stop Diefenbaker' campaign in Ontario, he was the instant favourite over his opponents, Donald Methuen Fleming and Edmund Davie Fulton. In his nomination speech Diefenbaker called on the party to banish a sense of defeatism. According to his Quebec supporter Pierre Sévigny, 'As he proceeded, the magnetism of the man, the hypnotic qualities which were to entrance a whole nation came to the fore. He spoke with an obvious sincerity and an inspired fervour.' Diefenbaker won a decisive victory on the first ballot.

The Liberal government remained complacent as it prepared for an early summer election in 1957. By contrast, Diefenbaker, despite his 61 years, injected energy and ideas into his reviving party with the assistance of his policy adviser, Merril Warren Menzies. Inspired by Menzies, and in his own visionary language, Diefenbaker put forward a program of national economic development aimed primarily at growth in the Atlantic provinces, the north, and the west. For three months he led a feverish national campaign with the assistance of campaign manager Allister Grosart, advertising director Dalton Kingsley Camp, and the efficient organization of Leslie Miscampbell Frost's Ontario Conservative Party. In Quebec the party received discreet assistance from the Union Nationale machine of Premier Maurice Le Noblet Duplessis. With freshly enhanced funding the party was able to contribute generously to local campaigns in all provinces. Diefenbaker's message to voters was positive, even utopian, recalling the party's role in the country's foundation under Sir John A. Macdonald. 'We intend to launch a National Policy of development in the Northern areas which may be called the New Frontier Policy,' he promised. 'Macdonald was concerned with the opening of the West. We are concerned with developments in the Provinces ... and in our Northern Frontier in particular. ... The North, with all its vast resources and hidden wealth – the wonder and the challenge of the North must become our national consciousness.' The party campaigned on a personalized slogan, 'It's time for a Diefenbaker government,' and the country awoke on 10 June to a surprise Conservative victory of 112 seats to the Liberals' 105; the CCF (with 25 seats) and Social Credit (with 19) held the balance of power. Diefenbaker took office on 17 June 1957 as leader of a minority government.

With over 60 new members in his caucus, Diefenbaker chose his cabinet entirely from sitting MPs. These included D. M. Fleming in Finance, Fulton in Justice, Gordon Minto Churchill in Trade and Commerce, Howard Green in Public Works, Douglas Scott Harkness in Northern Affairs and National Resources, George Harris Hees in Transport, George Randolph Pearkes in National Defence, George Clyde Nowlan in National Revenue, Michael Starr in Labour, Léon Balcer as solicitor general, and Ellen Louks Fairclough, née Cook, as secretary of state (the first woman to become a federal minister in Canada). In August Francis Alvin George Hamilton assumed the Northern Affairs portfolio and Harkness moved to Agriculture. The following month Diefenbaker drew his first minister from outside the house when Sidney Earle Smith, then president of the University of Toronto, became minister of external affairs. Drew became the Canadian high commissioner in London. The cabinet seemed competent and workmanlike, but it noticeably lacked French-speaking ministers in major portfolios. This failing Diefenbaker never corrected.

In his administration's early days Diefenbaker made a public commitment to divert 15 per cent of Canada's foreign trade from the United States to the United Kingdom. The promise would remain unfulfilled despite his government's continuing efforts to lessen dependence on the

American market and to promote trade with the British Commonwealth. Beyond this initial misstep, the new government proceeded boldly with an ambitious legislative program of farm price supports, housing loans, aid for development projects across the country, tax reductions, and increases in old-age pensions and civil service salaries. Public opinion polls showed strong support for the new government. When the Liberal leader, Lester Bowles Pearson, moved a motion of no-confidence proposing that the Conservatives hand power back to the Liberals, Diefenbaker seized the occasion to request a dissolution of parliament for an election in March 1958.

Diefenbaker's 1958 platform was a simplified and more exuberant version of the party's 1957 program, involving a new vision of the nation both economic and spiritual. He preached a populist, secular faith. 'Everywhere I go,' he declared, 'I see that uplift in people's eyes that comes from raising their sights to see the Vision of Canada in days ahead.' Diefenbaker's rhetoric caught the public mood. His campaign swept the country in a wave of euphoric enthusiasm. The posters called for voters to 'Follow John' and the electorate responded by granting the Conservatives an astonishing 208 of 265 seats, including 50 in Quebec. In his victory speech Diefenbaker declared that 'the Conservative Party has become a truly national party composed of all the people of Canada of all races united in the concept of one Canada.' His 'Vision' had raised public expectations beyond the possibility of satisfaction. He would need rare skill and good fortune to avoid a crashing descent from those heights.

Diefenbaker was soon accused of running a one-man government. This charge was true in the sense that his election victories and the political system focused public attention on his leadership, but untrue as a description of the governing process. In opposition he had been a loner in the Conservative caucus and in power he took pride in his dominating presence. He tended to distrust close advisers and was not at ease with his intellectual superiors – although he relied heavily on his clerk of the Privy Council, Robert Broughton Bryce. His cabinets contained few ministers of brilliance and he had no inclination to bring along potential successors. Throughout his term of office he held endless cabinet meetings in search of consensus, delayed decisions out of uncertainty, and (in the absence of crisis) left his ministers to manage their own departments with unusual freedom of action. Diefenbaker was neither an imaginative policy maker nor a skilled compromiser, preferring the stimulation of the hustings and debate in the house to any long-term promotion and brokering of his ideas. As he came under increasing attack, his suspicions, his tenacious fighting instincts, and his talent for the dramatic overwhelmed his capacity for calm judgement and his ability to lead a united political team.

The prime minister's initial decisions in foreign and defence policy, however, were taken confidently and decisively. They involved Canada's defence relationship with the United States, and were made in an atmosphere of cordiality with the American administration of President Dwight David Eisenhower – whose view of the threat from the Soviet Union during the Cold War was fully shared by Diefenbaker. The decisions grew naturally out of cooperation between the previous Liberal government and the United States and intensified Canadian absorption into the American military system. In July 1957 Diefenbaker and defence minister Pearkes – acting without consultation in cabinet – committed Canada to participation in the integrated North American Air Defence Agreement, known as NORAD. In 1958 Diefenbaker agreed with the United States to locate two short-range Bomarc anti-aircraft missile bases in northern Ontario and Quebec and to arm the missiles, once installed, with nuclear warheads. This decision at first caused little controversy.

In February 1959 (after ambiguous warnings had been delivered to the manufacturers in previous months) Diefenbaker announced the immediate cancellation of development of the Avro Arrow (CF-105), a Canadian-designed, advanced interceptor aircraft being built in Toronto. The Arrow decision raised questions about the government's style and judgement and eventually weakened Diefenbaker's confidence in his own political intuitions. In subsequent years the Arrow would become a cult symbol of mistakenly abandoned Canadian industrial and military opportunities, although in the cooler light of financial and military prudence the decision could easily be justified.

In opposition Diefenbaker had been a renowned champion of civil liberties. In 1958, as prime minister, he promised to protect rights 'defined and guaranteed in precise and practical terms to all men by the law of the land.' After two years of intense discussion on the merits of a constitutional amendment binding on all levels of government versus the passage of declaratory federal legislation, he opted for an ordinary act of parliament which would not become lost in controversy over amending the constitution. The bill, he declared, would serve to educate citizens on their existing rights and would act as a restraint and a guide for federal lawmakers. Diefenbaker acknowledged – in the absence of a constitutional amendment – that his bill was only a first step for Canada, but it was nevertheless a pledge to all citizens that their rights would henceforth be respected. He told the house what this change would mean for him: 'I know something of what it has meant in the past for some to regard those with names of other than British or French origin as not being that kind of Canadian that those of British or French origin could claim to be.' The bill was adopted unanimously in August 1960, and in retrospect Diefenbaker regarded it as his outstanding achievement. It contained two escape clauses, one permitting parliament to override the guarantees contained in the act, providing legislation specified that it had been adopted 'notwithstanding the *Canadian Bill of Rights*,' and a second exemption for actions taken under the War Measures Act. The act was interpreted cautiously by the courts, but had an exemplary political importance. Under Prime Minister Pierre Elliott Trudeau, it would be transmuted into the more comprehensive Canadian Charter of Rights and Freedoms, containing the same exemptions. In 1960 as well, parliament extended the federal franchise to Canada's aboriginal population.

The following year the Diefenbaker cabinet dealt with another issue of conscience long troubling to the prime minister. For three years after assuming power, cabinet had reviewed every criminal conviction involving the death penalty in time-consuming and anguishing detail, confirming some sentences and commuting others. Their task was eased after passage of justice minister Fulton's amendments to the Criminal Code, which created two categories of murder and limited the death penalty to a narrow range of deliberate offences.

The Diefenbaker government's first budget, in 1958, had held the line on further spending in the face of an economic slowdown, but the prime minister's preference for aid to prairie farmers and an uncoordinated program of development projects in the Atlantic provinces and the west progressively undermined the highly conservative instincts of finance minister Fleming. Annual budgets fell into deficit. Beyond his conviction that fairness required a new concern for the poor, the unemployed, the ill, and the elderly, Diefenbaker lacked any coherent economic strategy. As unemployment continued to grow in 1959, 1960, and 1961 despite infusions of fresh public spending, he was troubled by Liberal claims that 'Tory times are hard times' and haunted by memories of Bennett's loss of power in 1935. Under relentless pressure from the cabinet for expansionary policies, Fleming came to share Diefenbaker's belief that the restoration of prosperity was hindered by the Bank of Canada's restrictive interest rate policy and the outspokenness of its governor, James Elliott Coyne. For five months in 1961 Diefenbaker and Fleming engaged in an unseemly public battle with the governor, as they sought his resignation. Coyne's refusal prompted the government to introduce legislation dismissing him, but that was frustrated by a Liberal majority in the Senate. On 14 July, once Coyne was allowed to make his case before a Senate committee, he offered the resignation he had previously refused. The conflict resulted in agreements between the bank and the government to avoid similar disputes in the future, but the immediate political effect was to undermine popular faith in the competence of the Diefenbaker regime.

As prime minister, Diefenbaker was eager to make an impact on the international scene equalling that of his political rival Pearson. In the summer of 1958 he had welcomed both the British prime minister, Maurice Harold Macmillan, and the American president, Eisenhower, to Ottawa and in the autumn of that year he toured Europe and the Asian Commonwealth. In Europe he gained the respect of President Charles de Gaulle of France, Chancellor Konrad Adenauer of the German Federal Republic, and Prime Minister Amintore Fanfani of Italy. In Asia he admired the anti-communism of the new Pakistani dictator General Mohammad Ayub Khan and the political realism of Prime Minister Jawaharlal Nehru of India, while warning against the neutralism of Prime Minister Solomon West Ridgeway Dias Bandaranaike of Ceylon (Sri Lanka). He made a major speech to the General Assembly of the United Nations on 26 Sept. 1960, denouncing the Soviet Union for its domestic tyranny, its crude colonialism in eastern and central Europe, and its threats to the western alliance. The speech evoked praise from other western leaders.

Despite his vehement rejection of the South African policy of apartheid, Diefenbaker was hesitant to consider exclusion of South Africa from membership in the British Commonwealth on the ground that the association should not interfere in the domestic affairs of its members. Political pressure for action intensified after disorders and a police massacre of peaceful demonstrators in Sharpeville in March 1960. At a meeting of Commonwealth prime ministers in May Diefenbaker worked with Prime Minister Macmillan to avoid a split among the leaders along racial lines. They found their escape in convenient delay. The conference offered South Africa time to revise its policies by agreeing that in the event it chose to become a republic, it would have to request consent from other Commonwealth members for readmission to the association. When South Africa's whites voted that October in favour of a republic, Prime Minister Hendrik Frensch Verwoerd announced that he would seek continuing Commonwealth membership at the meeting in March 1961. Diefenbaker arrived at that meeting carrying divided counsels on South Africa, some calling for its exclusion, some for renewal of its membership coupled with a Commonwealth statement on racial equality, and others for further delay. As the conference opened he was undecided, but at the suggestion of Bryce he advocated a declaration of principles to be adopted before a decision on South Africa's readmission. The effect would be to force a choice on South Africa rather than on the other members. When Verwoerd called for additional wording which would exclude his country's practices from blame, Diefenbaker sided with the non-white leaders in rejecting the proposal. Verwoerd withdrew the South African application and left the meeting. Following South Africa's departure, the conference dropped the effort to adopt a declaration of principles, but Diefenbaker told reporters that non-discrimination was an 'unwritten principle' of the association and that it was 'in keeping with the course of my life.' He accepted the outcome as the least divisive one possible and received wide praise at home and abroad for his defence of the principle of non-discrimination.

As president of the United States, Eisenhower had showed constant respect and consideration toward his northern colleague. Potential points of friction in joint defence policy and other matters were handled from Washington with amicable deference or delay. As his last official act before departing office, Eisenhower invited Diefenbaker to the White House for a ceremonial signing of the contentious Columbia River Treaty on 17 Jan. 1961. The easy political relationship died when John Fitzgerald Kennedy became president. Kennedy was young, brash, wealthy, and an eastern sophisticate whose manner grated on the prime minister. To Diefenbaker's intense annoyance, Kennedy called him 'Diefenbawker' when he first became president. Although their initial meeting in Washington on 20 February was superficially cordial, Kennedy told his brother Robert Francis that 'I don't want to see that boring son of a bitch again,' and the American administration began almost at once to show impatience over Canada's hesitation to negotiate agreements on dual control of the nuclear warheads intended for Canadian Bomarc missiles. When Kennedy visited Ottawa in May 1961 tensions intensified. Diefenbaker explained his political difficulty in accepting possession of nuclear warheads in the face of growing anti-nuclear sentiment across the country; Kennedy responded that failure to arm the new weapons would turn Canada into a neutralist in the Cold War. When Diefenbaker accidentally discovered a confidential White House memorandum advising Kennedy 'to push' Canada on a number of issues, the prime minister chose to ignore the advice of his staff to return it, instead filing it away for potential future use against the president. (It would be leaked during the 1963 election campaign.) Formal negotiations for an agreement on the warheads made no progress in this atmosphere of distrust – although at the time Kennedy made no public complaint over Canada's hesitation.

Meanwhile, the Diefenbaker government's good relations with the British government were fading. Macmillan's initial respect cooled as Diefenbaker took an unexpectedly strong and decisive position on the subject of South African membership in the Commonwealth, and effectively disappeared when Canada criticized the British application for entry into the European Economic Community, or Common Market. Diefenbaker and his high commissioner, Drew, regarded the application as a betrayal of Canada's sentiments and economic interests and acted to subvert its success in the absence of firm trading guarantees for Commonwealth members. Diefenbaker made frequent complaints about Britain's lack of consultation with its Commonwealth partners on the subject and privately took satisfaction at hints of French intransigence. (The British application would be vetoed by President de Gaulle in January 1963.) Canadian opinion on the matter was divided, but the Canadian government's reputation was undermined by comments in the press that it had been overbearing and obstructive in its reaction to British policy.

Prime Minister John G. Diefenbaker governs with little concern for Quebec, in a caricature by Raoul Hunter from *Le Soleil* (Quebec City), 23 Aug. 1959.

John :ₒ La roue arrière...? sans importance..!

In Quebec the Quiet Revolution was transforming the province and elsewhere appeals were mounting for fairer treatment of the country's French-speaking minority. Diefenbaker, who had neglected the French-speaking members of his own caucus, was indifferent to the signs of change. He refused to consider proposals for a royal commission on French–English relations. In Ottawa the formerly admiring press gallery had grown disillusioned and hostile as the government's record revealed an ineptitude frequently traceable to the prime minister's character. Diefenbaker's disorganization and growing indecisiveness had discouraged and divided his cabinet. When the commons was dissolved for a general election to be held on 18 June 1962, reporter James Stewart of the *Montreal Star* described the entire parliamentary term as 'sometimes aimless, often ill-tempered, and always potentially explosive.'

As the election campaign began, the government faced a major monetary crisis. A lingering recession, a series of budget deficits, an unfavourable balance in the current trade account, and general uncertainty about government policy provoked a loss of confidence in the exchange market. For weeks the Bank of Canada sold foreign reserves to maintain the value of the floating Canadian dollar and in May the cabinet was forced to devalue and peg the dollar at 92.5 cents (U.S.) in order to prevent a cascading collapse of the currency. The devaluation was cruelly caricatured by the press and the opposition during the election campaign; phoney Diefendollars or Diefenbucks passed from hand to hand.

Diefenbaker campaigned defiantly in the face of vigorous opposition from the refreshed Liberal Party, from the newly formed New Democratic Party, and in rural Quebec from the Ralliement des Créditistes, which under its charismatic leader, Réal Caouette, had been allied with the Social Credit Party since 1961. The Conservative program offered no novelty. The Toronto *Globe and Mail* reported that 'the Conservative campaign has been essentially a one-man show with Mr. Diefenbaker the man. If they fail to win, he must take the blame; if they do win he can claim the victory, no matter how many seats they lose, for his own.'

For Diefenbaker, the election results were devastating. He kept his hold on the prairies, but in the Atlantic provinces, rural Quebec, urban Ontario, and British Columbia the Conservatives lost their dominance. Five ministers were defeated. Diefenbaker held 116 seats against 100 Liberals, 30 Social Crediters/Créditistes, and 19 New Democrats. Following the campaign, a new run on the dollar required the imposition of tariff surcharges, reduced government spending, and emergency borrowing from the International Monetary Fund, the United States, and the United Kingdom. Diefenbaker retreated into weeks of seclusion before reconstructing his cabinet and reconvening parliament in the autumn.

The cabinet was directionless. Up to a third of Diefenbaker's ministers speculated openly but indecisively on the prime minister's removal. In October 1962 the Cuban missile crisis diverted everyone's attention and Diefenbaker deepened his cabinet's divisions by responding hesitantly to President Kennedy's appeal for allied solidarity. In the aftermath, ministers insisted that negotiations with the United States on the acceptance of nuclear warheads should be reopened. The sudden impact of the international crisis and the prime minister's demonstrated inability to make decisions under pressure suggested that an agreement with the United States to supply the warheads had become a matter of urgency. Negotiations quickly foundered and Washington raised the stakes by accusing the Diefenbaker government of lying and neglecting its military obligations. Diefenbaker's minister of defence, Douglas Harkness, resigned. The opposition united to condemn Diefenbaker's indecision and on 5 Feb. 1963 his government was defeated in the house.

Diefenbaker entered the 1963 election campaign with a disintegrating cabinet. Harkness, Hees, Sévigny, Fleming, Fulton, and others had resigned or retired. His supporting newspapers, the Toronto *Telegram*, the *Globe and Mail*, and all but four other papers across the country, had abandoned him. The party organization had collapsed – although his chief campaigners, Grosart and Camp, maintained their loyalty. Diefenbaker set out on the campaign trail fighting 'the Bay Street and St. James Street Tories,' the American government, and his Liberal challengers. As he crossed the country in a whistle-stop campaign, greeting voters at little railway stations in the bitter cold, he was inspired by American president Harry S. Truman's 'Give 'em hell!' election of 1948. His rural, prairie, and small town public responded enthusiastically as he derided the Liberal Party and the American Department of State. Throughout the campaign Conservative support held steady while that of the Liberals declined until, on 8 April, Diefenbaker left Pearson five seats short of a majority. Diefenbaker resigned office and Pearson took power on 22 April, once he had received an assurance of support from six Créditiste MPs. In 1963 the journalist Peter Charles Newman published his vivid, best-selling account of Diefenbaker's career, *Renegade in power*, the first of a new Canadian genre of popular contemporary history, which romanticized the prime minister's dramatic rise and fall.

For three and a half years Diefenbaker carried on as leader of the opposition under siege from elements of his own party, but aggressive and menacing towards his Liberal opponents in the house. He ferreted out one embarrassing scandal after another – all of them involving Quebec ministers. The majority of his MPs, dependent on him for their success in politics, remained faithful. For eight months in 1964 Diefenbaker and his loyalists delayed approval of a new Canadian maple leaf flag because they said it lacked any historic symbols. The resolution was eventually adopted in mid December after closure was used to cut off debate. Most of Diefenbaker's Quebec MPs voted with the government. Pearson, harassed and distracted by Diefenbaker's relentless attacks in the house, called an election for 8 Nov. 1965, hoping to deliver a fatal blow to his nemesis. Old Conservative foes (including Hees and Fulton) returned to the fold in the hope of a political life after Diefenbaker, while the party leader himself dreamed of returning to power. At age 70 he conducted another vigorous national campaign. Pearson could find no clear theme beyond his call for a majority government and the final destruction of his foe, but he appeared to have little taste for the battle. Once more

Diefenbaker's Conservatives deprived the Liberal Party of its desired majority. The Conservatives, with 97 seats, held two more than previously, as did the Liberals with 131. The NDP, at 21 seats, gained four, while the Créditistes and Social Crediters (now separate) suffered losses.

By this time, the political conflict between Diefenbaker and Pearson had become malignant. The 1966 parliamentary year began with Diefenbaker's renewed attacks on the government's integrity, prompting countercharges against his own administration for having failed to act on a matter of security. A judicial inquiry under Mr Justice Wishart Flett Spence, appointed to examine what became known as the Munsinger affair, was in effect an *ex post facto* investigation of the political discretion exercised by the Diefenbaker government. Diefenbaker, Fulton, and their lawyers withdrew in protest from the inquiry midway through the hearings. The final report found no breach of security, but censured Diefenbaker for having failed to dismiss his associate minister of defence,

John G. Diefenbaker and boisterous western lookalikes dampen Lester B. Pearson's enthusiasm at the Grey Cup game (and in the previous election), as drawn by Duncan I. Macpherson in the *Toronto Daily Star*, 26 Nov. 1966.

Pierre Sévigny, six years earlier when he had learned of his extramarital liaison with Gerda Munsinger, who had apparently been a low-level Soviet agent. The *Globe and Mail* called the inquiry's terms of reference 'vague, vengeful, prosecutory ... setting a precedent for endless witch-hunts as government succeeds government in Canada.'

Diefenbaker's second battle of the year was fought within his party, where he struggled to control the party office and the national association and to hold onto his own leadership. Eruptions of discontent multiplied, but in the absence of any formal system of leadership review he took for granted that his term was unlimited. Once convinced that the leader would not take voluntary retirement, the party president, Dalton Camp, proposed a reform in the party constitution to require an automatic vote on whether to hold a leadership convention subsequent to the loss of a general election. Diefenbaker met Camp's challenge with charges of back stabbing, but failed to carry the annual meeting. It agreed on a leadership convention, to be held in 1967.

As planning for the convention proceeded, Diefenbaker refused to confirm his candidacy. Finally, he stood for re-election in opposition to a convention resolution emerging from the party's policy conference at Montmorency falls, Que., that spoke of Canada's 'two founding peoples' or 'deux nations.' (The draft resolution actually described a country 'composed of the original inhabitants of this land and the two founding peoples [deux nations] with historic rights, who have been and continue to be joined by people from many lands.') 'That proposition,' he told reporters, 'will place all Canadians who are of other racial origins than English and French in a secondary position. All through my life, one of the things I've tried to do is to bring about in this nation citizenship not dependent on race or colour, blood counts or origin.' Diefenbaker's vision of 'One Canada' meant equality for individuals and regions, but he could not accept the notion of 'founding peoples' or 'nations' which seemed to include some communities while excluding others. His familiar appeal to equality – always drawing on his personal experience – did not work in a period when the country had grown more complex. On the first ballot, he ran fifth behind Stanfield, Dufferin Roblin, Fulton, and Hees. He remained on the ballot through three votes. Stanfield was chosen leader on the fourth.

Through 12 more years and four more general elections, 1968, 1972, 1974, and 1979, Diefenbaker remained in the House of Commons. For a few years his prominent claque on the Conservative backbenches made life awkward for the new leader and for the rest of his life he could rivet the house's attention and embarrass ministers with his pungent and sarcastic questions. On his 30th anniversary as an MP, in 1970, he joked that he would live as long as Moses. Six years later he was named a CH in the queen's New Year's honours list and he travelled proudly to England for the presentation ceremony at Windsor Castle. In the mid 1970s he published three volumes of ghost-written memoirs. He conducted his last election campaign in ill health during the spring of 1979, returned to Ottawa, and died at home on 16 August.

Diefenbaker's state funeral was the most elaborate in Canadian history. He had planned it meticulously in consultation with the secretary of state's department. For three days the open casket lay in the parliamentary hall of honour before it was moved in a ceremonial parade to Christ Church Cathedral for an interfaith service. From Ottawa, an eight-car funeral train carried the coffin and more than 100 passengers westwards to Prince Albert and Saskatoon, with stops both scheduled and unscheduled for crowds along the way. On the high bluffs of the South Saskatchewan River, the old chief was buried beside the Right Honourable John G. Diefenbaker Centre, which had been constructed on the grounds of the University of Saskatchewan to house his papers and relics. The new Conservative prime minister, Charles Joseph (Joe) Clark, delivered the graveside eulogy, describing Diefenbaker as 'the great populist of Canadian politics ... an indomitable man, born to a minority group, raised in a minority region, leader of a minority party, who went on to change the very nature of his country and to change it permanently.' The body of his late wife Olive was moved from Ottawa to lie beside him.

Commentators and historians have not been kind to Canada's 13th prime minister. J. L. Granatstein and Norman Hillmer wrote that Diefenbaker's memoirs, 'arguably the most mendacious ever written by a Canadian politician, burnished his own image and refought all the old battles with only one victor. ... Yet the record remained, one of deliberate divisiveness, scandalmongering, and mistrust.' Historian Michael Bliss – perhaps slightly kinder – judged that 'Diefenbaker's role as a prairie populist who tried to revolutionize the Conservative Party begins to loom larger than his personal idiosyncrasies. The difficulties he faced in the form of significant historical dilemmas seem less easy to resolve than Liberals and hostile journalists opined at the time. ... But his contemporaries were also right in seeing some kind of disorder near the centre of his personality and his prime-ministership. The problems of leadership, authority, power, ego, and a mad time in history overwhelmed the prairie politician with the odd name.' For writer George Bowering, Diefenbaker was the wittiest of all the country's prime ministers, 'and he was the most amazing campaigner anyone would ever see or hear.' But he got everyone – the Americans, the British, the Liberals, the economists, the Quebecers, and his own party establishment – mad at him.

Diefenbaker's entire adult life was aimed at a political career. He was moved by ambition and a sense of injustice that was both personal and regional, a determination to succeed at the centre of Canadian politics in Ottawa and in doing so confirm the equal rights of those he believed had been excluded from power and influence in Canada. His attitudes were shaped in the 1920s and 1930s, when Canadian public life was dominated by a privileged circle of Ontario and Quebec politicians in the Liberal and Conservative parties. With his personal and western pre-occupations, however, he failed to sense the potential grievances of the French-speaking Canadian minority, who felt similarly excluded from a full role in national life.

Possessed of a rare determination that was reinforced rather than dulled by early slights and defeats, Diefenbaker had nurtured a dramatic and corrosive talent as a criminal defence lawyer which served him well as a member of the opposition, though less well as a member of government. He was a British Canadian with a sentimental attachment to the imperial connection and to Canada's parliamentary institutions. His convictions on welfare and employment policy were shaped in the 1940s by his experience of the great depression on the prairies and were broadly shared by colleagues in the Liberal and CCF parties. In his approach to fiscal and monetary policy, on the other hand, he remained an instinctive conservative, never fully absorbing the lessons of Keynesian economics.

By temperament Diefenbaker was never a team player. Once he was in office, it was quickly evident that he could not produce harmony in his cabinet, nor could he master the technical complexities of financial, defence, and foreign policies. He was overwhelmed by the problems of administration and was relieved by the prospect of escape into the House of Commons or onto the hustings, where his talents as a populist preacher could be exuberantly exercised. There, he was melodramatic and over-bearing, appealingly comical, whimsical, and sarcastic. He put on a great show. He was one of the last pre-television democratic leaders, who sought direction and self-confidence by face-to-face and intuitive con-nection with his voters rather than by polls, focus groups, and opinion management. He nursed resentments and in his later adversity his sense of isolation gave rise to dark visions of persecution and conspiracy. In politics he had little more than two years of success in the midst of failure and frustration, but he retained a core of deeply committed loyalists to the end of his life and beyond. The federal Conservative Party that he had revived remained dominant in the prairie provinces for 25 years after he left the leadership.

DENIS SMITH

Further reading

Denis Smith, *Rogue Tory: the life and legend of John G. Diefenbaker* (Toronto, 1995).

Knowlton Nash, *Kennedy and Diefenbaker: fear and loathing across the un-defended border* (Toronto, 1990).

P. C. Newman, *Renegade in power: the Diefenbaker years* ([new ed.], Toronto, 1989).

H. B. Robinson, *Diefenbaker's world: a populist in foreign affairs* (Toronto, 1989).

Dick Spencer, *Trumpets and drums: John Diefenbaker on the campaign trail* (Vancouver and Toronto, 1994).

LESTER BOWLES PEARSON,

professor, office holder, diplomat, and politician; b. 23 April 1897
in Newton Brook (Toronto), second of the three sons of Edwin
Arthur Pearson, a Methodist minister, and Annie Sarah Bowles;
m. 22 Aug. 1925 Maryon Elspeth Moody in Winnipeg, and they
had a son and a daughter; d. 27 Dec. 1972 in Ottawa.

B orn on St George's Day in the year of Queen Victoria's diamond
jubilee, Lester Pearson would be brought up in a home that
reflected fully the ambitions and character of Canadian Methodism
in the last decade of the 19th century. Although neither the Bowleses
nor the Pearsons were notably religious in Ireland before they emigrated,
they became enthusiastic and prominent Methodists after their arrival in
Canada, in the 1820s and 1840s respectively. Pearson's paternal grandfather, Marmaduke Louis, was a well-known Methodist minister; his
mother's cousin the Reverend Richard Pinch Bowles, later the chancellor
of Victoria University, Toronto, had officiated at the marriage of Annie
and Edwin. Edwin Pearson stepped aside from the heated debates about
the Social Gospel that marked early-20th-century Methodism. Athletic
and easygoing, he was a popular pastor who moved often because he
received calls from other churches.

The family's frequent changes of residence meant that Lester did not
have a home town, but the values of the various places in southern Ontario
where he lived were strongly defined. Alcohol was loathed, education
celebrated, and the sabbath holy. Edwin was a strong imperialist whose
scrapbook is filled with clippings about the royal family; his three boys
shared his enthusiasm for sports and the empire. An excellent student in
high school, Lester is revealed in the diary of his second year at Victoria
University as a polite young man whose enthusiasm for sports exceeded
his interest in his courses. He referred to his parents fondly and respect-
fully. His brother Marmaduke (Duke) had left university as soon as he
turned 18 to fight in Europe during World War I. As the war intensified,
Lester became ever more eager to volunteer. On 23 April 1915 he enlisted

in the University of Toronto hospital unit and became a private in the Canadian Army Medical Corps. His younger brother, Vaughan, would soon be overseas as well.

Although Pearson would later claim in his memoirs that the war was a decisive event in his development, his presentation of its impact is not supported by contemporary evidence. Like many others, he was to argue that his experience of the war disillusioned him. However, his letters home, his comments in a diary reconstructed from wartime scribblings, and his writings during the early 1920s indicate that he remained conventional in his attitudes. In common with most English Canadians, he had strongly supported conscription in 1917, continued to look to Great Britain for leadership, and honoured the fallen as heroes.

Pearson's own war service reveals an unachieved desire for heroism. After very basic training, he had arrived at the quiet front in Salonica (Thessaloníki, Greece) on 12 Nov. 1915. Greece was neutral, but the British and French stationed troops in the region of Macedonia to minimize contact between the Bulgarians and their Austro-Hungarian allies. Almost immediately, Pearson sought transfer to the Western Front. Thanks to the intervention of the Canadian minister of militia and defence, Sir Samuel Hughes, a fellow Methodist, a transfer to Britain finally came. After arriving in England in late March 1917, Pearson went for training to Wadham College, Oxford, where his platoon commander was the famous war poet Robert von Ranke Graves. When he finished training, he and his brother Duke decided in late summer to become aviators instead of infantry officers.

Lester B. Pearson on wartime service in Salonica (Thessaloníki), Greece, 1916.

In the most glamorous and dangerous of combat roles in World War I, the aviator had a life expectancy of months. Pearson joined the Royal Flying Corps in October and began his aerial training at Hendon (London). Two months later his career ended, as he later said, 'ingloriously,' when a bus struck him during a London blackout. His medical and other records indicate that the accident did not disable him, but that he broke down emotionally in the hospital and during recuperation in early 1918. He was sent home to Canada on 6 April, after a medical board declared him 'unfit' for flying or observer duties because of 'neurasthenia.' The war changed Pearson as it did his nation. His resentment of persons in authority, especially British officers, strengthened his democratic and nationalistic instincts. His emotional breakdown probably contributed to his tendency to keep his feelings private and to deplore irrationalism in public and personal life. The war also gave him the enduring nickname of Mike.

Pearson tried to return to the war, but the medical board denied him his wish. He had constant headaches, trembled, and could not sleep. He joined the staff of No. 4 School of Aeronautics at the University of Toronto and lived at Victoria once again. After the war, he enrolled at Victoria and became a star on the playing field and in the arena. Sports played a major role in his recuperation and would remain a central part of his life until his final years. He received credit for war service and graduated BA with a specialization in modern history in June 1919. He then began articling with the Toronto law firm of McLaughlin, Johnston, Moorhead, and Macaulay, but left quickly to play semi-professional baseball in Guelph, where his father was a pastor. Like many other young Canadians of the day, he found better prospects in the United States. He and Duke joined Armour and Company, an important meat company in Chicago of which their uncle was president. After a brief apprenticeship stuffing sausages in a Canadian subsidiary, Pearson went to Chicago in February 1920.

There he began work as a clerk in the fertilizer division of the Armour empire. The anti-British tone of Chicago politics, where the Irish and the Germans held sway, offended the young imperialist and business did not attract him. He told his uncle and his parents that he wanted to go to Oxford. With the help of a fellowship from the Massey Foundation, he left for St John's College in the fall of 1921. At Oxford, he achieved a solid second, but once again impressed his tutors and fellow students more with his sporting skills and his wit. He took a two-year MA degree and returned to Toronto as a lecturer in the university's department of history in 1923. In that small unit he made lasting friends, such as the future diplomat Humphrey Hume Wrong; he also met his wife.

The daughter of a Winnipeg doctor and nurse, Maryon Moody enrolled in Pearson's history tutorial for the fall term of 1923 in her final year at university. The attraction was immediate and within a few weeks the professor had persuaded his pretty female student to attend a party with him. On 13 March, five weeks later, Maryon wrote to a close friend, 'Don't tell a soul because we aren't telling the public till after term. I am engaged.' She admitted that she had 'known him really at all well [for] a little over a month' but they 'loved each other more than anything else in the world.' They were married in Broadway United Church, Winnipeg. Their son, Geoffrey Arthur Holland, who would become a diplomat, was born in December 1927 and daughter Patricia Lillian arrived in March 1929.

Maryon is one of the most interesting of the Canadian prime ministerial wives. Deeply religious as an undergraduate, she became a sceptic and, privately, a non-believer. Excited about the possibility of a life as a writer, she would never work in a paying job after her marriage. Against Pearson's enemies, she was a ferocious defender of her husband. After his death, she would be bereft and resentful of her widowhood. Yet when they were together, she was known for her barbed comments directed towards her spouse, as when she famously said, 'Behind every successful man there is a surprised woman.' They fought often and both had close relationships, perhaps affairs, with others. She despised politics but would take a close interest and would influence critical decisions, especially the selection of Pearson's cabinet. Her sharp and sardonic wit wounded some, but enlivened many dinner parties. She and her husband moved together along the modernist paths of the 20th century in their choices in literature, their attitudes towards religion, and even in their methods of child rearing, but they remained grounded in the traditions of Anglo-Canadian Methodism. In a later time, they might have divorced, but they would remain a couple, forming a partnership that deeply influenced their times and their country.

After their marriage the Pearsons lived close to the university and entertained young faculty in their home. Reports vary on Pearson's success as a lecturer, but all agree that he was a major figure in the athletic activities of the university and a minor contributor to the professionalization of the field of Canadian history in the 1920s. He proposed to write a book on the loyalists and spent the summer of 1926 at the Public

Archives of Canada in Ottawa. At the university, he faced a choice between accepting promotion through which he would become a major figure in the athletic department or demonstrating stronger devotion to scholarship and the classroom. Both options lacked the appeal of the Department of External Affairs in Ottawa which, under Oscar Douglas Skelton, the under-secretary of state, was hiring bright young Canadians with advanced degrees. Wrong, Pearson's closest friend in the history department, went to Washington as a junior diplomat in the spring of 1927 and Skelton expressed interest in Pearson, whom he had met in the summer of 1926. Pearson took the foreign service examination and stood first among a distinguished group of applicants. He had, at last, a *métier*.

Hugh Llewellyn Keenleyside, another academic who became a foreign service officer in the late 1920s, shared an office with Pearson in Ottawa after Pearson's arrival in August 1928. Pearson, he would later write, was in 'good physical shape, vigorous and alert.' He was 'cheerful, amusing, keenly interested in his work, ambitious for the service and for himself.' He remained so throughout his career in the department. There would be frustrations, especially with Skelton's lack of organizational skills and the idiosyncrasies of prime ministers Richard Bedford Bennett and William Lyon Mackenzie King. Nevertheless, Pearson's intelligence, artfully concealed ambition, good looks and health, and exceptional personal charm were qualities that identified him as an extraordinarily effective public servant and diplomat.

The times were bad in the early 1930s, but the opportunities for Pearson were many. In a small department attached to the office of the prime minister, he found himself with different tasks. He attended the London Naval Conference in 1930, meetings of the League of Nations, and the first World Conference on Disarmament in Geneva in 1932, but in Ottawa his major work was in the field of domestic politics. He served as secretary to the royal commission to inquire into trading in grain futures in 1931 and the royal commission on price spreads in 1934–35. His skills impressed Bennett, who recommended him for an OBE in 1935, the same year he posted him to London in the prestigious position of first secretary. As would occur often in his life, Pearson found himself at the centre of an international whirlwind and managed to keep his balance in turbulent times.

Pearson began his European experience badly when he advised the Canadian representative to the League of Nations, Walter Alexander Riddell, to put forward a proposal to impose sanctions on Italy after it invaded Abyssinia (Ethiopia) in October 1935. King, who became prime minister later that month, angrily repudiated the Riddell initiative in December, but Pearson escaped blame. King and Skelton had both lost faith in the League of Nations and fretted about British policy towards European border tension and the Spanish Civil War that they feared would lead to confrontations, not only with Italy but, more dangerously, with Adolf Hitler's Germany. Pearson shared some of these concerns in 1936 and 1937, but his views differed from those of his political superiors as Hitler's ambitions grew. When King 'rejoiced' at the Munich agreement of 1938 between Hitler and British prime minister Arthur Neville Chamberlain, Pearson dissented in a letter to Skelton. Munich was not a peace with honour, he wrote. 'If I am tempted to become cynical and isolationist, I think of Hitler screeching into the microphone, Jewish women and children in ditches on the Polish border, [Hermann] G[ö]ring, the genial ape-man and [Paul Joseph] Goebbels, the evil imp, and then, whatever the British side may represent, the other does indeed stand for savagery and barbarism.' It was fine to be on the side of the 'angels,' but Pearson knew that 'in Germany the opposite spirits are hard at work. And I have a feeling they're going to do a lot of mischief before they are exorcised.'

These comments reveal much about Pearson and his success as a diplomat and international security analyst. He was pragmatic but deeply principled and his principles were based upon a liberal conviction that brutal dictatorships not only repress many of their own citizens but also threaten the security of democratic nations. Moreover, he had sufficient confidence in his perceptions and his accomplishments to disagree with his superiors, a risky course for any public servant. Finally, he had become, by the late 1930s, a superb analyst of international politics and personalities. The British often turned to him for advice and he began to gather a group of international supporters who would assist his career. When the war began in September 1939, he was well placed to influence Canadian policy, particularly since he had told his doubting superiors that war would come and that Canada must fight.

The children, and then Maryon, returned to Ottawa, but Pearson stayed in England and worked ceaselessly to strengthen British–Canadian ties. Those times remained a cherished memory for him and their spirit is preserved in the diary of his colleague Charles Stewart Almon Ritchie and the novel, *The heat of the day* (London, 1949), written by Ritchie's lover, Elizabeth Dorothea Cole Bowen. The death of Skelton, however, forced Pearson's return to Ottawa in the spring of 1941 and the Japanese attack on Pearl Harbor, Hawaii, in December took him to Washington as minister-counsellor in June 1942. He arrived just as the centre of wartime decision-making was shifting to Washington from London and there was no doubt that the United States would dominate in reconstructing the international system after the war. The Canadian minister to Washington, Leighton Goldie McCarthy, was weak and Pearson quickly took on the major role in representing Canada, not only to the American government but also in the numerous committees that were the birthplace of post-war international institutions. Unlike many Canadians and most Britons, he had realized as early as 1940 that power had shifted from London to Washington and that the British Commonwealth of Nations would be a secondary actor on the international stage. For Canada, the political and economic implications of these changes were enormous.

Pearson quickly captured attention, especially from the American news media. He became a minor celebrity on a radio quiz program and, significantly, a close friend of several major American journalists. His diplomatic colleagues noted his skill in presiding over committees and in July 1943 he became the chair of the United Nations Interim Commission on Food and Agriculture. The committee was to become the Food and Agriculture Organization of the UN in October 1945. Pearson would decline the chance to head the new institution. From 1943 to 1946 he also chaired the important committee on supplies of the United Nations Relief and Rehabilitation Administration. On 1 Jan. 1945 he became Canada's second ambassador to the United States (earlier representatives had been ministers). He had become one of the foremost diplomats of the time and, in Canada, a public figure.

Pearson knew the United States well and admired its energy and creativity. Unlike his brother Duke, now a businessman and a Republican, he was an enthusiastic supporter of President Franklin Delano Roosevelt and the New Deal. He enjoyed American popular culture, especially its cinema, Broadway musicals, and, above all, baseball. Nevertheless, he thought American democracy too encumbered by major financial interests, its public life too vulgar, and its self-confidence sometimes abrasive. As Canada moved from its British past to its North American future, he anticipated many problems. Some in his department had written very negative comments on American policy, but he was always a pragmatist. In 1944 he had written: 'When we are dealing with such a powerful neighbour, we have to avoid the twin dangers of subservience and truculent touchiness. We succumb to the former when we take everything lying down, and to the latter when we rush to the State Department with a note everytime some Congressman makes a stupid statement about Canada, or some documentary movie about the war forgets to mention Canada.' This advice to a junior colleague neatly defined his central approach to Canadian–American relations throughout his diplomatic and political career.

Although unhappy about the shape of the UN and, especially, the dominance of the Security Council by the great powers, Pearson did not protest as strongly as the Australians did at the San Francisco Conference, where delegates met to draw up the charter in 1945. When the new organization took form, many favoured him for the post of secretary general. He was, however, too closely identified with American interests to satisfy the Soviets. He also knew that political changes were occurring quickly in Ottawa and he did not encourage friends who wanted to promote his candidacy. King was leaving and he had already spoken with Pearson about 'entering Canadian public life,' and the diplomat had the idea 'very much in mind.' To assure Pearson's presence in Ottawa as King slowly took his retirement, the prime minister appointed him under-secretary of state for external affairs. Pearson returned to Ottawa in September 1946. He served under the new secretary of state for external affairs, Louis-Stephen St-Laurent. The two quickly acquired confidence in each other and shared their doubts about the weary prime minister. As a minister from the traditionally isolationist Quebec and as King's favoured successor, St-Laurent gave Pearson valuable cabinet and political support for an innovative and energetic foreign policy. He needed such backing because King was wary of Pearson's enthusiasms and his tendency to commit Canada to international agreements and institutions.

Lester B. Pearson addressing a committee at the founding conference of the United Nations, San Francisco, April–June 1945.

The Cold War between the Soviet Union and the west was young but fierce during Pearson's tenure as under-secretary. The Soviet use of the veto handcuffed the UN's Security Council and Soviet influence in eastern Europe became control as coalition governments in nations such as Czechoslovakia and Poland fell to communism. Although the war's end did not bring depression as it had in 1919, the economic future was uncertain, since Canada's traditional European markets were either destroyed or, in the case of Britain, essentially bankrupt. Pearson took three major policy initiatives between 1946 and 1948. First, he continued to hope that the UN would gain strength and, much to King's despair, he backed UN involvement in the settlement of conflict in Korea and in other troubled areas such as Palestine. Secondly, he recognized the economic and political predominance of the United States. The shortage of American dollars in Canada was solved initially by a special arrangement and Pearson was willing to work out a free trade agreement with the Americans. King stopped the free trade negotiations, fearful of their political impact. Finally, Pearson tried to balance American influence by the creation of the North Atlantic Treaty Organization (NATO), and he argued strongly for a socio-economic component to the pact. He played a major role in the discussions and persistently urged Canada's chief negotiator, Hume Wrong, to take a broad approach to the treaty. By the time the pact was finally signed in Washington in the spring of 1949, his numerous accomplishments had gained him further recognition. With the strong encouragement of King and St-Laurent, he entered politics and was appointed secretary of state for external affairs in the St-Laurent government on 10 Sept. 1948. He ran successfully for a seat in the House of Commons in a by-election in Algoma East on 25 October and retained the seat in the general election of 1949, in which St-Laurent's government won a resounding victory. He would represent the riding throughout his political career.

Pearson would remain Canada's minister of external affairs until the defeat of the Liberals in 1957. Historians have called his times the 'golden years' of Canadian diplomacy. Although there are justifiable doubts about the glitter of the period, Pearson's own reputation retains its lustre. He had unusual freedom because of the consensus within the Liberal Party and the commons on the nature of the Soviet threat. His department was talented, strong, and well funded. The times were especially kind to him. He was a unilingual anglophone who had little experience outside London, Ottawa, New York, and Washington, but for a Canadian minister of external affairs in the 1950s little else mattered. He recognized that the rebirth of the European economies would make Canada a relatively less significant actor within the western alliance. He also acknowledged that Canada's relationship with the United States had become the principal concern of a Canadian foreign minister. He nonetheless retained his pre-war unease that the United States was sometimes an 'intoxicated' nation and, in that state, 'middle courses' were difficult to follow. Yet there was no doubt that the Canadian course in the Cold War years must follow closely behind the American juggernaut. Occasionally, a clever Canadian initiative could alter the course slightly, but Canada and the United States were on the same journey.

In the late 1940s Pearson worried that the United States would revert to pre-war isolationist tendencies and his rhetoric and policies reflected this concern. Beginning in the 1960s, critics such as Robert Dennis Cuff and

Jack Lawrence Granatstein would point to Pearson's strong and, in their view, strident anti-Communist speeches and his sternly anti-Communist policies in the first years of the Cold War, a position later adopted by historian Denis Smith, political scientist Reginald Whitaker, and journalist Gary Marcuse. These revisionists would suggest that Pearson overestimated the dangers of Soviet communism. Pearson equated communism with Nazism. He warned, for example, that 'we did not take very seriously the preposterous statements of the slightly ridiculous author of *Mein Kampf*. We preferred the friendly remarks of "jolly old Goering" at his hunting lodge.' *Mein Kampf* had been the true agenda; similarly, Soviet leader Joseph Stalin showed a gentle side to the American vice-president, Henry Agard Wallace, in 1944, but Pearson warned that the west should look at Stalin's harsh statements, 'which form the basic dogma on which the policy of the USSR [Union of Soviet Socialist Republics] is inflexibly based.'

This debate about the Cold War and the threat of communism, the so-called revisionist debate, has changed since the Cold War's end in the late 1980s. On the one hand, the opening of Soviet archives has revealed that Stalin was extraordinarily dangerous and cruel and that Soviet espionage had infiltrated Western security and foreign policy establishments more fully than revisionist historians had suggested. Pearson's evaluation of the menace was probably more accurate than his critics had thought. On the other hand, the opening of Canadian security files and greater attention to individual rights in Canadian society has drawn attention to discrimination against, and sometimes persecution of, not only political dissidents but also homosexuals in the late 1940s and early 1950s. The argument that Pearson's strident anti-communism had contributed to the climate of fear that stifled dissent has some merit. Pearson had little patience with those who made revisionist arguments and the second volume of his memoirs is a reply to the revisionist historians of the late 1960s and early 1970s. On the question of treatment of dissidents, he would have had some sympathy because his support of Egerton Herbert Norman, a Canadian diplomat accused by an American congressional committee of being a Communist agent, had made him very much a target of American extreme anti-Communists.

Although Pearson did not speak out publicly against the activities of the Royal Canadian Mounted Police in harassing dissidents, he did annoy the Federal Bureau of Investigation and some Republican politicians, including Senator Joseph McCarthy. He refused to allow Soviet defector Igor Sergeievich Gouzenko to testify in the United States before the Senate Internal Security Subcommittee and denied that Canadian information confirmed that Harry Dexter White was guilty of espionage. (White was a senior American public servant who is now known to have been an agent of influence for the Soviets.) His refusal to dismiss Norman made John Edgar Hoover of the FBI suspicious of him. The *Chicago Tribune*, owned by Hoover's friend Colonel Robert Rutherford McCormick, called Pearson 'the most dangerous man in the Western World' in 1953. These attacks and incidents deeply annoyed him, but they did not significantly affect his ability to work with the American administration under President Harry S. Truman and, after his taking office in 1953, under Republican president Dwight David Eisenhower.

The confidence in Pearson among senior Department of State and other American officials had come from his role in promoting the creation of the North Atlantic alliance, his support for American policy in the creation of Israel, and his encouragement of much higher Canadian defence spending after 1949. When the Korean War broke out in 1950, Canadian public opinion was not strongly in favour of Canadian participation. On 25 June, Pearson told journalists privately that he did not believe UN or American intervention would occur. Three days later, after learning that Truman had decided to intervene, he praised the United States for recognizing 'a special responsibility which it discharged with admirable dispatch and decisiveness.' He, like Truman, believed that such an intervention under the leadership of the United States and the auspices of the UN – which was possible because the Soviets were boycotting the Security Council – would call the Communists' bluff and strengthen the UN, whose first years had been very disappointing. At his urging, the Canadians raised their commitment from a token naval presence to a significant involvement in the brutal ground war.

Because of the war in Korea and the perceived threat of a Communist attack on western Europe, Pearson had unusual freedom from normal political restraints. He chaired the NATO council in 1951–52 and in 1952 became the president of the UN's General Assembly. As president, he had difficulties with the Americans, for he had become a critic of their policies in Asia. Canada had followed the United States in refusing to recognize Communist China, but he had been deeply concerned about the possibility that the war in Korea would become a broad conflagration after the Chinese entered it in November 1950. When American general Douglas MacArthur, the commander of the UN forces in Korea, spoke openly about extending the war, Pearson decided that he must protest. In a famous speech to the Canadian and Empire clubs in Toronto on 10 April 1951, he said that the UN must not be the 'instrument of any one country' and that others had the right to criticize American policy. He expressed his belief that 'the days of relatively easy and automatic political relations with our neighbour are, I think, over.' And they were, even though Truman fired MacArthur later the same day.

While sharing the American conviction that the expansion of communism must be halted and contained, Pearson deplored talk of 'rolling back' communism and worried about American excesses. The attack of Senator McCarthy and his allies on the Department of State was, in his view, dangerous and thoroughly irresponsible. The American policy on China especially bothered him. He told his son, soon to become a foreign service officer, that he had attempted and failed to moderate American attitudes toward China. In the winter of 1951 it seemed to him that 'emotionalism has become the basis of [United States] policy.' Canada would still 'follow' the Americans, but only to the extent of their strict obligations under the UN charter. The Korean War finally came to an end after Eisenhower became president. Pearson had irritated American secretary of state Dean Gooderham Acheson because of his insistence on advancing peace negotiations. Acheson's Republican successor, John Foster Dulles, was even more difficult and ideological in his approach and Pearson became more determined to find ways to end the Cold War chill, especially after the death of Stalin in 1953.

Despite Pearson's disagreements with the Americans, they recognized his skill and usefulness. When, in 1952, his name had come forward for the positions of NATO's secretary-general and the UN's secretary-general, the United States had supported his candidacy. He had resisted the NATO post and the Russians, as before, had rejected him for the UN appointment. He established strong personal ties with the Scandinavian countries and in the British Commonwealth he and Canada became an influential force. The Colombo Plan, which had been drawn up in January 1950, was Canada's first major commitment to assistance for developing countries and Pearson had been one of its architects. Although he thought Jawaharlal Nehru puzzling, he fostered the notion of a special relationship between Canada and India. Canada participated in the Geneva Conference of 1954 that sought, unsuccessfully, to bring peace to French Indochina. Canada became the Western voice on the International Control Commission that, again unsuccessfully, attempted to supervise and develop a peace settlement in the region. In October 1955 he was the first Western foreign minister to visit the Soviet Union after the death of Stalin. The trip, which featured a wild night of drinking and debate with Soviet leader Nikita Khrushchev in the Crimea, did not persuade Pearson that the post-Stalin Soviet Union was a more benign state.

Pearson's focus remained firmly on the Soviet threat and he believed the United States was weakening itself and its response to that menace by excessive attention to Communist China. He considered recognition of Communist China, but American warnings of retaliation quickly dissuaded him. He was furious, as were the Americans, when the British, the French, and the Israelis, angry about the Egyptian takeover of the Suez Canal, secretly planned and carried out an attack in Egypt on 29 Oct. 1956. The Soviets began to talk of sending volunteers to aid the Egyptians; the Americans, who had not been informed of the plans, moved to condemn their traditional allies in the UN. The Australians backed the British; Canada, for the first time in its history, opposed a British war. Working closely with the Americans, Pearson tried to craft a solution that would end the divisions among Western allies and would reduce the tensions of a broader war. Early on Sunday morning, 4 November, the UN supported a Canadian resolution that called for the creation of a peace force. The British and French backed down. On 14 Oct. 1957 Pearson would receive the Nobel Peace Prize.

Although Pearson gained international laurels, the Canadian position on the Suez crisis met with strong criticism in English Canada. Reluctant to abandon the British ties that had been the foundation of their identity for almost two centuries, many English Canadians linked the Liberal government and Pearson with the increasing Americanization of Canada. They complained that the Liberals had favoured the Americans and had 'knifed' Britain in the crisis. The irascible Conservative Charlotte Elizabeth Hazeltyne Whitton, mayor of Ottawa, quipped: 'It's too bad [Gamal Abdel] Nasser couldn't help Mike Pearson to cross Elliot Lake [in his constituency] when Mr. Pearson did so much to help him along the Suez Canal.'

The Liberals, with St-Laurent as leader, Pearson as his likely successor, and a Gallup poll forecasting another solid majority, called an election for 10 June 1957. The polls were wrong; Progressive Conservative leader John George Diefenbaker's appeal to Anglo-Canadian nationalism was effective in western Canada, the Maritimes, and British Ontario. His eloquent denunciation of the Liberal minister of trade and commerce, Clarence Decatur Howe, and the pipeline fiasco had also persuaded electors to vote Conservative. The American-born Howe had used closure to force a bill through the commons to create an American-financed pipeline which would bring western natural gas to Ontario. The Conservatives had opposed it bitterly because of American involvement and had sung 'God save the queen' to emphasize their traditional British-Canadian nationalism. The Conservatives won 112 seats with over 38 per cent of the vote and the Liberals 105 seats with over 40 per cent of the vote. After some indecision, St-Laurent resigned as prime minister and as Liberal leader. Pearson was the strong favourite in the Liberal leadership race, especially after he was awarded the Nobel Prize. He became head of the party on 16 Jan. 1958.

Pearson's victory left him foolishly confident and his first efforts in the commons were feeble. When he called upon the new government to resign, Diefenbaker, with his brilliant sense of parliamentary timing, ridiculed the motion and on 1 February asked for a general election, to be held on 31 March. The Liberals were in disarray and the campaign soon revealed how effective Diefenbaker could be on the hustings and how unprepared Pearson was. Although Pearson and Diefenbaker were of similar background and age, Diefenbaker was the more energetic and convincing campaigner. The Conservatives won the most decisive victory recorded in Canadian federal politics, 208 seats compared to only 49 for the Liberals and 8 for the Co-operative Commonwealth Federation. With characteristic black humour, Maryon Pearson remarked, 'We've lost everything. We even won our own seat.'

Pearson briefly considered resignation; Maryon encouraged it. He was over 60, a Nobel Prize winner, and aware that his speaking style did not suit an age when television dominated politics. He considered other offers, but his friends, notably Toronto businessman Walter Lockhart Gordon, encouraged him to stay. Diefenbaker was a better campaigner than prime minister and the economy was faltering after the long postwar boom. Pearson decided to stay on.

The election of Jean Lesage's Liberal Party in Quebec in June 1960 presented new challenges for the Conservatives, who had won in 1958 because of strong support from the Union Nationale under Maurice Le Noblet Duplessis. Pearson began to develop new policies that would reflect the liberalism of Lesage and, to some extent, of John Fitzgerald Kennedy, who was to become president of the United States in January 1961. In September 1960, just after the Liberals moved ahead of the Conservatives in a Gallup poll, the party held a study conference in Kingston. Pearson drew upon his network of friends in journalism, the universities, business, and politics to create a debate about the future of Canadian Liberalism and to draft a platform for the next Liberal government.

Prior to the conference, two of those friends, Gordon and journalist Thomas Worrall Kent, had been wary of each other. At the conference, they worked together to draft a progressive platform, one that reflected Kennedy's New Frontier policy and the ambitious programs of the Quebec government. Pearson became increasingly concerned about Quebec and he insisted that greater recognition of the French language and of the rights of French Canadians be part of the new Liberal platform. When Diefenbaker called a general election for 18 June 1962, many expected him to lose. The Liberal members had been extremely effective in the commons and Diefenbaker's ministers had fumbled badly. Nevertheless, the final results were 116 Conservatives, 100 Liberals, 30 Social Crediters/Créditistes, and 19 New Democrats. Despite the loss, it was a triumph for Pearson. Diefenbaker's government began to crumble. When he hesitated to support the Americans in the Cuban missile crisis of October 1962, not only the Kennedy administration but also many traditional Conservatives turned against him. The confusion surrounding the acceptance of nuclear weapons caused turmoil within the Conservative Party; the minister of national defence, Douglas Scott Harkness, was a strong proponent of acceptance and the minister of external affairs, Howard Charles Green, a strong opponent.

LE PÈRE NOBEL.

Nobel Peace Prize winner Lester B. Pearson is disguised
as *Père Noël* delivering nuclear weapons, in a Raoul Hunter
caricature, *Le Soleil* (Quebec City), 10 July 1963.

Pearson had opposed nuclear weapons for Canada, but on 12 Jan.
1963 he declared that the country must accept them because it had made
a commitment to its allies in 1958 to arm the Bomarc anti-aircraft missiles located in northern Ontario and Quebec with nuclear warheads.
Complaints came quickly from Quebec intellectual Pierre Elliott Trudeau
and, privately, from Walter Gordon and the young Liberal Norman Lloyd
Axworthy. Pearson's announcement split the Conservatives and some
ministers tried to secure Diefenbaker's resignation. They failed, but on
5 Feb. 1963 the government fell. Most expected Pearson to win the election, called for 8 April.

Pearson became prime minister on 22 April, but the majority government that public opinion polls had predicted and that he had craved
eluded him. The Liberals had obtained 129 seats and the Conservatives
95, while the Social Crediters/Créditistes and New Democrats held the
balance with 24 and 17 respectively. The following day he turned 66,
an age when many Canadians had retired. His cabinet impressed Canadian
journalists with its regional balance and broad experience. Paul Joseph

James Martin had served in parliament for 28 years. Newfoundland's John Whitney Pickersgill was Diefenbaker's equal in the house. Gordon, Mitchell William Sharp, and Charles Mills Drury brought business experience. Guy Favreau, the major Quebec minister, and Maurice Lamontagne were respected in Quebec and Ottawa. The poor results in western Canada, however, meant weak representation from that region.

During the election campaign Pearson had promised 'sixty days of decision,' but the first two months went badly. Gordon had supported Pearson financially since he had entered politics, had organized his leadership campaign, and had brought influential and capable friends into the Liberal Party. He expected to be minister of finance, but Pearson knew that many in the business community did not have confidence in Gordon's nationalistic views. Nevertheless, over his wife's objections, he made the appointment. Gordon turned to outside advisers to prepare the budget because he thought the Department of Finance would be unwilling to accept his nationalist policies. He presented his budget, with a withholding tax on dividends paid to non-residents and a 'takeover tax' on foreign acquisitions of Canadian businesses, on 13 June 1963. Bureaucrats complained about his use of outside advisers and many in the business community expressed hostility toward his nationalism. The lack of western Canadian voices in the Liberal caucus meant that their traditional suspicion of Ontario-based nationalism was not often expressed in party debate. The president of the Montreal Stock Exchange, Eric William Kierans, who would later become a nationalist ally of Gordon's, attacked the budget, claiming that 'our friends in the western world' would realize that 'we don't want them or their money and that Canadians who deal with them in even modest amounts will suffer a thirty percent expropriation of the assets involved.' The attack was unfair, but it and other criticisms led Gordon to withdraw the tax on foreign acquisitions on 19 June. The response was a call for Gordon's resignation by many major newspapers.

Gordon offered his resignation the next day; Pearson refused. Nevertheless, the distrust between the two friends grew. Pearson himself paid little heed to the details of the budget, but the appearance of a separatist movement in Quebec had captured his full attention. On 21 April 1963 a bomb placed by Quebec separatists had killed a janitor working in a Canadian army recruiting office. On 17 May dynamite had exploded in mail boxes in Montreal. Quebec journalist André Laurendeau had recommended, in January 1962, a royal commission to investigate bilingualism and Pearson had promised to act. On 19 July 1963 he appointed Laurendeau and Arnold Davidson Dunton co-chairs of the royal commission on bilingualism and biculturalism, and the so-called Quebec issue became the major domestic concern of Pearson's years in office. The royal commission was immediately controversial, although few suggested that the question of Quebec's role in Canadian confederation could be ignored. Critics, especially in the west, questioned the focus on the duality of Canada and, though the commission's terms of reference provided that other ethnic groups should be studied, argued for a broader approach that reflected the diverse origins of the country's population. The seeds of multiculturalism were born.

The Pearson government stumbled regularly between 1963 and 1965. Gordon never recovered from the budget debacle and Pearson proved no match for Diefenbaker in the cut and thrust of parliamentary debate. The most serious problem was Quebec representation in the cabinet. Pearson's support for the acceptance of nuclear weapons had weakened his position in Quebec. The nationalist *Le Devoir* (Montréal) attacked his stand and urged consideration of the New Democrats' stance opposing nuclear weapons; prominent francophones such as Trudeau and labour leader Jean Marchand retreated from flirtation with the Liberals. The result was weak Quebec representation in Ottawa. The veteran Lionel Chevrier was the major Quebec minister even though he was, by origin, a Franco-Ontarian. Justice minister Favreau was able, but he was a political novice. Lamontagne, an excellent academic economist, was an uncertain politician. When, therefore, the increasingly nationalistic government of Jean Lesage in Quebec countered the federal government in domestic jurisdiction and, more troublingly, in international relations, the government response lacked force. Pearson's Quebec ministers seemed ineffectual and unable to face the challenge of a strong provincial government. The impact was immediate in the area of social policy, where the Liberal agenda was ambitious. The Quebec government anticipated a federal contributory pension scheme by presenting its own plan. It argued, with the support of other provinces concerned about federal intrusion into provincial domains, that it was within its rights. Despite strong opposition in the Liberal caucus and cabinet, Pearson agreed that the Quebec plan should be the starting point for a national program. Quebec could 'opt out' of the national plan with compensation and could have its own scheme, aligned with the national one. He cleverly guided the agreement through the cabinet and the Canada and Quebec Pension plans would become a reality in 1966.

Despite its clumsy start and its minority status, the Pearson government implemented some social legislation over its two mandates, including the Canada Assistance Plan, which funded provincial welfare programs (1966), and the Guaranteed Income Supplement (1967). In addition, there was much more funding for university research and university capital expenditures. The government had created the Canada Student Loans Plan in 1964. Combined with provincial support for post-secondary education, these policies transformed the Canadian university system. Pearson was fortunate in that the Canadian economy was strong during his tenure as prime minister. Starting in 1965 and culminating with the creation of an apolitical Immigration Board in 1967, important changes were made to Canada's immigration policy. Under the leadership of the powerful Quebec minister Jean Marchand, who had been persuaded to join the Liberal Party and enter the cabinet, it was closely linked to the government's labour policy.

Although health is an area of provincial responsibility, the Liberals had promised a health care program in their platform of 1919, had dangled it before the electorate in 1945, and had made it part of the platform in 1963. The successful but very difficult creation of such a program in Saskatchewan by its socialist government in 1961 had set a standard that Pearson knew the Liberals must match, especially since the Saskatchewan premier, Thomas Clement Douglas, had become leader of the federal New Democratic Party that year. Pearson did little to shape the Canadian Medicare program, but he did challenge the reluctant provinces, notably Ontario, to accept that Canadians must have equal access to state-provided medical services. Parliament passed the Medical Care Act in 1966 but financial exigencies postponed its operation for a year. The effect of this social legislation was to make Canada more European and less American in its approach to social welfare. There had been no counterpart to Roosevelt's New Deal, but Canada caught up quickly in the 1960s and moved well beyond the American standard.

If Canada became less American in its approach to social welfare, it became less European in its symbols. The country had no national flag and Liberals had occasionally proposed one. Despite such musings, King and St-Laurent had wisely avoided the controversial issue. Pearson, however, was determined and in 1964, against the advice of many, he insisted on pushing forward. Diefenbaker rallied British Canadians in defence of the Union Jack and the Red Ensign; Liberals told Pearson that he was creating political difficulties over a purely symbolic issue. Nevertheless, he persisted and in the commons on 15 December, with the help of the New Democrats, he managed to secure approval of a design. Liberal MP John Ross Matheson, a war veteran who championed the flag, would later write that 'the fight for a flag became a crusade for national unity, for justice to all Canadians, for Canada's dignity.' Not all Canadians agreed; many Conservative members wept and the province of British Columbia would not raise the new flag in daylight on its inaugural day. As for the French Canadians, who one might expect to have welcomed the new flag, Trudeau claimed that they did not give 'a tinker's damn' about it.

This flood of legislation was broken up by a general election. The weakness of the Pearson government in the matter of Quebec representation had been made worse by scandals that left even fewer French Canadians in the cabinet. These scandals were the face of national politics that Canadians viewed in 1964 and 1965 and they did not like what they saw. There was, as journalist Peter Charles Newman would later write, a 'distemper' in Canada during Pearson's time in office. Writing in 1990 about his 1968 book on the Pearson years, Newman would recall that 'most of the people' he had talked with in airports, at dinner parties, and around hamburger stands were 'voicing a dismay at our politics that was hardening into cynicism or despair.' The scandals were the manifestation of profound changes in the Canadian political system that occurred during the 1960s. In the case of the Mafia-linked drug dealer Lucien Rivard, ministerial assistants and even Pearson's parliamentary secretary had supported Rivard's attempt to obtain release on bail. More seriously, a ministerial assistant had tried to bribe the lawyer acting on the American request for Rivard's extradition. Justice minister Favreau was drawn into the fray when he decided not to prosecute the assistant. He told Pearson about the developing scandal in September 1964 but Pearson left the impression that he had not learned about it until November. Finally,

Pearson corrected the impression in a letter to the special public inquiry, headed by justice Frédéric Dorion, which he had created to investigate the scandal. Favreau's reputation was shattered; Pearson's was damaged. Lamontagne and immigration minister René Tremblay saw their careers destroyed over their failure to pay for furniture from a bankrupt Montreal dealer. Yvon Dupuis, another Quebec minister, although later acquitted, was fired from cabinet because he faced criminal charges involving the acceptance of a bribe to accelerate the granting of a racetrack licence. In the commons, Diefenbaker's courtroom skills cut through the weak answers of the Liberal ministers and his list of French names linked with the scandals, pronounced in halting French, infuriated francophones.

Drug deals, bribes, and sleazy furniture sales were not as titillating as Canada's major political sex scandal, the so-called Munsinger affair. Gerda Munsinger had been involved with the Soviets in Germany. While living in Montreal she had had an affair with a Russian lover and, simultaneously, from 1958 to 1960 with Pierre Sévigny, Diefenbaker's associate minister of national defence from 1959 to 1963. The relationship attracted the interest of the RCMP and wiretaps. In the heat of debate in the commons on 4 March 1966, Liberal justice minister Lucien Cardin taunted Diefenbaker about the 'Monseignor case.' Rumours billowed about the involvement of a Tory minister with an apparently dead but once very sexy spy. Yet another inquiry engaged Canadians' curiosity and exposed Sévigny. Diefenbaker and Pearson had both behaved badly, the prime minister in calling for the RCMP file on Munsinger and, in Diefenbaker's view, threatening him with revelations unless the Conservative leader relented in the commons. For his part, Diefenbaker had dragged up old charges that Pearson had passed information to Communists when he was in Washington.

The scandals, the bad mood in the house, and the growing divisions in the Conservative Party persuaded Liberal organizers to call an election. The economy was strong and Oliver Quayle, the American pollster hired by Gordon, reported a Liberal upsurge in the spring of 1965. Although Quayle admitted that Pearson's image was not strongly positive and that most Canadians thought he was doing only a 'fair job,' 46 per cent believed that he would be a better prime minister than Diefenbaker, favoured by 23 per cent of Canadians. Faint praise indeed and enough to cause hesitations. Pearson finally called an election for 8 November after Gordon assured him that he would win a majority and that he would resign if the Liberals failed to obtain one.

Diefenbaker once again proved to be an excellent campaigner, overcoming a large Liberal lead in the initial polls. The Liberals pointed to a remarkable list of achievements: the Canada–United States Automotive Products Agreement (Autopact), the pension legislation, student loans, a revision of the tax system, greatly expanded support for post-secondary and technical education, bilingualism and biculturalism, and a more liberal immigration policy that appealed to new Canadians. Diefenbaker shifted debate away from these issues towards Lucien Rivard's 'escape' from prison, the free furniture for cabinet ministers, and Pearson's lacklustre leadership. Pearson's campaign was marred by protesters and, at the final giant rally in Toronto, the failure of the sound system. In Quebec, he had recruited three candidates to rebuild the shattered Quebec front bench: journalist and social activist Gérard Pelletier, Marchand, and, controversially because of his criticism of the Liberals' nuclear policy, Trudeau. When the campaign ended, the Liberals had won less of the popular vote than in 1963 and, with 131 of 265 seats, were denied a majority. The Conservatives had obtained 97 seats and the NDP 21, with Créditistes, Social Crediters, and independent candidates making up the balance.

Pearson offered his resignation to cabinet; it was refused. Gordon submitted his resignation to Pearson; to his disappointment, it was accepted. The Gordon team, which included Keith Davey, Richard O'Hagan, James Allan Coutts, and Kent left with him. In a study of the Liberal Party, Joseph Wearing correctly suggests that the Gordon approach concentrated on urban Canada and especially Toronto, Gordon's home. It was the achievement of the group that so-called Tory Toronto would be no more; however, the aftermath of 1965 was the shift of attention and power to Montreal and Quebec.

Quebec increasingly preoccupied the government after the election of 1965. Pelletier, Marchand, and Trudeau had entered federal politics because they feared that Quebec would drift towards separation as Lesage's Liberals became increasingly nationalist. The surprising defeat of the Liberals by the Union Nationale in 1966 created a sense of crisis. The new premier, Daniel Johnson, spoke of 'equality or independence' and the defeated Liberals, especially the highly popular René Lévesque, began to muse about an independence platform for their party. Simultaneously, the French government under Charles de Gaulle lavished attention on visiting Quebec politicians while regularly snubbing Canadian representatives. As a diplomat who had seen how the ties of the British empire came undone so quickly, Pearson believed that the French behaviour was profoundly dangerous and that Quebec's demands for its own foreign policy bore the seeds of the disintegration of Canada. Despite these doubts, which were not fully shared by his minister of external affairs, Paul Martin, Pearson accepted the demands of de Gaulle that he begin his visit during Canada's centennial year in Quebec City and that he arrive on a French warship, the *Colbert*.

De Gaulle toured Quebec City on 23 July 1967 and, after some controversial statements, travelled to Montreal the following day. There, on the balcony of the Hôtel de Ville, he made his famous declaration, 'Vive le Québec libre!' A furious Pearson declared the remarks 'unacceptable' and de Gaulle returned to France without visiting Ottawa. Although the event did not break the buoyant spirit of centennial year, it did underline the divisions within Canada. French newspapers tended to believe that Pearson overreacted while English newspapers expressed outrage. Within the government, Trudeau and several officials (notably Allan Ezra Gotlieb, Peter Michael Pitfield, Marc Lalonde, and Marcel Cadieux) met regularly

to counter what they considered the drift in the federal government's policies in the face of Quebec's initiatives. They began to formulate a strong response to French support for separatism and to the constitutional demands of Quebec. With Trudeau as justice minister, the agenda shifted to, on the one hand, a more coherent constitutional

A delighted Lester B. Pearson (middle right) and Queen Elizabeth II riding the Minirail at Expo 67 in Montreal, the highlight of Canada's centennial celebrations, 3 July 1967.

Lester B. Pearson with members of his revamped cabinet on 4 April 1967 (from left): Pierre E. Trudeau, John N. Turner, and Jean Chrétien.

program and, on the other, a more liberal social agenda that responded to the spirit of the times. Trudeau's famous statement that the government had no place in the bedrooms of the nation signalled a revolution in its attitude toward private behaviour, one that was far from the ethos of the manse where Pearson had been born or, for that matter, the Catholic home and schools of Trudeau's early years.

Because of Pearson's own distinguished background in external affairs, he had retained responsibility for a few issues in this department, delegating responsibility for the remainder to his minister, Paul Martin, and government officials. The Commonwealth was a prime ministerial gathering and there Pearson demonstrated his extraordinary diplomatic skills in dealing with Britain and others on the difficult Rhodesian and South African issues. There was one notable exception to his diplomacy: his decision in April 1965 to speak out against American bombing of North Vietnam. Pearson had had earlier meetings with President Lyndon Baines Johnson and had become concerned about Johnson's style and determination to achieve victory in Vietnam. Like other Canadians, he gave Johnson much latitude because of the difficult circumstances of his accession to power after Kennedy's assassination and because of the apparent extremist character of Barry Morris Goldwater, who had been the Republican presidential candidate in 1964. Nevertheless, the build-up of American forces in Vietnam troubled him greatly. He feared that the

United States would be drawn into a long war and that the North Atlantic alliance would be fundamentally weakened. After conversations with American friends, he decided to call for a halt to the bombing. Martin and the Department of External Affairs opposed the idea, but Pearson used the occasion of an award he was to receive from Temple University in Philadelphia on 2 April 1965 to call for 'a suspension of air strikes against North Vietnam *at the right time'* in order to provide 'Hanoi authorities with an opportunity, if they wish to take it, to inject some flexibility into their policy without appearing to do so as the direct result of military pressure.' These careful words brought an invitation to meet Johnson later that day at his Camp David retreat in Maryland. There Johnson berated and swore at Pearson and made his displeasure clear to the press. Their relationship never recovered, although later, in 1966, Pearson agreed to the use of a Canadian diplomat, Chester Alvin Ronning, as a messenger to the North Vietnamese. Canada, ironically, had benefited from the increased defence purchases that came with the Vietnam War and many Americans of draft age had migrated to Canada and contributed much to Canadian life, especially in the universities. Vietnam, the race riots in Detroit and other American cities, and the assassination of President Kennedy were causes of the surge of Canadian nationalism that occurred in English Canada during the centennial year of 1967.

Pearson called a press conference for 14 Dec. 1967 and announced he would resign in the new year. The Conservatives had a new leader, Robert Lorne Stanfield, and were ahead in the public opinion polls. Pearson's caucus and cabinet were restless as they prepared to face an election and a possible loss. More troubling to Pearson was the issue of Canadian national unity and he began to work quietly to assure that his successor came from Quebec. His first choice was Marchand, but Marchand recommended Trudeau, whose intellect had impressed Pearson, but whose political skills had not. Pearson did not designate Trudeau his successor, as King had done with St-Laurent, but he told his closest friends that Trudeau was his choice. It was, he believed, the only bet worth taking, given the challenges from Quebec. It was a bet he won. Despite his recent re-conversion to Liberalism, Trudeau won the convention and had parliament dissolved before Pearson's colleagues and foes could pay tribute to him. The journalist and former MP Douglas Mason Fisher later recalled that in April 1968, when Pearson left office, there was an atmosphere of 'indifference' and 'a notable keenness by his successor to separate his government distinctly from the bad Pearson years – scandals, leaks, messy, staggering parliaments and disorganized ventures.'

In 1968 Pearson became chancellor of Carleton University in Ottawa and he lectured there in history and political science until the fall of 1972. He chaired a historic commission on international development. Its report, *Partners in development: report of the Commission on International Development* (New York, 1969), called for a systematic transfer of resources and attention from the rich west and north to the poor south. The so-called 'Pearson Report' was the first sustained evaluation of international development assistance. It deeply influenced future debate and policy. Pearson had seldom seen Trudeau after 1968 and the new government's foreign policy review, with its criticism of post-war strategies, deeply wounded him. Still, he publicly and privately supported Trudeau in the general election of 1972. By that time he knew that he would not vote again. He told his old friend Senator Keith Davey that he would not be able to share his dismay if his beloved Toronto Maple Leafs did not make the playoffs in the spring. He had known since 1970 that cancer would soon cause his death. Despite Maryon's hopes, he would not retire. On learning of his cancer diagnosis, he rushed his memoirs to publication. The first of his three volumes appeared in 1972 and was an immediate best-seller. His elegant prose and self-deprecating wit made it the finest prime ministerial memoir. It contributed to what Fisher called the rapid 'hallowing' of Pearson after his death, which occurred shortly before midnight on 27 Dec. 1972.

The hallowing persisted as Canadians faced continuing challenges to national unity and political independence. When, in 2003, the journal *Policy Options* (Montreal) asked 30 Canadian academics and public figures to rate Canadian prime ministers since King, Pearson took the majority of first-place votes; Diefenbaker, his great antagonist, won none and finished sixth. One suspects Pearson would have smiled wryly and not taken the results very seriously. Neither should the historian.

One of the most severe critics of Pearson was his former colleague at the University of Toronto, historian Donald Grant Creighton, whose biography of Sir John A. Macdonald Pearson had generously praised in a personal letter to Creighton. Creighton, like Pearson, was the son of a Methodist parson, a graduate of Toronto and Oxford, and a historian by training, but in the 1950s their agreement about the character of Canadian history and nationality had dissolved. For Creighton, the loss of British identity and the post-war political and economic integration with the United States were giant steps on a path leading towards Canada's disintegration. The events of the 1960s – the rise of Quebec separatism and secular nationalism, the promotion of biculturalism and bilingualism, and the deluge of American popular media – made Canada's first century a study in decline and disappointment.

For Pearson, the British empire, whose traditions he had cherished as a youth and a young man, had become a hollow shell by the 1940s. Somewhat regretfully, he acknowledged its decline and recognized its flawed North American successor. Despite his doubts about American policy and about some elements of its society and culture, he linked Canada more closely with the United States in the 1940s and 1950s, mainly because he believed that the greatest threat facing Canada and the world was the Soviet Union and that the United States must give leadership in confronting that challenge. He also accepted that Canadians individually could benefit economically from integration with the strongest economy in the world. A politician had to deliver the goods and, in those days, the Americans had the most and the best.

It was Pearson's experience as a politician and as a diplomat that persuaded him in the 1960s that French Canada must become more integrally part of the Canadian political and economic system or it would go its separate way. Although he knew little about French Canada or about Quebec, he made Quebec's place in Canada the focus of his government, thus slowing the momentum for separation. The bitterness of Canadian politics during the mid 1960s derived in part from the sea change that came with the integration of French Canadian politics into the policy centres of the Canadian government. Never again would a Canadian cabinet have a few francophone ministers who could not speak their own language in cabinet and whose deputies dealt with them in English. After Pearson, no Canadian prime minister was unilingual. Ottawa became a different city, Canada a different country.

If he had not become Canada's prime minister, Pearson would still be a significant figure in Canadian history as the country's only Nobel Peace laureate and the most eminent Canadian diplomat. Some may cavil, as Creighton did, about Pearson's work as a diplomat, but few deny his skill and influence. His prime ministerial tenure, however, remains controversial. During his turbulent and fairly brief years in office, his governments transformed Canada. Although Canadians did not want a more open immigration policy, his governments introduced it, transforming the face of urban Canada. Although bilingualism was controversial, the Pearson governments adopted it and set the framework for an official policy that made the federal public service so different from what it had been. Although social welfare was, constitutionally, a provincial responsibility, the Pearson governments legislated boldly in the field and made Canada a country unlike its American neighbour, which had previously been the more generous North American nation in its social policies. Later in the 20th century, social disturbances in Canadian cities, separatism in the province of Quebec, and neo-conservative philosophies made some question the achievement of the Pearson years. Yet foes and friends already recognize that Pearson was a remarkable Canadian whose life and work profoundly changed the country he served.

JOHN ENGLISH

Further reading

John English, *The life of Lester Pearson* (2v., New York and Toronto, 1989–92).

Robert Bothwell, *Pearson: his life and world,* general ed. W. K. Lamb (Toronto, 1978).

L. B. Pearson, *Mike: the memoirs of the Right Honourable Lester B. Pearson, PC, CC, OM, OBE, MA, LLD* (3v., Toronto, 1972–75) and *Words and occasions: an anthology of speeches and articles selected from his papers by L. B. Pearson* (Toronto, 1970).

G. A. H. Pearson, *Seize the day: Lester B. Pearson and crisis diplomacy* (Ottawa, 1993).

PIERRE ELLIOTT TRUDEAU
(baptized Joseph-Philippe-Pierre-Yves-Elliott),

lawyer, author, university professor, and politician; b. 18 Oct. 1919
in Outremont (Montreal), son of Joseph-Charles-Émile Trudeau
and Grace Elliott; m. 4 March 1971 Margaret Sinclair in Vancouver,
and they had three sons; they divorced in 1984; he also had
a daughter with Deborah Coyne; d. 28 Sept. 2000 in Montreal
and was buried in Saint-Rémi, near Napierville, Que.

On his father's side, Pierre Trudeau (he would add Elliott in the
1930s and sometimes used a hyphen) was a descendant of
Étienne Truteau (Trudeau), a carpenter from La Rochelle,
France, who had arrived in New France in 1659. Pierre's father, known
to his friends as Charlie or Charley, was born on a farm in Saint-Michel,
south of Montreal. Although Charlie's father, Joseph, was semi-literate,
his mother, Malvina Cardinal, was a mayor's daughter who insisted that
their sons be given a good education. Charlie became a lawyer and practised in the heart of Montreal's business district.

Grace Elliott, Trudeau's mother, came from a prosperous Montreal
family. Her father, Phillip Armstrong Elliott, an Anglican of loyalist stock,
had married Sarah-Rebecca Sauvé, a French Canadian Roman Catholic,
and, as was required by the Catholic church for children of interfaith
marriages, Grace was raised as a Catholic. Phillip Elliott's wealth came
from real estate investments in Montreal. In 1903 he removed Grace from
her convent school there and placed her in the Dunham Ladies' College,
an Anglican women's finishing school in the Eastern Townships. Although
she spoke and wrote French, she preferred English, which would be the
language of the Trudeau home.

Charlie and Grace married in 1915 and they soon had children, first
Suzette in 1918 and then Pierre in 1919. Another child, Charles, whom
the family would call Tip, followed in 1922. By this time, Charlie had
largely abandoned his commercial law practice in favour of a business
career. Success had come with his creation in 1921 of the Automobile

Owners' Association, which comprised two Montreal gas and service stations and offered a program whereby car owners paid a yearly fee for guaranteed service. It was a brilliant device. The number of automobiles in Quebec swelled from 41,562 in 1920 to 97,418 in 1925 and would almost double again by 1930, when it reached 178,548. At the end of the 1920s the family moved from a modest row house in Outremont to a much larger but unpretentious dwelling there that could accommodate not only the Trudeaus but also a maid and a chauffeur. Although he would have apartments elsewhere, Pierre would consider it his home until he moved into the prime minister's residence at 24 Sussex Drive in 1968.

In the Great Depression of the 1930s Charlie Trudeau became wealthier and his automobile business, with some 30 service stations, was sold in 1932 to a subsidiary of the Imperial Oil Company for approximately $1,000,000, which he quickly invested. An ebullient, rough-edged businessman, he often gambled long into the night. There is evidence of hard living, including records of his large losses and wins, as well as family memories of his frequent absences. Yet he was a doting and demanding father who deeply impressed Pierre and they exchanged extremely affectionate letters. Subsequent rumours that Charlie abused Grace when he returned late at night are almost certainly false, although there is no doubt that the polished graduate of Dunham found her husband's antics difficult. They took their toll on Charlie as well. In the spring of 1935 he had a heart attack and died at age 46. His death deeply affected Pierre, who concluded, probably correctly, that it was the result of the social demands of the business world. Pierre became resistant to these practices and an ascetic in many of his own tastes. He did not gamble, disdained smoking, drank very little, and avoided wild parties. Such aloofness was made easier by the considerable fortune he had inherited, which gave him a freedom enjoyed by few others of his generation.

Charlie Trudeau's influence on his son was indelible; in assessing it, one must not conclude that his English-speaking home and association with the largely anglophone Montreal business class reflected his political views and private beliefs. Although Pierre had begun classes in English at the bilingual Académie Querbes in Outremont, he was quickly shifted to its French classes as soon as his English became fluent. In 1932 his father enrolled him in the Jesuits' new Collège Jean-de-Brébeuf, already the favoured school of the francophone elite and a centre for Catholic and youthful nationalist debate and thought in the 1930s. Charlie was a nationalist, supportive of the Catholic Church, the French language, and Quebec's place within the Canadian confederation. In politics he was a Conservative who was also a financial adviser of *Le Devoir* (Montréal), the principal voice of nationalism among Quebec newspapers. He was close to Camillien Houde, the mayor of Montreal and the former leader of the provincial Conservative Party.

Pierre Trudeau's pride in his father, which he never lost, derived in large part from his admiration of Charlie's success in business, a field from which francophones were largely absent in the early 20th century. He appears to have seldom discussed politics with his father, but Brébeuf was alive with political debate. Trudeau was introduced to nationalist thought and took part in rallies against perceived threats to the church and the French Canadian people. In a play he wrote in 1938, performed at Brébeuf, he satirized the tendency of his compatriots to patronize Jewish merchants and, implicitly, supported the Achat Chez Nous movement. An outstanding student, he reflected the milieu in which he thrived, one that was increasingly nationalist, supportive of corporatism, critical of capitalism and democracy, and wary of British and Canadian foreign policy as it moved hesitatingly forward on the road to war. Yet Trudeau could be a contrarian, cheering the victory of Major-General James Wolfe over the Marquis de Montcalm in class and challenging what he termed exalted patriots, those students who attacked bilingualism and mixed marriages. After he learned that another student thought he was 'Americanized, Anglicized,' he wrote in his diary that he was proud of 'my English blood which comes from my mother.'

After his father's death, Trudeau turned to his mother, who became the predominant figure in his adolescent life. He doted on her and she on him. His exceptional academic record pleased her greatly and she granted him the freedom that a favoured child so often obtains. With no financial concerns, he travelled frequently to New York, spent summers at Old Orchard Beach in Maine, took long canoe trips through the Canadian Shield, wildly drove a Harley-Davidson motorcycle, and bought books, records, and concert tickets few of his classmates could afford.

In his final year at the college, 1939–40, he edited the school newspaper, *Brébeuf*, in which he challenged the college administration, and finished first.

Brébeuf remained largely silent during the first months of World War II. Few students enlisted and indifference was the prevailing mood. Attitudes changed quickly, however, when France fell in June 1940 and the government of Prime Minister William Lyon Mackenzie King passed the National Resources Mobilization Act, introducing conscription for home defence. Earlier, Trudeau had casually suggested to his American girlfriend, Camille Corriveau, that he might enlist for the sake of adventure. Now he took

Pierre E. Trudeau, age 20, on his graduation from Collège Jean-de-Brébeuf, Montreal.

up the call of Mayor Houde and others who denounced conscription and urged French Canadians to defy mandatory registration for military service. Resentfully, he entered the compulsory Canadian Officers' Training Corps, which required regular drill and more extensive summer training. He began studies in law at the Université de Montréal in the fall and immediately attended lectures on Canadian history by the nationalist Abbé Lionel Groulx, but two other priests were far more influential in shaping his thoughts and actions at this time.

Trudeau had met Marie-Joseph d'Anjou and Rodolphe Dubé at Brébeuf. Father d'Anjou was one of his favourite teachers. Father Dubé was renowned not only for his teaching but also for his writings, published under his nom de plume, François Hertel. He became influential in debates about faith, politics, and Quebec's destiny, especially among the young. Charismatic, brilliant, and often outrageous, Hertel increasingly drew Pierre and his brother Charles into his circle. In the case of Pierre, he became a confidant, a confessor, and an inspiration in the early 1940s, even though his superiors moved him to Sudbury, Ont., because of his unorthodox approaches to religious teaching. Trudeau wrote to him regularly and visited him in Sudbury. An advocate of personalism, Hertel encouraged Trudeau to read philosophers Jacques Maritain and Emmanuel Mounier and the devout but rebellious young Catholic found their approach to personal liberty emancipating, although he also found corporatist thought and the conservative nationalism of Charles Maurras compelling. Personalism has many interpretations, but for Trudeau it meant that 'the person … is the individual enriched with a social conscience, integrated into the life of the communities around him and the economic context of his time, both of which must in turn give persons the means to exercise their freedom of choice.' Refined by later studies, this personalism formed the core of Trudeau's religious understanding of the relationship between the individual and society. That full understanding, however, would come slowly.

Hertel's unorthodoxy intrigued the young Trudeau as he sought answers to the question of identity. His anger mounting, Trudeau followed Hertel's counsel to become active in the struggle against conscription and to become revolutionary. He participated in the Frères-Chasseurs, who planned to rise up against the oppressors in Ottawa. Adopting a revolutionary pose, he signed his letters to Hertel 'citoyen,' took part in street riots, and worked in a secret society, the LX, with his friends François-Joseph Lessard, Jean-Baptiste Boulanger, and others to overthrow what they considered a corrupt system. Hertel placed the revolution within the anti-bourgeois and anti-democratic traditions in Catholic thought. He and Trudeau debated how the latter should be involved; radical approaches ranging from the anti-Semitic and conservative ideas of Charles Maurras to the revolutionary theories of Georges Sorel and Leon Trotsky all had appeal. Although Trudeau hesitated between being a 'philosopher' of the revolution or a 'man of action,' he certainly chose action in the streets during the conscription plebiscite of 27 April 1942 and especially during the federal by-election in Outremont in November 1942 when he gave a fiery speech, reported in detail in *Le Devoir*, which ended with a call for revolution.

Then, the spirit of violent revolution passed, although Trudeau was involved in the Bloc Populaire Canadien, which had taken the lead in the anti-conscription campaign. Father d'Anjou pressed him to take on the editorship of a nationalist journal promoting the notion of Laurentia, which at this time meant to Trudeau a French-speaking autonomous state. Trudeau's activism waned, however, as his law studies came to an end in 1943. Although he had disliked law school intensely, he finished first in his class. He continued to maintain close ties with Hertel, met several times with Abbé Groulx, favoured French marshal Philippe Pétain's government at Vichy, and supported nationalist causes, but he moved to the sidelines. He appears to have wanted to escape and to seek a new experience, initially soliciting a diplomatic post and then applying to Harvard University for graduate work. In the fall of 1944 he obtained permission to leave the country in order to study politics and economics at Harvard.

The university made a deep impact on Trudeau, although he frequently resisted the Anglo-American liberalism that pervaded it in the mid 1940s. His views changed while he was there. He was influenced by the numerous European exiles, many of them Jewish, who taught him brilliantly, notably Wassily W. Leontief, Joseph Alois Schumpeter, Carl Joachim Friedrich, and Gottfried Haberler. He heard about John Maynard Keynes for the first time and came to believe that his earlier classical education had been sadly deficient. He was also intrigued by liberal and democratic traditions and the separation of the spiritual from the secular in public life. He wrote in his notebooks, 'The spiritual will have [the] *decisive voice in education*, consultative in action.' And he began to reconsider what World War II had meant for the broader civilization he was learning to know better. He wrote to his girlfriend Thérèse Gouin that he had kept his eyes on his desk while 'the greatest cataclysm of all time' occurred. Puzzled, she asked what he meant. He replied, 'The cataclysm? It was the war, the war, the WAR!' In the mid 1940s Trudeau wanted to marry Gouin, a psychology student at the Université de Montréal, the daughter of Liberal senator Léon Mercier-Gouin and the granddaughter of former premier Sir Lomer Gouin, but she broke off the relationship, principally because of his intensity and his opposition to her desire to study psychology and continue her own psychoanalysis.

In 1946 Trudeau left Harvard with many questions, an abiding interest in the promise of Keynesian economics for democratic renewal, and a new scepticism about his earlier education and beliefs. He decided to continue his studies in France, where he audited courses at the Institut d'Études Politiques de Paris, but where his major interest was the stirring debates among French post-war intellectuals, particularly among Catholics. Like Trudeau, Mounier was discarding corporatist, collectivist, and elitist aspects of pre-war personalism and shaping the doctrine for the post-war era. Trudeau enthusiastically attended lectures and meetings with Mounier and other Catholic intellectuals such as Pierre Teilhard de Chardin and Étienne Gilson. In a nation where communism thrived, Mounier's attempt to find a balance between Soviet communism and Christianity impressed Trudeau, who decided that his proposed Harvard doctoral thesis should explore the potential areas of reconciliation between Catholicism and communism. From Paris he went to England in the fall of 1947 to study at the London School of Economics and Political Science. He quickly found that the eminent Labour Party intellectual Harold Joseph Laski shared his belief in the need for reconciliation between the west and Soviet communism and his doubts about the fervent anti-communism of Britain's Labour government. Laski and the London School of Economics had a greater intellectual influence on him than his experiences in Paris, particularly in spurring his understanding of democratic socialism.

While his views were changing, Trudeau kept in touch with old friends in Quebec. He produced articles for the conservative Catholic *Notre Temps* (Montréal) in 1947, denouncing Prime Minister Mackenzie King, the arbitrary internment of Quebec Fascist leader Adrien Arcand from 1940 to 1945, and the policies of the wartime government; simultaneously he argued for increased civil liberties, greater democracy, and more state involvement in economic life. There was an opacity in his writings; highly expressive language accompanied sometimes contradictory and confused views. To Lessard, he still wrote about the dream of Laurentia. After his London experience, he set out on a world tour in the spring of 1948. He justified the trip as research for his thesis, but there is little evidence of sustained work on the topic. He would never complete his doctorate, although he had received master's degrees from Harvard and the London School of Economics. His journey was, however, an adventure during which he was thrown into a Jordanian jail as a Jewish spy, eluded thieves at the ziggurat at Ur in Iraq, witnessed wars in India, Pakistan, and Indo-china, and barely escaped Shanghai, China, as it fell to Mao Zedong's

Communist army. Finally, he returned home to Montreal in May 1949 with a broad international experience, a solid knowledge of political economy specifically and the social sciences more generally, and a better appreciation of the possibilities of the law than he had had when he left the Université de Montréal as a celebrated but disappointed student.

In his own words Trudeau came back to a Quebec that was at 'a turning point in [its] entire religious, political, social, and economic history.' He believed he discovered that decisive moment when he set off with Gérard Pelletier, a journalist with *Le Devoir*, to the Eastern Townships to join striking asbestos workers. Pelletier, who had often met with Trudeau in Paris, sided with Jean Marchand, general secretary of the Canadian and Catholic Confederation of Labour, to press the cause of the strikers. The Union Nationale government in Quebec under Maurice Le Noblet Duplessis reacted harshly to what it considered an illegal strike, but the Catholic clergy was divided on the issue. Wearing a scraggly beard, Trudeau played a small role, marching in a head-cloth and shorts. The amused miners called him St Joseph; the police arrested him. He soon returned to Montreal, but the strike profoundly affected him as he linked the evidence of working class action with his study of socialism, labour, and democracy. He met with members of the Canadian Congress of Labour and considered becoming its research director. During the following years he acted as legal counsel for unions throughout the province. In 1956 he would use the strike as a prism through which to illuminate the social and economic development of Quebec in his most sustained analytical work, a chapter in *La grève de l'amiante* (Montréal); the volume, which he edited, would present a detailed study of the asbestos strike.

Trudeau now believed that in the new Quebec the 'social' should take precedence over the 'national,' as his close friend Pierre Vadeboncoeur put it in the summer of 1949. Although *Notre Temps*, in which he had invested $1,000 in 1944 and which had published his major articles while he was in Europe, became increasingly drawn to Duplessis's conservative nationalism, Trudeau moved in a completely different direction, towards the democratic socialism whose main Canadian expression was the Co-operative Commonwealth Federation. In the federal election of June 1949, he had been this party's agent in the riding of Jacques-Cartier. As the attraction of socialism intensified, his affection for Quebec nationalism waned, especially since nationalism was so strongly represented by the conservative forces within the Quebec Catholic Church and, of course, by the Duplessis government, which he regarded as archaic and out of step. Like many of his generation, he was angry. Once again, he left Quebec.

In the late summer of 1949 Trudeau became a federal public servant in the Privy Council at Ottawa. Although the choice shocked Pelletier and other friends, Ottawa beckoned to many highly educated francophones. Trudeau's experience there was important in providing him with a better understanding of the character of Canadian federalism. He came to believe that it had played an important part in limiting extremes while simultaneously affording the opportunity for political experimentation and the correction of social inequities. While retaining the notion that provincial and federal governments had clearly delineated responsibilities, he shared the assumption, common in Ottawa, that Keynesian economics provided the federal government with the opportunity and the responsibility to intervene in the economy to assure prosperity and security. He worked long hours and quickly impressed his superior, Robert Gordon Robertson, and his colleagues with his intelligence and diligence. His socialism and, even more, his criticism of Canada's Cold War alliances did not, however, fit well with Ottawa's mood as Canada entered the Korean War in 1950. He chafed against the anonymity imposed on public servants. He also concluded that Ottawa was an unwelcoming 'English capital' and spent most weekends in Montreal. Relief from Ottawa's bleakness came as well from an intense romance with Helen Segerstrale, a young employee of the Swedish embassy. In the summer of 1951, after writing an anonymous attack on Canadian involvement in the Korean War, he quit his job. His romance ended when Segerstrale refused to convert to Catholicism. Unlike many of his francophone colleagues, Trudeau would remain a devout Catholic.

In Montreal in 1950, Trudeau had begun discussions with Pelletier and, later, with others about the establishment of a journal similar to Mounier's *Esprit* (Paris), which had enormous influence on Catholic thought in post-war France. Pelletier had quickly persuaded Trudeau to become his principal partner in the creation of *Cité Libre* (Montréal) in the summer of 1950. He had a more difficult time getting his other colleagues to accept the wealthy and idiosyncratic Trudeau, who many believed would be 'a disturbing influence.' Writing in the 1980s, Pelletier would admit that he had been.

Despite the uncertain nature of his start at *Cité Libre*, Trudeau became closely identified with the magazine in the 1950s. His co-editorship carried him to the heart of the opposition to the Duplessis government and permitted him, in Pelletier's words, 'to find his place ... in his generation.' His presence was dominant from the first issue, when he wrote emotional but anonymous tributes to his mentors Mounier and Laski, both of whom had died recently. He also wrote an article on 'functional politics,' the first draft of the political program that he would develop in the 1950s. He urged Quebec to open itself to the world while still bearing 'witness to the Christian and French fact in America.' He concluded with a call 'to borrow the "functional" discipline from architecture, to throw to the winds those many prejudices with which the past has encumbered the present, and to build for the new man.' The new generation should break the old taboos: 'Better yet, let's consider them null and void. Let us be coolly intelligent.'

Things were not always cool. *Cité Libre* appeared irregularly, its finances were always wobbly, and it quickly attracted criticism. The conservative historian Robert Rumilly warned Duplessis that *Cité Libre*'s editors and contributors were 'extremely dangerous' and 'subversive.' Trudeau's earlier mentor Father d'Anjou wrote a savage attack on an article of his that claimed priests had no more of a divine right than politicians. As a result of these and other comments, Archbishop Paul-Émile Léger of Montreal summoned Pelletier and Trudeau. Despite some insolence on Trudeau's part during the meeting, Léger did not condemn the review, an action that could have had dire consequences. *Cité Libre* survived. Through his work as editor, Trudeau came to know the leading intellectuals of the time and Radio-Canada sought out *Cité Libre* authors and editors to comment on public affairs. English Canadian intellectuals became curious about the publication and invited Trudeau to their gatherings, especially the conferences of the Canadian Institute of International Affairs and the Couchiching Institute on Public Affairs. His flawless English, familiarity with contemporary social science, and striking physicality intrigued those who encountered him in such settings. So did his thoughts.

A close reading of Trudeau's writings and speeches in the 1950s reveals that some of his ideas changed little, others much more. He remained consistently wary of the Cold War and sympathetic to the view of *Le Monde* (Paris) and others that there was a 'middle way,' between the fervent anti-communism of North American governments and the stern communism of Joseph Stalin, a view rarely heard in English Canada or in the Quebec Catholic Church at that time. He also continued to call for francophones to be 'functional,' which towards the end of the decade came to mean a strengthening of the technical, scientific, and social science sectors of Quebec society, especially in the universities. However, his strong anticlericalism abated when it became clear that the church itself faced enormous strain in adapting to the rapid changes in Quebec as the economy became more sophisticated and modern communications, especially television, transformed daily life. He began to shift his attention to political institutions, notably the governments in Quebec City and Ottawa. He considered the provincial administration corrupt, autocratic, and socially regressive; the federal, he complained, ignored the French fact even when Louis-Stephen St-Laurent was prime minister, too casually embraced the American approach to the Cold War, and too often ignored the constitution. The last grievance became evident when Trudeau, to the surprise of many of his friends and some of his enemies, supported the Duplessis government's rejection of federal grants to universities on the grounds that 'no government has the right to interfere with the administration of other governments in those areas *not within its own jurisdiction.*' Yet even in agreeing with Duplessis he condemned his government. 'Let Mr. Duplessis establish an administration as efficient and honest as the federal government, and we shall then consider the rivalry to be a fair one.'

Trudeau, then, was never predictable. A social democrat, he became increasingly sceptical of the CCF and disappointed his friend Thérèse Casgrain, the provincial party leader, with his unwillingness to make a fuller commitment. A strong opponent of Duplessis and the Union Nationale, he refused to join the coalition that emerged under the leadership of the Liberal Party to defeat the government. The essay he contributed to the study of the asbestos strike of 1949, published in 1956, revealed his deep distrust of the Quebec Liberal Party and his disillusionment with the detritus of earlier political and ideological battles. The past, it seemed, bore mainly bad lessons for the future. In a 1958 article, 'Some obstacles to democracy in Quebec,' published in the *Canadian Journal of Economics and Political Science* (Toronto) and in French in his *Le fédéralisme et la société canadienne-française* (Montréal, 1967), he wrote, 'Historically, French Canadians have not really believed in democracy for themselves; and English Canadians have not really wanted it for others.' He increasingly argued that both English and French Canadians were imprisoned in their past, the English in the fusty British imperial tradition and the French in a sterile clerical nationalism, exemplified in his mind by the attacks on *Cité Libre* from conservative church voices such as Father d'Anjou or historian Rumilly. His assaults on Quebec nationalism, which had been less virulent than those of other *Cité Libre* authors in the early 1950s, now became intense as he blamed nationalism for closing the windows to the fresh winds of the modern world. He became an eloquent defender of federalism as a 'safety valve' through which individuals and groups might obtain redress denied by an autocratic provincial government and a strong supporter of the courts which, during this decade, began to establish a Canadian tradition of civil liberties. Like McGill University law professor and poet Francis Reginald Scott and journalist Jacques Hébert, he looked to the courts to protect individual rights that, in the past, had so often been denied.

As Trudeau became clearer in his writings, he seemed more muddled in politics. In 1956 he had joined with Pelletier, Hébert, journalist André Laurendeau, and others who lacked party affiliation to form the Rassemblement, which he would describe in his memoirs as a 'fragile and short-lived body [that] undertook to defend and promote democracy in Quebec.' While others began to rally behind the Liberal Party to defeat Duplessis, he continued to urge a non-partisan coalition. His vehemence in promoting the Rassemblement angered his friends both in the Quebec wing of the CCF, known since 1955 as the Parti Social Démocratique du Québec, and among the reformers who believed they were taking control of the provincial Liberal Party. He attended the Quebec Liberal Party's convention of 1958 and dismissed it as undemocratic. As the Rassemblement crumbled, he turned to a new grouping, the Union des Forces Démocratiques, which in October 1958 issued 'Un manifeste démocratique,' written mainly by him, in *Cité Libre*. Now a familiar figure on Quebec television and a target for attack not only by Duplessis but also by Quebec socialists, Trudeau took the leadership of the union. His decision to accept the position seemed a whimsical gesture to many. A student newspaper, the *McGill Daily* (Montreal), summarized the general perception of Trudeau, stating that 'the author is considered to be a brilliant man but to many [he] still remains a dilettante.' His ideas were interesting but his influence was limited.

The death of Duplessis in September 1959 dramatically changed the political landscape; the impact of his departure was amplified when his successor, Paul Sauvé, suddenly died on 2 Jan. 1960. The ambitious and the practical rallied to the Liberals under Jean Lesage, but Trudeau did not follow. He continued to lead the Union des Forces Démocratiques and to urge unsuccessfully the formation of a new coalition. On the eve of the provincial general election of 22 June he finally and grudgingly endorsed the Liberals in *Cité Libre*. His reservations about them grew after the election even though Lesage's determination to secularize Quebec society had his solid support. The administration was progressive but also nationalist and its nationalism increasingly troubled him. Although the Lesage government's nationalism or 'neo-nationalism' differed from that of Duplessis in its secularism and its fervent embrace of modernity, Trudeau saw in the official rhetoric and actions a nationalist approach in which the state was identified with the 'nation.' These doubts augmented during his regular meetings with René Lévesque on weekends when the new minister of public works and hydraulic resources returned from Quebec City. To Trudeau, Lévesque's anger and his determination to proceed with the nationalization of hydroelectricity seemed irrational. Trudeau believed that secularization and modernization were imperative but also that Quebec should, as he wrote in *Cité Libre* in 1961, 'open up the borders.' 'Our people,' he argued, 'are suffocating to death!'

That year Trudeau finally obtained the position with the faculty of law at the Université de Montréal which had been denied him by the Duplessis government. He found the atmosphere 'sterile,' with 'the terminology of the Left ... serving to conceal a single preoccupation: the separatist counter-revolution.' In 1962 he wrote a bitter attack on Quebec nationalism and separatism that placed the blame for these movements squarely on the intellectuals. In 'La nouvelle trahison des clercs,' published originally in *Cité Libre* and six years later in English in *Federalism and the French Canadians* (Toronto), he denied that decolonization was relevant to Quebec because the province had rights that colonists had never possessed. Nationalism had produced the worst wars of the century and the quest for 'complete sovereign power' was inevitably a 'self-destructive end.' Nationalism, then, was reactionary, an attempt by a new francophone bourgeois elite to consolidate its power through such devices as the nationalization of hydroelectricity. 'French Canadians,' he wrote, 'have all the powers they need to make Quebec a political society affording due respect for nationalist aspirations and at the same time giving unprecedented scope for human potential in the broadest sense.'

The Quebec election of November 1962 with the Liberal party's slogan 'Masters in our own house' and its major issue, the nationalization of hydroelectricity, placed Trudeau in a role he had often held, that of a critical voice without a party. After Lesage's triumph, he considered turning to federal politics at the urging of Jean Marchand, who had developed ties with the Liberals under party leader Lester Bowles Pearson. These plans collapsed when Pearson changed his position on nuclear weapons in January 1963. The reversal prompted an angry denunciation of Pearson in *Cité Libre*, where Trudeau echoed Vadeboncoeur's memorable description of Canada's Nobel Peace Prize winner as the 'defrocked prince of peace.' Other disappointments came with *Cité Libre*, whose expanded editorial committee bickered constantly.

More difficult were his breaks with Vadeboncoeur, perhaps his closest friend from childhood and adolescence, and Hertel, his early mentor. Both approved of separatism, but Trudeau became particularly enraged by an article in which Hertel seemed to advocate the assassination of Laurendeau for having accepted, with Arnold Davidson Dunton, the co-chairmanship of the royal commission on bilingualism and biculturalism in July 1963. He publicly attacked his former teacher.

Long ago Trudeau had heeded Hertel's call for revolution, but he now believed that what Hertel and Vadeboncoeur thought revolutionary was truly reactionary, an unrealistic approach to a world where science and social science offered real prospect for positive change. With some new friends – economist Albert Breton, sociologists Raymond Breton and Maurice Pinard, lawyers Marc Lalonde and Claude Bruneau, and psychoanalyst Yvon Gauthier – he issued a manifesto in both languages in May 1964. It appeared in English as 'An appeal for realism in politics' in *Canadian Forum* (Toronto). The group denounced the lack of realism in Quebec politics, argued that the traditional nation state was obsolete, and announced their refusal 'to let ourselves be locked into a constitutional frame smaller than Canada.'

Canada, however, seemed threatened as Pearson's government struggled with the pace of change in the mid 1960s. Hopes for an agreement on a way to amend the constitution through the so-called Fulton–Favreau formula collapsed, scandals undermined the cabinet ministers from Quebec, and Pearson groped for a new path through which his government could find a response to the challenge of Quebec nationalism and separatism. Trudeau had little faith in the royal commission on bilingualism and biculturalism, which he correctly believed was moving towards the recommendation of special status for Quebec.

In these circumstances Trudeau's long apprenticeship came to an end. On 10 Sept. 1965 Marchand, Pelletier, and he announced that they would be Liberal candidates in the federal election which Pearson had called three days earlier. The declaration stunned most of their *Cité Libre* colleagues, who expressed their disapproval in the magazine's pages and in later articles published elsewhere, and some of Trudeau's English Canadian socialist friends. Vadeboncoeur and other nationalists and separatists scorned Trudeau's decision. On the whole, the English press welcomed the 'three wise men' to the Liberal team. The French press called them simply 'les trois colombes' (the three doves). The eloquent labour leader Marchand was the prize candidate and it was he who insisted that the unpredictable Trudeau, who had so recently denounced Pearson, accompany him to Ottawa. After some delay, the party opened the strongly Liberal seat of Mount Royal for Trudeau. He won it with a large margin on 8 November and would hold it until the end of his political career in 1984. The Liberals failed to win a majority, however, and parliamentary disorder persisted.

Initially hesitant, Trudeau refused Pearson's request that he be the prime minister's parliamentary secretary. An angry Marchand rebuked him and Trudeau then accepted the position; his precise duties were not defined. Gradually, Trudeau found others in Ottawa who shared his concern that the government's policy towards Quebec was one of drift. He met regularly with Lalonde and with public servants such as Peter Michael Pitfield and Allan Ezra Gotlieb. They began to craft a more coherent response to Quebec's constitutional challenges, one that rejected

MARCHAND:

"TEL QUE JE CONNAIS PIERRE, IL N'A PAS BESOIN D'UN ENTREMETTEUR..."

Fellow MP Jean Marchand (right) explains that Liberal leadership candidate
Pierre E. Trudeau (centre) does not need a go-between to seduce the province,
in a Raoul Hunter caricature, *Le Soleil* (Quebec City), 8 March 1968.

what they perceived as the weakness embodied in the cooperative federalism of the first Pearson years. Trudeau became identified by political
commentators as, potentially, the most significant of the 'three wise men.'
He did little publicly in 1966 to justify these expectations, but Marchand
had noticed that his colleague possessed political magic. He told Laurendeau he 'bet his shirt' that Trudeau would quickly become the Liberals'
'big man in French Canada, eclipsing all the others.' Soon he did.

The close attention Trudeau had paid to the constitution while working
in the Privy Council in 1949 suddenly became valuable political capital
as constitutional discussions reached a deadlock in 1966. In March he and
Marchand gained control of the Quebec wing of the federal Liberal Party,
which had established its own administration. At its first meeting the
Quebec section supported motions drafted by Trudeau condemning 'special
status' or 'a confederation of ten states' and approving the concept of a
'bill of rights' within the constitution. On 5 June 1966 the provincial

Liberals went down to a stunning defeat. The victor, Daniel Johnson of the Union Nationale, was much more ambiguous about Canada. His slogan, 'Equality or independence,' directly challenged the platform drawn up by Trudeau for the Quebec federal Liberals. Behind the scenes in Ottawa, Trudeau worked with Lalonde and, especially, Albert Wesley Johnson, assistant deputy minister in the Department of Finance, to draft a statement presented by finance minister and receiver general Mitchell William Sharp at the federal–provincial conference held in September. It rejected special status for Quebec and opting out of federal programs by Quebec alone. Johnson's thrust forward met a well-conceived counterattack.

Trudeau was making his mark privately, not publicly, and he remained largely unknown in English Canada. Yet events were determining his fate. Centennial year, 1967, brought not only the celebration of Canada with its wildly successful Expo 67 in Montreal but also constitutional crisis as Johnson pressed his demands. On 4 April 1967 Pearson appointed Trudeau minister of justice and attorney general, strengthening the left wing of the Liberal Party and his government's constitutional expertise at federal–provincial meetings. Trudeau quickly went to work and displayed an astonishing discipline that shocked bureaucrats who had heard the many rumours about his playboy lifestyle. He concentrated primarily on the constitution and the much-delayed reform of the Criminal Code. The 47-year-old bachelor announced his plan to decriminalize homosexual acts between consenting adults, allow for easier divorces, and permit abortion if the mother's health was endangered. In a Canada that was suddenly becoming permissive and liberal, he struck the loudest notes. The house unanimously passed his divorce reforms in December 1967, shortly after Pearson had declared his intention to resign as soon as a new party leader was chosen.

The race for a successor began immediately. Pearson told Marchand he must run because the Liberal principle of alternation between French- and English-speaking leaders and the Quebec crisis required that he do so. Lalonde, Pitfield, and Trudeau's assistant, Eddie Rubin, were already considering how Trudeau might be drafted. In January 1968, after a vacation in Tahiti, where he had become entranced with the stunning Margaret Sinclair, daughter of a former Liberal cabinet minister, Trudeau met with Marchand and Pelletier. Marchand would not run; Trudeau must. Typically,

Trudeau hesitated even though he had seriously considered the prospect. The Conservatives under their new leader, Robert Lorne Stanfield, were ahead in the polls; there were powerful Liberals contesting the race, including the wily veteran Paul Joseph James Martin, finance minister Sharp, senior cabinet minister Paul Theodore Hellyer, and several other experienced candidates; and, finally, Trudeau feared losing the privacy he had long cherished. Yet he had dreamed of a public career since adolescence and he knew that, whatever its deficiencies, the royal commission on bilingualism and biculturalism was correct in stating that Canada was going through the greatest crisis in its history. It was no time to step aside.

Many agreed. Leading Canadian journalist Peter Charles Newman began to tout Trudeau in his columns. Marchand, who was a superb political organizer, told Trudeau that he would 'handle' Quebec for him but that Trudeau himself would have to 'handle' the rest of Canada. He did so brilliantly. In late December he had captured attention with his televised comment that 'there's no place for the state in the bedrooms of the nation.' He then received an enormous boost from Pearson, whom he had so often criticized publicly and privately. Despite the misgivings of other leadership candidates, the prime minister sent him on a politically valuable tour of provincial capitals and gave him the principal seat at the federal–provincial constitutional conference of 5–7 February 1968. Johnson had expected Pearson to be his debating opponent, but he faced Trudeau, whose biting tones, quick repartee, and well-defined positions quickly captured attention. Trudeau's sculpted face, penetrating eyes, and confident rhetoric dominated the nightly news. Marchand concluded that 'at the beginning of February he was really created.'

Not all were pleased with the creation. Claude Ryan of *Le Devoir* strongly criticized Trudeau's performance at the conference and his rigidity on the question of special status for Quebec and constitutional revision more generally, which became a frequent complaint of others contesting the leadership. His opponents were already reeling from the publicity Trudeau had garnered. Journalists had dubbed the resulting enthusiasm 'Trudeaumania' when Trudeau announced his candidacy on 16 Feb. 1968. Very quickly he rose to the top in the polls, but more important to his ultimate success was the defeat three days later of the Liberal government in the House of Commons on a money bill introduced by Sharp. Pearson returned from holidays to save the situation, but Sharp's leadership campaign was doomed. On 3 April, the eve of the convention, Sharp withdrew and announced that he was supporting Trudeau. Powerful Newfoundland premier Joseph Roberts Smallwood also offered valuable backing that same night, declaring before a riotous crowd that 'Pierre is better than medicare – the lame have only to touch his garments to walk again.'

Trudeau needed miracles nonetheless. Robert Henry Winters strongly challenged him after he overcame Hellyer on the second ballot. The fourth and final ballot saw Trudeau win with 1,203 votes to 954 for Winters and 195 for John Napier Turner, who had refused to withdraw. On 20 April Trudeau became prime minister and he soon called an election for 25 June. The leadership campaign had had the desired effect of boosting Liberal support and the election campaign saw the dour Stanfield overwhelmed as Trudeau, to the media's delight, shattered Canada's conservative electoral mould by kissing beautiful women, not babies, and doing jackknife dives clad in a European men's bikini. His many years of strenuous physical activity had impressively hardened his body and given him a quickness and fluidity of movement. His deserved reputation as an excellent swimmer and diver, skilled canoeist, practitioner of judo, and intrepid adventurer appealed to the young and the press. But there was substance too. He eloquently attacked the Conservatives and the New Democratic Party, accusing them of favouring a 'two nations' approach, and he directly challenged Quebec's international aspirations. His firmness gained credibility when, on the night before the election, Saint-Jean-Baptiste day, he took his place on a Montreal reviewing platform. A mob of students and separatists threw bottles, eggs, and stones, but Trudeau would not budge. Any doubts in English Canada about his personal courage, based on his lack of wartime service, seemed to disappear. He savoured his greatest electoral victory as his party won 154 seats, including 56 of the 74 seats in Quebec, the Conservatives only 72, the NDP 22, and the Ralliement des Créditistes 14. One Liberal-Labour member and one independent were elected, for a total of 264.

In the campaign Trudeau had promised a 'just society,' but contemporary observers remarked on the vagueness of his policy proposals apart from those on constitutional issues. As a scholar and a polemicist, Trudeau had urged greater democracy within political parties. His attack on

Pearson in 1963 had rested largely on the argument that Pearson had not consulted his party before he changed the Liberals' stance on nuclear weapons. Trudeau stressed political education and participation despite the doubts of Marchand and others. Lacking an explicit platform developed by a policy convention, he advocated the concept of 'participatory democracy.' On a range of issues, there would be broad public consultations that would serve to inform the citizenry while creating legitimacy for government action. The approach was not a success. It would be adopted most notably in a foreign policy review; the result, published in 1970, was a series of pamphlets whose content was so bland that the critical issue of Canadian–American relations went unmentioned.

Pierre E. Trudeau, newly elected as prime minister, playfully turns the camera on photographer Duncan Cameron, Ottawa, 28 June 1968.

This gap between hope and disappointment became quickly evident after the election campaign. As journalist Richard Gwyn wrote, 'The kissing stopped almost as soon as the ballots were counted.' Trudeau did receive some praise for the presentation of his cabinet on 5 July 1968, even from Claude Ryan, who commended him for the strongest-ever francophone presence. The cabinet included Léo-Alphonse Cadieux in national defence, Pelletier as secretary of state, Jean-Luc Pépin in industry and in trade and commerce (later combined as one ministry), and Marchand in forestry and rural development (the following year he would become minister of regional economic expansion). Outside the cabinet, Lalonde was made chief of staff and Pitfield took on major responsibilities in the Privy Council Office. The appointments signalled three important themes of Trudeau's tenure as prime minister: the strengthening of the francophone presence in Ottawa, 'French power' as it came to be called; the emphasis on regional economic initiatives or redistributive policies; and the streamlining of the Ottawa bureaucracy and political decision-making through the introduction of modern organizational concepts such as systems analysis. Trudeau would take special pride in the adoption of the Official Languages Act in 1969, a measure which reflected his political rhetoric and private beliefs. In these areas, the federal government had much freedom; in contrast, the unfinished business of the constitution required the cooperation of the provinces.

Daniel Johnson had died in September 1968. His successor, Jean-Jacques Bertrand, reaffirmed minority-language education rights in response to bitter confrontations in Saint-Léonard (Montreal), where a heavy concentration of Italian immigrants wished to educate their children in English. The second volume of the royal commission on bilingualism and biculturalism had just appeared and had called for federal support for minority-language education and for a constitutional guarantee of parental choice in the language of education. As the Union Nationale divided on the subject, the Quebec Liberals fractured. René Lévesque had left the party the previous year and he founded the Parti Québécois, which held its first convention in October 1968. Bertrand was weak, however, and in April 1970 the Liberals under lawyer-economist Robert Bourassa won a decisive victory, which appeared to open the path to resolving the thorny issues that had plagued constitutional discussion since the Johnson–Trudeau confrontation. In June 1971 the path led to Victoria, where the federal government and the premiers agreed on the Canadian Constitutional Charter, a compromise that, understandably, satisfied no one but which offered resolutions to the differences over a formula to amend the constitution, language rights, social spending, and the entrenchment of individual rights. Trudeau admitted the limitations but said at his final Victoria press conference that if all governments accepted the charter, as was required for its enactment, 'we'll all wear a crown of laurels.' Bourassa flew home the following day to a storm of criticism, since the agreement had not met Quebec's demands concerning greater provincial control of social policy. One week later he announced he would not present the charter to the

National Assembly of Quebec. For Trudeau, it was a defeat and even a betrayal by Bourassa who, he believed, had promised his support.

Trudeau's doubts about Bourassa had derived in large part from the October crisis in 1970, which remains, probably, the most controversial event of his prime ministerial tenure. The crisis began with the kidnapping in Montreal of British trade commissioner James Richard Cross by members of the Front de Libération du Québec on 5 Oct. 1970. Although there had been thefts of arms and rumours of possible kidnappings, the police forces at all levels were unprepared for the challenge and the governments of Quebec and Canada initially responded by agreeing to some of the kidnappers' demands, notably the reading of the FLQ manifesto and a guarantee of their safe passage.

Then on 10 October the Chénier cell of the FLQ seized the Quebec minister of labour and immigration, Pierre Laporte, at his suburban home in Saint-Lambert. The brazen act stunned the country. The Bourassa government hesitated. Trudeau had been irritated by the earlier decision of Sharp, the secretary of state for external affairs, to agree to the reading of the FLQ manifesto by Radio-Canada. Others, including Ryan and Lévesque, urged conciliation and considered calling for Bourassa to stand aside for a new coalition government. On 15 October the federal cabinet met to consider a request from Bourassa that Ottawa come to Quebec's assistance. Marchand took the lead by warning that the situation was 'much more serious' than had been believed. He claimed that the FLQ had two tons of dynamite ready to explode and urged an immediate raid on the organization, whose numbers he estimated at anywhere from 200 to 1,000. Trudeau agreed. According to cabinet reports, he concluded 'the longer we gave opinion makers in Quebec, the more we stood to lose,' a bitter reference to a document published that day in Le Devoir. Signed by Lévesque, Ryan, and others, it referred to the 'semi-military rigidity ... in Ottawa' and used the term 'political prisoners' for jailed FLQ members. Moreover, the prime minister advised that Bourassa did not want backbenchers 'to sit around too long.' They were 'falling apart.' This concern reflected Trudeau's belief that the Quebec Liberal Party was not united in its opinions. In answer to the Quebec government's request, the Canadian armed forces were called in to assist the police. Trudeau worried about what future civil libertarians might think but, after long debate, the War Measures Act was invoked on 16 October. The following day Laporte, whom Trudeau had known well, was found dead in the trunk of a car. The strong response had broken the momentum of the FLQ, however. Cross was released on 3 December and Laporte's murderers were captured on 28 December.

Trudeau's decision to suspend the normal legal process haunted him and it swelled the ranks of his detractors on the left and among Quebec nationalists and separatists. When he wrote his memoirs, he would defend the action, first, as the only one possible when the 'more interested parties,' the Quebec premier and the mayor of Montreal, pleaded for federal assistance and, secondly, as a step necessary to 'prevent the situation from degenerating into chaos.' The cabinet record and other evidence support his later claim that he had worried about the implications. They also suggest that the role of Marchand, who had overstated the threat posed by the FLQ, was decisive. However, information at the time was sketchy, confidence in the Bourassa government was lacking both in Ottawa and Quebec, and the War Measures Act, with its broad powers, was the sole means to act quickly.

The decision left an ambiguity concerning Trudeau's regard for civil liberties. His famous reply when asked how far he would go, 'Well, just watch me,' has lingered as evidence of autocratic tendencies. Moreover, many innocent people were arrested – some Trudeau knew well – and the police were careless in their use of their new powers. Although he had long been active in civil liberties movements and legal cases, he had also praised autocratic regimes in the Soviet Union in 1952 and China in 1960 and maintained a warm relationship with Cuban leader Fidel Castro. His views

Pierre E. Trudeau joins Cuban prime minister Fidel Castro in a singalong, Havana, January 1976.

fitted badly into the grammar of human rights that would be developed in the late 20th century by international non-governmental organizations such as Human Rights Watch, yet he would argue, as would his principal secretary, Thomas Sidney Axworthy, in 2003 that what is needed is 'an agreed-upon framework of law in order for us to make all of our individual choices.' Political and civil rights should be protected with whatever means were available if they were in danger. Hence in his memoirs he defended 'Well, just watch me' as an indication of his determination to maintain the rule of law in Canada. Opinion remains divided over Trudeau's decisions not to negotiate and to invoke the War Measures Act, but he is correct in stating that the terrorist threat abated and the FLQ disappeared after October 1970. Nevertheless, the death of Laporte, the government's response to the crisis, and the army in the streets marked a decisive moment in Trudeau's political life and that of his government. The buoyant hopes of the 1960s seemed to dissolve and the 1970s would be a difficult decade for Trudeau and other world leaders as the post-war boom came to an end.

Despite the opposition of many opinion leaders in English and French Canada to the government's actions, the immediate effect of the crisis was a surge in support for the government from across the country; 87 per cent of Canadians, with little difference between anglophones and francophones, expressed their approval of its actions. Enthusiasm for Trudeau and the Liberals was reinforced when he suddenly married 22-year-old Margaret Sinclair on 4 March 1971. The event attracted international attention.

The completion of Trudeau's foreign policy review in 1970 had resulted in few changes of direction. Diplomatic relations were established with China that year as they had been with the Vatican in 1969; the military commitment to the North Atlantic Treaty Organization was reduced; and Canada's foreign service accepted the need for bilingualism. Trudeau was initially so sceptical of the Commonwealth of Nations that only the strongest pressure from his staff persuaded him to attend its Singapore conference in January 1971. He nevertheless played a major role there in mediating the bitter disputes about South Africa. He also travelled to the Soviet Union, western Europe, Australia, and the United States. His relationship with the American administration was bad, however, principally because President Richard Milhous Nixon disliked him profoundly and Secretary of State Henry Alfred Kissinger played to Nixon's hostility and vanity. In turn, Trudeau barely concealed his distrust of American foreign policy. Yet despite nationalist calls for disengagement from the United States and dreams of a 'third option,' through which Canada would establish closer relationships with Europe and the developing world, the American presence remained dominant albeit difficult.

By 1972 the Canadian government was stumbling, as were the governments of other western countries, in trying to adjust to new international circumstances, particularly the combination of inflation and unemployment that challenged traditional Keynesian approaches to the economy. Ministers grumbled about Trudeau's staff, who, they claimed, lacked political experience; Hellyer and Eric William Kierans had left the cabinet complaining, respectively, about the lack of a housing policy and weak economic guidance; and others warned the prime minister that the Liberal grass roots were weak. Richard James Hardy Stanbury, the Liberal Party president, fretted in his diary about Trudeau's refusal to go to party fund-raisers and to pamper volunteer officials. This aloofness mingled dangerously with Trudeau's actions. Few believed he had really said 'fuddle duddle' in February 1971 to an irritating Tory MP. His explanation amused many, but commentators and even some colleagues thought it reflected his disdain for parliament and its traditions. Although an excellent debater, Trudeau did not conceal his contempt for much of the discussion in the House of Commons and for most parliamentarians. When he called an election for 30 Oct. 1972, the polls initially suggested another Liberal victory, but there was no Trudeaumania. The government had disappointed many. As John Gray wrote in *Maclean's* (Toronto), 'the outstanding impression is that, with few notable exceptions, Trudeau has remarkably few political goals.' The campaign strengthened that belief with its uninspiring English slogan, 'The land is strong.' The Liberal Party and Trudeau were not. On election night the Conservatives and the Liberals had to await a recount to learn who would form an administration. A chastened Trudeau then told the press that the government of the past four and a half years 'was not satisfactory.'

The recount saved Trudeau, but he now headed a minority government with 109 seats to the Tories' 107; the New Democrats under David

Lewis held 31 seats; the Social Credit Party had 15; one candidate was elected as an independent and another was elected with no designation. Trudeau quickly adjusted. He brought in new political advisers, slowed down the bilingualism program, and became warmer and less provocative in public appearances, when he was often accompanied by Margaret and baby Justin. He also moved to the left to maintain the support of the NDP. Some had said Trudeau was inflexible; his pragmatism was evident in the government's creation in 1973 of the Foreign Investment Review Agency, which the left had long advocated. Similarly, the government responded to the energy crisis of 1973 with a highly interventionist policy that protected Canadians from world prices. It annoyed Albertans, but there were increasingly few Liberal votes there.

On 8 May 1974 Trudeau engineered the government's defeat by producing a budget the opposition could not support. He made no mistakes in this election. He campaigned relentlessly, often in the presence of Margaret, who became a crowd favourite. *Le Devoir* spoke admiringly of the new 'Trudeau Express,' his campaign by train through the Maritimes. The smashing victory of the Quebec Liberals in the provincial election of October 1973 seemed to help the federal Liberals. Moreover, Stanfield had made a fatal error by suggesting that inflation should be halted by a wage and price freeze. Workers feared the wage controls and the Liberals gained New Democratic votes when Trudeau ridiculed Stanfield's proposal with the phrase 'Zap! You're frozen.' On election day, 8 July, the Liberals won a solid majority with 141 seats compared to 95 for the Conservatives and 16 for the NDP; the Social Credit had 11 and 1 independent candidate was elected. The *Globe and Mail* (Toronto), which, like nearly all Canadian newspapers, had supported the Conservatives, editorially declared the win 'a personal victory' for Trudeau, a tribute not to 'Trudeaumania, ... but [to] the work, effort and energy that he put into his campaign.' Yet it correctly warned that Trudeau faced problems of 'grave dimensions,' particularly 'runaway inflation,' often referred to as stagflation, in which high unemployment was combined with historically high rates of inflation. The inflation was in part the product of the global energy crisis whose political reflection in Canada was the absence of Liberal seats in Alberta.

Trudeau privately shared these concerns and the victory's glow soon dimmed, especially at 24 Sussex Drive. 'My rebellion,' Margaret Trudeau would write in 1979, 'started in 1974.' The day after the election in which she had campaigned so well, 'something' in her 'broke': 'I felt I had been used,' she explained. Despite her reluctance, Trudeau and his political advisers had thrust her to the forefront of the campaign even though she was emotionally fragile after childbirth. The next three years were excruciatingly difficult for Trudeau personally as his marriage came undone in embarrassing bursts in the media. The couple would separate on 27 May 1977, with Trudeau retaining custody of their three sons. His aides quickly noted how his concentration had diminished and how his usually assiduous work habits had altered under the strain. His attempt to impose order once again on the chaos of a government's daily life – steps which included making his friend Pitfield clerk of the Privy Council – could not cope with the rapid pace of change in the mid 1970s. A traditional Keynesian, Trudeau struggled to make sense of stagflation. He tried to establish a separate economic advisory group to counter the Department of Finance, which he distrusted. In September 1975 John Turner resigned as finance minister and an increasingly desperate Trudeau announced the creation of the Anti-Inflation Board to establish wage and price controls. It was a deed he had promised only a year before that he would never do.

Perhaps because of his personal problems but more likely because he believed a fundamental restructuring in the international order was near, Trudeau became more philosophical and more insistent that his government look towards the future. In a media interview of 28 Dec. 1975 he warned that the new controls reflected the failure of the 'free market system' to work. The Canadian business press reacted in horror to these remarks and denounced his assessment. Like Pitfield, Trudeau was intrigued with the projections of futurists such as the members of the Club of Rome and the possibilities of systems analysis to improve government decision making. In this spirit, he wrote to one of his ministers, Alastair William Gillespie, in 1976 that 'if we yield to the temptation of concentrating on today, we will default [on] our major responsibility to our children and to hundreds of millions elsewhere in the world who look to Canada with trust and who hope that we will contribute to a stable and just world order. ... We can shape the changes that face us; we can influence the future that awaits us.'

If the economy was perplexing, Quebec was disappointing for Trudeau. After his overwhelming victory in 1973, Bourassa had become more willing to respond to nationalist demands that he enact language legislation. The following year the Official Language Act, also known as Bill 22, retreated from bilingualism in Quebec. It made French the official language of the province, the government, and its services; expanded the use of French in the workplace; and restricted access to English schools to those children who had a knowledge of the language. It infuriated Trudeau. In a speech in March 1976 he lashed out at Bourassa; the bill was 'politically stupid,' the Quebec government's approach to constitutional revision obtuse, and earlier he had described Bourassa himself as no more than an eater 'of hot dogs.' Trudeau's speech itself seemed politically stupid when, on 15 November, the Parti Québécois under Lévesque trounced Bourassa's Liberals in the provincial general election. Although Bourassa had called the election to obtain a mandate for constitutional negotiations, Trudeau told Canadians that Quebec had not voted on the constitution but on 'economic and administrative issues.' It probably had, but the effect was to create a constitutional crisis because Lévesque was committed to a referendum on 'sovereignty-association,' a concept which Trudeau and his colleagues regarded as tantamount to separation but which Lévesque and his followers argued was an economic and political association similar to the emerging European Union. Initially, the Liberals soared in the public opinion polls across the country as the constitution, which had been so important in bringing Trudeau forward, once again became a major issue. In the first two months of 1977 Trudeau proposed discussions that would lead to the repatriation of the constitution and entrenchment of language rights, said he would resign if Quebec voted for independence, and told the American Congress that only 'a small minority of the people of Quebec' supported separation. Simultaneously, Quebec politician Camille Laurin, once a friend of Trudeau, prepared the Charter of the French Language. Also known as Bill 101, it went far beyond Bourassa's legislation in requiring the predominance of French in commerce, business, and communications and in compelling the children of immigrants to Quebec to study in French. It was passed by the province's National Assembly on 26 Aug. 1977.

In 1978, under their new leader, Charles Joseph (Joe) Clark, chosen in February 1976, the Conservatives began to move up in the polls as public attention turned back to the faltering Canadian economy. Union strife, low productivity increases, and a weak American economy combined to cause a string of budgetary deficits and a declining Canadian dollar. James Allan Coutts, Trudeau's principal secretary at the time, later remarked that the prime minister became exceedingly flexible and showed himself willing to consider full-scale review of the division of federal and provincial powers. On 5 July 1977 Trudeau established a task force on Canadian unity under the joint chairmanship of Pépin and former Ontario premier John Parmenter Robarts. It held hearings across the nation throughout 1978 and in January 1979 recommended decentralization and a special status for Quebec. These were not solutions Trudeau wanted.

There would be no further action because the government's mandate ended in 1979. Trudeau called an election for 22 May 1979 with the Conservatives, buoyed by the results of recent by-elections, slightly ahead in the polls. However, Trudeau was widely perceived to be a better leader. Coutts and Senator Keith Davey therefore decided to capitalize on this perception of the prime minister, making him the 'gunslinger' – 'standing alone, feet apart, thumbs hooked under his belt, with no podium or speaker's text, appearing to think on his feet and ready to take on all comers.' The image was symbolic because so many of his strong ministers, such as Turner and Donald Stovel Macdonald, had left; he now was the only 'wise man' in the cabinet, Pelletier having become a diplomat and Marchand having gone to the Senate. Trudeau's own performance on the hustings and in the televised debate was excellent, but Clark had the advantage of novelty and the peculiarities of the Canadian electoral system. Even though the Liberals took just over 4 per cent more of the popular vote, the Conservatives won a greater number of seats. The country was divided regionally. The Liberals, who had done poorly in the west since the 1960s because of the impression that the party's leaders had concentrated on central Canadian problems such as bilingualism, maintained support in Quebec and much of Ontario but the results elsewhere were disappointing. Of the Liberals' 114 seats, 67 came from Quebec and only 3 from the west, 2 of them in Manitoba; of the Conservatives' 136 seats, 57 came from the west and only 2 from Quebec.

Liberal leader Pierre E. Trudeau (centre), the New Democrats' Ed Broadbent (left), and the Progressive Conservatives' Joe Clark in a televised debate during the election campaign, Ottawa, 13 May 1979. This was only the second time in Canada's political history that party leaders debated on television.

In 1978 journalist George Radwanski had published a biography of Trudeau based upon extensive interviews that suggested the prime minister had begun to consider his own place in history. Although Trudeau was not yet a great leader, he concluded, he had 'governed intelligently in a difficult time.' He was 'not a failed prime minister but an unfulfilled one.' Trudeau probably agreed. He had told the American ambassador, Thomas Ostrom Enders, in August 1976 that his government had not been able to solve the constitutional problem or deal with the 'great wastefulness' of the 1970s. Worst of all, it had not vanquished separatism. Enders, one of the finest American ambassadors, shrewdly noted that Trudeau was 'convinced of his vision but [was] trying to govern by fiat rather than his very considerable skills as a practical politician.' It had not worked. In early June 1979 Trudeau seemed at ease as he left 24 Sussex Drive in his elegant albeit ancient Mercedes-Benz 300SL and prepared for a life as a single father without the burdens of the prime minister's office. On

21 November he announced his resignation as leader of the party, telling members of the press that 'I'm kind of sorry I won't have you to kick around any more.' They applauded.

Then, on 13 Dec. 1979, Clark refused to back down when told that the Liberals had the votes in the house to defeat his government on an unpopular budget which had also placed the Conservatives well behind in the polls. The Tory downfall was brilliantly managed by Allan Joseph MacEachen, the leader of the Liberal opposition, who immediately plotted with Coutts, Davey, and Lalonde to assure Trudeau's return. Trudeau hesitated briefly, but on 18 December he announced that he would lead the Liberals into the election.

During the campaign, Trudeau's advisers kept him away from the press, which was generally hostile, with the exception of the faithful *Toronto Star*. Yet the polls remained strong. On 18 Feb. 1980 the Liberals won 147 seats to only 103 for the Conservatives, a solid majority. The NDP had a record 32 seats. The Liberals carried only two seats in the provinces west of the Ontario border, but in Quebec they won an astonishing 74 of the 75 seats and over 68 per cent of the vote there, the greatest win ever in Canadian political history. Towards the end of the 1979 campaign, Trudeau had told a large Toronto rally that he would bring the constitution home even if it meant going over the provincial leaders' heads and seeking approval through a national referendum. The promise lingered. The Conservatives had shifted to the right during their brief period in office and Liberals recognized that their platform for 1980 should move to the left. With a second energy crisis, created by a revolution in Iran in 1979, redistribution meant taking account of the fiscal imbalances in confederation created by soaring fuel prices.

'Well, welcome to the 1980s!' Trudeau opened his victory address. He ended with American poet Robert Frost's 'But I have promises to keep / And miles to go before I sleep.' The major promise was to find a place for Quebec in Canada and that task was imminent after Lévesque, in December 1979, had set out the conditions for a Quebec referendum on sovereignty-association. The referendum, with an ambiguous question, was scheduled for 20 May 1980. Trudeau's old rival Ryan, now the Quebec Liberal leader, took charge of the No side and Jean Chrétien, minister of justice and attorney general, represented the federal government in the campaign. The No side initially stumbled badly and Trudeau finally entered the field in early May after polls showed the Yes side pulling ahead. His presence quickly irritated Lévesque, who foolishly said on 8 May that Trudeau had 'decided to follow the Anglo-Saxon part of his heritage,' a derogatory reference to the Elliott lineage. Trudeau responded brilliantly in a speech on 14 May declaring that Lévesque had said he 'was not as much of a Quebecker as those who are going to vote Yes. That, my dear friends, is what contempt is.' He also made a 'most solemn commitment' that if Quebec voted No he would 'take action to renew the constitution' after the referendum. With an 85.6 per cent turnout, 59.56 per cent of Quebec's voters rejected sovereignty-association. It was Trudeau's greatest victory, but not his last.

Lévesque told voters the night of the referendum that there would be another, a comment that infuriated Trudeau. The next day the prime minister announced to applause from all sides of the House of Commons that he intended to move forward with constitutional changes, among them patriation, an amending formula, and a charter of rights and freedoms. He had a new and dynamic constitutional team, including Pitfield, Lalonde, and Michael J. L. Kirby, which reflected his impatience with the federal government's conciliatory stance during the late 1970s. At the federal–provincial meeting which took place in September 1980, the premiers were divided among themselves, with most insisting on greater decentralization. Newfoundland premier Alfred Brian Peckford stated that he preferred Lévesque's vision of Canada to Trudeau's, which apparently meant that he favoured decentralization to the prime minister's apparent centralization. Trudeau had hoped for a better provincial response. Shortly after this inconclusive encounter, he met his caucus and asked whether they would go with 'the full package' even if the provinces hesitated. They enthusiastically agreed. On 2 October he told the country that because of the premiers' lack of agreement, he was forced to act unilaterally to patriate the constitution. Canadians needed to assume 'responsibility for the preservation of our country.' The great debate that followed split parties: Clark's Conservatives vigorously fought the plan while Ontario Conservative premier William Grenville Davis and New Brunswick Conservative premier Richard Bennett Hatfield supported it. The federal NDP were not unanimous; four Saskatchewan MPs sided with the province's NDP premier Allan Emrys Blakeney, who opposed it on the traditional British conservative argument that parliament must be supreme in the British system and not limited by the courts.

Provincial governments opposing the plan went to the courts and to the British parliament in London, where approval for patriation was required. In a still-controversial decision rendered on 28 Sept. 1981 the Supreme Court of Canada held that Trudeau's method of proceeding was legal but unconventional. Both Trudeau and his adversaries claimed victory; the court had forced a compromise. In the meantime, the opposing premiers had formed a 'gang of eight' in which Lévesque played a prominent part. They had agreed in April to a plan that permitted patriation and an amending formula involving compensation for provinces that opted out of future amendments. Quebec, in these discussions, did not insist on a veto, an instrument that had created many earlier constitutional quarrels. The federal government rejected this provincial plan; it nevertheless remained alive when the premiers and federal representatives met in November. Trudeau obtained Lévesque's consent to a national referendum on the constitution, which split the Quebec premier from his allies. Then, in a fateful evening gathering, nine premiers made a deal with Chrétien for patriation. Lévesque was not present; the evening became known as the 'night of the long knives,' when the anglophone premiers had figuratively stabbed Lévesque in the back by reaching an agreement without him. Lévesque, the other premiers complained, had broken their alliance and had accepted too quickly Trudeau's proposed referendum. Bitterness would linger long, but patriation went forward. The Canada Act, 1982, passed by the British parliament, ended that body's power to amend the British North America Act. It included the Constitution Act, 1982, which contained the Canadian Charter of Rights and Freedoms, recognition of the rights of aboriginal peoples, respect for the multicultural heritage of Canadians, a procedure for amending the constitution, and amendments to the BNA Act of 1867. At the insistence of Blakeney, a 'notwithstanding' clause that allowed the Canadian parliament or the provincial legislatures to override certain sections of the charter was also incorporated. The clause irritated Trudeau, but it was a small price to pay for the act that was proclaimed by Queen Elizabeth II in Ottawa on 17 April 1982.

Authors Stephen Clarkson and Christina McCall refer to the constitution as Trudeau's 'magnificent obsession.' It remains a remarkable achievement given the forces against change. While none deny the significance of the Canada Act and the charter, many critics in Quebec and elsewhere have claimed that Quebec was 'left out,' a criticism that Trudeau firmly rejected. The Quebec referendum and Trudeau's awareness that the election of 1980 had given him his last chance broke down the high barriers history and personality had erected. The charter would have far more impact on Canadian law and society than even Trudeau had anticipated. To his critics who complained about the treatment of Quebec in the constitutional discussions, he pointed out that Quebec MPs had supported the Constitution Act, 1982, and that in June 1982, 49 per cent of Quebecers considered the legislation 'a good thing.' His government's other policies had not fared so successfully, however. A bold attempt by finance minister MacEachen to revise the Canadian taxation system in April 1980 had failed in the face of unrelenting attacks by business and accounting interests. But the major target of the business press and the Conservative opposition was the National Energy Program, which was an ambitious attempt to respond to the rapid rise of energy prices after 1979. It had proposed a 'blended' price for oil that would be less than the world price, major incentives for Canadian oil companies to engage in exploration offshore and in the north, and greater state support for Petro-Canada, the federally controlled company despised in Alberta. The government's ambition was to achieve 50 per cent Canadian ownership of the oil industry by 1990. When introduced in the budget of 1980, the National Energy Program was presented as a means of securing the supply of a scarce resource that all expected would soar in price in succeeding years. In 1982, however, the price of oil began to drop and the National Energy Program fell apart, but not without leaving enduring memories of its confiscatory ways in Alberta and in the Canadian business community.

Such concerns were shared in Washington, where Ronald Wilson Reagan had become president in January 1981. Presidents Gerald Rudolph Ford and James Earl (Jimmy) Carter had worked well with Trudeau. Ford had been instrumental in having Canada join the wealthy countries represented in the Group of Six. The American Republican and the Canadian Liberal developed a fine personal relationship and would ski together with their families during their retirement. Reagan, however, represented a different strain of Republicanism and Trudeau found it difficult to take him seriously, treating him like an amiable but dull student at their meetings. American neo-Conservatives and their Canadian admirers could abide neither Trudeau's attitude towards Reagan nor his clear opposition to Reagan's confrontational policies against communism. Although Reagan was gracious, British prime minister Margaret Hilda Thatcher was not: Reagan wrote in his diary that 'I thought at one point [she] was going to order Pierre to go stand in a corner.' The tensions reached their height when Trudeau embarked on a 'peace initiative' in the fall of 1983. Although some of his colleagues, including Sharp, his former minister of external affairs, thought the initiative pretentious and politically self-serving, the journey through foreign capitals in the fall and winter of 1983–84 reflected Trudeau's deep concern about nuclear weapons. He accomplished little but, perhaps, he soothed his conscience.

Trudeau's time was coming to an end. In 1981–82 the Canadian economy had gone through its worst recession since the depression of the 1930s and the slump had left deep wounds. The collapse of the National Energy Program also hurt the government's reputation for good judgement. In June 1983 Martin Brian Mulroney, a 44-year-old, fluently bilingual Montreal lawyer, replaced Clark as Conservative leader and the Liberal caucus became nervous. Turner seemed an attractive alternative to Trudeau in the view of many Liberals and media commentators. After the constitutional battles, Trudeau's agenda for the future appeared thin. The growing scepticism about government intervention, which Reagan and Thatcher represented, made major social innovations difficult. Trudeau's peace initiative had revealed more limits than opportunities in the international field. He may also have considered that it was time to rest on the laurels he had gathered. Besides the constitution, there were other positive achievements to relish. The Parti Québécois was facing leadership problems and had temporarily retreated in its demand for separation. In the federal public service bilingualism was firmly enshrined. Above all, there were his three boys. On the evening of 28 Feb. 1984 Trudeau took a walk in the snow outside his official residence on Sussex Drive. The next day he announced he would resign.

In one last brilliant appearance at the Liberal convention in June, Trudeau roused the crowd to cheers and then left most in tears as he said farewell. Then he became silent. He joined a Montreal law firm, moved into an art deco home that he had bought during his first retirement in 1979, and travelled often. Though he took much pleasure in his participation in a group of former heads of state, he played no role in the Liberal quarrels that followed Turner's defeat by Mulroney in the general election of 1984. But in 1987 Mulroney and the premiers agreed to the Meech Lake Accord, which Bourassa, who had returned as Quebec premier, claimed would bring his province into the constitutional framework from which it had been excluded in 1982. Trudeau, who spoke out during a Senate hearing, was furious, partly because of Bourassa's interpretation of the events of 1982 but mostly because the accord created the potential special status for Quebec that he had so long rejected. Suddenly, the opposition to the accord, which all provinces had to approve by June 1990, gained support from two new Liberal premiers, Frank Joseph McKenna of New Brunswick and Clyde Kirby Wells of Newfoundland. The die was cast for its death in June 1990 when Wells adjourned the House of Assembly of Newfoundland and Labrador without a vote.

Trudeau retreated once more only to reappear when the Mulroney government and most premiers, reeling from the collapse of the Meech agreement and the rise of separatist sentiment in Quebec, brought forward the Charlottetown Accord in 1992. The accord had the support of the three federal parties as well as that of the provincial premiers, but this time there would be a nationwide referendum on 26 Oct. 1992 to approve the proposals. Once more, Trudeau emerged to offer criticism. He objected to collective rights and the hierarchy of those rights that gave francophone Quebecers special status. In a memorable evening at La Maison Egg Roll in the Saint-Henri district of Montreal, Trudeau explained to supporters of *Cité Libre* why he believed that Mulroney and the premiers had created 'a mess that deserves a big NO.' Immediately after his intervention, backing for the accord dropped significantly in English Canada. When the referendum was held, the accord was defeated in Quebec and failed to obtain the necessary level of support in English Canada. Was Trudeau's intervention decisive among anglophones? Certainly some who advocated the accord believe it was, although others suggest that Trudeau merely turned people's attention to its flaws.

Even though he fretted about the federal government's strategy, Trudeau took no part in the Quebec referendum campaign of 1995. He spoke out in 1996 in favour of the approach adopted by the minister of intergovernmental affairs, Stéphane Dion, which was to confront the Quebec government directly to achieve 'clarity' when it spoke of sovereignty-association and separation. But his health was deteriorating rapidly. The death of his son Michel in an avalanche in British Columbia on 13 Nov. 1998 shattered him and his weakness became visible to all as an ashen-faced old man left the funeral in tears. For a while, he questioned his Catholic faith. He refused treatment for prostate cancer and his memory began to fade. Before he died in Montreal on 28 Sept. 2000, he had made his peace with his family and his God. His body lay in state in Ottawa and then travelled by train along the Ottawa River as thousands came to the tracks to pay their last respects. His state funeral at the Notre-Dame Basilica in Montreal was memorable for the eloquent eulogy in English by Justin Trudeau, who ended it simply with 'Je t'aime, papa.'

Most of his obituaries in 2000 were generous in their praise, but Trudeau may be the Canadian prime minister who divides us most. Certainly he divided those journalists and academics who, when polled in 2003 on the post-war prime ministers by the journal *Policy Options* (Montreal), disagreed most strongly on his achievements and failures. Elsewhere historian Michael Bliss has ranked him very highly as an inspiring leader who saved Canada while political scientists Ken McRoberts and Guy Laforest have argued that his dream has died and that his attempts to realize it cost Canada and Quebec greatly. Yet even those who doubt his accomplishments agree that his presence in Canadian public life was remarkable. As the memoirs of his colleagues and contemporaries are published, Trudeau's personality and approach have become better known. His cabinet colleagues have remarked on his fairness and the respect he demonstrated for them in cabinet meetings. Yet he avoided close personal contact even with devoted ministers such as Marc Lalonde. Moreover, many problems he encountered might have been avoided had he been more open to criticism and less abrasive in personal relations. Although many ministers were fond of him, more shared the opinion of Jean Chrétien, who respected Trudeau but loved Pearson. His other successors as Liberal leader, John Turner and Paul Martin, in many ways framed their political approach in opposition to that of Trudeau. Still, Trudeau remains the Liberal leader and even the prime minister against whom his successors are measured.

Like John Fitzgerald Kennedy in the United States, Trudeau became the identifier for young people of his time. In the classic formulation of French academician Georges-Louis Leclerc de Buffon, echoed by historian Ramsay Cook, the style was the man himself. That style was a model for 'Trudeau's children,' those anglophone youths of the 1970s who took French immersion courses, travelled the globe with backpacks, and gained a self-confidence about themselves that expressed itself in Canadian songs and symbols. Trudeau's impact on 20th-century Canada is certain; Canada's fate in the new century will decide its meaning.

JOHN ENGLISH

Further reading

Stephen Clarkson and Christina McCall, *Trudeau and our times* (2v., Toronto, 1990–94; trade paperback ed., 1997).

George Radwanski, *Trudeau* (Toronto, 1978).

P. E. Trudeau, *Memoirs* (Toronto, 1993).

Max and Monique Nemni, *Young Trudeau, 1919–1944: son of Quebec, father of Canada*, trans. William Johnson (1v. to date, Toronto, 2006–　).

John English, *Citizen of the world: the life of Pierre Elliott Trudeau* (1v. to date (*1919–1968*), Toronto, 2006–　).

Contributors

BÉLANGER, RÉAL. Directeur général adjoint, Dictionnaire biographique du Canada/Dictionary of Canadian biography, et professeur titulaire d'histoire, Université Laval, Québec, Québec.

Sir Wilfrid Laurier.

BOTHWELL, ROBERT. Professor of history, University of Toronto, Ontario.

Louis-Stephen St-Laurent.

BROWN, ROBERT CRAIG. Professor emeritus of history, University of Toronto, Ontario.

Sir Robert Laird Borden.

BUCKNER, PHILLIP. Visiting professor, Institute of Commonwealth Studies, University of London, England.

Sir Charles Tupper.

ENGLISH, JOHN. General editor, Dictionary of Canadian biography/ Dictionnaire biographique du Canada, and professor of history and university research chair, University of Waterloo, Ontario.

Lester Bowles Pearson. Pierre Elliott Trudeau.

FORSTER, BEN. Associate professor and chair, Department of History, University of Western Ontario, London, Ontario.

Alexander Mackenzie.

GLASSFORD, LARRY A. Professor of education, University of Windsor, Ontario.

Arthur Meighen.

JOHNSON, J. K. Professor emeritus of history, Carleton University, Ottawa, Ontario.

Sir John Alexander Macdonald [in collaboration with P. B. Waite].

MILLER, CARMAN. Professor of history, McGill University, Montreal, Quebec.

Sir John Joseph Caldwell Abbott.

NEATBY, H. BLAIR. Professor emeritus of history, Carleton University, Ottawa, Ontario.

William Lyon Mackenzie King.

SMITH, DENIS. Professor emeritus of political science, University of Western Ontario, London, Ontario.

John George Diefenbaker.

WAITE, P. B. Professor emeritus of history, Dalhousie University, Halifax, Nova Scotia.

Richard Bedford Bennett, 1st Viscount Bennett. Sir Mackenzie Bowell. Sir John Alexander Macdonald [in collaboration with J. K. Johnson]. *Sir John Sparrow David Thompson.*

Illustration Credits

Bibliothèque et Archives nationales du Québec, Centre d'archives de Québec et des archives gouvernementales (Quebec City): Laurier, early 1900s (P1000, S4, D83, PL152-2); Diefenbaker's lack of concern for Quebec cartoon (P716); Pearson delivers nuclear weapons cartoon (P716); Trudeau needs no go-between cartoon (P716).

Archibald Dale, *Five years of R. B. Bennett* (Winnipeg, 1935), with the permission of the *Winnipeg Free Press*: Bennett the Grand Panjandrum cartoon.

Glenbow Archives (Calgary): Deynaka family (ND-3-6343).

Library and Archives Canada (Ottawa): Parliament Buildings on cover (PA-028565); Diefenbaker on cover (PA-130070); Trudeau on cover (C-46600); Macdonald, c. 1856 (C-003813); Macdonald, 1872 (C-010144); Macdonald's prorogation of parliament cartoon (C-078599); Macdonald's widow and daughter (PA-025744); Mackenzie, 1868 (PA-025303); astounded Mackenzie cartoon (C-078604); Abbott (PA-026319); Thompson, 1894 (PA-012206); Thompson vacationing (C-010111); Bowell (PA-027159); Laurier, 1874 (PA-025390); Laurier speaking for Parent (C-090230); Borden house (PA-034305); Borden decorating Medical Corps (PA-002738); Borden and McKenzie (C-046314); Meighen, 1920s (C-005799); King in Colorado (C-029350); King's residence, Laurier House (PA-008979); King at Kingsmere (C-009066); King and conscription crisis cartoon (C-044300); Bennett in Charlottetown (C-021528); St-Laurent wedding (C-010181); St-Laurent becomes party leader (C-023281); St-Laurent with grandchildren (PA-125907); Diefenbaker at combative best (C-080883); Diefenbakers at 24 Sussex Drive (PA-151038); Diefenbaker and Pearson at Grey Cup cartoon (C-113548) (with the permission of the *Toronto Star*); Pearson in wartime

(PA-117622); Pearson at United Nations conference (C-018532); Pearson at Expo 67 (E000996577); Pearson and cabinet in 1967 (PA-117107); Trudeau at graduation (PA-115081); Trudeau turns camera (PA-175919); Trudeau and Castro (PA-136976); televised debate (PA-142623).

A. D. MacLean, *R. B. Bennett: prime minister of Canada* (Toronto, 1935): Bennett as law student; Bennett at Waterloo Station.

Musée Laurier (Victoriaville, Que.): Lauriers with friends.

Le Nationaliste **(Montreal):** Laurier tightrope cartoon.

Nova Scotia Archives and Records Management (Halifax): Tupper (N-4844).

Robert Craig Brown Collection: Bordens, 1889.

Le Soleil **(Quebec City):** Meighen the imperialist cartoon.

Thunder Bay Historical Society Museum (Thunder Bay, Ont.): Macdonalds at Port Arthur station (N981.39.216).

Index